CW00793213

Trading Bible: 6 Books in 1

Cryptocurrency Trading, Stock Market Investing for Beginners, Forex Trading, Day Trading, Options Trading, Swing Trading for Beginners, Learn Technical Analysis for Crypto

Stock Market Investing for Beginners:

Mastery of The Market with Confidence and Discipline

Strategies to Earn Passive Income, Grow your Wealth and Start Making Money Today. Day Trade for Living.

© Copyright 2021 by Ryan Martinez - All rights reserved.
The content contained within this book may not be
reproduced, duplicated or transmitted without direct written
permission from the author or the publisher.
Under no circumstances will any blame or legal responsibility
be held against the publisher, or author, for any damages,
reparation, or monetary loss due to the information
contained within this book. Either directly or indirectly.
Legal Notice:
This book is copyright protected. This book is only for
personal use. You cannot amend, distribute, sell, use, quote
or paraphrase any part, or the content within this book,
without the consent of the author or publisher.
Disclaimer Notice:
Please note the information contained within this document
is for educational and entertainment purposes only. All effort
has been executed to present accurate, up to date, and
reliable, complete information. No warranties of any kind are
declared or implied. Readers acknowledge that the author is
not engaging in the rendering of legal, financial, medical or
professional advice. The content within this book has been
derived from various sources. Please consult a licensed
professional before attempting any techniques outlined in
this book.
By reading this document, the reader agrees that under no
circumstances is the author responsible for any losses, direct
or indirect, which are incurred as a result of the use of
information contained within this document, including, but
not limited to, — errors, omissions, or inaccuracies.

Table of Contents

Conclusion

Introduction

You might have probably heard of how good it is to invest in stocks. In fact, you might have even heard of how good this whole investment concept is. By putting in a considerable amount of money on something, you are bound to make that amount grow by each passing year until you get twice the amount you invested or more. At least, that's how an investment works in theory.

You might have even heard of how a lot of people became successful purely from investing in stocks at the stock market. With a few key investments here and there, they were able to earn from multiple sources within their investment portfolio. Perhaps with the right timing and knowledge, you too can turn a fistful of dollars into a 6-digit amount in your net worth or, better yet, in your bank account.

But here is the teeny tiny problem:

You know absolutely nothing about investing in stock.

That might be a problem because how are you supposed to succeed in any field if you don't have some level of experience in it? There are some key differences in the concept of investing which means success here is not as straightforward as earning a salary. In fact, investing has more similarities to gambling than with any other means of earning money.

However, here is the good news. Despite how intimidating the whole market could be, there is absolutely a way to be successful here even if it is your first time venturing into it. The stock market actually does not discriminate when it comes to who will make it big. Experienced or not and regardless of what stocks you invest in, everybody always has the same potential for success here.

So, how can an absolute beginner make their first successful steps in the stock market? In this book, Stock Market Investing for Beginners: Mastery of the Market with Confidence and Discipline, I will lay out a road map to your success. Investing in stocks is not exactly as complicated or glamorous as shows and movies make it out to be. There is an art and science to it. By taking advantage of what is available for you, you can eventually start making successes here and there.

To do that, you must first learn the basics. Now, the introduction to the market is always the intimidating part which is why it is necessary that you ease yourself in to the entire process. From learning what kind of investor you are, the types of stocks that you want to invest in, and how you could possibly earn from your investments, the basics will set up the foundation from which you can build on your successes in the stock market.

Once we get through the more basic concepts, we would now start going over buying stock. There are quite a lot of skills to learn here from research and speculating which stocks are about to go up in value a lot in the next few days. This is where the science part comes into play as you must learn how to become precise and methodical with your investments on a regular basis.

One other crucial aspect of investing in stocks is learning what not to do. Over the years, there are countless investors who made several mistakes that cut their stay in the market short. The best way to capitalize on these mistakes is to learn what they are, how you can perform them, and what you can do to prevent yourself from getting into such situations.

The risk will also be one other crucial aspect that you will learn over the course of this book. There is nothing certain in the world of investments. Things might take a turn for the worse in an instant due to factors that were beyond your control. By learning how to deal with risk, you could at least build on your successes without unnecessarily putting yourself in situations where you lost more money than you ought to gain.

Once you have made your first successful investment, the next thing to learn is how to build on your successes. In here, you will be taught how to carefully expand on your investment portfolio while dealing with new challenges that come from maintaining the momentum of your success. At the very least, this should make sure that your stay in the stock market does not become a short one.

Now, you will be asking yourself "Can I do all of this and be successful?". The answer is yes. In here, you will also get acquainted with several successful investors and learn how they themselves made it big tin their respective markets. With their perspective, you might be able to learn a few tricks for yourself and make your own path towards success.

All in all, this is but a bird's eye view of what you will learn as you go through each page of the book. Do not worry, all of this information is based on several years' worth of personal experience in the market and condensed in a manner that is easy to understand for the greenest of beginners.

Is investing in the stock market demanding? Maybe. Is it easy enough for beginners to understand and succeed in? Definitely yes. Again, all that is needed is for you to get the basics right, arm yourself with the right tools and knowledge, and make the right movements at the right time. The rest then, as they say, is up to sheer dumb luck.

If the very notion of reaping the financial rewards from a relatively high-stakes activity excites you, then let us dive first into the world of stock market investing.

Have fun!

Chapter I: Easing in on the Market

Picture this scene:

You are at home going through a news program. As soon as news about stocks come up, you suddenly switch to another channel. Why is this so?

There are quite a lot of reasons for this but the primary one is that you find the information being given to you a bit too intimidating. Those charts, graphs, numbers, and trends do sound important but they are presented in a manner that could scare off anyone who knows next to nothing about investments. It does not even help that they use industry-exclusive jargon which makes the segments even a bit more intimidating for non-investors.

Here is the thing, though: All that news about the stock market? They were meant for people who are already in it. So how can a beginner like you get an appreciation of the entire market?

To do that, there are a few basic concepts that you need to understand first.

(NOTE: The chapter will cover very basic stuff about stock investing. If you think you can get the gist of the chapter without reading it, you may proceed to chapter 2. But if not, I recommend that you go through this part first.)

What is Stock?

Let's get the most basic thing out of the way. What exactly is a stock? The definition of what constitutes stock can get rather complicated but the most basic concept of it is a claim of sorts on the assets and earnings of a company.

So how does stock exactly come into play? What you have to understand is that every corporation out there has a finite amount of capital to use in order to function properly. To get more capital, they need to ask for money in exchange for a portion of what that company owns and earns.

In essence, when you invest in stocks, you personally bind yourself to the existence, success, and overall longevity of a company. In short, you become a shareholder of that company. And when that company earns, you do.

Now, there will be a more extensive discussion on stock in the coming chapters. What you have to be concerned with now is that a stock always refers to a long-term relationship with a company. How you earn from your investments depends greatly on when you invested on a certain share and how that company from which that share came from performs on a regular basis.

What is the Stock Market?

The stock market is simply the place where stocks get issued, bought, traded, and sold either over a physical counter or through the various stock exchanges. Nearly every country has their own stock markets and dedicated stock exchange. Without these, the economy of that country tends to be rather stagnant or worse, non-functioning.

The purpose of any stock market is always two fold. The first is to **Provide Capital.** Now, as was stated a few paragraphs before, companies need capital in order to operate. And to get capital, they need investors. To get the attention of potential investors, they don't have to advertise over the radio or through print.

Instead, they get themselves publicly listed in the local stock market. Once they are listed, all of the stocks that they can trade will be publicly listed for trade. Once stocks are traded, capital comes pouring in to that company.

Here's an example: Let us say that Company A needs capital. As such, they get themselves listed in the local stock market where they issued 1 million shares for $5.00 each. Provided that all of these stocks are sold, the company gets 1 million shareholders each bringing in $5.00 per share to boost the company's capital by $5 million.

Of course, they could get the capital through loans but selling shares is one way of getting such amount without incurring debt and paying interest charges for such.

The second purpose is for investors to **Share Profit.** There are several ways on how you can profit from stock but they mostly come in two categories. The first is through passive means where the share earns in dividends for the investor over a period of time.

The second is through more active means by way of a trade. If, for example, the investor bought 6 shares at $10.00 each, he has the option to keep them under his name for as long as possible or sell them at a time when the same stocks for the same company are priced at $20.00 each. In essence, he got his initial investment back plus a 100% bonus. This helps the company gain more investors without releasing new shares while the investor gets to earn from each of their investments.

What You Need To Know About the Stock Market

As of now, the idea of jumping in to any stock market can be intimidating for you as a beginner. Just to make sure that your entry into the market goes as smoothly as possible, here are a few more things that you need to know about the stock market.

1. Market Indexes

When you watch stock market news, you might have noticed those little figures that go up and down. These are basically what are called market indexes which tells you how a certain class of stock or company is performing under the current market environment. Some news channels would use data from the S&P 500 or the Dow Jones Industrial Average to tell you the performance of one type of stock, corporation, or even an entire sector of the market.

A market index becomes important as it tells you, as an investor, on how to proceed in the next few days. Should you dump your shares and sell them cheap? Should you purchase new stocks on a certain company? Should you keep holding on to those stocks in the hopes that their prices go up in a few months or so? Your market index will tell you exactly that.

2. **Stock Trading**

A good investor knows to either diversify their portfolio or hold on to some stock index funds. These are actually legitimate strategies to sustain oneself in any market. However, if you are craving a bit more action, then you should consider trading stocks. If you time your trades right, you can earn quite a lot from your investments even if you just started with a fistful of dollars.

Stock traders are often classified by the frequency of their activity. There are those day traders who, simply put, trade stocks every day. There are also periodic traders who regularly make huge trades every few months or so. There are traders who do their activities exclusively on the physical stock exchanges and then there are those that do theirs online.

You will get to learn more of stock trading as you go through this book. What you have to understand now is that this activity will require a lot of research more than any other stock related activity. Tools, charts, and every other asset out there that can help you monitor and predict where stocks rise and fall can help you in this aspect.

3. **Bull or Bear?**

Do keep in mind that venturing into any stock market comes with a certain set of risks. It's up to you to pay attention of these risks in order to survive.

How would you know, then, that it is okay to venture into a certain sector of the stock market now? There are quite a lot of terms that seasoned investors but most use "bull" or "bear".

A bull market is simply a market where conditions are most favorable to investors. You will notice that you are in a bull market when the investors are quite confident in their transactions. Think of it like a poker table where the dealer shows his hand a lot. The players are getting cocky with their bets because they know what comes next and they can prepare accordingly.

A bear market, on the other hand, is where the prices for stocks are nearing free-fall. The threshold varies from market to market but you can be certain that investors here are either being more cautious with their transactions or, if worse comes to worst, start pulling out of the area.

As a beginner, you should know which economic pattern is present in your market so you would know how to take advantage of the situation. Your only solace is that markets tend to last longer as bulls instead of bears. If you find yourself dealing in a bear market, you can be certain that the downturn will not last for long.

4. **Crashes vs. Corrections**

Crashes and corrections are basically drops in the overall stock market. Where they differ is the percentage of the drop. When the drop is no more than 10%, that's a correction. But if the drop was sudden as symbolized by a downward spike in the trend, then this is a crash.

Crashes often tell you that the market is turning bear. But do remember that this downturn does not last long. Stock markets tend to rise up in value over time.

What you have to understand is that crashes and corrections happen more often than you think. Thus, discipline is necessary on your part to last long in the market. Long-term planning and careful allocation of resources should help you survive through a crash.

There are even tools out there that can help you determine how long you can recover from any sudden downturn. And you will learn of these a few chapters later.

5. Diversification

Although you cannot avoid downturns in the market, what you can control is your investment portfolio. A mistake beginner's make is failing to diversify on their investments. This means sticking to the stocks that they are the most comfortable with without venturing into other types.

This is rather precarious as you fail to provide a safety net of sorts on your investment. For example, if you invest solely on one sector, what happens to you when that sector drops? All of your investments would drop as well along with the overall value of your portfolio.

Believe it or not, a lot of things that are beyond your control can change the very outlook in a certain market. This could range from massive political upheavals, problems in economics and regulations, and even the outbreak of diseases.

Risk management is a key skill that you must develop when venturing into any stock market. You have to know which investments that you are bound to make carry the biggest risks and determine whether or not such risks can affect your overall portfolio.

Also, patience is required as building a portfolio takes a while. You can even look into mutual funds and index funds to instantly diversify your portfolio. There are other strategies that you can use to diversify your portfolio and, like always, you will get to know of them later on.

To Conclude

Is it intimidating to start out in the stock market?

Technically, it shouldn't be but that does not stop people from actually avoiding the market in its entirety. Some think that the market is too ruthless that anyone who is just starting might end up getting overwhelmed. Some are just too afraid of making bad investments that they end up not making any in the first place.

The truth is that, indeed, the stock markets are rather demanding. They are not that lenient to the point that you could be rewarded for a bad investment. However, they are not that completely ruthless that only those who have made it big can continue on earning here.

The point is that everyone has the same chances of success regardless of their experience in the market. Everyone can take advantage of the same opportunities and suffer from the same downturns. It is all a matter of being mindful of the current condition of the market and playing to your strengths accordingly.

Now, if that apprehension with the market is gone, it is time to get into the basics of buying your first stocks.

Chapter II: Investments

What are investments exactly? They are basically items that you put money in with the consideration that such thing would make that money grow for you. What makes investment different from gambling is that you are expected to know what you are exactly putting your money in and how it's going to make a profit for you unlike a wager.

But when we ask the WHAT when it comes to investments, what we are trying to ask is "in what form do they come in?". As such, getting acquainted with the stuff that you are about to buy and trade in the stock market and how you will eventually interact with them is rather crucial for any investor.

Stocks and The Stock Market

As was mentioned a few chapters ago, the stock market is a place where you can buy, sell, and trade all kinds of investments. As such, there are quite a number of ways to make money here.

But what exactly is the market's primary commodity? That comes in the form of, well, stocks. As was mentioned, stocks are proof of your ownership over a company's assets and income in exchange for providing for the company's capital.

What makes stocks so great as investment options is that their profitability is directly affected by the overall performance of a company. If the company does well, its value grows. And when the value of the company grows, so does the value of your share.

And this is where you can profit from your stocks by either trading your ownership of your stock to another according to the current value. If you bought stocks for cheap and that company's value grew by several digits in the market, you could effectively earn more than 200% of your initial investment through trading under the right conditions.

But if you do choose to hold over your ownership of the stocks, you can still profit from it. A company has the option of distributing a portion of its profits to the shareholders. As such, it is important that you read the fine print on the stocks specifically on what benefits you could reap from being a shareholder to the company before you agree to invest in that entity.

The point here is that stocks are generally viable options for first-time beginners. A lot of investors who succeeded out there have focused solely on stocks and made a lot of money before retiring like Warren Buffet. Of course, the potential for success in that stock is going to be dependent on that company.

This is why it is important that you can track and predict where a company is going performance-wise. For instance, if you feel that the company is failing, you may trade your stocks before the prices drop. This way, you can bail out on the company with a sizeable portion of your investments intact.

The Types of Stock

When we talk about stocks, we often think that they come in mostly the same form. However, the truth is that stocks usually come in two form. They are:

A. **Common**

When people talk about stocks in general, they most likely are talking about this type. As the name implies, common stocks are, well, common. They are publicly traded in stock markets and represent your claim of ownership over a portion of the company and its dividends. In short, most of the stocks you will find in the stock market fall under this category.

One neat feature with stocks is that they yield high returns as the years pass by way of a growing capital. In short, if a company performs well, the prices of their stock increases. This does not matter if those stocks have yet to be sold or currently in the ownership of an investor. All stocks will get a price increase so as long as the company performs well.

Of course, that works the other way around. If a company performs poorly or is in the verge of bankruptcy, the stocks become worthless. No matter the price you initially paid for them, those stocks will not be earning money for you.

B, Preferred

A preferred stock still offers the same benefits as common stocks in the sense that you get to own a portion of the company as well as a claim on its dividends. However, it is more limited in the sense that it does not give you the same voting rights as common stocks. In short, if you want to have a say on how the company is being managed, a preferred stock will not give you that right.

What it does offer instead is a fixed dividend. Unlike in common stocks where the value of the dividend can change according to the performance of a company, the dividends of a preferred stockholder will remain the same from the start to onwards. Usually, that dividend is several margins higher than what a common stock could offer.

One other benefit is that you will always get paid off first before common stockolders in case the company gets liquidated. However, just do keep in mind that creditors have to be paid off first before you.

Lastly, preferred stocks are callable. If, for some reason, the company wants to gain ownership of its stocks again, they can purchase your stocks for a premium.

At a glance, you can see that preferred stocks work more like bond than an actual share. It's something in between. But just to make things simple, preferred stocks are different in the sense that they allow you greater dividend sharing and the ability to get paid off first before the company closes.

Voting Rights and Stock Classes

Can a company make their own class of stocks? In a sense, yes. Although stocks are either common or preferred, companies have found ways to customize their stocks to come up with unique classes. Why would companies do this? Wouldn't they trade ownership of a portion of a company to complete strangers either way?

The truth is that ownership counts for not much when it comes to corporations. What matters more is voting rights. As the preferred stock has shown you, ownership really does not matter as much as having the right to determine how a company should be handled.

As such, companies are finding ways to get the capital from investors while retaining voting power to a select and often undisclosed group. As such, the different classes would often pertain to the different degrees of voting power being offered,

Here's an example, company XYZ would hold several shares to a select group with each share giving the holder ten votes. The other shares might just offer the standard 1 vote. So, if there are 100 shareholders split evenly within the two groups, that means that one group holds 500 votes while the other half holds only 50. Remember, majorities in companies are determined by the total number of votes owned, not the number of shareholders.

What are Stock Options?

Options are basically another form of stock with a more fluid pricing model. When you buy an option, you are technically close to gambling as the price of that stock could go up and down depending on how the company performs for that period.

Sounds risky, right? Not exactly. When you buy an option instead of the standard individual stock, you give yourself a stronger buying power over those stocks over a limited period of time. In other words, you have the option to either buy or sell that stock within a set period of time. Better yet is that you don't have to own the option in order to sell or trade them.

Of course, that fluctuating price could be rather risky. There is a change that the prices could drop severely for several periods. This means that you might be incurring losses for over a period of time depending on the performance of the company.

As such, stock options are great if you are aiming for a high-stakes, high-reward strategy in your investments. However, that also makes them risky for the uninitiated. Master the basics of the other stocks and investments first before you consider adding options to your investment portfolio.

The Other Kinds of Investment

Let's get this out of the way: in the stock market, there is no need to physically get a hold of the stocks and assets that you will buy and trade. In fact, what you are going to transact with over and over here will be documents signifying your ownership of such items.

That would make for a rather safe platform to do business in as there is no risk of the actual physical item being degraded or damaged through every transaction. In fact, depending on the nature of the stock, these items would not even move from where they are currently deposited. Their ownership only changes hands from one person to another.

Also, risk is directly affected by the nature of the stock itself. Of course, risk is directly proportional to the reward. There are stocks that are always good options to invest in regardless of the economy and then there are those that yield the best possible rewards but tend to be riskier depending on the situation. A good investor will know which stocks to invest in to balance the rewards with the risks.

With that out of the way, it is time to get to know which kinds of stocks you may want to invest in the market.

A. Cash and Commodity

At the bottom most portion of the risk ladder are cash and commodities. They are considered to be the lifeblood of any stock market as the frequency of trading activity regarding these stocks will often directly affect the performance of the economy. And even if the economy takes a turn for the worse, these stocks often remain viable investment options and could prove to be an effective safety net for your investment portfolio.

The only problem with this type of commodity is their comparatively low reward. Since they offer the least risk, their margin for profit growth for the investor is relatively low.

Gold

This metal is perhaps one of the oldest stock options to date. In fact, people have been trading gold for various commodities since way before the Egyptians built their pyramids. What makes Gold a safe first-time investment is its appeal. However, do keep in mind that much of this appeal is anchored on scarcity and fear. As such, the price of gold tends to fluctuate depending on factors beyond your control.

If you choose to invest in gold, you have to be mindful of the fact that your only protection against a price drop for this commodity is based on external factors. In fact, the price of gold tends to fluctuate a lot. Your only solace for this commodity is that never has the price of gold drop below the negatives.

An understanding of scarcity is also necessary to make the most out of gold. In essence, prices of gold rise up when scarcity and fear are quite high. Thus, if you are the person that would want to secure your finances in case something goes terribly wrong across the world, gold might be a good investment option for you.

Cash Deposits and other Bank Products

As the name imply, these investments are offered by banks. Bank products usually involve savings accounts and money market accounts. A cash deposit, on the other hand, is simply a loan that you give to the bank with the consideration that such amount will be returned to you with interest.

Like gold, bank products are still low-risk investments. In fact, you could expect no more than 2% for returns every year with these type of investments. If you know how inflation works, you would know that 2% will not be enough for profit out of these investments.

In essence, they are are safe options but are not great when you intend to make your money grow considerably over a period of time.

Cryptocurrencies

A newer form of investment, cryptocurrencies are unregulated digital investment options and are usually issued outside of the stock market. You may have heard one of these currencies, Bitcoin, which has been gaining a lot of traction in recent years.

However, since they are relatively new and contain too many unknowns, it is best that you stay away from these investment options. In fact, there are many governments considering regulating these currencies due to a rise of many scams that involve them. As such, it would be still quite a while before Bitcoin and its ilk would get widespread market acceptance.

So as long as stock exchanges do not recognize these investment options, hold off on cryptocurrencies as of now.

B. Bonds and Securities

Another form of low-risk investments, these options are usually offered by institutions like the government and your typical private company.

Government and Corporate Bonds

Bonds are basically like cash deposits except that they are not issued by banks. When you purchase a bond from the government or a private corporation, you are essentially loaning that entity with your money with the expectation that they will return the same to you some time later with interest.

Bonds are generally safe for the sheer fact that the only time that you are not going to get your money back is if the one issuing the bond, for some reason, defaults. With government savings bonds, that is not likely to happen.

As for corporate bonds, however, they are riskier as the chances of defaulting are higher with a private company. Also, unlike your typical stock or share, a bond does not confer to you ownership over a portion of the company's assets and income.

What you have to understand is that both corporate and government bonds can give you as much as 3% of a return of your money over several years. This would mean that if you were to take your money out of the bond, you might risk decreasing your buying power. After all, the 3% growth rate is not keeping up with inflation.

Mortgage-based Securities

A security is, again, like a loan. However, this time, that loan is going to come with some real estate mortgages.

What makes securities different from bonds also is the way that you can earn profit here. Unlike a bond where the payout only occurs after the expiration of the term, mortgage-based securities can pay to an investor their interest on a monthly basis.

However, what makes these securities intimidating is their complexity. There are too many factors to consider when you determine your regular payout. Also, the risks tend to be higher depending on the terms of the mortgage.

As such, this investment option should only be considered by investors if they already have considerable experience in the market. First-time beginners like yourself should try out the low-risk, easier-to-understand investment options first.

C. Investment Funds

An investment fund is basically a conglomerate of money which came from different investors which would then be used for different products which include but are not limited to stocks, bonds, and other trade-able assets. What makes funds great is that they are the best indicator of a market's performance since they track the market index.

Mutual Funds

This investment option is basically a proxy investment. It will be operated by an agent authorized by you who will invest your money in your behalf and find ways to make such profit.

What makes mutual funds safe is that it's very own concept allows for instant diversification. The way you get your benefits from these, then, is either through the interest that they generate or when you sell your funds if the prices for such go up in the market.

The only downside in this option is that you will spend more in keeping them functional. As a matter of fact, a portion of your money would go about paying the services of your manager as well as the agents that they might employ in order to investments running.

As such, do consider this investment option as a mid-tier option. Start with the other low-risk investments first so that you could learn how to invest your own money for yourself. Once you are confident with your skills, you can then use mutual funds to quickly diversify your portfolio.

Index Funds

Like mutual funds, this fund will help you diversify in your investments quickly. The only difference with them is that index funds are managed passively. This means that you would have to deal with fewer fees which then leads to you keeping more of the returns you will make out of your investment.

However, that amount you will get in returns is directly proportional to the market index. If the index is low, your returns will be low. And vice versa.

If you are the investor who wants to put money on something and then not think too much about it, then this investment option might be ideal for you.

Exchange-Traded Funds

An ETF will function similarly to other funds. What makes it different is that it is one of the only funds that can be purchased directly from the stock market. This gives you even more control over how much you are going to pay for them and you will have to pay fewer fees to maintain them.

But, of course, the fund's profitability is directly tied to the performance of the market index. This can be circumvented to a degree if the fund tracks a broader index like what the S&P 500 has to offer.
As such, for beginning investors, this is a relatively safe fund to invest in.

D. Retirement and Other Savings Options

These investment options come in the form of accounts issued by banks and other financial institutions. Since their purposes and duration vary from one product to another, the risk and reward for retirement options can vary. Beginning investors like yourself can consider these options early on but great care and research must be done first before you start investing on them.

Also, it goes without mentioning that the maturity periods for these investment options are notoriously long. Only include them in your investment plan if you are into long-term planning and a whole lot of patience.

Lastly, these are not purely investment options per se. Rather, your retirement plans can be a tool for which you can venture into other investment options. The only requirement is that you have access to the funds stashed in these plans which means that they must have already matures if you want to make full use of them.

401K

A 401K is basically a retirement plan offered by a company mandated by the US Government. What can draw you to such an investment option is that, in here, the employer can offer something that could match what you have already invested in or, at least, a portion of it.

This matching feature is what makes a 401K rather beneficial if you want to play it safe as an investor. However, 401Ks function like your typical Mutual Fund without diversification. This means that the funds are in the hands of a manager that you have to constantly pay for their services.

Of course, a 401K is only available if you yourself are currently employed. The company that you currently work in is the only entity that can offer you such. Thus, your 401K options are rather limited in one lifetime.

IRA

Known properly as an Individual Retirement Account, IRAs are either tax-deferred or tax-free. This means that a portion of the money you invested won't be taken out just to fill up the government's coffers.

Also, an IRA gives you better control on what you can invest with it compared to a 401K. If you want, you can use the money to invest on other products like stocks, investments, and mutual funds if you like.

In short, IRA is a good option if you want reduce the risks, exert more control over your funds, and quickly diversify on your folio. Your key to success here will most definitely involve maxing out on your plan as soon as humanly possible.

Annuities

An annuity functions more like a contract between you and a financial institution usually an insurance company. Here, you pay something in bulk to the insurance company with the consideration of getting payed regularly by the company. It's kind of like a salary if you are already retired in the sense that you get it on a regular basis.

The good thing about annuities is that there is absolutely no risk involved with them. The only problem? There is no reward with them either. It's a good way to get a steady source of income if you are retired but there is no room for growth here.

As such, they are not the most ideal option for any investor. Nor should you even consider them as a jumping off point for other investment options.

E. Real Estate

Whether it involves buying buildings, renovating them, or selling, real estate is one of the most rewarding investment options out there. But that high reward often comes with a laundry list of risks and expenses. There are some methods you can use to mitigate your risks here but it does not remove the fact that real estate is a high-stakes investment route.

Beginners should not take on this option right away until they master the basics of the other forms of investment. Also, having a sizeable capital is needed for your activities here.

Property

Whether for commercial or residential purposes, it is hard to find a building right now that is priced less then a $50,000.00 for the entire structure excluding repairs. This might give the idea that those with little to no capital cannot engage in this investment route but crowd funding has been a rather viable funding option for investors here. The only downside is that you will have to share the profits with others, depending on the terms you agreed with them.
What makes this investment option also hard is in finding the right safety margin. The safety margin simply means the difference between your initial expenses incurred in buying and flipping the property and your asking price for the same based on the building;s current Fair Market Value.

You can't have the margin too wide or people might not buy the property. You can't also have the margin too narrow or you'd end up with a loss. Finding that sweet spot between expenses and the price will help you earn considerably from your building.

Of course, buying low and selling high isn't the only means to make money from your building. You can also rent the property for tenants to use which ensures a steady stream of income from your investments on a long-term basis.

Investment Trusts

This investment option works similarly to that of a mutual fund. This is because it takes the funds of several investors and then puts them into several income-generating projects. Also, Investment Trusts can be sold and traded in the stock market which makes them the cheaper property-based investment option that you can resort to.

Since you don't have to buy, renovate, and sell property, an investment trust is one of the best property-based options that a beginner can take advantage of. You might not earn a lot compared to selling actual properties but the income you will get will be dependable enough over a considerable period of time.

What NOT to Invest In

Now, the investments above only cover a fraction of what is actually available to you in the stock market and beyond. Although cryptocurrencies and annuities are not recommended, they can still be viable if you know what you are doing or, at the very least, have a sizable safety net to fall back on if things get worse.

However, there are those investment options that you should avoid investing now. These investments are either bad because of current market conditions or are just bad investments by their nature.. As such, here are some of the options that you should never even consider as a first time investor.

1. Subprime Mortgages

If investment options are buildings, then a subprime mortgage is that seedy club at the farthest end of a red light district. In essence, these mortgages are meant for the least trustworthy of creditors who are most likely to default on a loan. To invest on one is to ensure that you are not going to see a single penny out of the money you just loaned to someone else.

2. Penny Stocks

Usually, companies offer their stocks for no less than $5.00 which is pretty cheap. But there are companies that go cheaper and Wall Street folk call these stocks they offer as "penny stocks". Mostly, they can go as low as $1.00 or 50 cents which can sound appealing for new investors. Also, due to their low figures, the smallest of changes in their price can translate to massive changes in your gains.

But what makes them deadly is their deceptiveness. A penny stock is usually a tell-tale sign that that company is going bankrupt. It's one way for deceptive companies to dump on their stocks and leave the stock market with a sizeable portion of money.

Basically, they are the fronts of many pump and dump schemes which will leave investors with a dud stock in the long run.

3. Junk Bonds

They are alternatively known as high-yield bonds today because, technically speaking, a high yield of reward often connotes high risk. Junk bonds can be enticing to investors especially in a market with low interest rates.

But like penny stocks, a junk bond is often a sign that the company is going bankrupt or will go into default. If you own a junk bond from a company, you are mostly going to lose that investment, hence the term.

You can mitigate the risks by choosing a bond by way of a mutual fund but this does not remove the problem entirely. If you do not have all the information about that company or do not know how to speculate on their performance, don't take any bond from them just to be safe.

4. Private Placements

A private placement is simply a stock that was not publicly traded in the stock exchange. Right from the start, they are a turn-off as you must become an accredited investor first before you can even start investing on them. And how do you become accredited? It's either you have an income of $100,000.00 per year or have a net worth over $1 million.

But what makes private placements risky by themselves is that they are often used by deceptive promoters, assuring you with a lot of upsides without telling you of the potential risks. In essence, you will be investing on something that you do not have full information of which is close to gambling.

5. The Double Digit Return

There are those stocks that are just too good to be true. If you have ever heard of an investment that promises more than 10% returns per year, you should be careful. This will be the first thing being promoted to you followed by usual malarkey like "it's government backed!" or "it's insured!" and the oh-so-common "it's the next (insert famous company here)!".

You have to remember that no investment option out there would promise any return. Yes, some are insured and some do get backed by the government but no stock out there will ever promise you returns by the double digits. In fact, the best companies out there rarely offer 10% returns. Some are generous enough at 5% and some do offer the usual 2-3%. Nothing more.

Just keep this rule in mind: if the offer is too good to be true, it is.

To Conclude

So which investment option should you go first? That really depends on you. But if you are the one to want to keep your momentum in this market strong, it is best that you build a strong base.

To do that, it is best that you start with stocks and then diversifying your portfolio with other investment options later on. It's a good way of getting the feel of the market without overspending. At the same time, it is easy for you to bail out in case something goes wrong.

In short, start with stocks first and then venture into other investments later.

Chapter III: The Investor

As was previously stated, the stock market has plenty of opportunities for a person to earn from their stay there. But you might be wondering to yourself just how could you make a name for yourself as a stock market investor.

To answer that question, you have to determine what kind of role you want to play in the market. Understanding this role is crucial for determining your path towards success in the stock market. For this chapter, we would discuss on what major goal you may want to achieve in the market and the tools that you will need in order to make a name for yourself there.

What Kind of Investor are You?

Buying stocks at the market is very basic skill. However, each person buying and trading stock does so for different reasons. The role that you will play as an investor depends greatly on the level of risk you want to regularly deal with, the amount of research that you can and want to do for each investment, how much you know or can speculate as to where the overall economy is heading to, and the length of your intended stay in the market.

Sounds a bit confusing, right? To simplify things, investors always come in three forms which are as follows:

Active Investors

An active investor is perhaps one of the busiest yet more cautious people in the stock market right now. They do everything in their power to stay in the know when it comes to market trends, keep up with the latest news, and spend hours of research on every viable stock option before they start investing.

Buying and selling is not exactly their primary goal here. They pay attention to trends in the market and form their decisions based on those trends. They might not hold investments in the long term but they do take care to make sure that each investment they make counts.

Passive Investors

Where other investors aim for the biggest possible rewards from each investment they make, the passive investor aims for more reasonable gains and a generally stress-free stay in the market. These investors do not care if they have to pay more from each investment as long as they enjoy their stay in the market.

As such, passive investors often go for mutual funds as this allows for quick diversification of their portfolios while others do the dirty work for them. They do not gamble their money on up and coming companies but stick with what has already been established as successful.

Their overall goal here is to coast through the market as easily as possible. If the value of their stocks rise by at least 20% of what they initially purchased it, they might start selling them. It does not matter if a better price is out there. What matters for the passive investor is to make things as easy for them as possible.

The Speculator

There is earning money in the stock market and then there is earning money *fast*. Like the active investor, speculators also do their research but focus on stocks that are about to go up a lot in pricing because of some impending change. Perhaps a merger is about to happen between two companies which can boost prices for their stocks.

Once they know what stocks are about to go up, they would then buy these stocks before the change happens. And when prices go up, they would then sell the stocks according to the new price tag. They then repeat this process over and over again..

Speculators have the highest frequency in trading activities among all other investor types. This also means that they don't hold certain investments for long, selling what they have at the first opportunity of a price change.

The Bargain Hunter

Unlike other investors that focus on buying cheap and selling high, the bargain hunter finds stocks that are really cheap and hold them. They are not essentially aiming for huge, instant profit but long-term growth especially if a floundering company still shows promise of bouncing back.

Their tactics might go against what we have covered a chapter ago but many companies that managed to regain traction in the stock market owe their survival to bargain hunting investors. KMart, for example, suffered through times so bad that they were effectively taken of Wall Street. However, they managed to make it out of their predicament with the investments from bargain hunters.

To be a bargain hunter is to play the game like you are gambling. There is absolutely no assurance that a failing company is going to rise again. But if it does, the rewards that a bargain hunter could receive are comparatively large.

The Retiring Investor

These investors are in the market for the long-term and they do change tactics once they get older. For example, an investor of this type would be quite aggressive at a young age, buying high-risk stocks. As they grow older, they mellow down and start moderating their risks.

Once they reach retirement age, this investor would now focus on dividend stocks that will make them money in lieu of a monthly salary. This investor owes their survival to an ability to manage their risks smartly. They focus on quickly increasing the value of their investments at a young age and then switch to making such investments sustainable as they get older.

The Player

This investor has more qualities to share with a gambler than any other investor role out there. They understand that chaos and uncertainty is always present in any market and thus try to take advantage of such.

Regardless of how they get their funding, the player aims to increase their money in the fastest time possible. Whenever a new company enters into the market or massive changes are implemented, the player would be at the very front trying to take advantage of the frenzy that is generated. Once they are confident with the value, they will then cash out before the market stabilizes.

It's a rather high-risk strategy but players tend to receive the largest rewards relative to the risks they take. By timing your investments right, you might just be able to take advantage of sudden opportunities without losing a lot of money.

What Kind of Trader Are You?

Trading is a wholly separate process from investing. In fact, it's requirements as well as the dynamics here can be quite different from investing.

As such, it is best that you know what kinds of traders tend to flourish in the market right now.

The Scalper

Although that word comes with some serious negative connotations now, scalpers in the stock market are simply those traders who are in it to fulfill short-term goals. Their turnaround time is shorter than that of day traders and they tend to stick to very specific niches in the market.

Scalpers do not necessarily need a lot of capital due to how quickly they can move from one stock to another. However, they will need to have a steady flow of cash ready at the side in order to take advantage of sudden changes in the market.

Since their capital size is small, their target profit is also comparatively small. In fact, they focus on small gains more which, in due time, would accumulate to a substantial amount. To make scalpers easier to understand, think of them as those bargain shop owners. They sell things cheap, mostly at a loss per individual item, but tend to clear up their inventories on a faster rate.

The Day Trader

One step above scalpers, day traders also focus on short-term trades but their turnaround time is comparatively longer. In fact, they often aim for short, 20-minute trades which is why they can do multiple trades per day (hence the name).

Like scalpers, day traders do not have a sizeable capital. This is why they trade often so they can soften the blow of losses on a daily basis. In theory, the frequent activity and the small capital base will allow for a day trader to survive under tough conditions or bail out without having to part with what used to be valuable investments.

Due to their frequent activity, a day trader does not leave a position open for too long. As such, their potential for profit is rather limited. Again, they can be like scalpers in the sense that their victory conditions can be expressed in terms of volume-based value instead of per-item value.

The Swing Trader

A swing trader tends to hold on their trades for longer periods of time. Patience and a bit of faith is required with these traders as they do not have the time nor the resources to constantly monitor their trades.

By the name itself, you can determine that a swing trader will hold on to their trades until times get better. A "swing" in the market, if you will. Thus, they require a lot of capital in order to keep their investments going under tought financial conditions.

A benefit of holding off on frequent trading is that it allows a trader wider profit margins when they do open their investments for trade. Again, this is dependent on timing. When things start to go up, you can expect a swing trader to be the first to open for trading and reap maximum benefits.

The Position Trader

These traders are the very definition of "long term". Like swing traders, they can hold off on trading but for a ridiculously long period of time. In fact, it is not uncommon for a position trader to open a stock up for trader years after purchasing it. As such, they tend to not frequent the stock market a lot.

Holding off on a stock is rather challenging as it's value can go up and down depending on market conditions. As such, a huge capital is needed in order for a position trader to survive with their chosen strategy.

But all that patience does pay off in time. Under the right conditions, the potential payoff for position traders are massive. This could be chalked up to long-term planning or the ability to accurately predict what trend that stock will follow in the years to come but a position trader is in the best position (pun intended) to earn thousands for each stock that they trade.

The Main Takeaway:

These different investor and trader personalities are just indicating that everyone has a place in the market. Though there will be winners and losers in every period, it does not remove the fact that everyone has a chance to make it big in the market.

What is essential is that you pick a style that you are most comfortable with or, better yet, confident with. In short, you must play to your strengths in order to make it big in the stock market. That is provided, of course, that you know what your strengths are.

Chapter IV: The Investor's Arsenal

What separates a good investor from the rest? If the firs thing that comes to your mind is "experience", you are basically half right. But, since we stand on the theory that you don't need experience to achieve your first-time success in the stock market, we can take that factor out of the equation.

What do we have left, then? That would the tools, skills, and even qualities that you must possess as a stock investor. As such, here are some of the things that you need in order to make your stint as a stock investor a rather successful one.

A. Essential Skills and Qualities

Let's start with the things that are innate to you or, at the very least, you will have to develop for yourself. Looking the part of an investor is just the start so that three-piece suit and capital will be where your baseline. From that point, you can start acquiring the essential characteristics of a stock investor which are as follows:

1. Analysis

A stock market investor is going to do a lot of analysis in order to remain competitive in the market. This is rather crucial as the stock market is rather dependent on trends and other outside economic factors.

A more practical explanation for the need of stock market analysis is that it allows you to determine what approaches, strategies, and tools are needed to respond to a trend in market. Later on in the book, you will learn the core characteristics of different market environments and how they are best responded to in order to survive. By using analysis, you will learn how to adjust your strategies while the market is approaching that certain condition.

The point here is that a good investor knows to find a balance between making the right amount of money and taking the right action at the right time. The former is for profit and the latter for survivability. Your analytical skill will help you meet these two different goals at the same time.

2. Research

What separates investing from gambling is that the former demands that you do not go in blind. You have to be armed with all the information that you could possibly gather before you place your bets on something.

When you encounter possible stocks in the market, you should resist all urge to invest on it ASAP. You have to take the time to learn everything about you can about that company, what trends would affect the performance of that sector, and even who runs that company before you start buying and trading stocks.

And how exhaustive is research in stock market investing? You will have to keep track of whatever economic changes, political movements, and inter corporate announcements to make sure that you are investing on the right stock.

In fact, you must develop a preference for reading through charts and tables to keep track of how stocks are performing. This is also quite crucial in downturns as a well-informed investor can take advantage of such and make a profit where others are losing money. At the very least, the right amount of information will help you make better-informed decisions.

3. Calm

Remaining calm is a crucial yet oft-overlooked quality in stock investors. A common mistake beginners make is to panic when they are at a loss. Thus, you get all those pictures of distressed stock investors gnashing and pulling their hair at the Stock Exchange during the economic crisis of the 2000s.

Do not get the wrong idea. There is actually no way out there to fully avoid stress in high-stakes environments like the Stock Market. However, getting overwhelmed by your stress tends to make you do some stupid mistakes which makes things worst for you.

There have too many instances in the past when panicking investors dump all their stocks at the first sight of a downturn, not realizing that the entire problem could have been solved without them incurring losses. A calm investor, on the other hand, carefully adjusts their strategy in order to take advantage of the sudden change of plans.

4. Records Management

A stock investor must also keep a record of every transaction they have ever made. This will serve two purposes. First is for archiving as a record will help you keep track of all investments you have made and how they are faring currently.

The second reason is more personal. By keeping documents, you can at least track your progress as an investor. Are your strategies doing well? What sectors have you yet to venture into? Is it time to call it quits? Your records will tell you that and more.

5. Discipline

I've gone on many times on the difference between investing and gambling because a lot of investors treat the former as if it were the latter. In fact, many go to the stock market thinking that it's just some fancier casino minus the slot machines.

Your overall goal as a stock market investor should not primarily be around making money. The reason for this is that you are bound to make money (and lose it) whenever you buy, trade, and invest in stocks.

What your goal should be must revolve around longevity. You have to stay in the market for as long as possible to truly understand how it works. By understanding how things work in the market, you will have an easier time taking advantage of changes in it.

This is rather crucial especially in those conditions where losses are constant. Nearly every investor will have to deal with a losing streak for reasons that are outside or within their control. With a bit of self-discipline on your part, you can survive under these conditions with most of your capital intact and in a position to start profiting at the next upturn.

B. Tools and Assets

Now that the more personal stuff is out of the way, it is time to look into the things that you could personally arm yourself with to remain competitive in the market. The tools of a stock market investor can vary from person to person.

But, to keep things simple, here are some of the tools and assets that you should get acquainted with before you start investing.

1. Capital

It goes without saying but you should never venture into the stock market without a solid financial plan. The reason for this is that profiting in the market is not cut and dry. There is no assurance that you will be profiting here regularly but the chances of you losing money is always high. In short, you will not earn money in the stock market if you are not willing to spend the same or more in return.

It does not matter how much you have saved for stock investing, if we are to be honest about it. The point is that you should never become a stock investor on an empty wallet. But, just to be safe, save up to a $1,000.00 at the very least before you start investing.

2. A Trading Platform

A trading platform is simply the place where you do all your investment activities in. However, it is a rather crucial place to decide on before you step into the market. What you will have to consider here are the commissions offered or even the requirements necessary to access the platform.

There are brokers that use trading platforms that give high commissions for each trade but require a minimum account balance or a number of successful trades in the past in order to sign up in. In short, they may be good, but they are not ideal for absolute beginners like you.

Conversely, there are trading platforms out there that might work for your current setup. TD Ameritrade, for example, has no minimum account balance requirements although the commission you have to pay for your middlemen is quite high at $10.00 per trade. OptionHouse might be cheaper with a $5.00 trader's fee but more robust trading options and tools.

If you become more confident with your investing and trading skills, you can invest in more robust platforms like the Ameritrade one mentioned above or Interactive Brokers.

3. Mobile Apps

A serious investor and trader will have to take their work wherever they go. Fortunately, there are applications out that help you do all of your stock market activities in one handheld devices.

There are quite a lot of these apps out there which begs the question: What should you look for in them?

For starters, what you need is a diverse set of in-app tools and options. Choose an app that allows you to quickly search for and screen potential stock investments while also monitoring their performances in real time. If you want to be more advanced, choose an app that allows to you seamlessly move from your desktop computer to your handheld through a unified account system.

Lastly, choose an app with a reasonable subscription fee. Some mobile apps go for the $20.00 which might be pricey for some investors. If you do opt for an expensive app, make sure that you have access to a lot of features that will make your investment activities easier regardless of your location.

4. Stock Screening Tools

Looking for the stock that will fit your needs can be hard if you are a beginner. This is where a stock screener comes into play as it helps you look for stocks in the market based on a set of criteria that you yourself will determine.

For instance, you could be looking for stocks based on their market capitalization, the potential dividend yield, and the prices for each share being offered. Fortunately for you, most trading platforms and apps offer screeners as a basic feature.

However, there are dedicated screening apps out there like Finviz which offers more specific screening criteria. Of course, you will have to pay a subscription fee in order to get access for its advanced features but the basic services are free for all investors.

5. Charts, Charts, and More Charts

What you have to remember is that the stock market is not exactly the easiest thing to describe with mere words. The amount of number crunching and computations that happen here means that you are better off understanding the whole thing from a non-verbal viewpoint.

This is where charts come into play as it helps determine what actions to take by laying and connecting different points of data in a relatively easy to understand format. A simple look at a chart will tell you where a company is going performance wise, where the value of their stock prices are currently, what trend it is following, and what might happen in that sector within the next few hours or so.

Here's the caveat, though. It's a bit hard to understand these charts if you don't know what to look for and what each term means. Also, do keep in mind that these figures will change by the minute which means that stock charts have relatively short lifespans as far as relevance is concerned.

Fortunately, there are different services out there that will help you understand what the figures are saying in the simplest terms possible. It is up to you to get subscribed to them so you know how stocks are performing in real time.

6. Brokerages

Consider this one as the training wheels for every newbie stock investor. Since you are new to the market, there is always a chance that you might get confused and make mistakes in your activities. You can mitigate this by getting subscribed to a brokerage service who will assist you in getting a hand of the stocks that you want.

However, brokers require a fee which means a portion of your earnings will ultimately end up being used to pay other people. You can lessen your costs by looking for a discount brokerage which can offer all the basic amenities at a fraction of the price.

As of now, the best brokerages are Robinhood, TD Ameritrade, and Fidelity. E-Trade is also good if you are looking for a brokerage that can focus solely on buying and selling stocks. The point is that there are actually services out there that are inexpensive yet effective. The less money you will have to pay for good services, the more money you could use to go through the market.

7. Portfolio Analysis

Aside from the diversity of your investment portfolio, you also need to determine the risks and opportunities that are present with it. Portfolio analysis will help you go through all of your investments and understand which ones possess the best possible yields given the current market conditions.

However, the problem with a portfolio analysis is that they are rather expensive. That is if you don't know where to look for free services.

Portfolio Visualizer is a website that will offer a free analysis of your portfolio using data models that go several decades back. Their services will help you run simulations, find points of interest base on historical data, and test all current investments using a number of calculation tools.

The process might be intimidating to some but the results they produce are rather easy to understand. You can also use the data being given to you to further optimize your portfolio as a whole instead of looking at it by individual investments.

8. Financial Ratios

Stock market data are mostly numbers based. This is why the first order of the day for any investor is to make sense of every financial data being provided to them, A financial ratio will help you do just that while also locating and isolating those bits of information that you need the most. In essence, they help you understand the figures as a collective and as individual strands of data.

Financial ratios are quite diverse but they often fall under the same categories which are the following.

Price

As the name would imply, these ratios assess stocks according to their price. More often than not, you can use them to track the performance of a company since prices rise and fall according to how good a company is in that period.

As such, Price Ratios can use a number of models which include:

● Price to Earnings
● Price to Sales
● Price to Book
● Dividend Yield
● Dividend Payout

Profitability

Like the Price Ratio, Profitability Ratios track a company's performance. But, instead of the changes in their stock prices, this ratio determines performance by how a company earns comparative to the expenses they made. As such, profitability ratios use the following metrics:

● Profit Margin
● Return on Equity
● Return on Assets

Liquidity

This metric is used to determine how good a company is meeting short-term goals and obligations. You have to remember that companies tend to create debt just to function properly. Thus, what separates a good company from the rest is its ability to pay out such obligations as soon as possible.

A company that has low liquidity tends to create more debt or, worse, make decisions to raise money that does not bode well for the company in the long-term. In short, liquidity will tell you how well a company manages itself under tough financial conditions.

Under this ratio, the metrics below will be used:
- Current
- Quick

Debt

This ratio focuses more on how a company manages its obligations on a long-term basis. By looking at its starting capital and current financial structure, this ratio will help you understand the overall health of a company which indirectly tells you of their validity as an investment option.

With this ratio, the following metrics are to be used:

- Debt to Equity
- Interest Coverage

Efficiency

Under this ration, a company will be assessed on how it uses its capital and assets in order to function properly. It is mostly a management issue but this metric will help you determine just how good a company uses the investments it makes while also delivering on the promises it has made on investors. When using efficiency, the following will be looked into:

- Turnover of Assets
- Turnover of Inventory

Important Reminder: Do keep in mind that these ratios just tell you what MIGHT happen with a company based on currently available data, and know what will happen. As such, do not be dependent on them for information but do refer to them when making crucial investment decisions.

9. Budgeting and Portfolio Management

Although not exactly a tool for your investment activities, budgeting software will help you track how much you are spending on your activities and how much you have left on your current capital.

A budgeting software should help you manage your payments while checking on the prices of stocks.

As such, here are some of the budgeting apps that you should look into.

- **BlackGold -** This financing app will focus more on the prices of commodities like oil. It checks mostly for the prices of gasoline as well as the stocks of energy companies on a statewide and international basis.
- **PageOnce -**This app helps you keep track of all due bills **in** your investment and track their performance. It can send out regular notifications to inform you of an upcoming payment so you wouldn't miss out.
- **Venmo -** This app helps you do all of your payments on one platform. It links to your existing investment accounts and bank numbers and sports an interface that is ideal for those new to investing. Also, it's free.

- **Wikinvest Portfolio -** A mobile portfolio analysis tool of sorts, this app helps you keep track of how your investments are faring in the market. It will import brokerage information and provide news on investors as they happen in real time.

10. A News Source

As was stated earlier, knowledge is crucial in order to survive as a stock investor. And any knowledge is not enough, however. It has to be up to date and based on the most accurate of figures.

Being subscribed to a news source is a must for any investor as this allows you to know what is happening in the market, which stocks are going up, and why. Of course, this is only effective if coupled with a habit of reading the news before you start the day,

Nevertheless, knowing what is new in your market is important as a stock investor. Fortunately, there are quite a lot of news sources out there that you could subscribe to and they tend to get updated on an hourly basis.

C. Technical Analysis Tools

Due to how robust their features are, it is best to separate these tools as their own category. The ability to accurately evaluate stock market data is crucial for any stock market investor. It removes a bit of the uncertainty that comes with investing while also preventing you from being too rash with your investment decisions.

Fortunately, technical analysis tools are readily available for all investors and traders right now. Yes, some might charge a free for premium features but most do not require you to pay up just to enjoy the bare essentials.

Brokers

A lot of brokerage firms right now provide technical analysis tools to ease in newcomers in the field. They mostly draw their data from Recognia, a Canadian Third Party company that provides stock market data for a lot of trading platforms and brokers.

By analyzing changes in the price of stocks, Recognia will give investors and traders the insight needed to see if certain stock options are worth the while to invest in or not. Recognia itself is not available for those who are not operating brokerages. However, you can be certain that most of these brokerages who offer technical analysis will have Recognia incorporated into their services.

- **Charles Schwab**

This broker operates a trading platform named StreetSmart Edge. This platform, in turn, analyzes data being streamed in real time which allows users to go through stocks and ETFs with the already existing Screener Plus feature. The platform also provides a number of charts which track the progress of the stocks you were looking for in real time. You can customize what each chart would present based on several parameters.

- **E-Trade**

E-Trade uses a system called the Live Action Scanner. As the name would imply, it scans the market in real-time for stock prices as well as analyze technical information that would affect any changes to such. It is also a rather robust screening feature as it uses at least 100 pre-defined screening options that investors can mix and match.

Also, the scanner can do a portfolio analysis for you by tracking which of the investments you have made were overbought, underbought, dropping, or rising in prices. And if one of your stocks meets criteria you yourself have set in the scanner, the program will alert you. On paper, this should help you adjust your strategies in response to those changes.

- **Fidelity Investments**

This broker uses the Active Trader Pro system which can track stocks in real time and alert you of any changes in the stocks that you have invested in or are planning to. For instance, if a stock in a company is open for trading, the system will alert you if you have tagged that company previously.

There is also an advanced charting option that lets you peer way back several decades of a company's stock history. If you want something more recent, the system can also track changes that have occurred in the past month or, better yet, in the past 60 minutes.

And if that is not enough, Fidelity Ivnestments does offer several online courses through the system that help traders get a handle of their technical analysis tools as well as improve on their stock strategies.

- **Interactive Brokers**

What Interactive Brokers have that others have yet to offer is a more extensive charting option. Using the data that they got with Recognia and pairing that up with hundreds of performance indicators, what IB gives to investors is the chance to really see how stocks have performed or are performing based on a number of criteria that they prefer.

Also, you can use your IB account and attach it to a third=party analytics tool. In theory, this should allow you to chart stocks in a manner that truly fits your overall investment strategy.

- **Lightspeed**

Catering to day traders, Lightspeed uses a scanner called LightScan to search and filter through hundreds of trading options. How it works is that goes through multiple markets looking for the stocks that will meet the criteria you have set in the program.

The program can also chart up to 20 years of historical stock data to give you an idea as to how certain stocks have been performing in multiple market conditions. The entire program is still in beta as of now but you can download the demo if you want to try things out for yourself.

- **Thinkorswim**

The trading platform of TD Ameritrade, Thinkorswim is primarily catered for options trading but it has some features that do make things easier for equity traders as well. In here, you will find several drawing tools, data visualization tools, and hundreds of technical indicators.

What Thinkorswim does is it allows traders to create their own analysis scheme in order to analyze stocks based on criteria that they think works for them best. Thinkorswim is best used on the desktop as the mobile version has some optimization issues.

- **TradeStation**

Out of all the broker-based technical analysis tools out there, TradeStation is perhaps the one that was designed for technical analysis from the ground up. It traces its origins from the software made by the Omega Research firm which should tell you that this was designed specifically to analyze stock options.

TradeStation offers an automated analysis feature that monitors trade stocks in real time. It also sports an AI which seemingly adjusts its monitoring in response to the criteria you often use in previous activities. It's charting feature can also draw from several decades of historical data while also simulating future stock performances.

Standalone Programs and Websites

- **ESignal**

.The most current iteration, ESignal 12, is a downloadable program that comes with a number of technical analysis and consultation packages. It is also compatible with the services offered by Tradier and Interactive Brokers which makes this a handy inclusion if you already use those services already.

The downside? ESignal is rather expensive. The basic version is $54.00 per month and comes with a paltry 25 technical analysis features and a 15-minute delay in data streaming. If you want a more real-time streaming service and several hundreds of data analysis services, you must pay for the Signature version which comes at a whopping $176.00 per month.

- **iVest MarketGear**

This program sports charting features that allow you to track stocks using customizable performance indicators. Aside from that, you can use drawing tools to determine market trends, look back on all the past trades you have made, and schedule when and how you are going to start trading certain stocks.

The basic version offers 100 technical indicators that should help you find the stocks that meet your preferences. Also,

MarketGear sports compatibility with TD Ameritrade, and E-Trade. As for subscription fees, you only have to deal with a $38.00 per month price tag.

● Meta Stock

Having been in the market since the 1980s, Meta Stock is one of the oldest technical analysis tools for traders and investors out there. There are a number of versions of the tool available in the market right now but the best one happens to be Meta Stock R/T which features real-time analysis and tracking.

The basic version comes with 150 performance indicators plus a number of interpretations to help you understand what each indicator is telling you. If you opt for the advanced version, Meta Stock comes with an Indicator Builder feature that lets you create your own indicators. In theory, this means that you should be able to come up with analysis based on strategies of your own making or for those that the tools were primarily designed for.

Subscription comes at $100.00 per month and data live feeds are purely optional. Also, Meta Stock is quite compatible with Interactive Brokers.

● TC2000

Known formerly as Worden's TC2000, this program is compatible with a number of operating systems and can be linked to the Interactive Brokers system. It's the most basic package, the practice version, which allows for charting, screening, and trade monitoring. It is also free to download.

However, if you want to have access to more scanning options and performance indicators, you will have to get the gold and platinum versions which are priced at $30.00 and $80.00 per month respectively. Data feeds have also be paid separately. Regardless of this steep asking price, the TC2000 system has been known to be rather dependable for investors looking at stock performance under specific market conditions.

The Habits of Highly Successful Investors

Having the right tools and qualities will be enough in order to succeed, right? Not quite. You see, these assets, tools, and personal qualities are good but only if they manifest into something actionable. And the manifestation should not be a one-time thing but must be executed on a daily basis.

In other words, arming yourself with the right skills and tools is not enough if you don't actually use them on a constant basis. Sustaining this effort is thus the key to becoming successful as an investor.

As such, you need to develop habits that increase your chances of success as an investor. These habits include:

1. Saving Money

Regardless of your intended strategy as an investor and then as a trader, you should never come to the market with less than the ideal amount you have set up for your investing activities. Remember that you are going to spend here in order to earn more which is why you need a sizeable capital to sustain your efforts.

So what's the ideal amount that you should have saved before becoming a stock market investor? There is no exact figure but the generally accepted figure would be 15% of your yearly income. Of course, that is the baseline as some people would actually put off more than 20% before starting on their careers as investors.

Whatever the case, it is important that you must have more than a few hundred dollars saved up for investments if you want to be in the market for as long as possible.

2. Diversify

Risk is something that you will have to deal with regularly as an investor. It may be something light as sudden but minor changes in company performances to drastic ones like massive economic downturns.

There is no escaping risk in stock investing but you can soften its blow by spreading your activities in different sectors and stock types. Diversification works by adding new stock types from different fields to your investment portfolio.

The goal here is to create a safety net that will prevent your entire portfolio from losing value in case one industry falls. For example, let say that there are two investors, A and B. Both of them have invested $1,000.00 in stocks. A invested all of it in crude oil and metal. B, on the other hand, invested in energy, electronics, finance, real estate, and retail.

Now, if stock prices were to drop in the oil and metals scene, A has a greater risk of losing all of his $1,000.00. B, on the other hand, might lose some of his money if the sectors he invested in took a turn for the worse but not all of his money will go to waste if the other sectors continue performing well.

Of course, diversification does not guarantee profit nor does it ensure that you will not suffer a loss. At the very least, it lessens the blow if things get worst The best part is that diversification does not work on a per-stock-class basis. You can further diversify stocks in their own categories. Some smart investors do diversify according to investment types, geographic location, size, and stock exposure.

3. Sticking to a Plan (Despite Market Volatility)

When the value of an investment falls, it is natural to entertain thoughts of bailing out. A good investor, on the other hand, resists such an urge.

Instead of taking their money and running with it, an investor will maintain a sizeable allocation of stocks that can help them live regardless of the market condition. When the financial crisis of 2008 happened, a lot of investors scrambled to get the most of their money before things eventually went south.

Although they might have recovered a portion of what they invested, they had a harder time starting from scratch when things picked up again in the early 2010s. In fact, those that did not panic in '08 were able to maintain a presence in the market even as things got worse until 2010. But when things got better, they were the first to open themselves to better trading and investment options.

This habit tends to go along with a diversified investment portfolio. The point is that you do not bail out when things get worse. Instead, you adjust your strategies so that you can still meet your goals even when the market is in a downturn phase.

4. Focusing on After-Tax Returns

The taxes you have to pay often affect how much you can earn from your investments, depending on the situation. As such, you should consider adding in options that yield higher after-tax returns to get the most out of your investment. For example, a 401K, an IRA, and other annuities can generate higher after-tax returns due to their nature.

You should also learn how to perform asset location and account location. The former is the practice of putting in your investments on different accounts based on their tax treatment and efficiency. The latter, on the other hand, focuses more on putting your investment on accounts depending on how taxes are treated in them.

In practice, this means putting in your investments with the least amount of tax efficiencies like bonds in accounts that are tax-deferred by nature such as an IRA or a 401K. On the other hand, if the investment is more tax-efficient, you must place them in a taxable account.

Taxes should not be the sole focus of your investment decisions, mind you. This is habit is purely effective in making sure that you get the most of your investments while still complying with tax laws. And we know how much Internal Revenue can be ruthless when it comes to getting the government's share in personal profit.

To Conclude

Now, does having the right skills, mindset, assets, tools, and strategies lead to a successful investor? Not exactly. Remember that there is no assurance of success in the stock market. Everyone gets the same opportunities and deal with the same threats. It is up to the individual stock investor to play to their strengths and take advantage of changes in a situation.

That being said, it does not hurt to arm yourself with the best possible tools in the industry to increase your chances of succeeding. You may not even use all the tools mentioned here or even use strategies outside of this book. The point is that your creativity and persistence will play a huge role in becoming successful as an investor.

With all of those out the way, let us begin preparing you for making your first steps into the market.

Chapter V: Buying Your First Stock

As of this point, we have only talked about what you must be and what you must have in order to succeed as an investor. But there is still one question that remains to be answered:

What should you DO in order to succeed in the stock market?

Do not get the idea that this is a rather easy question to answer. In fact, it's a rather loaded one, and how you answer it depends greatly on how well you applied all that you have learned so far. As such, from this point on, we are going to talk about how you could make the best of your time whenever you are in the stock market.

To start things off, let's focus on actually acquiring stocks and other investment options. Here's how.

1. Finding a Broker

Now, we've talked exhaustively about the different brokers that you can subscribe to as an investor. However, that still does not answer the question as to which brokerage firm will be best for you. Keep in mind that the best ones cater to different styles and needs.

Also, do remember that commission is no longer a problem when it comes to some brokerage firms like Charles Schwab and TD Ameritrade since they have already removed that. In other words, the cost is not exactly going to be your biggest concern for and the rest of the foreseeable future.

As such, you ought to ask yourself a few questions when you pick a broker.

A. **Do They Have All that You Need?**

When you ask this question, you should look be focusing on the services that they offer. For example, a broker might be content in providing you with more investment options which is why they might offer trading options in foreign stock markets or the option to buy fractional shares in a company.

Other companies might want to invest in your development which is why they also want to make you a better trader/investor. Some brokers offer educational programs, sources, weekly newsletters, and other information sources that you can draw a lot of knowledge from.

Each broker has its own set of features and advantages on offer. As a rule of thumb, you must pick the one who's promised amenities are worth the subscription fee that you will eventually pay for.

B. **Are They Easy to Deal With?**

Assuming that you are going to be tech-savvy and do all of your investing and trading in multiple devices, you need a broker whose platform is optimized for handheld devices. It's a common feature nowadays for brokers to allow investors and traders to do on-button transactions which should speed up the process without sacrificing comfort and safety.

One other aspect you could look into here is navigation. A good brokerage platform should allow for seamless transitions between pages and processes so that you don't have to go back frequently just to make sure that your information is correct.

Also, check if that brokerage firm allows for "trial phases" for their programs. This is not a chance for you to test the quality of the broker for free but to also get comfortable with how things are done in the platform.

But if you are a stock investor/trader that is not comfortable with doing all your activities online, then find a broker with a physical branch near where you live. This should reduce a lot of time fumbling through pages and charts while also getting direct, uninterrupted consultation with a broker.

C. Narrowing the Field

Now that you know what you need and intend to do with the help of a broker, the next thing to do is to limit your choices down to a handful. Every broker has its own features, advantages, and disadvantages but a good one tends to check certain boxes which include:

- Membership at a Stock Broker Regulation and Trust firm like the Securities Investor Protection Corporation.
- Membership at the Financial Industry Regulation Authority.
- Coverage from the Federal Insurance Corporation especially if they offer Cash Deposit, Money Market Deposit Accounts, and other similar accounts.
- Insurance amounting to $250,000.00 at the very least in case of problems.
- Fraud Protection guarantees
- Account protection protocols to prevent online attacks.
- A consistent customer review score ranging from good to above average

What all of these qualities imply is that the firm knows how to facilitate your online activities for you without leaving you unnecessarily exposed to threats coming from outdoor threats and even in-door system deficiencies. After all, you are dealing with huge amounts of money here which is why you'd rather do it on a secure platform.

2. Opening an Account

Once you have found the brokerage that fits your style and needs the most, the next step is to actually open up an account in their firm. It is a fairly straightforward process and will involve you disclosing certain basic yet vital information about yourself.
What that in mind, it is still best that you take into consideration a few points.

A. How Are You Going to Be Funded/Paid?

As of now, there are multiple ways to funnel money in and out of your brokerage account. When opening an account, do consider the following options:

- **Electronic Funds Transfer -** This is one of the more convenient options as it connects your account to an already existing checking or saving account that you already have. At best, the funds that you have wired will show up at the account on the next business day.
- **Wire Transfer -** This is a direct bank to bank transaction which would mean it takes minutes for a single transaction to be completed. If you are looking for a fast transaction, this option is the best for you.
- **Checks -** One of the more variable funding options, checks do not allow for instant transmission of money but trades it for a more secure transaction. Of course, the availability of funds in an account is never assured but, at the very least, you can demand payment if that check does bounce.
- **Assets Transfer -** This option is ideal if you have more than 401K in your account or intend to transfer investments that you already have to another broker.
- **Stock Certificates -** You are not exactly transferring money here but direct ownership of the stock. If you have a paper certificate and want to trade that stock to another,

you can have the certificate mailed into an online account. It's not the most efficient funding option but it does work.

B. What Privileges are Being Offered?

Privileges are simply the incentives that you are bound to enjoy in consideration of opening up an account with that firm. These benefits are divided into two groups which are:

- **Margin Privileges**

These benefits provide the ability for an account holder to borrow money from the firm in order to buy stocks. Investing on a margin is not always a good path to take but having margin privileges can help you get out of a bind.

For example, there are some instances where you cannot use the funds you deposited unless you opened a margin account. If this requirement is present in your account, then have a margin account opened but make sure that whatever amount you borrowed will be paid in time.

- **Options Trading Privileges**

Stock options are generally best avoided if you are a new trader but it would be best to know if you have options trading privileges being offered by the firm. Do not worry as there are several levels of options trading privileges that you can choose from. You can even change such privileges once you get used to being an investor/trader.

3. Research

This is where the bulk of your time buying your first stock should be focused. In no circumstance should you go in on an investment blind. Instead, you should know everything that is to possibly know about that stock before you purchase them.

And that does give rise to the question: What should you look for when going through investment options. Here are some factors to consider.

A. Earnings Growth

First things first, you have to determine how well the value of those stocks has increased over the years. What you should be looking for here is not one-time, massive changes but a gradual improvement of value over time. A "trend", if you will.

Use your broker platforms and see if they can plot a chart on the price of that stock for years. What you should be looking for is an upwards trend. There might be drops occurring through the years but it should generally follow a path where the value now is quite better than what that company had at the start.

Once you know that that stock follows an upwards trend, the next thing to find out is why. As a rule, always pick company whose stocks enjoyed upwards value trend is sparked by changes in the quality of their products and/.or services. This is an indicator of strong performance and viability.

B. Relative Company Strength

When looking for a company to purchase stocks at, you have to first look at the industry it operates in. Normally, a strong industry performance will tell you that a company will thrive there.

But, of course, you have to know how that company is performing relative to its competitors. What advantages does it have? Has it used those advantages or played to its strengths? Is there a potential threat to its viability to you as an investment? These are crucial questions that you need to be asking as you'd rather invest in a competitive company than a failing one (unless that's your strategy, of course).

To evaluate a company's relative strength, you have to look at its sales figures as well as its cash flows and income statement. You can make this easier for yourself by lining up that company with its competitors and gauging how it is performing compared to the rest for a certain time period. There are broker apps out that there that can help you draw this performance up quickly.

C. Debt to Equity Ratio
Out of all the financial ratios that you can use, this is perhaps the most crucial when looking for stocks to buy. To use this, you have to get a hold of the company's income statement. If you have the figures, you have to divide the total liabilities that a company has in its sheet by the total number of shareholders.

If you are looking for a company with a low risk tolerance, the figure that you should come up with should be no more than 0.3, Of course, this debt to equity ratio works for most companies not all. Construction firms, for instance, have higher debt to equity ratios due to their reliance on funding incurred by debts.

Whatever the case, just make sure that that company's debt to equity ratio falls within the norms of the industry that they are part in. At the very least, a good debt to equity ratio tells you that the company, if things get worst, will have more shareholders to pay than creditors.

D. Price to Earnings Ratio

As the name would imply, this ratio determines how much a company's price in its stocks is doing compared to how much it has been earning. As a matter of fact, this ratio will tell you if a company is either overvalued or undervalued.

To find this ratio, what you will have to do is to divide the company's current share price by the price of its earnings per share. For example, if a company is trading it's stocks for $30.00 per share and it's   earnings per share is at $1.875, then the price to earnings ratio is at 16 which is a rather strong figure.

You can even use this ratio to compare stock prices between competing companies I the same sector.

E. Dividends Management

To be straight to the point, a company should be paying its dividends in order to be seen as a stable company to invest in. This is quite important if that company has shown an increase in payout over several years. In other words, it is earning more than enough to pay itself, its staff, and then all those shareholders who invested in it.

Here's a caveat, though: that an increase in dividend yield should not be sudden so as to form a spike in the chart. That is a rather telltale sign that the company is not investing in itself much or is getting desperate in reeling in new investors.

Also, the dividend yield is not always necessary to determine how good a company is performing. When the economic times get hard, it is common for companies to cut on their dividends in order to stay afloat. It's not a sign that the company is about to go under but, rather, it is shifting its goals so that creditors are paid first and its employees are taken care of.

But, if the conditions are good in the economy, then look for a strong dividend payout when investing.

F. The Leadership

You have to know exactly WHO runs the company. Effective leadership means that that company can last long in different economic conditions while managing a stable flow of income.

Aside from having a strong baseline performance in leadership, the executives must also show signs of innovation as well as flexibility in the markets that they choose to operate in. Under the best conditions, this means that the company's stocks are not only following an upwards trend in price but that the trend itself is being charted on a higher point than most of its competitors.

G. Long-Term Stability

If there is one term that you need to really understand when it comes to the stock market, it would be volatility. Nothing is ever certain here and what performs well today will be losing hundreds or thousands of dollars a few hours later. That's the rather peculiar dynamic in the market that everyone else has to keep up with.

As such, do not make profit as your sole factor in determining a company's strength. Eventually, every company is going to lose value in the stock market for reasons within and outside of its control. What you should be looking for, on the other hand, is a company's stability in the market over a long-term basis.

This should be reflected in your chart as a smooth yet upwards trend. It may hit a few downturns here and there but the company should be able to pull itself back together and come back stronger than ever.

This should also be reflected in a number of factors we have already discussed in this section. A stable company has strong revenues, low debt levels, a strong competitive advantage, and is ran by people who exactly know what they are doing.

4. Deciding on Share Quantity

Now that you know what company to invest in, the next part would be determining how many shares you'd want to purchase. Compared to the previous step, this should be a rather straightforward process so there should be no pressure on your part on how many stocks you'd want to buy.

But what is a good range for newbie investors like you? Just to be safe, start with the smallest quantifiable number out there: 1.

Starting with just one share does have its benefits. For starters, it helps you get the feel of that company without overly exposing yourself to risk if you happen to buy at an inopportune time. Once you feel confident with that company, you can add in more stocks,

You may also want to consider what are called as "Fractional Shares". This is something new in companies where you get to buy a portion of a share, not the full thing. The advantage they have to offer is they allow investors to get a hold of more expensive stocks without having to go over their budget,

However, not all brokers offer this option. Only a few brokers like Charles Schwab, SoFi Active Investing, and Robinhood offer these fractional shares, Either way, it is recommended that you ask if such an option is offered by your broker. On paper, they would allow you to earn more stocks, pay for the entire stock gradually, and diversify your portfolio in an instant.

5. Choosing Your Stock Order Type

This is one of the more deceptive parts of the buying process not because it is actually easy. Instead, the opposite applies as choosing the right stock order type for you looks complicated but, in application, is one of the easiest parts of the process.

How so? For starters, you are going to be encountering a lot of fancy words and terms that companies call their stock orders with. You might start thinking that you are now going to deal with a lot of complicated trading jargon just to get survive in this field.

The truth? You don't need to learn a lot of complicated order types and terms just to successfully buy stock. In fact, a lot of successful investors made careers for themselves buying two order types only. They are as follows.

A. Market Order

A market order is simply the type where you buy the stock at its best and current available price in the market. One notable advantage that this stock order type has is that it allows for immediate execution and fulfillment of your order. The reason for this is that there is no price parameters set for the purchase. Of course, the order is immediately executed if you are not buying shares worth over millions or are taking part in a shift of majority votes in a company.

However, since there are no price parameters, do expect that the price that you are given will not be the same price quoted to you when you were contemplating buying that stock a few moments ago. Bidding and selling prices would actually fluctuate by the hour. As such, a market order is great if you are ordering stocks with more stable price swings.

In other words, this order type is great if you are buying stock from a larger, reputable, and stable company.

Protip: Timing is the key to making the most of a market order since prices fluctuate by the hour. As such, do your market order "after hours". this means that you must purchase the stock when the stock market has closed for the day.

Why? This will cause your order's price to be placed at the most prevailing price of that stock for the day when the stock exchange opens for the next day. So as long as the prevailing price was good on that day, you can be sure of a rather good purchase price for your stocks.

Also, do check the terms of execution by the trader of your choice in this order type. Some brokers that offer their stocks cheap will often bundle all the orders of their customers and execute them all at once under that stock's prevailing price for the day. At least, you'd know why your stock orders are taking so long to be executed if ever that happens.

B. Limit Order

Unlike the market order, limit orders give investors and traders better control over the price range of stock. How it works is quite simple.

Let us say, for example, that company DEF is trading their stocks at $200.00 per share. However, you think that the stocks should be priced at $180.00 given the performance of the company currently. Add to that, there is a chance that the price would drop at $180.00 or below within the next few hours or days.

As such, a limit order works by telling the trader to hold off on executing the trade with you until the price drops to $180.00. Think of it like going to the department store and telling the cashier to place all your orders in a secret compartment so you could pay for them once the shop has a sale.

This type of order is quite favorable for investors that want to invest in smaller and more volatile companies or when the market is experiencing some short-term volatility period.

Also, you can even further customize your limit order by adding certain conditions. You can go for an All or None Order where your order will be executed only when all the shares that you wish to buy have reached a certain price point.

Alternatively, you could for the Good for the Day type where your order will either be executed or expire at the end of the day even if not all conditions are met. Lastly, you can go for the Good Til Canceled type where your order will never expire until you say so or 2 to 4 months have passed and the stocks have not met your conditions.

Other Points to Consider

Keep in mind that a limit order does not exactly guarantee the fulfillment of your order. The order type actually operates on a first-come-first-served basis. The orders that have parameters that are easier to complete will be fulfilled first and will only happen if the trade actually benefits the trader as well.

Also, a limit order can be more costly to an investor in the long run. Limit orders that were not completed or fulfilled for a day may continue on being fulfilled in the next few days which can increase costs on your part. As such, temper your conditions with the actual figures in the market. The more feasible your conditions are, the quicker it is for your limit order to be fulfilled.

If all goes well and you follow all of the steps above, then Congratulations! You have finally purchased your first stock. Now, the question is what will you do with it?

An investor has several options on what they could do with their stocks in the foreseeable future. We will discuss them intently in the chapters to follow.

Chapter VI: The Basics of Trading

As was previously stated, trading is perhaps one of the quicker methods to earn from your stay in the stock market. But just because you own stocks does not mean that you have what it takes to be a successful trader.

There is an art as well as a science to trading your stocks. Depending on your chosen strategy, the entire process could be a breeze or a total hectic nightmare on your part.

But since it is an integral part of the stock market, it pays to know just what it takes to succeed in the field of trading stocks. Aside from that, you should know how to manage some of the more inherent risks and opportunities within this sub-field of the market. Here's how.

The Basics

Since this will be your inaugural attempt at trading, it is best to keep things nice and simple. That being said, the entire process of trading stocks can be broken down into a handful of steps.

1. Owning a Brokerage Account

It goes without saying that you can't trade if you are not affiliated with a brokerage firm. The previous chapter has gone into considerable detail on the intricacies of opening one up so you should know how to do one for yourself now.

That being said, this is the easy part as you are merely setting up the platform where you are going to do all of your trading-related activities.

2. Understanding Market and Limit Orders from a Trader's Perspective

"Haven't we discussed this already? You may ask and, yes, that is true,

But what you have understood so far as market and limit orders are concerned is how they work from a buyer's point of view. What about the trader, then?

As with a buyer, a trader can choose to use limit or market orders depending on what they want. However, there are some key advantages that a trader can get from these order types which are as follows.

A. **Market Orders -** Since these order types require that an order be executed ASAP, you can actually determine when that day will that order be executed. This works in two ways. First, it helps you take advantage of the prevailing price of that stock so you also get to profit considerably from the trade. That is, of course, if the order was done before the exchange closes for that day.

As a matter of fact, you can have all orders executed at any time of the day that you want so that you don't spend all day doing repeated order fulfillment processes. At the very least, this is a more convenient order type for you.

But what about "after hours" trades? Well, the prices of those stocks will be fixed at the prevailing price for that day which will be used as a baseline for the next day when the exchange opens.

Also, the price that the stock will be bought for may not exactly be the same as the price that you quoted to the buyer.

Depending on the time when the trade was done, this might work to your advantage.

B. **Limit Orders** - Due to the placing of parameters for the execution of stock, you might think that this order type would not e beneficial to you. However, this also means that you have more control over how the order is going to be fulfilled.

If the buyer, for example, places a condition that the order will be fulfilled if 20% of stock prices drop before a certain period but another buyer will purchase the same stocks ASAP, you can at least put more preference in the latter instead of the former.

In essence, you get to dictate who can purchase your stocks and in what period depending on which buyers have the least amount of "demands" before they start paying up for certain stocks.

3. Practice

Arguably, there is a certain level of intimidation when it comes to trading. You can soften your entry into the process by going for some low-pressure practice rounds with the brokerage firm of your choice. Some firms like TD Ameritrade and Interactive Brokers allow for first-time traders to do some "paper trading" transactions where you trade actual yet low-priced stocks for a small amount of money or none at all.

The goal in these practice trades is to let you hone your skills in trading without putting a serious dent in your budget. Also, it helps you build your record as a trader so that other buyers will have more confidence in doing business with you.

Just to be safe, ask for this option from the brokerage of your choice. Some do not offer practice trading opportunities but offer alternatives like training courses and consultation.

4. Benchmarking

The goal for trading stocks is to always be a few steps ahead of a certain performance index. So what exactly is a "Performance Index"? It could simply be the index used by Standard & Poor known as the 500 Index. It could also be the composite index used by NASDAQ. It could be any of those smaller performance indexes used by agencies and focusing on certain factors like geographical location, size, and industry type.

Whatever the case, you should have a good idea of how the market is faring as of this minute. If an investor you are dealing with is not able to keep up with that performance benchmark, then you should aim for low-cost investment options like mutual funds or ETFs. The point is that the stocks that you have to offer for that day must align with what the benchmark index is telling you will be profitable for that day.

5. Trade!

If you are ready to place in your first trade, all you will have to do is fund your brokerage account through the funding system you have placed for it. If the funds are already processed and ready for use, you will then have to select the stock that you want to trade, pick the type of order you want to use, and then place your order.

What is important here is that you make sure that the order actually executes. A market order will be processed immediately while a limit order takes a good bit of time to get processed. As such, try to make your parameters a bit more reasonable and achievable so that your limit order will be processed quicker.

Survival Tips for Beginners

Your ability to go through the trading process safely is a hallmark of a good trader. Things can get rather "intense" when trading. In fact, it is at trading where that misconception of the stock market being ruthless could be traced from.

However,that does not mean that absolute rookies like you can't survive their first stint at the trading process. Here's how:

1. Build Your Base Slowly and Gradually

Look, you must never come to the trading process with guns blazing. That's a surefire way of getting yourself into a position where you are going to lose a lot of money from more experienced traders and buyers. Get the feel of the process first by doing some low-cost activities like:

● Dollar-Cost Averaging:

Here, you are only controlling yourself on how much you will trade and when you will trade. The set amount will be what you will use to buy shares when stock prices are low and fewer when prices rise. The point is that your costs will even out after a period of time has elapsed.

Here's an example to make things easier to understand. Let us say that you have a budget of $1,000.00 per month for investing. When you apply dollar-cost averaging, here's what your budget will look like:

- Month 1: $30.00. Hence, $1,000 divided by $30.00 will be 33 shares.
- Month 2: $25.00. Hence, $1,000 divided by $25.00 will be 40 shares
- Month 3: $20.00. Hence, $1,000 divided by $20.00 will be 50 shares

- Month 4: $50.00. Hence, $1,000 divided by $50.00 will be 20 shares
- Month 5: $40.00. Hence, $1,000 divided by $40.00 will be 25 shares

Within 5 months of using the system, you would have acquired 168 unique shares without overspending. You can do this by setting up a schedule for yourself but there are brokers out there that can automate the scheduling process for you.

- **Buying in Thirds**

Here, you will divide the amount you have set up for trading by three and pick which of the three areas you want to focus the most. You can either choose for regular intervals like months or quarters or on specific events like company anniversaries or improvements in their performance.

- **Basket Buying**

Now, what if you cannot decide which of the several companies you have picked has the best chances of success since both are equally viable? The next best option is to buy or trade stocks from both. This immediately takes the stress of having to pick the best company to invest in while also taking advantage of any sudden changes in either company's performance.

This strategy is also great for determining which of the two companies will eventually be the better option so you could invest more in them.

2. Never, Ever Fall for a "Hot Tip"

There are a lot of pump and dump schemes out there looking for suckers who would invest in cheap stocks. They usually drum up hype in the market (usually on the Internet) and even pay seemingly trustworthy Wall Street gurus to ensure that everything is okay.

Once they have enough investors, they would then drive prices up to attract more investors. If enough money has been generated, these people would then bail out of the market, sending all the prices of their stock crashing.

The point here is to never fall for any stock trading tip that assures you massive profit yields at a short amount of time and companies being backed by people you can't seemingly find notable credentials off in the Internet. A little bit of care and common sense will help in preventing you from becoming the next target of a stock market money trap.

3. Make Friends with the Tax Man

If you are trader that is not using a 401K or IRA account, then you are not enjoying a tax-favored status. This means that you are going to be taxed on your capital gains considerably which can complicate things.

However, the IRS does have different rules and tax rates depending on your income as well as well as the type of trading that you do. And if discrepancies do arise from the computation of your taxes, you can dispute such and present proof that you have only earned this much for that period. The excess that you have paid will then be off-set in the next tax period (refunds are not possible with the IRS, sadly).

4. Don't Anticipate

If you have made the decision to buy or trade stocks, you might feel the urge to get the orders done PRONTO. As such, you start watching the charts and wait for the right moment to pounce and purchase/trade those stocks.

This is where a lot of frustration as the charts might get close to your desired price but then drop down again. What you should be doing instead is find the "sweet spot" where the price is good enough for you and the buyer. It might not be close to what you want but, at least, you have a nice point of entry where you can start negotiations for the price of your stocks. If you wait too long to start trading, you might come to a point where the trend starts taking a downwards turn.

5. Time it Right

If the goal of the investor is to buy cheap, then a trader's goal is to buy and trade at the right time. So what is the "right time", exactly?

When you see that the stock is getting strong I.e. heading towards an upwards trend, then it is time to start buying. And if the stocks are showing signs of following a downwards trend, then it is time to sell.

The key emphasis here is that the stocks "show" either strength or weakness, not when they are actually strong and weak. if that happens, then the price is too costly for you or too low for you to make a profit when you want to start trading.

Here's an example. Suppose that the stocks of the company are at $10.00 per share but are going to $25.00 in the next few days due to strong performance. Don't wait for the stocks to actually reach $25.00 per share before you start buying. And if the reverse were to happen, don't wait for stock prices to go to the $10.00 mark before you start trading. At least, you won't put yourself at a disadvantage by timing your activities right.

Alternative Trading Strategies

If you have mastered the more basic concepts of trading, you might want to try out the other tactics that experienced traders have been using.

Everybody has their own way of going about trading stocks but which of these strategies have proven to work? Their effectiveness will vary depending on the situation but here are some of the tactics that experienced (and successful) traders have used in the past.

1. IPO

Known formally as Initial Public Offerings, IPOs are a direct consequence of a company shifting from a private firm to a publicly traded one. In most cases, the IPOs of a company is the first stocks that it offered to its first stockholders and can be traded publicly once the company enters the stock market.

Profiting from an IPO can be done in two ways. The first option is to watch and wait for how the value of these stocks changes as time goes by. If the price is fair given the circumstances, then buy it then wait for prices to go up to trade them again.

The second option is to buy the IPOs as soon as the company gets publicly traded. However, there is no assurance that the value of that stock will rise as it is dependent on the company's long-term and short-term performance rate. But, if the company does grow in the market, you can then sell the stocks at a higher price.

2. The Short Sell

This strategy is great for traders who are a bit adventurous with their activities. The entire premise of short selling is that you sell stocks (not owned by you) in the belief that their value will rapidly decline in a few weeks or days. And when that price drops massively, you can purchase them again at the new low price and return the stocks to their owners.

However, this trick only works if the stock in question actually drops. If the stock is poised for a drop but, instead, soars in price, you'd end up losing money. As such, the potential losses you can get from a short sell is greater than the potential gains you might generate. A bit of meticulous speculating will be necessary in order to make this strategy work.

3. Trading by Margins

If you have a margins account, you are given the option to borrow money so you could trade stocks. With the money you borrowed,   you can increase the number of stocks that you can purchase without having to wait for additional funds to get wired into your account.

Here's an example. Let us say that the entire price for the 10 stocks you purchased is at $200.00. If you do not have a margins account, you are going to pay the total sum of money directly from the available amount in your account. But with the margins option, the stockbroker might lend you half or $100.00 while you supply the rest.

If your stocks yield a profit of $20.00 per stock which gives you a profit of $400.00. You return the $100.00 you owe to the stockbroker while you keep the rest of the money.

Here's a caveat, however. Do use the Margins Option only when you are in a pinch. It's easy to get reckless and abuse the option. What happens if stock prices drop and you actually generated losses? You are still obligated to pay the amount you owe to the broker.

Even More Advanced Strategies for Day Traders

Day trading is where things can get exciting. If you want to try your hand it is, you must understand that the overall goal for survival here is to find the best trend for the day and exit at the right moment.

So what makes for a good day trading tactic? It must follow certain elements like:

- **Trading Signals -** The strategy should clearly lay out how it is going to open and close trades. The clearer the technical rules will be, the easier it will be for you to implement them. And the more logical they are, the less room for interpretation and impulsiveness there will be on your part if you start trading.

- **Rules for Stop-Loss -** Risk is a definite factor in day trading and your goal is to mitigate much of it to the best of your ability. This is where a stop-loss rule comes in as a good one can limit the risk exposure of your investments to 1-2%. Any trader will have to do 50 to 100 losing trades in order to lose all of their funds in an account. How good would it be if those 50-100 bad trades were actually good ones? This only happens if you have a clear stop-loss rule and can follow it easily.

- **Moderate to High Success Rate** - The strategy you will use must have a success rate that is relatively high compared to the risk that you are going to expose yourself to it. In other words, the rewards that you are going to potentially get from it should be worth the risk that you will eventually suffer if things get out of hand.

For example, if you have a strategy with a success rate of 50%, then that means 5 out of 10 trades will be successful. Now, combine this with a risk to return ratio of 1 to 10 where there is 1 risky trade for every 9 moderately risky trades. That means that in 50% of all trades, you will guess correctly.

Just keep in mind that you are still crunching numbers as of this part. There is no telling how every trade will happen. Whatever the case, your discipline as a trader, and your ability to exit before losses start piling up will be crucial.

With that out of the way, here are some of the more advanced day trading tricks that you can use.

1. The Ichimon Cloud

This strategy makes full use of the chart wherein 5 lines are being plotted on a price action indicator, two of them consisting of the "cloud" or top performance indicator limit for specific stocks. Another line will be the baseline which reflects the actual performance of a certain stock's price. The fourth and fifth lines would indicate the stop-loss order line that your price line must never meet if you want to profit for that day.

How this strategy works is that you open up a stock for a trade whenever the prices reach or go out of the cloud lines. You will then keep that trade open until it reaches the blue line or the day ends.

Since you are expecting a stock price to follow a trend, the third line must closely follow the trend plotted by the cloud lines. Put some considerable distance on your price and performance lines with the stop-loss order line then close if the price cloud interacts with the performance line.

The overall goal here is to make your price line follow the performance line at a close yet safe distance to protect your investments against sudden spikes in the trend.

2. The RSI/Stochastic Oscillator Strategy

This strategy will take full use of the Relative Strength Index and what is known as the Stochastic Oscillator. These indicators usually track the value of stocks and determine whether they are overbought or oversold

The premise here is to scalp the market and check for the smallest of price movements and then look for high trade activity. As such, this strategy will require multitasking and an ability to reach and adapt to sudden changes in the chart.

To use this strategy, you must first open for trade when you get signals from both the RSI and Stochastic Oscillator that certain stocks are overbought and oversold. Then, look for areas in the graph where both RSI and Oscillators meet at the lowest points, indicating a double oversold instance.

Now, if both indicators go up, that means that the stock was overbought and you should respond with a short trade. That trade should happen as often until one of the indicators go their opposite direction which should signal an opposite signal and an unfavorable price move.

For stop-loss, what you will have to remember only is that your stop-loss orders must be rather close by safe. Better yet, you should decide on a sizeable stop-loss distance and follow that trend.

3. Post-Gap with Price Action Trading

If you are the person that trades with stock-based trading assets, then this strategy might just work for you. The premise here is to set up a gap in order to properly apply the rules of this strategy. Also, you should have a list of financial assets to trade for that day as these have gaps in between the different trading periods.

This strategy begins at the start of the day which has the morning gap for the assets. Then, in between 30 minutes to an hour after opening, your financial assets will be there to be the most stable stock you have on offer.

It is important that you observe what happens in those 30 to 60 minutes after opening. If the stocks start with a strong upwards gap and then the price fills in that gap in the next hour, then there is enough reason to believe that the prices for that stock will continue to increase in that hour. But if the price continues to decrease, then maybe there is no strong growth for that stock for that session.

One other feature of this strategy is that it constantly uses price action rules to determine where and how you will exit for that session. The goal here is to end the day with a strong figure so your start of the next day will be strong as well.

For your stop-loss rule, it should be placed on the opposite side of the gap. If you open for a strong bull trade, then the stop-loss order should be at the lowest point of the gap. But if you are starting with a bear condition, then the stop-loss order should be placed at the highest point of the gap.

The Main Takeaway:

All of this talk about trends and figures only tells you that discipline is a key component for success among day traders. A mistake day traders often make is that they do not stick to their strategy, resulting in missed entry and exit points as well as massive losses by the end of the day.

Also, it takes time before you realize that you are already deviating from your strategy. As such, it might be too late to course-correct and come out strong.

Thus, it pays to write your strategy in someplace where it is easy to see and remember. Also, the apps that you will use will help you chart the performance of stocks for that day. It is up to you, then, to follow the movements of stocks closely and time your actions right.

Getting good with these strategies will take time and practice but, eventually, you'll be able to confidently open your trading day and close it with strong figures.

Timing Your Trades Correctly

Traders actually thrive by exploiting whatever conditions are present in the market that affects stock prices. In short, it is doing the most profitable action and at the right moment.

That does beg the question, though: When it is right to buy and trade stocks in the market? We're not talking about the moment that the exchanges open or close for the day. We are talking about those little windows of opportunities that you can enter in a day and start trading.

There is no exact hour for you to start trading on a single day as that depends greatly on the stock in question.However, you can look at certain aspects like:

A. Liquidity

This factor simply indicates when it is good to enter or exit a trade based on the price. What you should be looking for are "spreads" in the graph, the distance between the asking price of a stock and its bidding price. Or you could also be looking for a low slippage where the difference between the expected price of a trade and the actual price is not so wide.

What you should be looking for is a distance that is close enough but should never meet. This would tell you that you can trade stocks on that day with minimal risk of a loss.

B. Volatility

This simply indicates the expected daily price range for a certain stock. This will be the range for which any trader must operate with. The general rule is that the margin for profit or loss is greater when the volatility is high. After all, the differences in the chart will be larger if there are more figures in the range.

What you should be looking for in a manageable range of volatility. If you feel that the difference between profit and loss is quite high for that hour, maybe you should hold off on trading that stock until the gap narrows down considerably.

C. Volume

This measures frequency of activity with regards to a specific stock. To be more precise, it measures how much of that stock has been bought, sold, and traded at a given period of time. What this indicates for you is the general interest for that stock which, in turn, can tell you of an impending price jump.

More often than not, an increase in trading volume will be followed by a spike in the graph. This might be alarming for any trader but you can use that impending jump to your advantage by trading early.

Now that you know what assets to look for and how they might perform for that day, what you should be looking for is your entry point. There are tools that can help you determine this which includes:

- **The News -** There are quite a lot of market-moving news items being published by the hour. Your news source of choice should tell you when such events might happen so you could prepare accordingly.

- **ECN Quotes -** An electronic communications network will provide you with crucial information like the bidding and asking quotes from multiple market experts while also matching and executing orders for you.

What you should be looking for is a Level 2 subscription service as this provides you with access to an order book from NASDAQ. At best, this gives you an idea as to when you should buy stocks or execute orders.

When to Sell

Now that you know when to enter, the next challenge is knowing when to get out of the market before it closes for the day. Your exit strategy will be dependent on your overall strategy but common exit strategies include:

A. Fading

This strategy will involve short stocks and is best applied when the prices have been moving upwards for a while. However, such a trend should be considered only on the presumption that the stocks were either overbought, their buyers are now ready to start profiting from them, or that the buyers want to bail out ASAP.

This makes for a rather risky yet rewarding strategy as buyer activity will almost always affect stock prices for the good. At best, you can exit the market with a strong figure.

B. Scalping

One of the more popular strategies out there, scalping involves merely you selling your stocks at the moment that they start becoming profitable. It does not matter that if a better price is existing and can be achieved for that day. So as long as you are about to start making money out of that stock, you can start selling them as soon as possible.

C. The Pivot

This strategy takes advantage of a highly volatile daily market. To do this, you buy stocks at a low price at the start of the day, wait for them to rise significantly, and sell high before the market closes for the day. This strategy is rather dependent on a possible reversal of figures for stock prices. As such, the amount that you will earn at the end of the day is dependent on how much the price has risen for that day.

D. Momentum Selling

If you are the one that constantly reads the news and knows when market-changing events are about to happen, you can use this strategy. If a trend appears and is supported by a high volume of stock activity, you trade such stocks and end the day with a sizeable figure. Alternatively, you can anticipate a price surge and fade out of the market before the day ends.

Just with your entry point, you need to set up the conditions on when you want to end the day for your trading activities. Once the criteria have been set, all that is left to do is to stick to the plan.

Chapter VII: Playing the Long Game, Part I:

Understanding Risk

Regardless of how well equipped you are and how experienced you might be in trading stocks, there is never an assurance that you would profit hugely in the stock market. You can only do so much but there are just things inside the market that are beyond your control.

All of these factors can be summed up in one word: Risk

It does not matter what type of stock you invest in. Risk will always be there. As such, understanding your relationship and reward is absolutely crucial to your success as an investor/trader.

How Prevalent is Risk in Stocks?

Remember the notion that a higher risk yields higher rewards? That, technically speaking, is not correct. The more accurate statement is that a high risk yields a high potential return but the latter is less likely if the former is considerably high. That might sound confusing but that is the core premise of risk tolerance.

If you decide to invest that are riskier than the standard types in the market, there is always the chance that you will:

- **Lose your principal amount -** A poorly thought of investment at a high-yield bond runs the risk of you losing a massive portion of your funding, if not all of it.

- **Get Outpaced by Inflation -** The value of your investments is rising at a rate slower than prices. This usually happens if you invest in bonds like the ones offered by the government.

- **Lose your Retirement Money -** The money you yield from your investments is not equal to the amount that you are supposed to put up for retirement.

- **Get Overwhelmed by Fees and other Transactional Expenses -** The returns you made are barely enough to cover the expenses you have incurred in your investments.

So, how does risk come into play when it comes to your investments? Each stock type carries certain types of risk which is why it would be best that we talk about risk according to the top three common investment options.

A. Stocks

This investment option has a rather reliable return rate of 10% which is higher than what other investment options can offer. However, this also means that you have to be extra careful with them as not all companies have the same level of exposure to risk for investors.

For instance, an older and better-established company with a history of strong and consistent performance might have a high reward potential but the risk is low which makes them safe investment options. However, the same could not be said for a startup. Here, volatility is quite high which means that the chances of a high reward are rather low.

B. Bonds

A bond is one of the best ways to mitigate risk exposure in your portfolio. Since a bond is basically a reverse loan (you lending money to the company instead of the other way around), the company is obligated to pay you first as you have more to share with a creditor than your standard investor. Due to this, bonds have a generally higher rate of safety despite their lower reward rate.

And this safety is even higher if that bond in question comes from the government since they are required by law to pay you back plus interest. However, on the opposite end are the junk bonds which provide high returns but accompanied with equally high risk.

C. Mutual Funds

Since Mutual Funds are a collection of stocks and bonds, they work as a hedge that could potentially lower the risk exposure of your portfolio to a nearly negligible degree. Of course, it matters what kinds of stocks and bonds are being invested in your mutual fund. If your broker of choice decides to put your funds in bad stocks and bonds, the risk exposure not only remains but increases.

Investment-Specific Risks

Regardless of the investment type and the company offering them, you are bound to face some risks whenever you buy or trade stocks and other investment options. Here are some of the more popular risk that comes when investing in stocks.

1. Commodity Prices

This risk is inherent in companies that deal with certain commodities like gas, gold, and metals. When the prices of these commodities go up, the company benefits. But if the prices drop, then the performance of the company suffers as well as prices for their stock.

And if you think that only companies dealing with commodities can e affected by this risk, you'd be mistaken. There are some instances when companies get to suffer from price drops in a commodity especially if such a company relies on the commodity company as a supplier or as their client.

2. The News

This risk is proof of the power of media. Since they provide information that forms part of public opinion, how headlines mold the public's perception of a company will ultimately help or hinder the values of their stock.

This risk often occurs in headline-worthy events that could affect stock value such as a crash in a local economy, natural disasters occur. A company's ability to respond to such changes will matter in maintaining investor faith.

More often than not, this risk is purely "simulated" in nature. It does not have to be real or factual. So as long as the news can cause people to react en masse, the risk that a bad headline can bring to a company is rather considerable.

3. Ratings

Whenever a third-party organization assigns a certain rating to a company, such a rating will also affect how investors would perceive the company. For example, the analysis rating that a company gets in the stock market will cause swings in public perception and the company will have to do damage control just to prevent losses. Again, this is like the news but with more number crunching.

4. **Obsolescence**

The fact that the very nature of a company or its products and services is going to be out-phased can deal a serious blow on its stock value. This is a problem that long-running companies often deal with as they have to keep up with the pace of technology.

One common example of this is when a younger company enters into the market, offering a product that is similar to what older companies offer but is better and cheaper. This risk is expected to increase as the years pass with more technologies being created and the knowledge gap of consumers getting narrower and narrower.

5. **Public Scandals**

Let us say that an auditor performs an analysis on the company and discovers that there are discrepancies in its financial statements. Worse, let us say that the leadership of that company is involved in embezzlement schemes, are not paying their taxes honestly, and other news-worthy scandals.

If such were to ever happen, the damage to a company's standing among its investors will be severely damaged. This is what happened to Enron when the company was involved in a series of high-publicized schemes as well as a massive environmental calamity. As soon as investors are made aware that company leadership is unethical, their most natural response would be to bail out. This causes a massive drop in stock value as well as a near-irreparable reputation.

Systemic Risks

We've only talked so far about the risks that you encounter when investing in stocks. However, the risk is so prevalent that it is even inherent to the market itself. In other words, there are factors out there that are absolutely out of your control and yet would throw a proverbial wrench in all of your plans.

If you listen closely to the stock market news, you'll come across certain news items about seemingly unrelated events that investors fear would affect prices in the stock market. Seriously, how does a person getting elected as the US President or the British Prime Minister have to do with prices for stocks? What does a worldwide pandemic have to do with the stock market?

The truth is that, regardless of the explanation, the occurrence of such events would generally influence activity in various stock markets. To understand how you need to know in what forms these risks would take.

A. Politics

This risk comes from changes in administration, governmental policies, shifts in political movements and ideologies, and other events that could impact the movement of commodities across the world.

For instance, the war in the Middle East caused massive changes in the stock market in the 90s to 2000s while the UK stock market experienced a period of volatility when the country decided to leave the European Union. Another good example is the political turmoil in Venezuela in the 2000s which obliterated its stock market.

B. National Debt

This risk usually happens when a state cannot honor the debts it has incurred at the World Bank or the International Monetary Fund. Due to the debt, all financial products like stocks, bonds, and mutual funds are the ones that are the first to get hit. This happened in Greece in 2009 when the country was unable to pay off its debt and, as a consequence, stock prices in the Greek economy plummeted.

C. The Environment

These events are either unforeseen or, if foreseen, unavoidable. A single natural disaster can do quite a lot of damage in the stock market, especially in a major financial center.

D. Market Value

Due to prevailing trends, the value of investments will eventually fluctuate. However, in some cases, they will lose quite a lot of value which leads to a crash.

Recessions are perhaps one of the most direct threats to your portfolio's value. When the US real estate market collapsed in 2008, the value of investments in the US Stock Market declined as well. Of course, this sparked a frenzy in investors scrambling to bail out before they lose all their money.

E. Interest Rates

A change in interest rates at the market is known to slow an entire economy down. The reason for this is that companies and investors are now a bit more cautious with their spending activities. This primarily affects bonds but stocks can also be affected by changes in interest rates.

How to Tell If You are in a Bull or Bear Market

How could you ever possibly know what you are in a bull market or a bear market. So far, we have been talking about taking advantage of whatever conditions are in the market but how does an investor prepare themselves for an upcoming change of trends in the stock market?

First things first, there is no proper definition of a bull or bear market. Nobody can tell you exactly what these market conditions are. You can only tell that the market is entering the bull or bear phase by paying attention to changes in stock trends or figures.

A. Bull Market

The bull market is where the market follows an upswing phase. You can tell that things are going well when performance indexes grow by 20%. however, that growth is not enough. It should immediately follow a decline of 20% or more.

So, if the market's drop is at 25% but this has risen to 19%, then the market is entering its bull phase. The market will remain in that phase so as long as the index does not go back to 20% and above range.

If you want to be a bit fancier, you can also declare a bull phase if the rise and drop occur at the closing of a market. As such, if the market closes at the 20% limit, then you as an investor are exiting it at a bull phase.

B. Bear Market

If the bull market is an upwards swing, then the bear market is the complete opposite. When the index drops to 20%

following a gain of 20% or more, then the market is entering its bear phase.

Also, unlike bull markets which follow one after another, bear markets only follow after a bull market. There is no bear market after a bear market. So as long as the index remains at the 20% drop, then it is a singular bear phase no matter how many times the market has closed for the day.

The Bottomline

The prevalent presence of risk in the market will tell you that there is no such thing as a risk-free stock market. Also, there is no right or wrong response to risk. Whenever a potential risk pops up, there is the option to hold on to your investments until things get better or bail out and take whatever portion of your money remains.

That being said, there is a way for you to mitigate the risks that you encounter without necessarily deviating from your plans.

Chapter VIII: Playing the Long Game, Part II: Mitigating Risk

Now that you know that risk can come from anywhere in the stock market, the next thing that you'll have to do is to reduce its effects on your investment portfolio. There are multiple ways to mitigate risks in the stock market and they could be used by you regardless of your overall strategy.

But, before we go to those, it is best that we settle something else first.

Managing Debts

Your capital is your most important asset like a stock investor bar your skills and tools. After all, you cannot invest without money. However, just remember that brokerages like the S&P 500 get a 10% return as an average every year. Although that is a rather healthy return for any investment, that is still considerably lower than any interest rate that a credit card could impose on you which could go as high as 15%.

As such, if you have credit obligations, it is best that you clear them first before you start or resume investing in the stock market. The same also goes for personal loans.

But, in some instances, credit card debt is unavoidable. So, when should you start prioritizing your credit card and personal debt before investing? There is no exact figure but, just to be safe, hold off on investing when you have a credit card or loan with an interest rate over 5%.

If you are serious about investing in the stock market regardless if you have debt or not, then it is recommended that you set aside money specifically for investing. An emergency fund should be some savings of sorts by you where you have set aside a portion of your monthly earnings in preparation for investing.

This means that you should have already prepared years in advance before you start venturing into the stock market. If that is not possible, then make sure all of your debts are clear before you start investing.

At least, this way, you don't have to juggle two different obligations at the same time.

Dollar-Cost Averaging: Advantages and Disadvantages

A few chapters ago, we talked about how dollar-cost averaging is used. But what benefits does it offer? The most direct one would be that it spreads your risk exposure evenly over time.

The other advantage is automation. With a set price every month, you won't have to spend a lot of time mulling over how much you are going to spend every month and how many shares you should acquire. There are even apps that allow you to automate not only the allocation of budget but also the actual investing in stocks,

Another advantage is that it removes the need on finding the right entry and exit point every time the market opens. At the very least, you can do your activities without having to wait for a good market swing.

But if there was ever a disadvantage with dollar-cost averaging, it would be that it is not enough to deal with the cost of long-term averaging. The strategy is good only for returns that are below the average.

AI-based Index Funding

As of now, you should realize that actively managing your funds is rather expensive. After all, you are paying someone to do all the investing for you   so you could beat the average market returns. In the long run, this is going to consume a huge portion of your money.

Of course, you cannot remove the element of error since another person is running the operation on your behalf. As a result, a lot of actively managed funds underperform in the market.

As such, it would be better if you opt for a passive index funding platform. Their system works by the use of an AI that can accurately mimic the movement of indexes like the S&P 500. Since this is an AI, there is no need to pay for a fund manager, and human error is likewise removed.

What you will be paying for instead are the expense ratios which are lower in cost than the salary of a fund manager by 90%. In other words, you can protect keep more of your money by letting an automated computer system do your funding activities for you.

Surprises in Earnings

Picture this scenario: have you ever closely monitored the earnings of a certain company, expecting them to follow a certain path, only to deviate in one key point? For instance, you were expecting the earnings for one company to plummet further only for them to rise significantly in just one day.

It's a welcome surprise, right? After all, the earnings have actually beaten the predictions of industry experts. Technically, you should be worried. Surprises are a major indication that forecasts for that day were not as accurate as you want them to be.

If the stocks that you have invested in are known to earn in large amounts and the analysts' forecasts are way off, then the risk is greater for you. This level of uncertainty can make you feel apprehensive in speculating where a company's performance will take them in the future.

Think about it: if a lot of people were wrong in their earnings forecast for that one company, where else did they screw up in that day?

So, how could you tell that there will be surprises in a company's earnings? Here are some aspects to look for.

- **Limited to No Coverage** - Not a lot of analysts are monitoring that stock.
- **The Company is New** - New companies have not a lot of history to indicate good performance. Thus investors and analysts do not have much to go about in predicting their earnings.
- **No Consistent Trend** - When analysts do cover that stock, their estimates, and predictions do not share any common point or trend. This only reflects the fact that there is a lot of uncertainty regarding that company.

Naturally, predictions for a company become stabler the longer they perform in the company. Whether good or bad, a history and a sizeable performance index can help analysts predict what might just happen next, with key emphasis on the word "might".

Low P/E

A lot of investors have this thinking that bargain-level trading is the best way to succeed in the stock market. And to find such cheap bargains, these investors use the Price to Earnings ratio.

If the stock is earning a level of profit higher than its price, the P/E ratio would classify this stock as undervalued. This means that they can buy the stock cheap and then sell it at a higher price later on.

However, looks can be deceiving. The P/E ratio might be low but it does not account for the wider range of risks that could ultimately affect stock prices in the future. The point is that you should never be completely dependent on P/E to determine which stocks are cheap.

As a matter of fact, you are better off using other ratios like the Cash Flow Per Share ratio and even the analysis of industry experts.

Diversifying Your Portfolio

Perhaps one of the most potent strategies you can use in mitigating risk is to diversify your portfolio. The act of diversification simply pertains to adding different types of investments to your portfolio. The concept here is that a higher variety of diversification in your portfolio will yield a high return while lowering risk by spreading your presence in different sectors of the stock market.

Diversifying your investments is not exactly a new idea. It really takes care and attention to detail in order to diversify your investments instead of being reactionary and impulsive. In essence, you diversifying your investments should have been part of your plan and not just you responding to any exposure to risk.

With that out of the way, here are some tips to remember in order to diversify your investments.

1. **Vary Stocks**

Your individual stocks should not be identical to one another as this is a surefire way o losing value in case the worst were to happen. For instance, you should not invest in one type of stock for $100.00 per share every time you enter the market. Try to look for cheaper stocks that allow you to buy more on the same budget.

Also, there is nothing that says that you cannot invest in the competition. Each company stock has its own rate of return, growth, and other performance metrics. The same goes for bonds as you want varying levels of credit features, term duration, and maturity periods.

The less homogenized your stock is at a glance, the more secure it will be as time passes.

2. **Mind the Quality**

Having a lot of investments does not make for a diversified portfolio on its own. What you should be focusing on is the variety of such investments which means your portfolio should not be focused on stocks,   bonds, funds, commodities, and other options on their own.

To truly make your portfolio diverse in quality, you need to understand what each investment type brings to it. A diversified portfolio will have:

- Stocks for growth
- Bonds for an income boost
- Real estate funds as a safety net against inflation
- Global investments for further growth and buying power
- Cash for stability

3. Diversify by Investment Categories

You can take diversification even further by investing in different stocks within the same category. For instance, if you are started with some healthcare companies, perhaps you can look into stocks offered by financial companies, food services, and retail. At the very least, this prevents your portfolio from losing value if one sector faces a serious crisis for a period of time.

If you do not have a lot of capital, diversifying your portfolio by buying individual shares might become expensive. As such, your next best option is through mutual funds. As was discussed extensively a few chapters ago, mutual funds are like a collection of investment types coming from different sectors at a fraction of the cost.

To truly take advantage of mutual funds, look for types that feature investment options at a global scale or coming from different seemingly unrelated markets. They should instantly protect and diversify your portfolio.

4. Spread Out

Sticking to the stocks or sectors that you are most comfortable with might be good but it's best that you don't get stuck in those areas for too long. You can quickly spread out with the help of a mutual fund where you can choose to invest in other companies. These companies do not even have to be new ones. They can be the companies whose products you use every day or, at the very least, are ran by people that you know.

Of course, stocks are not the only thing to consider when you are an investor. The different investment options provided in Chapter II have their own set of advantages and potential reward yields which you can use to create a safety net for your investments. As of now, commodities like gold offer the highest rate of security as they are known to perform reliably even under bad economic conditions.

Also, don't just invest in your local market. Think about going national or global as there are a lot of other companies out there who are looking for overseas investors and whose local markets have a more lenient margin of competition that you can take part in.

However, do take care that you do not spread yourself too thinly. You should keep your portfolio at a certain manageable size. At least, add 20 or 30 new stocks to your portfolio for a year to diversify it.

5. Finding a Good Balance Between Stocks and Bonds

You could take things a step further by adding more individualized stocks and bonds to your portfolio. The ratio of stocks compared to bonds in your portfolio will depend greatly on your tolerance and overall investment strategy but make sure that the bonds do not overwhelm your stocks.

If, for example, you have 30 shares acquired this year, you can add somewhere in between 5 to 10 bonds into your portfolio. Experts even recommend that you stick to an 8:2 or 9:1 distribution between your stocks and bonds.

The reason for this is that stocks and bonds actually behave differently in the market. Bonds already have a high rate of security but they do not have a high yield. On the other hand, stocks have a high yield but a low rate of security. You can use the bonds to make your portfolio more secure while stocks are there to increase the flow of cash.

6. Mind the Risk Exposure

One way to mitigate risk is to pick stocks with different rates of return. This is to make sure that you can still enjoy fro substantial gains in case on company or sector under-performs for a period of time.

This is where going global can also help you as some countries have stock exchanges with different dynamics, competition, and risk exposure which should balance out the inherent disadvantages of your local stock market.

However, while diversification protects you from losses, it leaves you open to another risk: the amount you pay in annual returns. This is because anything that increases or lowers risk will also increase or lower the potential for rewards.

7. Know When to Make an Exit

One mistake that a lot who use dollar-cost averaging and automated funds as strategies make is that they do not bother to pay attention to what is going on. Those systems and fund managers can only do so much but an investor still has to make judgment calls here and there to optimize their investments.

Keep in touch with the market and pay attention to any potential change. You should also be aware of whatever changes are being made in the companies you invest in. This will help you make informed decisions and determine when it is time to start cutting on your losses.

114

The Basics of Hedging

Since risk is unavoidable, the last counter you could use some form of loss protection. This is where hedging comes into play and it simply involves an investor setting up fail-safes to protect themselves from the negative impacts of an unwanted event.

The best way to understand Hedging is to think of it as insurance. Whenever something happens to the assets being covered which, in this instance, are your investments, something will protect you from the losses you might potentially incur.

Funnily enough, some Hedging measures act like actual insurance. For example, let us say that you own shares at Company 456 which operates in the foodservice industry. Although the company has a long-standing history of good performance and profit, you are worried about its short-term performance due to a massive downturn in the industry.

To protect yourself in case of losses in Company 456, you buy a put option where you are given the right to sell your shares in the market at a fixed price. Now, if stock prices were to fall way below the put option price, the losses you incurred will be offset by gains in the same put option.

Hedging also works in instances of a company relying on certain commodities. Let us say that Company 963 produces beer and is thus reliant on the prices of yeast in the market. As such, 963 would find themselves in a bind should prices for yeast increase tremendously.

To protect against such an event, 963 might enter into either a future or forward contract which allows the company to buy yeast at a set price for a period of time in case of the aforementioned price increase.

These are just some of the so-called hedges that can be put up by investors and companies in the preparation of unwanted events. However, you yourself can put up a hedging system for your investments using some of the strategies below.

A. Don't Forget About Cash

Savings accounts, cash deposits, and certificates of deposit are partially unaffected by market volatility. The reason for this is that cash posses agility and versatility that allows it to thrive where other investments can get hampered. Of course, this comes at a price as cash has little to no returns and does not provide a lot of buying power in case of inflation.

B. Invest in Gold

Gold has perhaps one of the most dependable track records out of all commodities. Even though prices would fluctuate, it's performance has never dipped below the negative for over a century now. Having some gold investments should at least provide some stability to your investment in case of a massive economic downturn.

C. Do Covered Calls

A covered call involves you selling out money call options against long equity positions. Although it does not reduce your exposure to risk whatsoever, it at least offset the potential losses you might suffer. Just remember that this strategy works well only with individual stocks that are set to drop in prices. Should the stock price rise above the strike price, the losses you might incur at the option position will offset whatever gains you were to receive on equity.

D. Inverse Returns

As of now, you can buy ETFs and other financial securities that seem to appreciate their price when other stocks are losing money. Just keep in mind that most of these products are leveraged which will require capital in order to be hedged. However, they can also be traded through an ordinary stock trading account.

D. **Go On the Defense**

Investing in defensive sectors like utilities, consumer products, and even bonds is not exactly a purely hedging maneuver. It's a mix between hedging and diversification, in fact. But what makes this strategy work is that it shifts the focus of your portfolio towards low beta assets.

What that simply means is that your investment's exposure remains the same (which keeps the potential reward at the same level, too) but gives enough leeway for you to keep yourself active even under unfavorable market conditions.

To Conclude

Even as you attempt to apply these risk mitigation strategies, you have to remember that they are just as effective as how you applied them. If you do not time your strategy right like in options or futures, you might end up spending more where others are dealing with cheaper prices.

Also, none of these strategies would ultimately remove risk. There is still that off-chance that, even with all your fail-safes, you would still end up losing at the closing of a day. However, they do at least minimize the effects so you only end up losing some of the value of your stocks, not all of it.

Conclusion

At the end of the day, after everything that you have learned, there is still one question to ask:

What does success look like for an investor like me?

That might sound like a loaded question because, in reality, it is. Every stock investor has their own way of answering this question. But, as a way of summarizing all that you have learned in this book, success does take a certain form for every stock market investor out there.

First, and the most basic of all, would be an investing lifestyle that is grounded on the basics and discipline. In all honesty, you must never treat the whole investing/trading activity like gambling. This activity is not about pure luck (although that does factor in some way) but a careful study of what's going on in the market.

Also, it involves fighting off the more negative tendencies that you might develop as an investor. This includes becoming impulsive with your decisions or abandoning your plans at the first mention of trouble. More often than not, it is the disciplined traders and investors that last long in the market.

The second would be an intelligent usage of all the tools, skills, and strategies at your disposal. Every trader/investor has their own unique experience in the market even if they trade the same stocks and use the same analysis tools. You have to remember that there is a high degree of uncertainty within the market despite all those forecasts and speculations.

As such, you should strive to apply what you have learned in a way that fits your situation, not the other way around. A good investor not only knows what analysis tool to use or ratio to look into but can also adapt to sudden changes in the market. Your adaptability and creativity as a stock investor will matter more than your ability to quote complex analysis formulas.

Lastly, and perhaps the most important of all, is that feeling that you have a greater degree of understanding about the variables in the stock market. There is actually no way to "beat the system". Regardless of how much you earn at the end of the day, the stock market gets to function the same way as it did ever since the 1920s. Regardless of which companies and traders won big that day and what conditions there are in the market currently, the stock market will open again the next day to do the same thing. And the day after that.

As such, what you can only hope to achieve here is to end the trading day on your terms. This means finding the right stocks to trade and open, trading the same at a price most valuable to you, and exiting the market with way more value or money than you started just a few hours ago. And once all of this done, you can get to open with strong figures in the next day.

That might not inspire a lot of confidence but that is true if your sole parameter of success is earning a lot as a stock investor. As was stated in the beginning, what shall determine victory for any stock investor is not profit but survivability. If you can get to do what you want to d in the stock market every day without bleeding your funds dry, then you can consider yourself a successful stock investor.

And with that comes the end of this book. I hope you have learned a lot regarding the basics of investing and moving around the stock market. All that is left to do now is to apply all that you have learned and achieve whatever degree of success you have set for yourself.

Good luck!

Bibliography

Books

- Graham, B., Zweig, B., and Buffett, W.E.,"The Intelligent Investor: The Definitive Book on Value Investing"., 2006
- Mladjenovic, P., "Stock Investing for Dummies", 2020
- Aziz, A., "How to Day Trade for a Living: A Beginner's Guide to Trading Tools and Tactics, Money Management, Discipline and Trading Psychology", 2016
- Malkiel, B., "A Random Walk Down Wall Street: The Time-Tested Strategy to Be Successful", 2020
- Snow, T., "Investing QuickStart Guide: The Simplified Beginner's Guide to Successfully Navigating the Stock Market, Growing Your Wealth & Creating a Secure Financial Future:, 2018
- Bogle, J., "The Little Book of Common Sense Investing: The Only Way to Guarantee Your Fair Share of Stock Market Returns", 2017

Journals

- Peavy, J.W., and Safran, J., "How Efficiently Does the Stock Market Process News of Price Anomalies?', The Journal of Investing, 2010
- Foster, J.D., Reidy, D., Misra, T., Joshua, S., "Narcissism and Stock Market Investing: Correlates and Consequences of Cocksure Investing", Personality and Individual Differences, 2011
- Clark, E.A, and Tunaru, R.,"Emerging Markets: Stock Market Investing with Political Risk", SSRN Electronic Journal, 2001

Website Articles

- Chen, J., "Risk", Investopedia, October 6, 2020. Link: https://www.investopedia.com/terms/r/risk.asp
- Kay, M.F., "3 Reasons Why Investors Fail and What We Can Do About It", Forbes.com, October 29, 2013. Link: https://www.forbes.com/sites/michaelkay/2013/10/29/3-re

asons-why-investors-fail-and-what-we-can-do-about-it/?s
h=71624871a17b
- Beers, B., "Hedging vs. Speculation: What's the Difference?, Investopedia, May 4, 2019. Link: https://www.investopedia.com/ask/answers/difference-between-hedging-and-speculation

FOREX TRADING FOR BEGINNERS

The Ultimate Comprehensive Guide

For Any Forex Aspirant, Top Trading Strategies, How to Make the Right

Investment and Make Money Online! Create Wealth in 2021 and Beyond…

© Copyright 2021 by Ryan Martinez - All rights reserved.

The content contained within this book may not be reproduced, duplicated or transmitted without direct written permission from the author or the publisher.

Under no circumstances will any blame or legal responsibility be held against the publisher, or author, for any damages, reparation, or monetary loss due to the information contained within this book. Either directly or indirectly.

Legal Notice:

This book is copyright protected. This book is only for personal use. You cannot amend, distribute, sell, use, quote or paraphrase any part, or the content within this book, without the consent of the author or publisher.

Disclaimer Notice:

Please note the information contained within this document is for educational and entertainment purposes only. All effort has been executed to present accurate, up to date, and reliable, complete information. No warranties of any kind are declared or implied. Readers acknowledge that the author is not engaging in the rendering of legal, financial, medical or professional advice. The content within this book has been derived from various sources. Please consult a licensed professional before attempting any techniques outlined in this book.

By reading this document, the reader agrees that under no circumstances is the author responsible for any losses, direct or indirect, which are incurred as a result of the use of information contained within this document, including, but not limited to, — errors, omissions, or inaccuracies.

TABLE OF CONTENTS

Understanding Forex: Getting To Know The Basics

"I don't know what Forex is, and since I don't understand what it is, I'm sure I haven't participated in that yet." – this is something that you might have heard from yourself, or from someone you've known. When something appears or sounds strange, it is quite natural for people to frown upon it, or avoid talking about it.

But the truth is, if you have already visited other countries, then you already took part in it. Forex is obviously just a shorter term for "Foreign Exchange." Even though it sounds really simple, the logistics behind it are actually broader and much more interesting, especially if you're the type of individual who wants to make the most out of your earnings while just staying at home.

To make it easy for a layman to understand the complexity that Forex might spell, it can just be perceived as a major business institution where money from various places around the world are traded from one form into another. We might say that whenever money transcends across other national borders, it needs to be converted into something else so it can be useful.

It is dubbed as "The world's biggest financial market," which makes it clear that it really does contribute a lot to the over-all flow of the world's economy. Within its virtual halls, great amounts of money are transacted, traded, and dealt with by a lot of huge business entities as well as average persons. And we're not only talking about millions of Dollars here, but trillions of Dollars, Euros, and almost any other global currencies you can think of.

The exchange of currencies that take place within Forex is very crucial for the international business world. Forex enthusiasts and participants range from government institutions to private corporations, to plain individuals like you and me. Governments are known to utilize the power of Forex for the furthering of their country's interests.

For instance, when a particular country wants to conduct some business deals with other countries such as in lending money, borrowing funds, or even in giving aid whenever crises arise, a country needs to convert its existing currency into foreign currency.

With business entities, they leverage the Forex market to facilitate business deals within the international trade. While they do so, they might need to convert the value of goods and services in exchanging payments from customers into the currencies they prefer.

Individual investors, or those that we call ordinary traders also use Forex as they monitor the rise and flow of global currencies. In just a span of a week, or even in just a few days, currency prices my hit really high or hit really low, mainly because the market doesn't sleep.

Though it is just open from Monday to Friday, it functions round-the-clock during those days, conducting a day's business starting at 4:00 pm central time and ends at the same time the day after. Forex operates this way because it encompasses the demands and activities of the global economy.

How Forex Trading Can Change Your Life

Trading is one of the best money-making trends in the world these days. It is here to stay and will mostly likely be even more attractive and marketable in the next decades. According to the data given by Brokernotes, one of the most recognizable trading publication websites on the web, there are 9.6 million people around the world that are joining the online trading bandwagon.

It means that for every 781 people you meet, there is one of them that's actually doing some trading on a regular basis. Now, with online technologies become more advanced with each passing month, that figure could rise even higher in the next few years. People's lives are changed because of the trading habits… it would be unwise of you to not join the fray.

Now let's tackle another important question, "How much can you really earn with Forex trading?"

To have a rough but simple idea, let's take a look at the success of this very popular Wall-Street guy named Marty Schwartz. He is dubbed as "The Pitbull," and with good reason. Why? Because he has one of the highest levels of aggression, when it comes to investing in Forex.

He is not only about plain attack though, because he is very methodical and smart with his decisions. He has an estimated income of 25% per month. So if he invested a million Dollars in a particular moment, it would mean that he will be twice as rich in the next 4 months.

You can be as rich as him... if you set your mind into believing that you can, and if you work on your trading skills and decisions. That can happen of course if you take the time to perform these 3 very important things: practice, practice, and practice.

Compared to other forms and methods of investments, Forex really pays a lot more. For instance, typical banks will just give you an increase of 2% per year. Mutual funds reward you higher, for it gives 10% per year. The same happens in the stock market. Even if all 3 forces get combined, they are still low compared to the 25% increase that Forex gives. Forex is the ultimate champion, so to speak.

But you may say, Mr. Schwartz might have been a rich guy already before he participated in Forex. He already got a big capital at his disposal already even before he got interested with currency exchange. While that might be true, you have to know that many people have been through a story that we can really call as a "rags to riches tale." Forex really is a life-changer, and it is for the following reasons:

It can make you obtain great amounts of money, in the a very short time.

That's how attractive Forex trading can really be. Some traders put in a certain amount say, 100 Dollars. By trading wisely and carefully, many of the are able to double that amount in just an hour, or even in a few minutes. Some who invested on thousands of dollars are also able to triple that amount in also just a few hours. Needless to say, some of them became millionaires in just a matter of weeks.

It can give you huge returns of investment, with just very little effort.

When you engage in trading, all you will be doing is the act of staring at charts, picking up news about the market, make decisions and implement a set of trading actions. You wait for a while, and then your money increases in value, even though you were just sitting down, at the confines of your own home. Some people's idea of getting rich means you have to invest on real physical capital and work in real workplaces. But as a Forex trader, you will achieve the same level of wealth even though the physical effort your pouring out is just a minuscule one.

It is a safer, better version of gambling.

Truth to be told, Forex trading is every bit as similar to gambling in a casino. You place your bet, and wait for how the dice may fall, or where the arrows may point to. It is a very addictive kind of activity. But here's the good thing about it, it's not as harmful as gambling, and not as illegal as the most common forms of gambling are, when they are placed in unregulated places. This is not to say that gambling is really a bad thing, it's just that with Forex trading, you're not only helping yourself, but you are also contributing to the profits that the global market can accumulate.

Upon reading the above statements, you're getting very excited, and that's very understandable. But here's something that you should know: Forex trading really can in fact make you the richest person in the neighborhood, but before you reach that position, you need to undergo through a series of self-education, risk-taking, and failure absorption – all of which are not easy sets of undertakings

The 3 major advantages of Trading stated above are now contradicted within the same chapter of this book, and perhaps, you're starting to get mad. But Forex trading is not as easy as it may appear to your ears, it is for this reason that writings of this kind exists, because trading really can be difficult, but it can be made to appear easy, if you have the initiative and bravery needed for such an endeavor.

To motivate you even further, let's take a peek at the life of Daniel Martin. During his younger years, he was a Migrant in London. The bad thin about him during those times is that he can't speak English, even in little doses.

Fast forward to the future however, he has amassed some popularity within the field of Forex trading. While he is not to boast of his exact earnings, he has one been given with this cool tagline which is "Turning The 2020 Crash Into $222,000 Cash."

That might not be as big as the amount that Mr. Schwartz is earning, but Mr. Martin's story can make us say that plain, ordinary people like you and me can be greatly changed my Forex. It just goes to show that even without millions at our disposal, we can get a truly attainable set of earnings by just trading strategically.

Mr. Martin's formula for success is declared by himself as 95% psychology, 4% capital, and 1% action. This means that what you need at a greatest measure is how you set your mind into doing what needs to be done. In that case, let's delve into the topic deeper.

How Forex Trading Really Works

Maybe the statements above are still too vague, or maybe it's too technical for you. Let's break the definition down in the simplest analysis possible. Here's a simple example of basic foreign exchange activity:

Let's say a certain company buys a bulk of products from another country. To make the purchase happen, the company owner needs to acquire some currency for that country first, just like when you go on vacations and holiday trips. The only notable difference is that the exchange of amounts that take place are just in a greater scale.

When that company goes through the process of exchanging of those amounts, they contribute to the changing the corresponding prices of those products as well as anything related to it.

When there are more people who actively use a form of currency, the demand for that currency also increases. When the demand decreases, so does the price of the products – it is one of the core concepts of business that everyone can understand easily. With all of these exchanges happening all over the world, the exchange rates constantly move.

Like in any market, the price of any currency is based on the laws of supply and demand. For instance, if there are more people or business entities who exchange Euros into Dollars, the price of the Dollar will rise in comparison to the price of the other, which will change the exchange rate.

Here's a much simpler example that we can see every day so that we can clearly understand how anyone can benefit from foreign currency trades:

Let's say a guy named Greggy lives in Europe and went on a vacation in the US. The guy would certainly bring some European cash with him, and will surely exchange it with some Dollars. During his stay in the US.

Now, let's say Greggy exchanged his 1000 Euros into US currency with a rate of 2.8 Dollars for every Euro. He would get 1400 USD. Let's assume he didn't spend that money, and brought it back to his hometown in Europe, and have managed to keep the money until the exchange rate dropped to 2.8. Instead of getting back his original amount which is 1000, he would actually gain 77 Euros more, so he will now have a total of 1077 due to the lower value that the US Dollar got during that time.

He gained additional earnings just for holding on to a currency that he obtained from a foreign land. That is how Forex basically works – just the simple act of exchanging one form of currency to another, from a certain country to another country, and vice versa.

A trader or investor buys one form of currency, holds on to it for a while, wait for the rates to rise, and then make the move to change his money back, increasing earnings along the way. When to do the exact act of trading is what makes Forex trading very tricky. It can be really hard if you are just starting out. But with careful analysis and repetitive investing, you will find it very easy over time.

Based on what you have understood so far, you might begin to think that traveling from one country to another can actually make you richer than you ever were. In that sense, you are correct... but expert traders would advise you against that. Unless of course if you really love to travel and visit different places.

Aside from the fact that traveling from country to country can be truly burdensome, it isn't also very practical, especially with the current global health crisis we're experiencing today. Thankfully though, there is a much easier alternative to trading foreign currencies – doing it with online means.

Today, many people are getting richer by the minute as they tap into the existence of internet entities called "Forex Brokers." By working with such online businesses, you can take advantage of the rise and fall of foreign currencies right at the screen of your laptop, or even your phone.

Just like what that guy Greggy experienced as he traveled from Europe to the US, you can trade one currency into another and make your earnings significantly higher as you witness the fluctuations of currencies all over the world. Trading within the Forex market via the internet has lots of great advantages.

In addition to the convenience of doing it within the confines of your own home, you can also take advantage of the idea that Forex never sleeps. This means that you can do some trading activities at absolutely any time of your convenience, though you can just do it 5 days a week.

To participate in it, you don't even have to procure a really huge budget. For the moment, you can just start with just as little as 10 USD. Some say it could be as low as 5. You can't expect it to grow really big though. However, you can use that amount as some sort of "trading startup and practice" money.

To be truly successful with Forex Trading, you need to invest not only in a certain monetary amount but in a huge portion of your time as well. Success with money matters is not a walk in the park. You need to learn, take risks, and improve on your methods and techniques. Rich people, as well as anyone who has attained success in all areas of life, attained their royalties because of patience and hard work. You as a Forex beginner should not be any different at all.

The Mathematics and Logistics Behind Currency Exchange

Here's something that you should really accept in becoming a Forex trader: You have to be great in Math. This is not to discourage you, it's just something that you have to be good at so you can be truly profitable with this new undertaking you're considering.

Do you need to learn complex Math? No. Actually, what you need is just very simple mathematics – the set of Math that can make you understand basic numerical operations and some understanding about decimals. If you're good enough with that already, then we shouldn't have any problem at all.

Successful traders are not all excellent mathematicians, however all of them are people who really love working with numbers. They might not be that good with Algebra or anything similar, but they are the kind of people who can think mathematically in the most efficient manner. As a Forex neophyte, do your very best to adapt to that skill – it's the best and only way so you can proceed smoothly with your trading journey.

Now, let's hop into the typical act of trading. Whenever you do business with Forex, you're not only dealing with one currency, but 2 currencies at the same time. Such an intertwining is called a "currency pair." The main concept of gaining or losing revolves around the value of 1 currency in comparison to another.

Comparing and trading currencies can be easily understood by putting them side by side, or by looking at them from left to right. Let's break down a simple example of pairing the most popular currencies ever: Dollars and Euro. When the "Euro to US Dollar pairing" is equal to 1.20, it means that your 1 Euro will be converted into 1.20 if you do some trading at that particular moment.

For another pairing, let's say the US Dollar to Canadian Dollar pairing is equal to 1.25. It also means that your 1 Dollar will also be raised to 1.25 if you trade it with that currency from Canada. Even though there are 2 currencies involved in a trading act, they act like a single currency from the eyes of the Forex market itself. Just like in investing on a particular stock, an investor will gain some profit when he buys a currency pair. When the value of those currencies rise, so does his investment.

Another way investors make money is through speculation. For instance, if an investor feels that the economy of Europe will rise way faster than that of the US, it will make him believe that the Euro will have more power than the US Dollar. The investor will then buy the Euro-Dollar pairing based on his analysis. If that pairing's value becomes high, he will gain money. Conversely, when the value of the Euro-Dollar drops, he will lose some of his earnings.

Now, let's dig a little deeper into the main key aspects of the Forex market. Let's talk about the term called "Margin." When you trade using this method, it means you will only put up a certain percentage of the total investment given by a Forex Broker. The amount you need for that is often called "Margin Requirement."

There is also this term called Stock. With it, you are allowed to borrow funds from your Forex broker. However, trades can only be covered using your existing Forex account. This means that a new investor can't borrow funds to begin. A newbie trader needs to put in some funds into a newly created Forex account. Only then can he start trading.

In using the Margin method, you have to be aware that how much you can earn is dependent on the value of the currency pairings and the price of the trade that's taking place. The size of a pair is basically called "Lot." The most notable sub-categories for this are standard lot, and mini lot. A standard lot is known to carry a value of 100,000 units, while a mini lot has 10,000 units.

Depending on you broker firm's policies, you may also start with just 1,000 units. Such a value is called a "micro-lot." The value of a Margin requirement can be as small as just 2% of the total investment or it could be as large as 20%. But for most trading activities, the average margin requirement falls within the 3 to 5% range.

Let's understand how margin requirement value is calculated with another example. Let's say the pairing of Euro-Dollar has the equivalent of 2.40 and is invested with 2 standard lots. That should make us calculate 2.40 x 200,000, resulting into a capital of 480,000 Dollars. That's a huge amount, one that can surely make you acquire big profits along the way.

The good thing is that you don't really need to pay that exact amount so you can begin trading. What you really have to pay is just the margin requirement. If it's value is just 5%, then you will only need to pay 2400 Dollars.

From that concept, another term called "leverage" should be introduced. It is something that enables an investor to control a huge amount with just a small value of money. We can say that if an investor has 120,000 Dollars, he can control that with just an amount of 3,600 Dollars because it's the 3% of the real amount – the actual value of the margin requirement.

The existence of the leverage method is one of the most important elements of the Forex market, as many analysts claim. But many experts also claim that it is one of the biggest risks investors may come across. It may give an investor the highest earning potential, but conversely, it can also make way for the greatest of losses.

Whenever a trading act happens within Forex, we have to remember that there are 2 currencies involved each time. And as stated above, the 2 is actually viewed as just one. It means that while you're lending 1 currency of the pair, you're also borrowing on the other side.

Such an activity is what the lending rate policies of a certain country is really all about. To sum all of the technicalities up, we can just arrive into the understanding that the entirety of the trading within the Forex market is this: when the value of 1 country's currency goes high, the currency of another country goes low.

By taking advantage of such kinds of events, a Forex investor can be a very big winner in the shortest time imaginable. Consequently though, a careless trader could also become the biggest loser of all time.

Forex Then and Now: How Forex Has Changed Due To Technological Breakthroughs

If we take a look back in history, we would understand that because of the existence of technology and the ease and comfort it gives, the underlying processes that revolve around money are also revolutionized. Just after a few generations when the concept of money has been transformed into paper bills, the act of money-making and investing has changed dramatically as well.

Because going to the bank has become too burdensome for people as well as for the bank owners themselves, they invented "wire-transfer technology" – a process in which transferring of funds can already be done via-electronic signals, which can also be reinforced by telephone conversations.

There also came the Automated Teller Machine, which really offered a great convenience for anyone who wants to avoid the hassle of bringing large amount of real physical cash on their wallets with them.

But such methods were revolutionized even further, because apparently, the business world as well as the people within it are working non-stop in a really speedy way to get things done much simpler and easier. As a result, monetary transactions are now executable on the internet which greatly changed everything.

Gone are the days when you need to actually travel into another country just so you can participate in currency exchange. In the past, people need to be physically present in trading and money-exchanging firms so they can have their foreign money changed. With the existence of computers in homes and offices, transactions became more accessible via keyboard strokes and mouse clicks.

And what's more amazing is that today, such activities can already be done within the comforts of just nearly everywhere. Apparently, mobile technology hasn't only changed the way we communicate, but on how we use and view money as well.

People nowadays, even those that belong to the lowliest of the lows, can actually use their cellphones as their wallets.

Furthermore, many online portals are providing tools and apps that can make financial transactions much easier even for the not-so-rich individuals. Also, many experienced traders are sharing their knowledge and expertise within video streaming sites like Youtube. Truly, there is no excuse for anyone who claims that Forex trading is hard, and only for the ones with a silver platter handed over to them since birth.

About the online trading platforms mentioned earlier, literally all of them offer great assistance in helping anyone who's new to modern-day trading. Some of them even offer "trading mimicry options" in which all a novice trader needs to do is just copy the trading activities of an experienced trader.

By just clicking on a button or an a certain link, the trading methods and exact actions of that trader will manifest on your trading acts too. It means that if that trader wins it hugely, then so will you, although your actual profit will be dependent only on the amount you invested.

That goes to say of course that if that trader loses, you will lose too. But the point of the matter is, trading is really so much easier these days because you can choose to copy the trading practices of successful Forex investors who rarely fail.

Such benefits are widely available these days, which can help us arrive with the conclusion that with Forex, your financial worries can really vanish… if you have the right motivation and mindset to trek into the amazing path of digital trading. If you want to learn the most effective means by which you can make a living out of Forex Trading, sit back and read on.

Starting Forex Trading

Knowing the basic requirements so you can start your first Forex adventures.

First, you have to be within the "legal-age bracket." This means that if you're lower than 18, you can't do some trading just yet. Sorry kids, you're gonna have to grow up for a few more years before you can get rich with the Forex market.

The cool thing though is even if you're a kid, you can make a "practice account" in which you'll have the benefit of enjoying some "Forex play money." When you are already old enough and have gained some knowledge and experience already, you can then use that to your advantage later in adulthood.

Another thing to have is your valid ID. Government-issued IDs could really come in handy in this requirement. You can also use your driver's license, your passport, or whatever ID card that can declare proof of your real identity. You need these as pertinent documents so that your presence in the Forex world can be validated.

You also need proof of your address. Those billing sheets about your electric bills, water bills, and similar related documents should be ideal enough as they can give sufficient proof that you really are a resident of a certain area of your town. Or you can just get a residency clearance from your government municipality's office, that should also be good enough.

You also need to have a bank account, or some of those platforms that can hold digital accounts for your finances such as Paypal, Skrill, or Stripe. There are so many of them out there. What you just have to bear in mind is that almost all of the long-running platforms that are similar to the ones mentioned can be a really good storage area for your Forex earnings.

For the equipment needed, your smartphone will do. You may also use a laptop, a desktop PC, as long as they are connected to the internet. You will then use such devices to connect to the online Forex brokers that are practically just very easy to find.

Before you begin with your trading journey, you need to make sure that you are prepared to lose. Although Forex can really make you extremely rich in just a few moments, it can also make you more broke than you ever were in your life. Speaking of losing, you need to pay attention to the following.

Dealing With Failure: Reasons Why An Aspiring Forex Trader Will Fail

If you want to be truly successful as a currency trader, avoid the following mistakes by all means:

Not having enough understanding of the market.

Truthfully, no mistake is bigger than this. Successful traders, regardless of their area of expertise be it cryptocurrency, the stock market, Forex, or any other similar realms you could think of having this thing that they call their "domain of confidence." As they go about what they do like choosing new forms of investments, collaborating with like-minded people, and making decisions, they stay on that domain.

As they stay within that area of business where they plan to make huge amounts of income, they do their very best to learn about it because they know it for themselves that the best way to be successful with the business, you have to really understand how the structure of the business works.

Most Forex newbies approach the business as just a simple piece of object that they can plug themselves into and hope that money will just flow through their wallets. Such people think that by simply sticking themselves into the business without doing anything, they can get rich easily. If you're that type of person, then there's no hope for you as a Forex trader.

So the main emphasis of this first item is that before you proceed with the real mechanisms of Forex trading, do your homework and do some reconnaissance like that of a highly trained assassin. Although you won't be killing anybody within the business, you really need to truly grasp and understand what is Forex, and how it really works.

Not having a solid and actionable plan.

Since trading is a very serious undertaking, you need to really come up with a solid plan and have the guts and the rock-solid willingness to put those plans into action. The natural reaction for novice investors when hearing about something that can increase their income is this: they put in some money, expect it to grow, and just wait for that quick moment in which they can siphon their earnings into their wallets and bank accounts.

Many newbie investors are having that mindset within themselves, and it is exactly why most of them fail miserably. Some of them also think about retiring early, having some passive income generators, and doing things just to enjoy themselves.

While such plans are good things to execute, it would be a really bad idea to just think about that end scenario without really laying out some solid plans. Some of them don't even think deeply about the proper amounts of money that they need for those plans, thinking that things will just fall into place automatically.

Most newbie investors in Forex are too excited about the money they can earn and are willing to trek into new money-making territory like blind men walking near a cliff. Such a notion is really bad and not to mention a very dangerous idea. So here's what you should do, take a pen and a paper, write down your plans, think about them deeply, and take intense and strategic actions in doing them when you are ready enough already.

Unwillingness to invest time within the market.

All things exist because of 2 important elements: space and time. Ask any physicist, and all of them would surely agree with the statement. Income is a very good thing to have, no argument about that. But thinking about income and actually having income are 2 very different things.

No matter how good you are at dreaming about the physical objects that you can buy with your income, and about how you will store those piles of income, all such thinking and planning will not amount to anything, if you don't invest in a very crucial element: time.

Forex trading is one of the most sought-after activities conducted and engaged in by the richest people in the world today. Do you want to know why they're so good and why they're so successful at what they do? It is because they put a lot of time into learning about the thing, and doing the thing constantly and repeatedly until they become masters at the art of trading and investing within the Foreign Exchange Market.

Successful traders do not only invest in money matters, but they also invest in time because they want to learn. The good thing about Forex investing is that it's never too late for anyone to start investing. Even if you're already past your prime or even if you're within the "senior age bracket," you can still have a profitable trading journey ahead of you.

You might not be as young and energetic as those teenagers who are now getting so good within Forex (Yes, there are very successful youngsters in their late teens who are well-known within the Forex market. We will talk about them later if you keep on reading.), but you have one decisive power that those kids don't have: the wisdom of an experienced man.

Even though you are not yet well-versed with the art of trading currencies yet, you are most likely experienced with other things from other areas of life. You can then apply those experiences in your trading undertakings. Those kids might have the energy, but you have the advantage of wisdom and experience as you have lived certainly longer than all of them.

Doing a lot of wrongful buying practices.

Everyone makes mistakes. And in order to really learn, it is understood that errors and wrong decisions will be made along the way. But if you can prevent those errors from taking place

152

in the first place, why not utilize such an advantage? This is something that most Forex newbies should really put into the highest of considerations.

When you are about to embark on your first trading steps, you will surely be lured and tempted to buy currency pairings that appear to be very cheap but are actually so overpriced. For instance, when looking at Forex charts, which you will surely do if you want to get serious with the business, you might see the rise and fall of monetary value in an erroneous way.

Oftentimes, newbies would surely get excited when there is a sudden rise of a particular currency when compared to another currency and will quickly jump into the trading act, not realizing that they could earn a lot more, if they waited for just a longer bit of time.

Conversely, one of the most common mistakes among newbies is the desire to earn more when the rise of a currency's value is actually the highest that it can get at a given moment. The trick to getting around to this is to play within the mid-level approach: don't get too greedy, but don't be too slow either.

To simply put it, invest in ample time to learn the basics, and improve on them with thorough practice. As you do them more and more each time, you will have the wisdom that can be equated with the most successful Forex traders within the market today.

Not having the proper mental conditioning about trading

If put the advice of Daniel Martin's into high consideration, then we need to really set our minds properly into the game of trading. Some very strong warriors are known to lose to inferior fighters because of one thing: they lack the proper mindset needed to win the battle. Being victorious, even in the aspect of physical fighting is not only about having a strong body, but about having a strong will too.

Now, if you are not someone who has the iron will to step into the digital halls of the trading world and have the guts to win or to lose, you'll never get anywhere near the avenues success. During your first trading actions, you will surely have the initial feelings of getting overwhelmed, that's natural. But in the midst of that, you need to rise above the very moment of sinking and get yourself to the top quickly.

What you really need to do is to learn to balance impulse with patience, greed with wit, and quickness with tarrying – those are natural manifestations of all businessmen. You have get along with that pretty well… it's the only way by which you can step into the first doorsteps of financial success.

Getting Into The Real Action: The Trading Tasks That A Forex Newbie Must Undergo

We've discussed the concepts that revolved around Forex already, and we've had enough statements that should have motivated us to delve deeper into the business. Now, Let's get right into the real action. Let's get into the "nitty-gritty" so to speak.

Without further ado, let's talk about what you really need to do and undergo as you go about your trading tasks each and every day of your dear existence? Wait a minute, every day? Yes, my friend, every day.

Successful Forex traders, as well as any kind of businessmen for that matter, became very well-seasoned and extremely popular at what they do because of one thing: they really love what their profession, and they deal with their business so religiously that missing a single day with their routine would make them feel like they're sick with a very infectious diseases.

Of course, they take breaks from time to time and go on vacations occasionally because after all, what good is money if you can't spend it? But as soon as they're back from their strolls and their tours, they once again deal with their business with the deepest and most intense of seriousness.

You as a Forex neophyte should condition yourself to do the same too. Now, let's get into the real action.

As stated in the earliest discussions, Forex revolves around the idea of exchanging one country's money for another country's money, that's just the simple framework of the business. No magic there, that's just it. Now the real question would be attaining the desired profit you can get from it. Beginners are often scared about taking the first steps.

Don't get too scared though, because there are actually brokers who will lend you a starting amount like 30 Dollars, that you can use as your starting investment. If in any case, you will not gain anything from that, you will not be liable to pay anything. Pretty cool right? But if you are successful with your first trade though, you will pay that amount. It's a win-win for both parties, and people have been taking advantage of that already.

You can participate in Forex for free. You can just visit the website freeforexmoneynodeposit.com and you'll be given a 30-Dollar practice money that you can use for your first Forex adventures. Aside from the free goodie that you can have, there is also a tutorial video there that will guide you on how to create and open a Forex account.

You might ask this, "Who gives away money for free just so more money can be attained?" Nobody can blame you if you won't believe that some people would actually give that amount totally for free. But here's the truth about that… it's simply advertising, some kind of propaganda.

If you visit that web page, you will see that there are 4 internet firms there that are actually brokers. By choosing to tap into them for your first Forex trades, they are actually announcing to the world that they are among the best Forex brokers that you can trust. 30 Dollars is just a small amount for them, even if there are lots of us who will take advantage of it.

It's actually a win for them. Because it is a very clever way of advertising their Brokerage's existence.

One of the most popular brokers among beginners is XM. Should you choose it, you can begin with as low as 5 Dollars from your debit card or 20 Dollars via online banking. The good thing about XM is that it has zero-fee policy for withdrawing your earnings. It is actually one of the most appealing things about XM.

The reason why Forex offers an increase that high is actually due to the fact that each and every day, its market gains around 5 trillion Dollars. This means that the more active you are with your participation within the Forex market, the more you can actually gain a huge portion of that 5 trillion.

It is the total amount shared among Forex investors with each passing day. Statistically speaking, all the stock markets in the world combine are still a little thing compared to the entirety of the Forex market.

Now, about that free 30-Dollar capital for Forex trading, would that be good enough? For someone who has no solid knowledge yet, absolutely. Now suppose you want to hit it big, or if you want to do some real, big-enough trading, You need to use your bank account on that aspect.

You need to siphon some big-enough amount into your chosen Forex broker so you can expect to have higher returns too. But if you want to just have a feel of what trading really is all about, you can just experiment with that free 30.

Any bank account you may have, as long as those banks are engaged in online banking can be used for all your trading adventures. All of them for sure have online connectivity of some sort. Which bank doesn't? Nothing, right? So you can choose any bank at all. Or you can use those digital financial account platforms mentioned earlier too. You can actually just use any of those at your convenience.

Once you hop into your first act of trading, one of the most crucial things you need to figure out is the importance of the word "low." Why? Because your very first Forex deed must be this: buying a currency at its lowest possible value. This is just like buying a very cheap and affordable product that will be very useful for your metaphorical store when the time is right to sell it.

As you should have understood already by now, a time will come when the value of that currency you bought will rise high, way higher than the price when you originally bought it, that will be the best time to let go of that piece of monetary commodity, which will then usher in your very first Forex earnings.

The profit you'll get will not be at a constant rate because as what's told previously, the value of a certain currency can really rise and fall… sometimes unpredictably. Just bear in mind that whenever you engage in a Forex trading act, you will be buying and selling at the same time. Think of it as being on a see-saw: You and a playmate will experience a rising and a falling, not at the same exact second, but throughout the entire time when the 2 of you are see-sawing for enjoyment.

Now speaking of the see-saw act, there will be that specific moment when you get the high-ground position. In Forex trading, if you see the value of a currency rising really high, and you have this feeling that it will drop in the next moments, then it will be the best time for you to sell that currency – that is where you can get your much-awaited income from.

Let's have a simple example. Let's say you bought a currency that's priced at 5.50 and after a few hours, its value has become 7. If you decide to sell it at that moment, it means that you gained 1 and a half of that currency. By waiting for a few hours, you can really earn more, many traders are so good with it that they become so much richer in just a very short span of time.

But as a beginner, you should not risk it too much. Having a little earning during your first tries is so much better than having no earnings at all, or worse yet, losing your money due to some bad decisions. This should make us think about…

The Risks And Dangers In Doing Your First Trading Acts

The concept of losing money as a trader can be simply understood by looking at an event that often takes place within the currency world. Sometimes a currency starts to depreciate. Like for instance, the price of the US Dollar compared to an Asia currency like the Philippine peso could drop relative to each other. Sometimes, it is priced at 50 Php while sometimes it could be 48, or even lower.

The same goes with other currencies out there. As an aspiring trader, you really need to watch out for such trends. Don't worry too much though, there is an easy way to get get the hang of this problem. There are actually mental conditioning drills that you can implement on yourself so that such an exhausting chore will be a bit easier for beginners like you.

So if you're a Filipino and you're seeing that the value of Pesos is at an all-time low for a set of weeks, it would be easy to say that it's a bad time to go to the US. Because your money, which is of course so much lower compared to the currency of that country, will be pushed even lower once you do some exchanging there.

But when you see that the value of the Peso compared to the Dollar is priced at around 50 or a bit higher, then we can say that it would be a good time to visit your American friends. Don't expect the Peso to be even close to 60 though, such an event couldn't happen for now, at least, not yet anyway.

But when trading with currencies such as the Japanese Yen, or the Euro, that is where you can get the best profits possible. There will be more discussions about such currency lists a little later.

Aside from talking about highs and lows and rising and falling, let's talk about liquids. Like water? Like oil? Like alcohol? Something like that, but a different kind of liquid. Known for their characteristic of being "incompressible," they are highly of use to the processes that govern this dear world of ours. So how are they related to the Forex market?

In a lot of ways, they are highly relevant. Because when we study liquids, we can figure out the volatility of the events around us... including what goes on within the money-making and money-trading field. We see oceans rise and fall as tides get controlled by the moon. And if we acknowledge it, changes in the water will rise all boats or sink all of them.

Another relevance about liquid as a term in the Forex market is the "liquidity" that you can execute as you go around buying and selling currencies. Whenever you are interested to buy a particular currency, you can execute that plan at will. All it takes is just a few seconds, or even just a single second, provided of course that the internet connection in which your phone or computer is attached to, is quite stable and reliable.

Knowing The Best Time For Trading

The Forex market works round the clock, 5 days a week, you knew that already. Does it mean you can do some trading and make money any time of the day as long as they fall within that 5-day scope? Yes. However, you also need to be aware of the most ideal times of trading so that you can make some really good choices and decisions about the exact currency you need to buy or trade for.

To understand the paragraph above, we have to grasp some understanding about Greenwich Mean Time. It is a system by which time zones all over the world are cohesively weaved together so the events that take place within them can be recorded accordingly and appropriately. Tourism, as well as currency exchange rely heavily on time zone schedules so they can conduct business in the smoothest ways possible.

Why do we need to know about it? Because it will give you a better understanding of how the Exchange market really works on a global scale, as a business that never sleeps. Forex experts claim that from the perspective of the GMT time zone, the 3 major components of the market operate according to the following sessions.

Asia: 5:00 am – 4:00 pm

Europe: 3:00 pm – 12:00 am

USA: 8:00 pm – 5:00 am

By looking at that, we can grasp the idea that the Forex sub-markets within a particular group of countries are active within those given timeframes. It means that if you are quite knowledgeable with how the market within the areas listed above, you can make some smart trading within those schedules.

Does that mean you can't trade within the other markets if you live outside a certain country or continent? You still can! What that time list simply implies is that the market of those groups of countries, which happen to be the biggest factors that play within the Forex world are most active during those respective times.

If you prefer a trading schedule in which the country where you live is not that active during a certain session, you can always trade for currencies in other countries that are active in your free time. Like what's mentioned earlier, the Forex market doesn't sleep technically. You can trade, buy, sell, and make profit 5 days a week, 24 hours a day, as long as you choose the right currency in almost any given time at all.

Difference Between the Forex Market and Stock Market

Aside from the fact that it's bigger than the Stock Market, Forex has no main office, in contrast to the former which has a main office for every country you can think of. If you heard about cryptocurrency which is also one of the biggest trading markets today, you may have heard about the term "decentralization."

Such a term means that there is no single person or business entity controlling the whole system. This is where the cryptocurrency business becomes very similar to the Forex market – which is defined by experts as a huge network of trading entities from practically everywhere in the world as long as a certain form of currency exists.

Those entities that comprise the said network are banks, private business firms, fund management companies, and even government institutions. As they merge together with their day-to-day operations, that is where the trading and profiting takes place.

Since those business entities vary in sizes and mode of operations, it's the main reason why currency values and prices rise and fall. If something goes wrong with the economy of a certain country, we can surely see that the price of its currency is affected too. Conversely, if the economy of another country goes so well, we could see its currency performing nicely too.

That is actually how Forex trading experts base their decisions from. Their speculations are based on what goes within the over-all business world of a country. If most of the big names in the commercial field are raking huge incomes, then that country as a whole should experience a great rise in its finances too.

Also, if the government of that country is actively doing business with other governments as well, like maybe if a political leader is buying petroleum or all sorts of fossil fuels from another country, then it should go without saying too, that the recipient government would experience some revenue spikes on its over-all economy.

When situations like that happen or fail to happen, that actually determines the rise and fall of the currency value. Since all countries are contributors to the overall structure of the Forex market, they are all important nodes or elements within the network mentioned. We can also say that the currency of a country is kind of like its "share" to the overall global market if we are to treat the Forex Market as a corporation.

Another major factor that contributes to the rise of a country's currency value is the employment rate that's taking place within it. If there are more jobs that are offered therein, it would mean that more people are working and are gaining some regular income. Furthermore, it will be very likely that workers from other countries will also be hired there, which would usher in currencies from the countries of those outsiders – trading and exchanging of money will rise significantly.

Now, I know you're thinking that there is a lot of information that you really need to grasp. Do you really need to understand all of it just to start trading? Not really. With just very small capital, and just a few hours of your time each day, you can already start trading. No hardships there.

However, if you wish to be a truly successful trader, you have to learn about the currency of the target countries that own the currencies you want to trade with. Itwould be a really huge deciding factor for your investment choices. The most successful businessmen are those that know their craft very well. You can't expect to be a good warrior if you don't know your weapons and the battle techniques of your enemy.

Of course, we won't be dealing with real villains within the Forex market, although you might encounter some really villainous people along the way as you hone your trading skills. The only enemy you'll ever face as a Forex trader is yourself, making bad decisions. We can then say that to beat the enemy, you need to make some very smart decisions, and to do that, we really need to have at least some basic understanding of how the economy works.

But if we think of it and summarize the tasks of a trader, all you need to understand is this, there are only 2 main actions that you will do: buying and selling. If you think that a currency is doing so well, then you buy it. If you think it's gonna go down, then you sell it. Think about the see-sawing analogy mentioned earlier. If you mix it up with your knowledge about the economy of a certain country, then you will always be on the good path of successful trading practices.

Knowing The Most Profitable Currencies

Like a good warrior who has good knowledge of his weapons and battle equipment, you who plan to be transformed into a wise Forex trader must know the basics of the most popular currencies that you can make a profit with. Currencies are named with some abbreviations. Let's iterate them one by one.

For the US we have the Dollar which has the symbol of "USD", also called "Buck"

For the European Union we have the Euro which has the symbol of "EUR", also called "Fiber"

For Japan we have Yen which has the symbol of "JPY", also called "Buck"

For the UK we have the pound which has the symbol of "GBP", also called "Cable"

For Switzerland we have the Swiss Franc which has the symbol of "CHF", also called "Buck"

For Canada we have the Canadian Dollar which has the symbol of "CAD", also called "Loonie"

For Australia we have the Australian Dollar which has the symbol of "AUD", also called "Aussie"

For New Zealand we have the New Zealand Dollar which has the symbol of "NZD", also called "Kiwi"

They are not the only currencies out there. However, most successful traders focus on these 8 major currencies because they are the most traded forms of money in the world. Looking at the given list would also give us the understanding that in connection to the "economy knowledge" stated above, there are also 8 countries that you need to really watch out for.

Such countries are the major key players within the Forex market so by default, being knowledgeable with all of them will surely give you the greatest advantage as a Forex trader.

Understanding Symbols Pairings

Let's understand what currency pairing actually means, and why they are paired in these ways:

EUR/USD

USD/JPY

GBP/USD

USD/CHF

USD/CAD

AUD/USD

NZD/USD

You might wonder why in the list above, the US Dollar appears in all items. It's because it has the most number of transactions going on in the world at all times. While the US might not be the ultimate richest country in the world, its currency has become the favorite single side of any Forex trading that ever exists.

When doing your actual trading acts, bear in mind that the position of USD is fixed and locked which means you can't really change it – Online platforms program their systems that way, for easier comprehension. If it appears on the left or on the right said of a certain pairing, you have to leave it as it is. Such a method makes the acts of trading much more simple for everyone especially for novice traders like you.

Exotic Pairs

When physical looks are focused on as a topic there is this thing called "exoticism." And although we're not talking about any outward beauty in Forex, we have to know that there is another kind of beauty going on within the market, and it is an exotic currency pairing at its finest.

Why exotic? Because they don't really belong to the "8 big leagues" in the Forex trading business. They are those that come from "not-so-popular-countries" in terms of currency power. Here they are with their corresponding symbols:

Currencies	Symbols
Euro – Turkish Lira	: EUR/TRY
US Dollar – Swedish Krona	: USD/SEK
US Dollar – Norwegian Krone	: USD/NOK

US Dollar – Danish Krone   :   USD/DKK

US Dollar – South African Rand   :   USD/ZAR

US Dollar – Hong Kong Dollar   :   USD/HKD

US Dollar – Singapore Dollar   :   USD/SGD

They are the most popular currency pairings within the "Exotic Category"

About Forex Quotes

To understand Forex pairs further, let's break down each part meticulously. Reading Forex quotes is one of the most fundamental things that an aspiring trader must learn, you have to know it this early. For this example, let's take a look at USD and Euro. As of this writing, the pairing of the 2 would give us a value of "1.1500" so it would give us this Forex Quote:

EUR/USD = 1.1500

That line simply means that if you invest on that pair, you'd get the amount stated by their equivalent numbers. So if you exchange your European money for American money, you'd have a total of 1 Dollar and 15 cents. The 2 components of that quote are actually labeled as "base currency" and "quote currency" – the one on the left side (EUR) is the base, while the one on the right (USD) is the quote.

To make it easier for traders to remember the respective values for each currency pair, the base currency is always assigned with the value of 1. As what's discussed earlier about trading as the act of buying and selling at the same time, we can say that a currency quote is what reminds you the amount you're dealing with.

So in the EUR/USD pair, you are actually selling Euro money while buying US Dollars at the same time. If you have it this way, USD/EUR, then you're actually selling USD money while buying Euro. Just bear in mind that the base currency, the one on the left, is what you'll be selling.

To make it simpler, we can write the formula this way:

EUR/USD : buy Euro, sell US Dollar

USD/EUR : buy US Dollar, sell Euro

The same applies to all currencies in existence. All you need to really understand and take note of is the symbol for each currency.

About Pips

What are pips? To simply put it, we can just say that "pips" is the plural form of pip. I'm just humoring you, don't get mad. As acronym that means "Percentage In Point," They are actually the rise and fall of the equivalent value of a currency pair. For instance. If you hear a statement that from a Forex trader that goes "My pairing is up by 1 pip!" it means that his EUR/USD transaction becomes 1.1501 from 1.500.

Likewise if you hear that trader say, "My pairing is down by a pip!" it means that his EUR/USD transaction becomes 1.1499. Counting pips is what determines your losses or winnings if you play the Game of Forex Thrones. The higher the pips are, the higher your income will be, the lower the pips go, the lower your profit will be. This is something that you should be good at if you wish to be truly profitable as a Forex trader.

Dealing With Brokers

In being a Forex trader, let's not forget one important entity: the broker. They are a group of people or maybe just one person that facilitates your money flow within the Foreign

Exchange Market. If they are tasked to do one important thing, then they should get paid, right? So how much should we pay them?

Actually, they will just take a very little amount – very, very little. The transaction cost that the broker gets is actually called "spread." This term can also be referred to as the difference between the "buying price" and the "selling price."

For instance, if you frequently go to a bank or a money-changing firm, you would have most likely known that you are always shown with 2 price values: the value of the currency you're holding, and the one you'll be given once you go through with the exchange.

Now let's say the current buying price of Euro is 1.1511, and its selling price is 1.1513, then it means there is a 2-pip difference, that is then the amount the broker gets. Don't be too sad about it. Because it is just a very, very small amount considering that 0.1500 actually just means "15 cents."

So whenever you deal with the EUR/USD pair, and you buy them, you will be automatically subtracted with 2 pips, depending of course on the currency value at a given situation.

Pips In Relevance To Lots

We talk about Lots in the previous paragraphs. Now let's discuss them in relevance to Pips. We already understood that a Standard Lot is comprised of 100,000 units and has a volume of 1.00. Now that would give us a cost of Dollars per pip which is 10 Dollars. It means that it will be the multiplier that determines your profits or losses.

So if you have 100 Dollars it will be multiplied by 10, because it is the current price per pip.

So for instance, if the current Pip value moves to 20, then you'd have the total earnings of 200 Dollars. Likewise, if you lose, then you'd lose with the same amount, although actually, you just lose the original amount you staked during the initial trading process.

It goes to show that higher pips equate to higher wins, while it results as well in big losses too. Now if you're a bit scared about it, you can always switch to a Mini Lot, or to make it less scary, you can also choose Micro Lot, which is way smaller.

A mini lot has the equivalent of 1 Dollar which will give you a profit of 20 Dollars. A smaller win, but a smaller loss too. Micro Lot is 10 times smaller, which again, results in a much smaller win, and a much smaller loss. The math is pretty easy to grasp, right?

Understanding Candlestick Charts

"The world today communicates visually" – This is a statement that today's marketers and media creators can openly declare with zero-doubt indication. Whenever we see signages of all kinds, we now see drawings and symbols instead of words. In publications, magazines, books, and even their digital counterparts are so replete with diagrams and infographics that text and numbers are kept very minimal.

Undeniably, graphics and visuals are now becoming as important as words in making people understand something. With Forex trading, even though you will mostly deal with numbers, you will also deal with graphics a lot… illustrations that represent the rising and falling of monetary pricings from all over the world, graphics that are actually known to the trading world as candlestick charts.

Believed to have been popularized by Munehisa Homma, a Japanese rice trader during the 18th Century, it is now the basis used by traders all over the world in this digital age of ours. Even outside Forex, this kind of chart is also used in other fields such as cryptocurrency.

The candlestick chart is super-important for a Forex trader – it is the ultimate tool that one must use in order to come up with the best trading decisions. Trading is an art that can really make you rich, no doubt of that. But it isn't something that you can just put money into, and wait for it to pile up without really doing anything.

You really need to understand how money within the exchange market flows and to do that, you need to understand what a candlestick chart is, and how you can use it as a guide to embark on your trading adventures.

Candlestick charts are often regarded by some traders as more than just a trading tool that can read and predict prices. For them, those charts are also a means of behavior analysis – something that can make them them understand the possible outcome of market practices tomorrow, and in the next period of months, or even years.

Some experts even claim that candlestick charts are actually objects that can spell out human emotions because they tell us the buying and selling patterns made by people within the Forex market every day, and what could they be thinking as they go on about their transactions.

Before breaking down the elements of a candlestick chart, let's grasp a simple analogy from a rope-pulling game called "tug-of-war." Even if you haven't participated in that kind of game, you can certainly discern that it can be summed up by knowing which side pulls the hardest, and which side gets dragged over into the opposing side's domain.

When a tug-of-war battle begins, we can see that the 2 teams start at an even point: no winner, no loser. But as the battle ensues, we can then see that one team could be in greater power compared to others for a few seconds, but then would start to get overpowered by the other due to some underlying forces at play.

When the battle finally commences usually after just a few seconds, we can then see the true victor and the true loser. In Forex, that can then be declared as the closing of a trading day, or week. Bye then, you should be able to see if you've gained more, or lost more than what you have actually expected.

Such an analogy could be one of the best methods for understanding a Forex chart. When a particular currency is pulling a currency closer to its domain, it means that it is gaining higher value compared to the other currency it's paired with.

There are times when one team pulls strongly for a few seconds, but then gets easily trampled down as the opposing team unpredictably pulls back harder. In currency exchange, things can also be like that – unpredictable and erratic. But by gaining some experiences with charts constantly, you can somehow make productive predictions that can help you grow your money fast.

The Anatomy Of A Candlestick Chart

The very reason why it is named as such is actually due to a very obvious reason – it really does look like a candlestick, with protruding fuses on both ends. It has basically four parts:

High point – is the topmost part a Forex candlestick. It is kind of like the tip of the candle's string fuse.

Close point – the bottom of the high point line, or where the main body of the candle begins.

Open point – is the bottom of the candle's body, the tip of the low line.

Low point – the tip of the candle's bottom string fuse.

To have a clearer picture in your head of what a Forex candlestick looks like, we can say that it looks like a tube with short protruding strings on both ends. The candle's main body or the tube actually represents a trading duration. It could represent a single day, an hour, a day, an entire week, or even an entire month.

In the open point, it is where a trading day opens, and the corresponding price for a certain currency of that day. The "low point string" is the duration in which the currency at hand is at its lowest point. Conversely, the higher part of the candlestick is just the opposite of those.

Green candles are often referred to as "bullish candles" because well, they are raging like bulls in terms of making a currency attain a higher value. Red ones are called "bearish candles" because traders think of them as slugging the value of your money like a slow-running bear.

When a candle is in full green, meaning it has no string fuses at all on either end, it means that it is a strong candle, representing a currency that performing extremely well. Conversely, a totally red candle with no thin lines at all means it's doing badly.

You have to note that when the candle's body appears red, it means that the value is lower than the expected lowest point, so it means that the currency is appearing really bad. We can think of it as the value becoming negative if we compare it to Algebra. Another way of saying it could be that a currency becomes lower than the original value when it was opened on a given day.

By looking at various candlesticks within a Forex market chart, we can then create our own analysis about the market's direction. It is then when we can make a smart decision about what particular currency to trade, and how long will we hold on to our money, and how soon should we let it go and trade it with something else.

Bear in mind that a good comprehension of candlestick charts is very fundamental to the success or failure of any Forex trading activity. When the direction of a chart is going up, it means that there are lots of currency buyers doing some purchases.

It means you should consider buying too because the value of that currency you're buying could be raised really high. It could be raised to a quarter, a half, or even many full times over... depending on trends and other factors.

When a candle is very short compared to its strings on its ends which are really long, and if that little candle is in the middle, it means indecision. It means that people find it hard to decide whether to sell or to buy currencies at a particular time.

Understanding Dojis

Let's understand another important set of symbols. A long vertical line with a very short horizontal line (the very shortened candle body) is called a "Doji" It means that the opening price of a currency is the same as the price when it got closed.

Dojis are actually shown as a typical plus sign, a plus sign with an extremely long vertical line, and a "T" with a rather long bottom. It is also called a "Dragonfly Doji."

There is also the "Gravestone Doji" which can be seen as an inverted T or the reverse of a Dragonfly Doji. When a candlestick looks like that, it means that the price of a currency opens and closes at the low point or very near it, and has a long topping tail. When a chart shows a Gravestone Doji, it would mean that trading at this point isn't a good thing. You have to wait for a while before the situation improves.

184

The lengthening and shortening of a candlestick could be due to people hearing about an economy or financial news, or a major event within a certain country's monetary status. It could also mean an increase or decrease in a country's tourism revenues.

But for a typical trader like you and me, the reasons could just be irrelevant. What we will just be focusing on is the simple fact that a currency's value is high enough and that we should take advantage of it.

There is also the "Spinning Top Doji" – one that looks like a plus sign but with a vertical line that becomes fat, very fat, and goes back to being thin again. From an emotional perspective of the currency buyers, there is almost no emotion depicted on the buying habits that are represented by spinning tops. It means that prices are not moving up or down significantly. It generally represents indecision to either buy currencies or sell them.

"When a real candle is long, it means it has the burning power to stay longer of course." The same is true with candlesticks in a chart. If the "wick of a candle" grows long, it means the value of the currency it represents is rising too. It also means that there are lots of emotions in it too – people are buying and selling efficiently within the real world which boosted a country's economy. Such kinds of candles are also referred to as "expanded range candles."

When looking at a chart as you formulate your analysis, one of the major factors you have to highly take note of is when a sudden lowering of prices happens. When it rises again higher than the previous high point, it is called a pullback, and it could be a sign that the currency can still rise higher.

Recurring pullbacks are actually beneficial to a long-term trading strategy because it represents a currency's consistent increase throughout a certain duration. Such a set of events within a Forex chart can just be regarded as a 3-point action, the rise of the value, the sudden lowering of it, and the rising which is way higher than the previous high point.

As long as you take notice of those 3, and if they are higher than the previous sets, then it means the currency is performing so well. By looking at the exact point of the pullback, you can think of it as your "support level." It means that you should hope that the next low point in the direction of the chart shouldn't go lower than that.

The opposite of that point is called the "resistance level." It is the next indicator that the next low shouldn't be lower than that too. If it does go lower than that, then the currency could be in a bad scenario. Another way of determining if the value is going desirably higher is that the current support level should be higher than the previous one, and so on and so forth.

If they continue to be displayed with that pattern, it means that the currency at hand is in an "uptrend," and that many traders are enjoying the benefits it gives. By consistently looking into that, you can really do some little tradings, or big tradings, depending on what your gut is telling you.

If you see that the current support level is lower than the one before it, then we have to expect that the currency is now on a downtrend, which means that there are more sellers than buyers.

The best way to deal with that gut feeling is to remember the "don't get greedy advice" from the previous pages. Little profits accumulated over time would result in big profits. It is so much better than expecting a big win but attain a big loss as well in just a single stroke.

Here's one crucial fact that you really need to bear in mind, no matter how good you become in analyzing candlestick charts, there is no guarantee that the analysis you can derive from them will always work at all times. Here's the truth about Forex charts, or any other trading chart for that matter: they're not really 100% accurate.

The rise and fall of those green and red candles are just representations of what could be possibly taking place, they're not actual-real time data that truly represent what's actually happening within the financial setting of a certain country.

While trading charts are created using the most sophisticated software and hardware technologies there are, they can't really predict human behavior and choices that are taking place in various global markets every hour or every day.

The most productive treasure-hunters don't just rely on a hunch or luck to locate and dig up buried treasure chests. They need maps and homing instruments to find what they're looking for. As a Forex trader, candlestick charts are your maps and compasses – treat them with the utmost importance, and success in trading will surely await you in the very near future.

Understanding the Market's Direction

It has been stated earlier in the discussion that becoming a successful Forex trader has something to do with understanding the international market flow. To achieve that, we can just stare at the 3 kinds of analysis that a Forex neophyte must just look into: fundamental, technical, and sentimental. What are they?

Fundamental analysis – This revolves around this simple idea: a bad economy means a decrease in currency value while a good economy is an increase in currency value. It would mean that you need to have some comprehension regarding a country's government debt, inflation rate, employment status, and other similar stuff. It's pretty heavy to grasp at first, but it's something that you really should have some high consideration of.

Technical analysis – The easiest way to deal with that is understanding Forex charts, which is something that we will discuss in the next chapters. There are basically 4 factors that comprise technical analysis: price action, supports and resistances, trends, and indicators.

Price action is simply about the rise and fall of the prices that correspond to each currency. Supports and resistances on the other hand represent the low and high levels of a currency that it is able to reach over time. Support gets manifested when a value drops to a point that should be the motivation for traders to buy some currency.

Trends will show the steady direction of a currency, often for prolonged periods. For instance, if a currency is going up steadily on its course, or if it drops in the same manner, they are called trends. Expert traders often use it to predict upcoming value changes within the Forex market.

Indicators are those points that tell exactly how high or how low a certain currency is. Seasoned traders consider them as tools that can help them with precise and specific trading decisions.

Sentimental Analysis – Are they things that can make you cry because of nostalgic past memories? No. they are actually sets of analyzed data regarding the positions of major players that participate within the Forex market. These are often the biggest banks and biggest business entities around the world. They are actually members of a huge group within the business world know as the Commitment of Traders.

Attaining Forex Expertise: Learning About Top Trading Strategies

Since you really want to be greatly successful in your dealings with currency exchange, you probably want to answer questions like:

How do the experts conduct their trading businesses?

What are their entrance and exit strategies?

How are they leveraging economic news and events?

How are they running their lives as they invest huge time and effort in their trading activities?

Those are questions that you really want clear answers for, so let's tackle them here. Let's get acquainted with crucial key points that truly define rich traders and poor traders. You can call them techniques or strategies, either way, is preferable. What matters is your absorption for each of them.

Strategy 1: Working On Your Attitude Towards Trading

Let's talk about habits. Are they crucial to the very essence of being a good Forex trader? Absolutely. Why so very few traders become rich and why plenty of Forex enthusiasts don't become wealthy is defined by this important factor called habit – because good traders make it their second nature to habitually trade for most of their daily routines.

While they may not do it each and every day of their lives, they do it a lot, obviously. Habits greatly matter in this discussion, so let's get right to it. Here are the traits that you need to learn:

Balancing patience and impatience

Can you patiently wait while being impatient at the same time? That sounds impossible. But the truth is, the big leagues of Forex have the 2 traits in a perfect balance. So what does it mean? In all of their trading acts, literally all of them, they get anxious and worry a lot all the time. They are quick to jump into whatever trading advantage they can see, but then, there are also times when they quickly get out of them too based on the chart trends they're seeing.

Although they can manage the levels of such feelings efficiently as they gain more experience, they really worry about how their day-to-day trading might eventually turn out – it is the chief reason why they always do their very best to come up with the best decisions.

While there are times when they are quick to get out from a strategy they're executing, there are a lot of moments too, in which they will just say "I will wait for a little longer to see how

194

this move pans out." The best way to describe the patience/impatience trading balance is this: being patient with winning trades and being impatient with losing ones.

If we are to illustrate such a principle, we could think of it as a picture with a set of small red dots, and a single occurrence of a big green dot – red being an indicator of waiting, and green being a symbol for proceeding. Another set of small red dots, and another presence of a big green dot, the cycle goes on and on.

The bigger the dot, the bigger the move or monetary value that should be involved. And since red is represented as small objects, it means the action or value to be staked at those moments should not be very big too. If you understood that pretty well, and if you plan to make it a habit, then you should be on your way to becoming an excellent trader.

If you think that many of those great traders succeeded easily during their first tries, you'd be hugely wrong. In fact, most of them lose a lot more than you can possibly imagine. Even during their expert days, they still lose heavily. But what they do is they become impatient with their losses, that's why they are quick to come up with more solid plans and actions on how to improve on their methods.

Be impatient if you're learning less than you should, but be very patient on those things that you can't control – this a statement that should belong to your main driving force with Forex.

Focusing on higher profit instead of proving smartness

Everybody wants to prove they're brilliant, who doesn't? But sometimes, the smartest of us get too blinded by our own perception of ourselves in terms of knowing the right stuff to buy and invest on, that we fail to realize they don't get the highest returns of investment. No matter how wise or intelligent you are, you can't just implement your knowledge into how the Forex market works all the time because there are lots of people therein that are just way smarter than you.

You have to listen to what the market tells you, not the other way around. You cannot tell the market "Do this because my experience tells so," or "Do that because the knowledge I attained will prove me right." The market is what's right all the time, so listen to what it says.

You have to set your mind in choosing those actions that make the most money, not on how beautiful an investment object is, according to your own definition. So in Forex trading, you have to focus on the winning side always. Even if you dearly love a certain currency because of some nostalgic elements attached to it, you have to be quick to switch from one portion to another. Forget about currency loyalty. Instead, focus on one major aspect that can really make you succeed – your own money.

Using charts and visuals wisely

In the candlestick topic we discussed in the previous pages, it is emphasized that they should be absorbed and understood thoroughly because they are among the most useful tools in trading. Successful traders don't just look at charts, they internalize them deeply because aside from telling them the best directions the market is going, they can also tell where other good traders are lining up.

All traders perform technical analysis of some sort. It would be foolish to just trade without really thinking. While typical traders look at charts as nothing but bars and lines, rich traders look at them as pictures of other traders that line up as they move into or away from a certain buying act. They always picture in their mind that something is going to happen whenever they look at a particular behavior of a chart.

Before engaging in a certain trade, they identify the right spots to enter, but also look for a quick exit strategy, should something go wrong – that's one of the traits of successful traders. Novice traders are often too fast to get into a good trade because of too much excitement. Great traders don't think like that. If they can't tell where the exit points are in a chart, whether it's an increase or a decrease, they don't get in, it's power wisdom at play there. They gain big time by pointing out entrance and exit points clearly.

Learning from mistakes by moving on quickly

As you gain more trading experience, you might experience successive trades like 4 to 6 times that are so against what you hope for. Conversely, you might also encounter successive trades that go with you in a very positive way. This is natural. You have to absorb that in a statistical manner and accept that stuff like that could happen again and again.

When they do, you have to know that it's not because you are interpreting the market in the wrong way. It is simply because the market is just unpredictable at times that even the smartest analysts could end up very wrong too.

Although the importance of reading the charts right is emphasized in the previous item, you have to acknowledge that they don't work 100% of the time. Experts even claim that they just work 60% in most cases. Shocking and disappointing, right? But that's one of the realities that you just have to accept.

Another thing about big-time traders is that as long as there have been a series of wins with their past methods, those methods will prove in time that they will be effective again. They are not bothered by some of the losses they get as long as their previous statistics prove them to be profitable.

In dealing with the lows and disappointments of your previous trading, you have to think about those moments when the odds are in your favor. Learn from your mistakes but be quick to move on, there are better opportunities that ahead that await you.

Strategy 2: Choosing The Right Broker

Whenever you engage in any money-trading transaction in Forex, you need some kind of middle man. Not exactly a man, but an online business entity that will facilitate the transaction for you: From you Dollar to Euro, from Swiss Franc to Pound, from Peso to Yen, et cetera. Such a kind of entity that handles the changing of any of these currencies into another is called a "Broker."

Like any middle man in a real-world business setting, you need someone you can trust. After all, why would you entrust your hard-earned money to someone who has earned the reputation of swindling people's money away? While the money-making mechanisms that make Forex function is definitely not a scam, there will always be those that will use the very nice functions of the market as a scam.

Just like the statement in the Bible that goes "The love of money is the root of all evil," The problem is not money itself, but in the idea of how people deal with money and how they lie and cheat for the sake of attaining it. Forex, as a giant money-making system is also used by a lot of scammers and swindlers too, that's why it is really important that an aspiring Forex trader must know the proper steps in choosing the right broker.

In this section, let us talk about the proper guidelines and checklist in tapping into the right brokerage firms on the internet. Even experienced traders constantly look for truly trustworthy traders that might help them increase their profits even more. You as a newbie should do the same too since failure for you is never an option since you are someone who's super-excited to hit it big with Forex.

Traits of A Good Forex Broker

A good broker can be identified as having the following:

Looks for its own interests, but makes sure yours are looked upon too

Most brokers just want to gain profit from you but are not really interested in seeing you grow, and in witnessing you succeed with your trading endeavors. A good broker is someone who seeks really high gains but makes you tag along with it. Yes, all brokers are businessmen whose goals are to make money, and anyone who doesn't acknowledge this would be a fool. But a good broker would not just be focused on getting something from you, but also in getting something from the market, which he can then share with its clients, such as you.

If you remember the facts about Spreads in the previous sections, they are the amount that the broker earns by facilitating a trading act. Of course, all traders are doing the best they can to make the most out of their clients' Spreads, and you are of no exemption. But good traders attain their spreads in the fairest manner, they wouldn't be in the business for extended periods if they are bad at it.

Has excellent trading demos that anyone can openly view

Whenever we hear about the success of a businessman and wish to follow in the footsteps of that person, we would most likely see that person "walk the talk." A person who babbles about his success but has no concrete proof of it would be something that we annoyed listening to. To really know if your broker has the business prowess that can grow your money, you have to see for yourself if they have good trading demo videos that you can easily view and understand.

All legit brokers have their own websites of Youtube channels and in them, you should see some of their videos in which they perform video tutorials or live trading that you can take inspiration from or learn from. If you can see that their recorded videos produce almost exactly the same results as their live ones, then it is a surefire indicator that the broker you're considering to partner with has the business execution that can really make you rich.

It would be quite natural for brokers to upload videos in their channels about how they're better than their competitors. It is understandable that all businesses advertise their advantages and none of their disadvantages to all of their potential clients. However, it would be far better for you to focus on their demo and live videos more than on their advertising and promotional videos.

Many Forex brokerage firms will offer you trading courses for a certain fee giving you promises of doubling, tripling, or quadrupling your income. Some of these claims could just be an exaggeration, though some of them could also be very real as well. Tapping into such courses is fine, you should take advantage of them too if you're truly serious with your trading endeavors.

But bear in mind that there are free tutorials out there too. Sometimes, paying for training doesn't really pay off any better than the free ones. Some online course lovers highly prefer paid training with a coach instead of self-learning in which they just become lazy and sluggish.

Demo trading video streams are meant to show you the transition of the uploading and receiving of funds and you have to see if you can easily duplicate what the demonstrators do on screen. Pay for such skills or learn them on your own, the choice is yours.

Whatever works for you, just bear in mind that a good and successful trader doesn't rely on the decisions made by others. Although taking heed of the decisions of the best traders out there surely gives lots of advantages, the real advantage is having the skill to make decisions on your own. It will not only make your trading adventures so much emotionally rewarding, but more prolific as well in terms of self-growth and self-worth.

Has a wide selection of market options

One way to discern if a certain broker can be successful for the long haul is by looking at its selection of markets. The most-traded currencies are of course the Dollar and the Euro. But are they the only currencies out there? No. While they are truly the currencies that you can make the greatest money with, there will be times when other alternatives are also showing profit promises that could be truly rewarding.

If your broker has no easy way of changing other currencies that could just be minor key players within the entirety of the Forex market, it could be a huge indicator that they are not something that you should always work with. In the business world, opportunities come and go. Some of the best opportunities could arrive now, and be gone in a very short span of time.

In the Forex market, the rise and fall of money are really volatile. What's very high now could be very low in a matter of hours. What if you want to switch from one currency into another but your broker couldn't handle such a trading speed that suits your transaction preferences?

The best brokers should be instantly there whenever you want to immediately hop into a trading transaction that you want to hop into at nearly the speed of thought. While it's not really a beneficial habit when you constantly jump from one currency pairing to another, there are special times when you really need to, that's why it's super-important for a broker to be capable of handling speedy transactions especially if there are plenty of traders like us who wants to quickly attain the earnings we dream and wish for.

One of the trends in Forex trading nowadays is that Spreads are quite thin and small. Years ago, the fees that we need to pay to the brokers are quite high. But with the number of traders grown rapidly with each passing month, fees are getting smaller and more affordable, making anyone with very small capitals be able to participate in the games of trading.

This is a good opportunity for small-time individuals to increase their means of living. And all successful brokers do their very best to cater to even the smallest players who just want to start trading with their very small amounts. If a broker has a relatively high-rates of Spreads, you should avoid it because for sure, there will be lots of more affordable options out there.

The best way to find out who they are is to spend enough time practicing on your own account and connect with other new traders out there. Surely, there are plenty of individuals out there who are as non-educated as you in terms of Forex trading. You might think that you are Forex-ignorant, but there others out there who are more ignorant than you.

Do you know what's really cool? Many Forex broker experts don't care if your ignorant or not. They will surely have the means of helping you. Many of them are actually very friendly and helpful – it is one of the traits that make them very successful within the market.

If your chosen broker firm shows some unfriendliness, then then it is not the right one for you. Move on to the next ones on your list, some of them could be more worth your time.

Shows professional transparency

In dealing with friendships and partnerships in our social circles, we hate nothing more than those people who have hidden ulterior motives as they conduct those processes that they claim could benefit both parties: yours and theirs. Although they may sure do work hard in attaining some profit that can benefit both of you, knowing later on that your partner actually gains more than you could have without really explaining it to you would surely make you feel uncomfortable.

If your broker is showing such signs, then it is also an indicator that it is not a good brokerage firm. Even top-notch broker businesses in other areas that have very little thing to do with the Forex market are very clear with what they're doing. They don't show any signs of cheating on their clients are gaming the entire system just to their advantage.

Whenever you ask them questions, they will give you a straightforward answer as long as such answers don't breach their company's trade secrets. They are quick and swift in dealing with clients' queries and will waste no time in reaching out to us whenever we speak about troubles of any kind.

They are the kind of business firms that are very evident in their 2-way dealings. They are good at increasing their revenues, all the while showing great indications as well that their clients and partners as well are properly rewarded. They are the types of entities that make sure that it's a win-win situation between them and their prospective clients, inasmuch as in their dealings with the clients in the past.

Has excellent customer support

In connection to the "Forex never sleeps" adage, good brokers have customer service sections that never sleeps as well, and one that deals with problems in the quickest ways possible. While Forex isn't really 24-7, more likely being just 24-5 because it is closed during Saturdays and Sundays, the best broker firms have some staff that works even on those days, just to handle clients' inquiries and problems.

It doesn't mean though that those firms that are closed during weekends are bad ones. There are actually good brokers that are also closed during those days because the markets are also closed therein. However, when they do open, they are very quick and are highly reachable whenever you want to communicate with them through phone or through e-mail. Some of them even cater to video calls and teleconferences just to give the best possible services to their clients.

Has a wide range of trading tools

Aside from the excellent services and nice etiquette that they're capable of displaying, a good broker firm to pick would be one that has a wide variety of software tools that you can utilize to maximize your trading efforts. The best way to know this is by looking at the links and menus of their websites.

Are the links and link descriptions easy to grasp and comprehend? Are the sub-menus fast enough to access and learn from? Those are questions that you should find so easy to give answers to, by simply navigating through the interface of their web portal.

Since you already have some in-depth understanding of charts in the earliest chapters, you should also check if the broker's website has previous charts that you can check out and study – they will be excellent guides that can help you decide on your next trading moves.

Many popular broker firms have the habit of sending newsletters and press releases straight to your e-mail or social media accounts. Such methods are very cool strategies that can make their platforms even more attractive.

The online portal of a good Forex broker is something that should be a complete recipe on itself. Whenever you log on to their site, you have to be ushered into a set of tools, demo videos, and images that you can instantly use. They have to be so good and very comprehensive that you don't need other tools or supplements so you can understand the latest trends or methods better.

The Best Known Forex Brokers

XM – This is by far the most popular among beginners. Their most notable feature is their free $30 that you can use for your first trading experience.

IG – Globally speaking, this is the most trusted broker by most traders worldwide.

Saxo – If having a more in-depth knowledge about the Forex market is your goal, this should be your first choice.

CMC – This one shows you the widest options for currency pairs. This is where money connections can be found best.

Etoro – The best platform for those who wants to trade in the easiest way possible. Its main feature is "cop-trading."

Strategy 3: Mastering Your Own Demo Account

What's the next best thing to having a real dog? By having a stuffed-toy dog, or by having a figurine dog, that would be the safest answers to give. Of course, owning a dog is not really an extremely serious undertaking, unless you have the mind of an animal-rights activist. If you really know what it feels like to own a dog, why take an object that looks like a dog? Why not take a real, live dog that barks, wiggles its tail, and plays with you in your dull moments?

But here's the thing about real dogs: they will bite you, especially in situations when you will be harsh to them, or if you don't feed them enough. Now, what do dogs have in common with Forex trading? Well, nothing directly.

But if we're going to look closely enough, we might get to see that if you don't trade wisely enough, your Forex efforts will bite you, albeit painfully, because you will lose some precious earnings that should have been better investments somewhere else. That's where Forex and dogs are a bit similar. – Lame analogy, but one that you have to contemplate on.

Using A Forex Demo Account: The First Crucial Step To Take

Now, let's get a bit more topic-centered. How can you be truly well-versed in the very acts of trading? Should you invest real money on a real trading act right on? What if you'll lose? What if you'd gain regret instead of more motivation to proceed with your endeavors as a successful Forex investor? Fret not and fear never, because most Forex brokers offer something that all trading newbies would be very pleased with: demo accounts.

With such an account, you will be granted access to an online portal in which you can conduct some trading practice using digital money that represents your first trading amounts. All you need to key in are some numbers like your supposed dollar deposit, the currency pairing of your choice, your entry point, and your exit point. You will be then prompted to begin the trading simulation which actually looks and feels like it's a real trading activity.

By doing it again, and again, you will surely begin to understand the ins and outs of a trader's life. Which will gradually transform your mode of thinking. Demo accounts are free and are easy to acquire. It just usually involves the following:

- having an email account

- having a computer or smartphone that you can regularly use

- choosing the right broker

- logging on to your chosen broker's website and signing up

- waiting for a confirmation email

- downloading their trading interface and installing it to your phone or computer

- configuring your trading settings and starting the actual trading

Performing all of these steps may vary a little depending on your chosen broker's platform. But they basically work the same. There is no need to worry about not learning how to start, as their menus and guides are very comprehensive.

Choosing the best trading practice platforms is also very simple. All it needs is just the proper keywords in Google's search bar. To make it even easier for you, you can just simply go to Forex.com where you will be guided easily to your first trading experiences. In case you want to have a feel of social trading, going to Etoro.com would also be a very wise choice.

What is the importance of practicing using a demo account?

Because jumping right into real trading using real money is often emotionally painstaking, using unreal money that simulates real trading scenarios would be very ideal for a Forex beginner. You can begin trading right away, experience failure, and then restart the activity again and again. As you get into the habit, you will attain some considerable wisdom along the way and will be having lesser levels of fear whenever you decide to conduct real trading acts in the future.

But like an aspiring boxer fighting punching bags and sparring partners in the gym, using demo accounts has some disadvantages as well. Let's talk about them so you'll have better insights into the act.

Brokers may intentionally let you win more

Forex brokers are businessmen who want to attain more clients. And in order to do so, they will surely do their very best to make their platforms very attractive. Since that is the goal, they will most likely show that within their domain, you will surely win most of the time. Although expert traders will easily spot that, you as a novice will not see that through easily, as you are someone who really wants to get rich quick.

Although what happens in a real trading act is what's depicted in a demo account simulation, it's just exactly what it is: a simulation, unreal, fake, an imitation. The psychology behind the deed is there, but the actual learning gain is much lower.

You might get encouraged to overtrade

"Too much of a good thing is actually bad." – This is a very famous adage. Even in Forex trading, the same principle applies. Ask any experienced trader, and he or she will most definitely tell you: "Don't overtrade my friend, it does more harm than good." If doing the same thing again and again can make you better and wiser, wouldn't overtrading make you a better trader? No. Becoming a good trader is built on trading at the right time with the right mindset. Much like the idea that "The best sex is not due to oversex."

212

If you eat a top-class pizza delicacy, it will be very tasty during the first few slices. But eat an entire jumbo order by yourself, and you'll be sick physically and mentally as well. If you're forced to commit such an act, multiple times, the resulting outcome would be severe vomiting and withdrawals. You will then have it in your head to avoid eating pizza for the next years to come.

Of course, trading is different from eating. Experts have this to say: "Overtrading will make you see things in charts that aren't really there, and will let you make foolish decisions." Bear in mind that gamblers in casinos really can win, but most of them lose because they don't know when to stop or when to take a rest.

To be truly efficient in Forex, never overtrade. And in spending too much time with demo accounts, you just might fall into that trap. Avoid it at all costs.

You might not get the proper psycho-emotional learning.

Forex trading is an emotional undertaking – that's something that you should highly put in mind. Why many businessmen become so successful is they don't only invest time and money in their endeavors, but emotions and mental efforts as well. They formulate plans, review them methodically, and put those plans to work. How those plans get changed or executed differently will be based on what people feel or how they may react to the products they bring out into the world.

Because you're not actually dealing with real money, you won't be expecting real failure should anything go wrong. For that, you will be less scared, which makes you hop into false bravery, which will eventually push you into making wrong decisions.

But before you become too discouraged in signing up for a Forex demo account, you should take heed of this declaration: the advantages of demo accounts far outweigh the disadvantages. Here's why.

They will teach you better than tutorials and articles can.

There are tons of videos and articles that serve as Forex trading guides all over the internet. Many of them are actually very helpful resources that can really make you an expert in the shortest time possible. But as what's stated earlier, experience is still the best teacher. Although watching those videos and reading those articles can surely help you get into the vibe, nothing feels better than being on an actual trading exercise. It is the only way of truly illustrating from a mental standpoint what the action is really all about.

They will show you the realities of the daily life of a trader, minus the financial expense.

Successful trading is a way of life, and you can't be rich with it if you don't make it your second nature, or at list within the list of your regular "to-do list." But making trading as a way of life would be very expensive money-wise for a beginner like you. Demo-trading is the cheapest and most accessible way of replicating the daily dealings of an expert trader and for the time being, no better option is there yet.

Those are only 2 advantages, but their weight should be understandably heavier than the disadvantages. Start your own Forex demo account right now so that the expertise you're hoping for will only be a few steps away from you.

Strategy 4: Using The Scalping Method – The Key to Attaining $10,000 a Month

If you truly believe that "slow and steady wins the race," then you have to highly consider learning the most effective trading strategy yet: Scalping. Before we begin discussing this technique, you have to go back into the topic "The Trading Tasks That A Forex Newbie Must Undergo," so you'll be refreshed with the technicalities that this discussion will show you.

So what is scalping? As the root word suggests, it is a technique in which you will scrape some earnings little by little, usually just a small percentage of the capital you're trading. Most traders who are fond of using it has a 10% rule – They make it a habit to put in 10% of their capital, make a trade, take the 10% increase of their profit, and get out. They do it 9 more times and by adding all of the profits, they would then evaluate and calculate if they got the winnings they hope for.

Some trading experts say that the risks involved with scalping are very high, while some view it as a means of attaining the best stream of income because the rewards are quite high too. Whenever you consider applying this technique to yourself, you should weigh it carefully from your own perspective.

But many traders are getting some decent success with it, that's why you should give it time to try it out to see if it works for you. For the next few pages, you will be ushered into the one of the best keypoints promised in this book: *how to attain a 10,000-dollar income each month.*

Steps to take in using scalping

Observing pivot points – Knowing exactly where a currency begins to drop or where it starts to rise is highly important, that's one of the key factors that make many Forex investors successful. There is no definitive way of predicting when exactly a pivot point happens. However, understanding the highs and lows for the previous days is really helpful in making a good trading decision.

A pivot point can be viewed as an indicator coined by floor traders so it will be much easier to determine possible turning points of whether a certain price will go up or go down. By understanding pivot points, you can easily detect if the market's sentiment can go from bullish to bearish – bullish meaning green candlesticks and bearish meaning red.

They are the means of determining the exact "support and resistance levels," of a chart. We will have to draw lines in the chart the levels of the rise and fall of the market so we can know exactly when to get in and when to get out.

Observing yesterday's chart movements – This is also important so we can have the idea of the market's direction for the present day, and in the next days. Because 2 of the elements that make Forex function is tourism and product exporting/importing, they are among the chief reasons why charts show some rising and falling of currencies. And the thing about such events is that most of them happen for days, which means that yesterday's trend could just be the same today.

Since we understood already that pips determine our profit, knowing the average pips of yesterday's charts would be a good move to choose. For instance, if you entered a trading act using a currency pair that's equivalent to "1.6400" and it can be seen that most of the pips during the previous days are around 50 to 75 (that's today's common range for the EUR/USD pair), it would mean that you'd get an estimated earning of "1.6450"

You have to take into account that the value of a pip can be calculated this way: 1 divided by 10,000. That would give us an exchange rate of 0.0001. Remember, 50 to 75 pips are just the typical rise or fall of candlestick movements; they are not always exact not accurate, that's why it is essential to observe yesterday's chart movements. If you've clearly understood yesterday's chart visuals, it should be safe to do some scalping trading for today.

Scalping is actually done as a series since we will just be scraping little earnings and gathering them altogether to assess our winnings. For that, it would be wise to have a money management strategy as you get on with it.

Money Management With Scalping

For this example, let's work with a capital of $100 for a beginner, that is not a small amount. But let's just use the number for now so the Mathematics behind our following analogies would be a bit easier to follow. And also, it would be profitable for you anyway, as long as you already got the logistics right. Bear in mind that small capitals will also result in small profits.

If you want to take some considerably high profit as a beginner, it would be good to start with a hundred bucks. Now, in using scalping with that amount, let's say we engage in a trading series comprised of 10 trading moves. For each move, we will put in 10 bucks so we can attain that 10% rule which should be the goal too.

The ultimate objective of scalping is to attain a tenth of our capital each time, to maximize our winning trading potential. Just think of this strategy as making a 10% risk, which should also result in an estimated 10% result of profit.

For this example, let us use the EUR/USD pair as they are obviously the most popular currency pairing in existence. Let us set the number "5" as our "take profit" point and "50" as our "stop-loss" point. This means that once our earnings have equaled 5 pips, we should already take that as a win, and take our earnings already. If we see that the pips have gone down to 50 pips, then it would be time to stop since we are apparently losing.

You might begin to think that if our possible win is just 5 points and our possible loss is based at 50, does it mean that we will lose more than we could win? Actually, we shouldn't view it as such. Why we set 5 as already a win is because it is a good amount already. If we wait for it to rise higher, we could lose – it is a good practice to take the win even though it's just a small one. By habitually doing that, your "little earnings" will pile up and become "big earnings in the long run."

About that 50-point stop loss, it means that even though the values are getting lower, it means that we're not giving up just yet. It implies we need to wait for a while because the values could rise higher in the next moments. If it goes lower than 50 though, it would be wise to call it day and wait for greener opportunities in our next trading sessions.

Understanding the effectiveness of scalping

The success rate of this technique, according to the experts themselves, is 90%, which means that for a series of 10 trades you will do with scalping, you could lose only once... provided or course that you have studied and understood the charts of yesterday clearly. Experts claim that 90 is just the safest margin. They declare that if you mix up your endeavor with excellent technical analysis, your success rate could be much higher.

Some seasoned traders can attest that with scalping, you can already attain a success rate that high within an hour if you get lucky. But if you have more time to spare, it would be nice to not make it too short, just to keep it safe.

If you remembered the previous pages' recommendation of the XM Broker as an ideal choice for beginners, it would be best to use the company for scalping because they have this

Ultra-Low Spread Account that could be as low as 0.6 spreads.

In case you missed what a spread means, it is that amount that you will pay to a broker like XM, who facilitates a trading transaction within Forex. By choosing a broker with a low spread, it is a means of maximizing your possible earnings.

In starting the actual scalping method, the presence of another account which should serve as your "storage account" is recommended. Inside it will be that a hundred bucks we mentioned earlier and the other account will be the recipient of the ten bucks that will hold the amount that we will use for each element of our trading activity.

In trading, there is this term called "slippage" – a term that describes those damages or wasted portions of our earnings. This can be viewed as those little droplets of the drinks we're sipping during mealtime or those little grains of rice that got lost during transport if we are a rice trader. Such a scenario is natural. It would be unwise to fail to recognize it.

So to prevent your main account from suffering some damages, it would be wise to deposit an amount into another account so that our main account will not be affected. Once you deposited the $10 already, we can then begin trading.

The Math behind scalping can be easily understood by just looking at the first few wins of your trading series. For instance, if in your first trade, you have a $1 win, your total earnings have just reached $11 as it gets added to your initial capital of ten bucks. If you stake it again for the next trade, it could grow by 10% each time.

Now if you execute the same process 10 times in a row, provided that you win each time, you'd accumulate a total amount of $115.939, that is after you've completed the entire series of 10 trades. Once you've done that. It would be good to withdraw your earnings, and stake in another 10 bucks for your next series of trades. You repeat the same process, again, and again.

But does this technique always makes you win? No. like what you've been told in the previous pages, there is no exact way of accurately predicting chart movements and market direction at a 100% rate. For this reason, experts suggest that if you've experienced 2 losses or more losses with scalping, you should stop trading for a moment.

Let's get back to your goal: Accumulating $10,000 a month. Is that a realistic goal? It is, if we adhere to 3 solid approaches: 1.) a realistic mathematical formula, 2.) a realistic perspective on how many trades you can make for a month, and 3.) a much bigger capital. Experts claim that for each single day, you can only make 5 effective and reasonable trades. And since there are only 20 business days in a month, it means it would be unwise to exceed 100 trades for that duration.

If we are to accept that, then it also means that having a $100 capital is not enough. If we increase it into $110, it means we could attain an estimated total earnings of $127.53 for 10 trades. And going back to that ideal 100 trades per month, it means we can accumulate a total of $12,753. Seems good, right?

But we have to remember that there's no guarantee that you'd have 10 straight wins, let's just say that the 2,000 is the slippage we mentioned earlier. We might say that it is our "margin of error." Remember, no strategy, no matter how smartly crafted is ever perfect.

Bear in mind, don't overtrade. You must constantly remind yourself that greedy traders don't get too far in the trading business. When there are times that you're experiencing some losses, it means that the currency pair you're focusing on could be in a bad situation. In that case, give it a rest and pick another good time to trade. Take some time to analyze what went wrong with your previous efforts so you can formulate better plans and better strategies in the future.

Best Methods of Making Forex So Much Easier

While getting through the previous discussions, you might have this notion that "Forex trading has a lot of deep analysis requirements that you need to get by." Hate the idea for what it truly is, but that's just a reality for a market trader. You can't get rich with the art of trading without getting through the mental processing needed to be successful at it.

But is Forex really that difficult? Must a novice trading enthusiast really have to go through all the seemingly unbearable difficulties mentioned earlier? With all seriousness, all expert traders will really say yes. That's just the best way to answer it.

But what if you want to take the easy way? Isn't there a much more convenient set of methods that can give you profit with Forex without experiencing extreme hardships? Thankfully for you, and for all those Forex aspirants who want to take the easy path, a comprehensive guide awaits you. Keep reading.

Engaging in copy-trading

Because Forex has been around for nearly 50 years already, many successful individuals are already very well-versed at it. As such, many of them are so good at what they do that failure is almost an impossibility whenever they conduct trading acts on any given day of their profitable lives. In that case, wouldn't it be best for the enthusiasts to mimic what they're exactly doing?

The best approach for that would be to study what they're doing: read writings about them, or watch videos of them as they perform such actions. After having some comprehension, we would then take some actions based on what we've learned. Amazingly though, that's not what copy-trading is all about – it's actually employing an automated system that imitates exactly what those expert traders are actually doing.

To simplify it further, we're talking about a computerized procedure that will facilitate the linking of your account with that of the trader whose actions you want to copy. Whatever are the outcomes of that person's choices and decisions, so will be the outcome of your account.

But there is actually a catch with that technique. By doing copy-trading, a small portion of our profit will be directed to that trader you're linked with. You are benefiting from his actions, it would be unfair for you to just take profits without paying anything to the one who does all the action. It just seems justifiable for the system to work that way.

Copy-trading is closely related to mirror-trading. It works basically as something that would pop into your mind if you'd think about mirroring. It means that that the actions that will happen within your account is a duplicate of someone else's. Both copy trading and mirror trading are components of a system called "social trading" – a system that takes advantage of the network of traders that are actively participating in the Forex world.

With the accumulated knowledge gathered from the network, any Forex aspirant can greatly benefit from tapping into an array of benefits. It started as a trend in 2005 and since then, it has been a favorite thing for aspiring traders. The fact that people are attaining some success with it should make us think that it must have some reasons that make it so attractive:

Advantages of copy-trading

- There is very little effort that you need to pour into it.

- You just set the amount you want to trade, and wait for the expert trader you're copying to make a profit for both of you.

- You are gaining earnings with trading, but are also able to do your daily chores in life

But you have to take heed to the following too.

Disadvantages of copy-trading

- It has lesser returns of investment

- An expert trader's failure will be your failure too (Yes, they fail at times too, though such failures are dependent on their reputation so you can just look them up and make your decision of copying them.)

- You will learn very little with actual trading, which means becoming an expert is something you'll never be.

If you want to hop into the ease and comfort that copy-trading can offer, here are 2 good platforms you should check out:

Etoro – A trading company established in Israel. Founded in 2007, it has been one of the most profitable firms in the field of trading having accumulated an estimated total value of $800 within its 2-decade operation. Israel is a country known for its successful startups and sophisticated technological breakthroughs, which makes it easier for us to put our trust in Etoro.

Zulutrade – Also founded in the same year as Etoro, it is a Greek-managed company that's declared by Daily Telegraph as one of "The Best 100 Startups" in the category of Finance and E-commerce. One of its most notable features is ZuluGuard, a system that automatically you to unfollow a certain trading act if something changes with the acts of the trader you're copying.

So mirror-trading and copy-trading work basically the same. What is the notable difference between the 2? The simplest answer to the question would be this: That the former is better suited for those who want to have bigger volumes of profit, while the latter is more applicable for those who want to have smaller incomes.

Mirroring works best with higher capitals because it is often related to major trading entities. Copy-trading works within the framework of one individual trader to another. This can give us the understanding that it is most suited for small trading investments. So as a beginner and as someone who has only a small amount at your disposal, copy-trading might just be the best option for you.

Does copy-trading really work? Yes, it really does. In fact, most experts have the estimate of a 10% profit that one can attain yearly, which shouldn't be so bad for someone who doesn't want to invest on a huge amount of time with trading on a daily basis.

Working with trading coaches and consultant

Because Forex trading is a very serious undertaking indeed, you might want to consider seeking professional help in attaining success with it. As such, tapping into the wisdom that trading coaches and consultants can give shouldn't be a bad idea. They have been trading consistently for years which means that their experiences have given them concrete methods already that can make anyone learn quickly and easily.

When choosing consultants, you will surely meet people who make exaggerated claims. That should be something you have to consider as something that's natural. Not all of them are all promises though. Some of them actually have the skills to truly deliver, and some of them can actually make your dreams come true.

But how do you find the best Forex trading consultant? While finding the best is not really easy, and not to mention expensive, choosing a good consultant might be something that's attainable and more realistic.

Here are the best traits that you should look for in a good trading consultant or coach:

1. **One that has been in the business for years already –** Sure, longer doesn't always mean better. But let's not forget that experience is the best teacher. One who else to look for a good teacher than someone who has been doing the act for longer periods already?   A good Forex coach has to be a

trader who has been to a series of ups and downs already. It is the only means by which he can give you the best indications of when to proceed, and when to halt or back down.

2. **One that you can communicate with easily** – In every relationship, communication is a very vital key. Without it, any undertaking would collapse before it even starts. In planning to hire a consultant, be very sure that he or she is very reachable and accessible.

One of the best ways of figuring this out is knowing if the consultancy services being offered has a website or social media page that you can easily exchange messages with. Also, be very sure that the consultant in question is available for video calls because seeing the face behind the business transaction is something that should be highly considered.

3. **One who has a great understanding of your goals** – The most successful trading coaches are the ones with the greatest understanding of how to attain the goals of the business. But what about your personal goal? Do you have the indication that the consultant you're planning to hire completely understands your own objectives? If that coach often talks about his own success but can't clearly give details about how the 2 of you might achieve your goals, avoid that person, he will not be worth your time and investment.

How much would consultancy cost you? It's hard to come up with an accurate answer. But the safest bet would be that it would surely fall within the 10% fraction of your earnings. Ten is actually that magic number that works so well in any digital-information dissemination. For instance, it can be observed that for every internet promotion of a product, nearly around 100 people will respond to every group of 1000 people reached.

It means that even though a product ad will show up to a person's wall news feed, only 1 for every 10 of those ads will be checked out by that person. The response rate could be higher or lower, depending on the beauty or usefulness of the product therein. Given that fact, it would be safe to say that consultants and coaches will never take a commission that's equal or higher to 10% of your earnings.

With online courses and webinars, the figure could be much different. For a certain payment, you could enroll in some kind of training where you can understand the ins and outs of trading, which you can employ to your advantage whenever you decide to embark on your first trading adventures.

Here's the plain and simple truth, hiring professional consultants or coaches is actually expensive. As a beginner, it would be best to just connect to a trader within your social circle. By choosing someone who's just within your arm's length reach, you can get the wisdom you need, provided of course that the person does not belong to the "douchey, a-hole category." Choosing this action would be very low-cost on your part as it would just be a "friendly partnership" of some sort.

What if you have nobody in your social circle who's into trading? You can find an endless sea of people who are very much on the same page as you, and they can be within reach via Youtube, Facebook, LinkedIn, or any social media website you can think of. Surely, there are lots of pages and online communities out there that you can tap into.

Join them, communicate with them, reach out to them. You can find countless like-minded individuals who can guide you and motivate you into taking huge undertakings within the Forex world. You can also just self-educate yourself, there are countless video tutorials out there that you can binge-watch anytime at your convenience.

Employing Trading Robots

We live in a generation that's replete with computers and a bunch of other digital things. Without a doubt, their existence has automated a lot of processes. What's so time-consuming in the past can now be done in a matter of minutes or even seconds.

How cool would it be to just utilize the presence of computers and the software inside them to do the trading for us, instead of ourselves staring at screen displays so we can come up with the analysis needed to make money? It is very cool of course. Do you know what's even cooler? Is that there are actually Forex Bots that you can employ to make trading even a lot easier.

What is a Forex Bot? It is a computer program employed by some brokers that automates trading decisions based on typical patterns generated by currency charts. Powered by Artificial Intelligence, it is designed to remove people's burdens of the psychological aspect of trading. Like real physical robots making heavy jobs in factories a lot lighter, these software bots are also helping beginning traders enjoy their trading acts greatly.

How does a trading bot work? The concept of its operations can be understood with a trader's habits and patterns being keyed into a certain bot's interface. It could also happen by letting the bot run along with a particular trading act. Once the bot's AI already figures out a certain trader's strategy, it will then create an automated procedure that can be executed without intervention.

All a trader needs to do is configure some commands and numbers, and the bot will perform its task, raking in some income as it does so tirelessly and relentlessly, even while the investor is sleeping, or doing whatever chore he can get his hands on. Brilliant and convenient, right?

What are the best Forex Bots? There are so many automated bot traders out there that declaring who's the best will be very hard for even the best analysts. The following are the ones worth checking out. They are listed along with their corresponding deposit rates:

Bot Name:	Minimum Deposit:
GPS Forex Bot 3	$100
Forex Trendy	$250
X Trade Premium	$100
Cento Bot	$250
Walls Street Forex Bot	$1,000
Forex Diamond	$1,000
Forex Gump	$4,000 on a regular account, $400 on a nano account

What's up with those deposit rates? They actually speak for the effectiveness of those bots that correspond to each of them. Basically, the higher the price, the higher the chance of earning big. To know the success rates for each of them, it would be good to Google them up for a better understanding.

Do Forex bots really work? Because they are systems built by experienced traders and really smart people, they really do. Many Forex popularizers are actually gaining big profits out of their acts of selling Forex bots. The existence of lazy money-rakers is undeniable, and many software developers and Forex businessmen are exploiting such a fact.

But here's something that you should really put in mind: The best racers never rely on the auto-gear features of even the best cars. While very good cars can really spell the difference between an excellent racer and a mediocre one, which makes world-class racers the best of their kinds are their skills and wits. They don't use auto-gear, that's just a solid fact.

To sum all of this up, you have to engrave this in your mind: copy-trading, mirror-trading, and trading bots, can really help you, and they can make your Forex undertakings so much easier. But they're the type of techniques that you can use if you just want to make trading as a side-hustle. Think of them as little tools that can augment your earnings.

But If you really want to get serious with Forex trading, never rely on the presence of anything that can automate the process for you. They're great tools to learn from, and they can really do the work if you don't have the time for some actual trading. But if you're in it for the long haul, or if you want to hit it big, learn from real experiences and from real people – there is no substitute for the golden knowledge and wisdom that you can attain from them.

How to Get The Right News for Best Investment and Make Money Online

When you get a stream of wins with Forex, the most likely thing to happen is that you'll be adding the habit of trading as a very important part of your daily routines in life. If it brought you massive amounts of income, would you ditch the habit? Definitely not. You will be trading some more tomorrow, and for the next years to come. That will be an infallible prediction that is if… you have made some success out of currency trading.

But as what you have truly understood by now, all global financial markets that use Forex as the main driving force changes a lot dramatically from time to time. By acknowledging that fact, we have to also embrace the idea that being many steps ahead among other traders is one of the key elements that will make us remain successful in the field of trading.

Knowing this, it is quite clear that we have to learn some skills in getting the right news to come up with better investment decisions.

Here are 2 tips on how you might be able to achieve it:

1. Knowing about how the employment system works

The employee-to-employer scheme of things play a very crucial role in the entirety of the realm of Forex, let's not forget about that. This means that we have to pay attention to it too if we plan to be truly serious with our trading endeavors in the future.

In connection to the previous item, we really need to have some solid idea about the flow of financing on a global scale. It's really hard to make predictions about this but to play it safe, it would be wise to be at least be advanced for "half a year to 18 months." There is statistical data that supports such a claim. For instance, most young people, who comprise a great majority of the workforce in nearly all companies in the world today usually hop from 1 workplace to another in a span of that duration.

We have to acknowledge that many young professionals rarely stay at their jobs for 2 years. 18 months should be a fair assessment as an average. Given that, we should consider accepting that the economy can really change within that span of time.

So in your trading activities in the next months or in the next few years, studying how the employment system works should be a wise investment of your time as well. For sure, you can come up with a much deeper analysis and speculations about how currency prices could rise or fall.

The world is virtually smaller now because of the existence of telecommunication along with the presence of high-speed planes and ships. In this era where the concept of "work from home" is becoming extremely popular, its effect on currency exchange could be really vital for the over-all scenery of the global economy. That's something that you really have to watch out for.

2. Advanced understanding of the status of the Euro and the US Dollar

There is no argument needed about the supremacy of the EUR/USD pairing. Since they are so relevant today, it is very unlikely that they will become quickly irrelevant for the next few years, or even decades. The very smart traders of today always look into these 2 currencies closely, as an Eagle would on its prey, as a high-definition camera would to an object being shot at. To be very good at such efforts, it would be truly wise to look at the economical flows of the countries within those financially bustling areas. It would be a huge mistake in choosing not to.

You may find it a bit trivial, but some expert traders take hold of information that isn't directly related to daily dealings with Forex. For instance, some traders absorb the idea that the physical design of the US Dollar Bill hasn't changed since 1929. To simply put it, existing paper bills that come from that era are still usable today. So if your grandpa has some treasure chest buried somewhere with some dollar bills in it, you could still use it now. Seriously.

Such a fact could make us discern more about the significance of the US Dollar. If you add it up with some daily small doses of what's happening within the economy and government settings of the Americans, you should be on the right path of a much broader understanding of Foreign Exchange. Consequently, better trading decisions from your head will just get channeled outwards, as you conduct more trading transactions each day.

Also, poking closely into the financial flows and events that traverse among the countries near England would be helpful too. The reason why the Euro is a much stronger force than the US Dollar is mainly due to this one simple truth: the economy is much more stable there, and that there are significantly richer business entities in Europe altogether, compared to those that are in the United States.

Although many US-based companies are also existent somewhere else, they will still be a minority compared to the vastness of the sea or mega-rich entities across Europe. By understanding the economies of the governments there, as well as the "money-funnels" that thrive within the area, you can have a good understanding of where the Euro will go in the next years or decades.

Now let's talk about ideas that can help you earn some additional income online.

5 Ways of Making Money With Your Forex Knowledge Online

Let's say you've been into trading for quite some time, and have been gaining some wins with most of your trading gigs. You've been pretty successful and are starting to have some considerable augmentation of your income. What do you do? Keep on trading without sharing your knowledge? No, because you as a noble person are somehow under the realization that such a kind of thinking would be an unkind trait to have.

Even if you're not considering it, let me encourage you that imparting your trading skills and learnings would be a cool thing to do, because it would not only make you earn more, but could also make you a hero to others. If there are ways that you knew about but are not sharing them to people who might need them, wouldn't that be selfish?

"But I don't want to be a hero!" you might blurt out. Yeah, perhaps. But what about the fact that you can make some extra earnings with some techniques that aren't directly connected to the very acts of trading, wouldn't that be some sort of amazing accomplishment?

Before the argument gets too long, let's just get right to it. Here are some ways in which you can make profit with your knowledge about Forex trading:

By publishing your writings on the web

For this option, blogging would be a very good first choice. A great bulk of the internet websites that exist today is mostly a pile of blogs. If they are that plentiful, then it means many writers are exploiting the very idea of publishing their knowledge and experiences every day, while making great piles of income along the way.

Take note, many of these bloggers are actually just plain, household individuals. They're not even the kind of people who were able to attain degrees in journalism or those who attended a series of writing workshops. They're just people who are into the habit of writing regularly and consistently.

The cool thing about article-publishing on the internet today is that people don't really care if you're a good wordsmith or not. All you have to be is someone who can put your ideas into writing in a simple-enough manner that they can figure out what you're trying to say in a "street-level approach."

As long as you can just explain your ideas into a form of writeups that would be simple enough for an elementary-grader, you are already a profitable blogger in the making. To make the idea simpler, learning about the likes of WordPress, Wix, and Blogspot would be a good start.

In terms of hosting your blogs within a webserver, Googling up Godaddy or Hostinger would be a great way to start your journey. You need not worry about how to actually start, as there are countless tutorials on the web that you can use to self-educate yourself. It shouldn't be that difficult for a novice, aspiring blogger like you.

How much can a blogger possibly earn? Novice bloggers, or those that we can categorize as writers who have been blogging for a year mostly claim to earn around $200 a month, and that's just a side income.

For those who blog seriously for 2 years or so, many of them claim to earn around $800 to $1000 a month. And again, that level of income is just for the average blogger. What if you become a well-loved blogger who discusses about Forex? You could earn a lot higher!

Another option you might want to choose is by publishing ebooks. They might not be as expensive as real books but that's basically the point. Because ebooks are cheaper, they're more affordable from people's perspectives, which make them very attractive kinds of stuff to buy. Should you hop into this method, selling your Forex ebook at $5 per download would be a good price level for a startup.

As your reputation gets noticed, you can then raise your pricing a little bit higher. The key idea is don't make it too expensive especially if you're just starting out as an ebook publisher. Bear in mind that hubris will make you fail easily, that's not what successful people are made of, just reminding you.

If you find the idea of establishing your own blog, or writing an ebook too tiring and exhausting to think of, you might want to consider blogging in existing "blog for payment" platforms. The best options for you would be sites like Medium, Hubpages, and Vocal.Media. Those platforms are popular, and have very high internet page-rankings.

Within them, you can discuss nearly any topic under, or over the sun. And if you are someone who is very well-versed with money-making especially in Forex, your ideas would be most welcome there. The good thing about writing on those platforms is there is no "audition drills" or something, you can just write and publish, although if you don't put some extra deep thought and effort into your articles, you might not get enough attention that can merit you with some earnings.

For Medium, you can get paid via audience claps. Meaning if a reader clicks "the clap" icon in your article, you could get paid up to $5 for each clap. Just imagine how much you can earn if a hundred readers clap on your single article!

With Hubpages and Vocal.Media, it's a bit different, you can get paid via advertising, much like you'd be with your own blog. The more viewers you attain with your articles, the higher your earnings would be. But take note, they are not the only blogging platforms out there! They're just mentioned here because by far, they are definitely the most popular of their kind.

There are also crypto-blogging websites that can really benefit from your trading knowledge. Even though Cryptocurrency is a bit different compared to Forex, the core concepts are actually the same. Many successful Forex investors are actually also hopping into the likes of Bitcoin and Ethereum. Since you have already understood solidly the ins and out of Forex trading, writing something about crypto coins shouldn't be that difficult.

You can just tweak you knowledge a bit, publish it in crypto-blogging platforms, and you can just wait for some additional dollars to get added to you already rising pile of income? Wait dollars? Yes, dollars. Most crypto-blogging sites today are run by a certain crypto-coin, but the equivalent money you'll get will be easily covertible to US dollars. Not all of them, but most of them basically works like that.

Here are the most popular crypto-blogging platforms today:

Steemit – Launched in 2016, it is the first of its kind. It is a micro-blogging social media site that's very similar to Twitter and Tumblr. Users can make money by posting articles that don't need to be very long, just enough to make other users be interested and give tips to the author. It is powered by cryto-coin Steem.

Hive.Blog – It has very notable similarities to Steemit. As a beginner, you can't post as often as you can as you need to buy more coins so you can make multiple posts. It was conceived when some users and co-owners of Steemit were disgruntled by how the latter was run. For the time being, many authors are earning with the same level as what they earned with Hive, as they are with Steemit.

Publish0x – Powered by Ethereum, it is currently the most attractive crypto-blogging site today. It enables you to post articles that are not your own, provided that you have the reprinting rights for those articles. You can also make money by just reading articles written by others, and also by giving tips. When you click on the tip button for each article, a portion of it goes to the writer, while a portion of it goes to your own wallet as well. For the time being, becoming a writer can only be achieved through application and invitation.

Read.Cash – It is the newest platform of its kind, and is declared as the closest cousin of Publish0x. When blogging for this platform, you will earn Bitcoin Cash, which is currently the 4th-ranking crypto coin. The best thing about it is that even without too many views, you can still earn from the tips given by their software robot called "The Random Rewarder." By just showing hard work, you can earn some amounts everyday.

How much can you possibly earn in those platforms? Bloggers who have been around for quite some time in Steemit and Publish0x claim that by using platforms side by side, they have an average earning of $200 each month.

Not really a big amount, but here's the thing about cypto-blogging, you can post the same articles for each of them. So if you have 20 articles for Steemit, you can post the same for other similar sites as well, as long as you can prove that you're the author of those articles.

200 Dollars is just an average. But if you look at the top posts in Steemit or Hive, you can surely see that many authors are earning hundreds of dollars for just a single post. Most of these posts are about how to make money with cryptocurrency. Will your Forex articles be as attractive as those? Certainly, they will be.

What makes those platforms teem with users who read, give tips, and provide additional earnings is because they are always eager to learn about money-making. If you've earned some reputation with Forex already, you'd be most welcome there.

Even those who write about articles that are not related to trading are making great incomes with the likes of Publish0x and Read.Cash. Wouldn't you as a knowledgeable Forex trader make a higher stream of profits? Writing can be a very powerful tool, use it to rake in some passive income with your currency-trading knowledge.

By teaching Forex on video

"But I hate writing. Even though I love talking non-stop about Forex, I really hate the idea of having to write my knowledge and publish them on the internet!" Cool down friend, you can still make some extra income if you have that mode of thinking. How? By videoing yourself and explaining your trading adventures and techniques on screen.

The best way to achieve that would be to launch a Youtube channel. Much like launching your own blog, becoming a Forex vlogger would be very profitable too, although a bit much easier. People argue that anyone can write articles, but not everyone can shoot videos, edit them, and upload them online. Many of them actually think that vlogging is easier than blogging.

But the truth is, becoming a great writer, which is the key ingredient to blogging success is more difficult to master, than in becoming a great YouTuber. In becoming a good enough vlogger, you need to learn at least some basic videoing and editing skills. In addition of course to some communications skills.

You don't really need to talk like a TV host to attain vlogging success. Many YouTubers who can't even speak properly have a great number of viewers and subscriptions. To reinforce the idea further, it would be good to acknowledge that becoming a good vlogger requires you to watch a lot of videos.

But in becoming a good blogger, you need to read, and read a lot. Now which is easier, reading 50 books or watching 50 videos? Another reason why people are more attracted to becoming a vlogger than in becoming a blogger is that it's much easier to get an audience in the former.

Many Youtubers can attest to this. And many bloggers who are also vloggers can really be live witnesses that vlogging can get you a higher number of viewership quickly than with blogging. In Google, the average time for your blog to get searched and gain income is around 6 months. But within Youtube, your vlog could already gain viewership in just 24 hours.

It is estimated that a vlogger who has 1 million subscribers can earn up to $57,200 per year. But that could change though depending on where your channel is actively viewed from. With web advertising, the countries with the higher buying power actually pay more than those who just view ads but don't buy that much.

Another way by which you can share your knowledge through videos is by conducting webinars. By encouraging people to join your online discussions which of course needs promotion beforehand, you can ask them to put up some payment. Online courses are among the hottest money-making systems that are going on every day, endlessly on the internet. Many web-content publishers are getting extremely rich because of it, so to speak.

To help you set up a Forex webinar easily, Demio, WebinarJam, and Livestorm would be great platforms to check out. Youtube would be a great place to just conduct it too, although there are some strict requirements that you need to pass through to totally pull it off. The best way to get past that is to launch a channel with some attained viewership first. Once you've achieved that, conducting webinars should be fairly easier.

By podcasting and publishing audiobooks

But what if you just want to discuss your Forex knowledge but you hate to write, and also hate being videoed? Is there a way to make some extra income? Yes! – through podcasting or audiobook publishing. Witch such undertakings, all you need to have are just some guts, some good-enough speaking skills, a recording device such as your phone, and you're good to go.

While reading and watching videos might be the most-loved learning activities by a great number of people, there are those who prefer listening to instructional materials while they do their household chores or while they are out strolling in the park.

Research conducted by TheBestMedia website claims that, "If your podcast has about 10,000 downloads per episode, you can expect to make between $500 – $900 in affiliate sales. With audiobooks, voiceover artists who are just starting out can expect to earn $100 for each hour of finished audio. For industry veterans, those figures can reach up to $500 for a completed hour." That data is according to Business Insider.

Another brilliant option you can choose is by becoming a trading coach, or consultant. How you can make money out of that is by of course, establishing your web presence first. By setting up a Facebook or LinkedIn page that showcases your trading achievements, you can then put some promotional posts that should reach thousands of people for just a very small fee.

In Facebook, for instance, you can pay for an ad that could run for a week, which could reach up to 10,000 people, for as low as $3. How they would respond to that ad snippet is another story though. When you advertise your accomplishments as a Forex trader, the number of respondents greatly depends on your credentials: how many successful trades you already made in the past, and the rate at which your future trades could succeed… stuff like that.

Of course, becoming a productive trading coach or consultant could be very tiring and exhausting on your part, that's why extreme patience should come with the package as well. If you don't have the patience of a kindergarten teacher, maybe this gig is not for you. On the flipside though, many trading instructors are becoming richer too, in addition to their trading activities that they still do a lot.

As a trading coach, you'd be doing most of your tasks via phone calls, or via video conference apps. You need to have a steady setup of internet connection at home for this, alongside a reliable computer too. But all of that would just be irrelevant if you don't have the skills and conversational attitude that's the real important element for such an undertaking.

By Joining Forex Affiliate Programs

If you have established yourself as a Forex educator already via writing, videoing, or consultancy, you can actually make some more income by joining Forex affiliate programs. What are they? And how do they work?

The concept revolves around the idea that for every trader you can motivate into joining a certain Broker, you'll get paid with commissions. So basically, Forex Affiliations are those tasks that you do to promote or advertise an online brokerage firm so it can be made known to others.

For instance, check out In The Money Stocks, a company with a well-established affiliate program. They claim to have a 94% success rate in all their trading endeavors. By being an affiliate of theirs, you could earn $21 for each transaction. Another is Admiral Markets. The pay from their program is quite big, you could be paid up to $600 per client, and they take 0% commission from you. However, you need to have a deposit of $300 upon signing up.

Of course, they're not the only Forex Brokers with very good affiliate programs. There are literally dozens of them all over the internet. Search engines could really help you with that. Just make sure you've read enough reviews before putting your trust in any of them.

So far, those are the best methods by which you can earn by sharing your Forex trading knowledge on the internet.

By Taking Advantage of Forex Giveaways

Everybody loves free stuff. Who doesn't? When you're a bit exhausted with all the analyzing, speculating, and the over-all pressures trading has brought upon you, maybe you should exploit the giveaways that Forex enthusiasts can enjoy. They might not be money that you can add to your next trading capital, but they could be those tools that you can use to make the most out of your trading acts.

So what are those giveaways the likes of you and me from benefit from? They could be laptops, desktop PCs, cellphones, or some other handheld gadgets that you can connect to the internet with. Since trading can only be done with an internet connection nowadays, those who choose to hand over giveaways to various Forex traders took it upon themselves to give related equipment to them too.

So who are those generous people who are so willing to give us some free stuff? Most of them are actually Forex brokers and establishments with trading-related businesses. Technically, their very acts of giving free stuff that we can enjoy are nothing but advertisement tactics. For sure, nobody wants to give away something for nothing. When they offer you something, it means they usually want something in return from you too.

But most of the time though, those giveaways have no disadvantages whatsoever, except maybe for the annoyance that you'll get as those people will unleash their marketing tactics on you. Forex giveaways are there for the taking, you just have to know where to look.

Creating Wealth in 2021 and Beyond

As what's stated in the opening pages of this ebook, Forex has been through great changes already throughout the decades. We have to acknowledge that *in order to stay profitable within the market for the next years, we have to find other ways of attaining income from it*.

Whenever you Google up the long-tail keyword phrase "making money with Forex," all you will ever find are countless lists of articles that's about trading, which would be naturally so. Obviously, that's what Forex is all about, trading, trading, trading.

You've heard about overtrading being a bad habit. But is the idea of still making money with your Forex knowledge in a passive way, like when you're doing nothing at all so horrible? Not at all. In fact, many expert traders area still accumulating huge piles of wealth with their trading skills even when they are sleeping, literally. Because their knowledge are stored in internet content that people can access and study anytime, anywhere.

But what if you want to make money with Forex without actually trading? Can that be possible? Such would be a weird manifestation of one's curiosity. It would be like learning how to swim without immersing yourself in water. Sounds counter-intuitive, right? But here's something that might amaze you… you can really make money with Forex, without really trading… but by doing things that are just connected to it, in some ways.

So how can you still be an effective trader even in the next coming years? If only there's a crystal ball that we can look into for guidance, that would be extremely cool. Unfortunately, there is none. However, we can look into the following guides that can condition ourselves into becoming better and wiser traders.

Let us be clear though, the following tips and methods may not be about the very act of trading itself,   you need to have acquired some pretty handful trading experiences along the way, in order for you to execute them properly and convincingly, Let's just say that the following are very cool side hustles with the wisdom that you got from your trading journey in this present year, and the years that await us.

6 Tips In Becoming an Effective Trader For The Years Ahead

1. Knowing about the future of money

Since money is one of the most important commodities in existence, its relevance to our daily lives in the future will still matter a lot. For that, we can be so sure of. As a trader who wishes to be even more productive in the years ahead, you have to take huge efforts in understanding how money will evolve.

Today, financial analysts, scientists, businessmen, and statisticians make predictions about how money-making will be like in the next decades or centuries. Do we really need to take great heed of those predictions? Yes. Though not to a very high extreme.

It is important for an effective trader to be aware of future trends. But from a realistic and practical standpoint, it wouldn't be wise to look too far ahead, because we might miss out on what really matters at these times, and in the next months as we go about on our trading endeavors. "Letting tomorrow worry about itself" might be a good mantra to remind yourself of occasionally, if you wish to balance things out between the now and the alter of trading.

For now, futurists seem to have this forecast that the likelihood of a "cashless society" will be more feasible. This was heralded by the arrival of the ATM and the debit card that goes with it. Since then, money-usage has never been easier and more convenient for people.

These days, mobile and internet banking are becoming more accessible for anyone. When cash cards became commonplace, they were only meant for the rich, but with online money-storage platforms like Paypal and Coinbase, anyone with very small amounts of money and an email address can take advantage of the benefits they're giving too. Since daily processes are digitized, cash became digitized too, which greatly diminished the very act of printing money and making metallic coins.

Then there's also online buying and selling. Even without spending real paper bills, people can now purchase products online and pay those items with just numbers that represent the actual money that they possess. In just a few clicks and confirmations with short phone calls, any product can be delivered to anyone's doorstep, without ever needing to deal with tangible cash.

In the next few years, it can be understood that the physical banks that we know today can be really obsolete. They're becoming irrelevant now, they could be totally gone not too long from now. Many financial analysts are declaring this us something that's inevitable. As a trader, you have to be aware that the future of money is digitization, and not understanding how digital cash works would be foolish idea.

From now on, try your best to learn about the likes of Paypal, Stripe, Payoneer, and anything similar. They could be the ultimate replacements of the banks where you deposit your money. Yes, it would be totally impossible to actually predict the future of money, but by looking carefully at how it is being managed now using digital technology, we can have a fairly reasonable assessment.

2. Earning by making a PAMM system

By far, this is the only technique here that's the most closely associated with an actual trading act. This is about letting people entrust a certain amount to you, so you can do the trading for them. All they need to do is hand you the money, and just let your magic fingers do the work. Of course, your success is also their success, which is also another way of saying that your failure is also theirs. Because nobody would ever trust a failing trader, you need to establish your reputation first before broadcasting into the world that you are a trader that they can wisely invest with.

The acronym actually stands for Percentage Allocation Money Management. Apart from Forex, such a kind of system has been applied in other business ventures as well. It has been known to really work in most cases, as long as done strategically by well-decisive businessmen.

In trekking into this, you need to explain to your clients clearly what happens if their investments win, or if their investments fail. You need to let them know what the risks are, and how high is the success or failure rate of your partnership. More often though, people who invest in this kind of system are those who expect that they would always win, so you need to really come up with a system that succeeds at all times, or at least, one that can be profitable for both parties.

Of course, this is quite hard to get by. The best way to implement this is by cutting down on the wins of the clients to a point in which they will have an almost fixed amount each time even if the wins are actually bigger than expected. This calls for some scenarios in which you will not totally reveal your trade secrets or methods to them although for sure, they would not love that.

The best thing to do is to always be transparent, so your renown as a businessman will not get damaged as you build your network within the trading business. The bottom line for this is that you need to emphasize and be very clear to the client about the percentages that you'll take from them, as payment for the trading efforts you pour out.

You do all the labor, but both parties will earn the rewards. Be very clear with that in accordance with reasonable transaction fees. By sorting that out fairly and squarely, your business endeavor should turn out just fine.

3. Studying Cryptocurrency

In the earlier chapters, we have compared Forex against the Stock Market as they are obviously 2 of the biggest money-making metaphorical machines in modern history. But we haven't talked that much yet about another major player – Cryptocurrency. Is it a threat to Forex? Very… and a very big threat at that, although it would be unfair for either major forces to pit them against each other.

Financial analysts bravely declare that since everything is going digital these days, the money will be ultimately digitized too in the not too distant future. Experts even claim that paper bills, coins, and even debit cards will vanish too because all you need to carry with you is your phone – which will act as your personal accountant as you buy, sell, and consume everyday commodities in your daily living.

Some even insist on outrageous claims that your money, as well as your entire identity, will be embedded into your wrist or forehead so that all the information about your being can be accessed whenever the need arises. This might happen, yes. But it would not be so until at least for another 100 years.

The point of such possible advancement is that money is really becoming digital. Without a doubt, cryptocurrency is the thing of the future, because it is the best proof that cash can really be transformed digitally. Businesses all over the world are now profiting efficiently as they are run by purely crypto coins alone.

As a smart trader, although you just deal within Forex, it would be foolish not to learn about Cryptocurrency. Even if we don't look upon it deeply, we can easily grasp that it has so many similarities with Foreign Currency Exchange. Crypto is taking the financial world by storm, and the force it's showing must never be belittled.

Since that can't be disputed, conventional trading wisdom hereby advises you that as you study about Forex, take another side course: learning about the likes of Bitcoin, Ethereum, and Ripple. They are 3 of the biggest name in the Cryptocurrency business, and they are surely the biggest players in that industry for the next foreseeable future.

4. Understanding the economy of China

Many people, especially those belong to the "western-category countries" hate this idea, but as a smart trader, you have to acknowledge that understanding the economy of the country known as "The Sun's Origin" – as their tagline is used by many journalists.

In case you haven't known it yet, China will be the next world power. Hate the idea as much as you can, but such an outcome is inevitable. Historians, political analysts, as well as world leaders, in general, have this separately unanimous conclusion that China will indeed be the most powerful nation on the planet in approximately less than 2 decades from now.

To reinforce this claim, let us delve a little into how a country becomes a world power. It's not because of the strength of a nation's army, or the number of citizens that live within it, but of the strength of its economy. That's how a country can gain global dominance, at least in this modern generation. Gone are the days when a nation needs to wage physical war against another nation to prove its power over the other.

Today, what needs to be done is to come up with a robust economy, one that can be effectively extended into other countries and continents. If a government can do that in the greatest measure compared to others, then that government is surely on its way to becoming the most powerful nation on the globe.

While it would be outrageous to expect that the Renminbi will gain supremacy over the Dollar and the Euro in the next few years, it will most likely be an equally strong currency force in the next decades. The best way to deal with this fact would be to study closely the economy of China in the same manner that you studied Europe's and the USA's.

Furthermore, acknowledging that Chinese-made products will be even more commonplace in the global market in the next set of years would be truly beneficial for a trader who wishes to be many steps ahead compared to common traders who rarely analyze things.

5. Understanding web-advertising

When Satoshi Nakamoto, the person behind the creation of Bitcoin came up with the idea of digitizing money, one of the main driving forces is computer networking technology – it is the very essence of the world's connectivity in this digital generation where we happen to exist. Now more than ever, the world is becoming smaller and smaller due to the existence of this digital universe called The Internet.

Even our beloved Forex. which can still dwarf out the crypto-giant easily is still highly dependent on the power of cyberspace to conduct business. And since it is one of the most important truths of all, a smart Forex trader needs to also learn a lot about web-advertising.

Like the business that revolves around television and radio broadcasting, websites heavily rely on advertising as well so that they can continue to exist on the web. Without the viewers and potential buyers of the products that those ads are showing, the internet will surely collapse under its own unimaginably heavy weight, though such mass is not to be taken from any physical sense.

Although web advertising has no direct thing to do with Forex just yet, it has now a lot of involvement already with how businesses in the world today are presented and made known to people. For that reason, a good trader must also be ever-ready to grasp the framework that makes internet advertising works so well.

6. Earning by becoming a Forex broker

When all the above methods fail, you could get into the last, but greatest resort of profitably earning with Forex without actually trading – becoming a broker yourself. Truth to be told, this is no small undertaking. Back in the days, all a Forex broker needs are a telephone line, an office, a set of record books, and some marketing skills. Today, however, you can't be like that anymore.

Forex brokers nowadays, literally all of them are modern-day offices equipped with high-end IT infrastructure. They are the kind of facilities that are almost exactly like those high-tech buildings you see in movies where humans are cloned or get transformed into superheroes. Okay, that might just be an exaggeration. But the truth is, you can't be a Forex broker today if you don't invest in expensive computer equipment with some technically savvy staff tasked to operate them.

Becoming a Forex broker is one of the most serious business endeavors you could ever hop into, that's why it's not actually meant for beginners. However, it should be something that you would want to think of from time to time because maybe, it could be the best direction for you as you get more experience and renown as a profitable Forex participant. This item is included here just to give answer to the question that pertains to making money with Forex without really trading.

The above-mentioned tips are a new set of methods. Take time on learning them because they are the best ways of *keeping ahead and in making additional income with Forex for this modern times of trading… and beyond.*

Parting Words For The Forex Aspirant

About 5 centuries ago, when the Europeans invested on building ships so they can embark on expeditions that can help them conquer the world, those who were the very first to partake on such an undertaking were declared as either "too ambitious" or "foolish" by people within their social circles. Centuries later though, we consider those people as heroes.

As you embarked on your first trading acts, you might have heard about people who are too dumb to understand what currency exchange is. By now, you could easily prove them wrong because as what you have understood already, trading can be a really profitable kind of business, one thing that can significantly change your life, in ways you never would have thought possible.

Whether or not you will take the habit of trading as a major part of your life is mainly up to you. You've been shown with the right mindset, the right tools, and the right guidance on how to take your first steps towards it. In addition, you've also been given proper directions which path to take in the future, as you continue the exciting and profitable life a Forex trader.

This book has been a good companion for you. While this might not be a totally complete guide that can make you fully understand the entirety of the currency market, it was a great motivator – for it surely did give you the right kind of ignition… to have that spark needed so you can be an efficient trader today, while there are still ripe trading fruits that you can pick and harvest.

Trends could rise really fast, and could fall even faster. That's why it is also very important that you remain updated with what's happening to the world, especially within the currency exchange market. Being well-versed with technology can really be a great help too – it is the ultimate tool that can help any businessman. It would be utterly foolish for anyone to endlessly wish to be rich, yet not planning on investing time to learn about how technology could be leveraged for the augmentation of someone's wealth.

To proceed further with your trading endeavors, it would be good to tap into the nearly-limitless resource that other, more experienced traders are giving to anyone who has access to online technology. Scour through Youtube, peek through the endless sea of blogs, and you will see multitudes of them. Some of them might not be that friendly, but most of them will surely provide you the help you need so you can become as smart as them, as you grow on your trading efforts.

Study their writings and listen to them carefully, you could end up just like those people. If you improve the techniques ans strategies they're giving, you could even be more profitable than they ever were. It just requires the proper mindset and since you have it already, things should be much easier now.

Hope you'll have the best of luck as you trek into your trading journey.

Cryptocurrency Trading:

The Ultimate Guide for Beginners to Start Investing in Bitcoin, Ethereum, Litecoin and Altcoins in 2021 and Beyond. Create Wealth with Mining and Best Strategies in Blockchain

Copyright: Ryan Martinez

All rights reserved. No part of this publication may be reproduced, stored in retrieval system, copied in any form or by any means, electronic, mechanical, photocopying, recording or otherwise transmitted without written permission from the publisher. Please do not participate in or encourage piracy of this material in any way. You must not circulate this book in any format. Chana Cohn does not control or direct users' actions and is not responsible for the information or content shared, harm and/or actions of the book readers.

In accordance with the U.S. Copyright Act of 1976, the scanning, uploading and electronic sharing of any part of this book without the permission of the publisher constitute unlawful piracy and theft of the author's intellectual property. If you would like to use material from the book (other than just simply for reviewing the book), prior permission must be obtained by contacting the author at
  Thank you for your support of the author's rights.

Table of Contents

Introduction

I want to thank you and congratulate you for downloading the book, *"Cryptocurrency Trading – The Ultimate Guide for Beginners to Start Investing In Bitcoin, Etherium, Litecoin and Others In 2021 and Beyond. Create Wealth with Mining and Best Strategies In Blockchain World"*.

For the past few years, you may have heard of the words 'cryptocurrency', 'bitcoin', 'blockchain', and 'mining' and wondered what they meant. Well, these terms have indeed been ubiquitous on the Internet, appearing across social media platforms, websites, and online advertisements. Cryptocurrencies are here and they are very likely to stay. In fact, they are considered to be excellent investment opportunities in the highly volatile market.

In this book, you will learn about its history, benefits and drawbacks, and why it continues to gain popularity on the markets worldwide. You will learn about buying and selling cryptocurrencies, opening and maintaining accounts, and everything else you need to know as a beginner.

What's more, it has something great for more experienced traders. Even if you think that you already know everything there is to trading, you will be surprised to find out about new trends and developments. This book is not only ideal for beginner cryptocurrency traders, but for experienced ones as well.

This book will give you a good insight on how to trade, mine, and invest. It will also give you sensible pointers on how to make the right investments. You will know how to choose the right investment method so that you can identify your preferred risk level. You will learn how to maximize returns while minimizing risks.

You will learn how to make a personalized trading plan as well as how to create a mining machine. In essence, you will be able to make intelligent assumptions into the future of cryptocurrencies.

So, what are you still waiting for? Make the most of today and start learning about the digital gold of the future!

Thanks again for downloading this book, I hope you enjoy it!

Chapter 1: An Introduction to Cryptocurrency Trading

Trading has always been profitable. Those who are into this kind of moneymaking opportunity typically buy and sell financial instruments like stocks, mutual funds, derivatives, commodities, and bonds. Recently, however, a new kind of trading has emerged – cryptocurrency trading.

Cryptocurrency trading is a unique form of trading. Although quite new on the market, it is legit. Once you understand how it works, you will be confident to trade it. Today, you will find a variety of platforms that help individuals start cryptocurrency trading.

Of course, as a beginner, you might feel doubtful and hesitant at first. You might think that it is a scam or that it has no real value. A lot of people think and feel this way. Some of them think that many countries will not recognize cryptocurrency, so there is no point in making investments. Others feel that cryptocurrency trading is merely a fad that will fade out in just a few years.

However, these negative assumptions are incorrect. In fact, the biggest economies in the world recognize Bitcoin as an official currency. India, Japan, and the United States are only some of the major countries that consider cryptocurrency as an asset.

So, what is cryptocurrency trading exactly?

What Is Cryptocurrency Trading?

Cryptocurrency trading refers to the holding, buying, or selling of cryptocurrencies such as Litecoin, Ethereum, Ripple, and Bitcoin among others in order to generate a profit from their price fluctuations. Those who are into cryptocurrency trading generally trade on platforms and exchange fiat currency, including the United States Dollar (USD) and Euro (EUR), for cryptocurrency. They also tend to exchange a certain cryptocurrency for another.

When you delve into cryptocurrency trading, you have to learn how to speculate on cryptocurrency price movements using a contract for difference (CFD) trading account. You also have to know how to use an exchange to buy and sell underlying coins. With CFD trading, you can make speculations on the rise and fall of prices on financial markets including currencies.

Contract for difference (CFD) trading involves derivatives. You can make your speculations on the movements of prices without obtaining ownership of the coins. So, for example, if you believe that a particular cryptocurrency is going to increase in value, you can buy or go long. On the other hand, if you believe that such cryptocurrency is going to decrease in value, you can sell or go short.

Take note that these are leveraged products. So, you simply have to put up a margin or small deposit in order to acquire complete exposure to the market. All your losses and profits will still be computed depending on the full size of your position. The leverage will magnify the losses and profits.

When it comes to using an exchange to buy and sell cryptocurrencies, you have to set up an exchange account to buy the coins. You have to put up the asset's total value to open a position. Then, you must keep your cryptocurrency tokens in your wallet until you are ready to sell them.

It is crucial to learn the ropes when it comes to exchanges since they tend to come with steep learning curves. You have to understand the data as well as find out about the limits on deposits. In addition, you have to keep in mind that account maintenance may be very costly.

Cryptocurrency Markets

Cryptocurrency markets are actually decentralized. This means that they are not backed by the government or any other central authority. They are run online across a network of computers. Nonetheless, they can still be bought and sold through exchanges as well as stored in digital wallets.

Cryptocurrencies also merely exist as shared digital records of ownership that are stored in a blockchain. This blockchain is a shared register of recorded data. It basically shows the transaction history and reveals how the ownership of cryptocurrencies changes. It records the transactions in blocks.

So, if you wish to send some cryptocurrencies to a friend or business partner, you can send them to his digital wallet. Your transaction can only be completed once it is verified and added to the blockchain through mining.

Commonly Used Terms in Cryptocurrency Trading

Experienced traders are familiar with the words, expressions, and terms that are commonly used in the world of trading. Fundamental and technical analysis, resistance and support levels, Bollinger bands, and swing trading are just some of the most commonly used terms.

In order for you to do well at trading, you have to familiarize yourself with these words. This way, you will not have a hard time practicing your strategies. With cryptocurrency trading, you have to know about the following:

Associated Crypto and Blockchain Technology

Blockchain refers to a special kind of software technology upon which cryptocurrencies are built. It makes use of a peer-to-peer computer node network to verify cryptocurrency ownership and transactions.

Cryptography is used in the verification process. It involves the usage of complex mathematical formula and is the bases of the cryptocurrencies' names.

Nodes refer to the computers in the network that runs software programs. There are specialist nodes that solve cryptography problems and are used to secure transactions. These specialist nodes are also given newly minted units of cryptocurrencies. They are also referred to as miners since they eke out new units of cryptocurrencies.

Tokens and Coins

Tokens and coins are also commonly referred to as utility tokens. They are used to purchase and sell different types of services and goods as an alternative to the traditional fiat currencies. These fiat currencies include the pound, yen, euro, and dollar.

Bitcoin is actually the first cryptocurrency introduced to the public. It is an example of a coin cryptocurrency. Other coins like Litecoin and Bitcoin cash are also coin cryptocurrencies. Due to the 'hard fork' in Bitcoin blockchain, Bitcoin cash came into existence. At least fifty-one percent of the nodes that make up a blockchain must agree together to implement a change in order for the blockchain software or underlying protocol to be made.

Such hard fork in a blockchain was created when some parts of the Bitcoin network desired to make technical changes but did not have the fifty-one percent majority required. Nevertheless, they still went on to make the change in protocol. They thought that this would make the blockchain more effective. As a result, however, the hard fork was created.

This means that the blockchain was split into two coins. One of them rejected the changes while the other one approved them. Bitcoin cash emerged when the part of the blockchain that had the changes turned into a new cryptocurrency.

A fork is created each time a blockchain of the cryptocurrency gets updated. A hard fork, on the other hand, is created when a side of this fork is continued as a standalone and new cryptocurrency.

You should also know about Altcoins, which refers to the other cryptocurrencies. These are every cryptocurrency that is not Bitcoin. In essence, they are the alternatives to Bitcoin.

Take note that cryptocurrency tokens are not meant to be used in the same manner as traditional currencies. They are connected to blockchains, so they have a specific function. Such function can be a smart contracts blockchain like the Ethereum, which is used in building decentralized applications called Dapps as well as payment blockchains like Ripple. As for the tokens, they are used to pay for single-purpose blockchain platforms.

Rules that are software-based are known as smart contracts. If you combine them in complex and difference ways, you can use them to create applications, just like software applications.

However, they are enforced and verified through peer-to-peer blockchais. Because of this, the applications they create are called Dapps or decentralized applications.

Chapter 2: Basic Facts on Cryptocurrency

Bitcoin is also known to many people as "liquid gold". While money, on its own, doesn't have an intrinsic value, it is still valuable. This is because we think that it is. Money is actually just a tracking system. It is used to track the things that we owe and own. It is basically a ledger. So, whatever monetary form exists, it is given value due to its functionality as a tracking system or ledger.

For more than five thousand years, gold has been the primary means of exchange. Then, metal coins and paper money came along. Gold was used to back up paper money and had to be kept in the bank. So, if anyone had to go to the bank to have their money exchanged for gold, they can do it. This was the norm until 1971, when Former United States President Richard Nixon let go of the Gold Standard. The US Dollar was then cut loose from gold.

The United States was the first country to do this, but other countries soon did the same. The governments of the world were able to print as much paper money as necessary because gold was no longer required to back it up. Banks began lending out five to ten times the money account holders had. This caused more money to be circulated. This money is what's known as "fiat" money.

While this may have sounded great, it actually wasn't. You see, the more fiat money was printed, the less its value became. Fiat money was typically used to fund wars, pay back debts, and staved off recessions. Its value became less and less each year.

Gold, on the other hand, has value due to its scarcity. The supply is limited and it is very hard to mine. Gold has actually been the best ledger until blockchain and Bitcoin came along. However, gold is also difficult to send, store, and divide up. So, it cannot be used for selling and buying on a daily basis. Because of this, people started to turn to cryptocurrencies such as Bitcoin. Unlike gold, this type of money is easy to send, store, and divide up.

The Characteristics of Money

Money actually has five characteristics: scarcity, divisibility, transportability, durability, and recognizability.

Fiat money is not scarce, but gold and cryptocurrencies are. More fiat money can be printed but there can only be 21 million Bitcoins. This makes the value of fiat money less and less over time.

Both fiat money and cryptocurrencies are divisible, but gold isn't. It is not possible to pay for basic commodities with gold. Likewise, both fiat money and cryptocurrencies are transportable. You can transfer fiat money via electronic money systems and you can send out cryptocurrencies like digital files to other wallets. Gold, on the other hand, cannot be easily sent overseas in bulk.

Both gold and cryptocurrencies are durable. It is not even possible to destroy Bitcoins. As for fiat money, only coins are durable. Notes are not, because they have to be reprinted each year.

With regards to recognizability, it really depends on where the fiat money is used. For example, a particular currency can be considered recognizable if it is used in a particular country and everybody recognizes it. On the other hand, if it is not widely known and you have to pay using another currency, then it cannot be considered recognizable.

For example, if you travel abroad and you use that country's currency, you will be able to go around easily if all the people there recognize this money. You will be able to buy food, book hotel rooms, go shopping, and visit tourist spots. There will be no need for you to use your own country's currency.

Gold can be both recognizable and unrecognizable. You see, there are countries that like its relative safety. Then again, even though this is the case, gold is still not accepted as a payment method in a lot of places. It may not be easy to produce fake gold, but it is also not easy to recognize real gold when it is handed to you.

Bitcoin is recognizable. In fact, it is now accepted by many different merchants as a means of exchange. You can get it from your Bitcoin wallet to pay for goods and/or services. The great thing about Bitcoin is that it cannot be copied and counterfeited.

With this being said, you can say that Bitcoin is akin to gold in the sense that its value is protected against inflation. Then again, unlike gold, it is a daily transactable currency because it can be easily divided into any amount.

Bitcoin Gold and Bitcoin Cash

Bitcoin Cash and Bitcoin Gold were both created in 2017. The previous was created in August 2017 by a group of miners while the latter was created by another group of miners in October 2017. These groups of miners 'hard forked' from the main blockchain by turning to a new software version with better transaction capacity. As a result, millions of users were gifted with Bitcoin Gold and Cash tokens even though the fork did not have any effect on the Bitcoin balances.

So, what is the difference between tokens and coins? Is there any difference, at all?

Each time a new token or coin arrives on the market, people tend to call them "ICO". However, this is actually incorrect. Tokens and coins may seem alike, but they are really different from each other.

Coins, such as Dogecoin and Litecoin, are variations of the open source of Bitcoin. On the other hand, tokens, such as Ethereum, are secondary assets for Decentralized Applications within the blockchain system.

Bitcoin Mining

You may have also heard of Bitcoin mining and wondered what it is all about as well as whether it is profitable or not. Well, Bitcoin mining is vital in maintaining the blockchain that underpins the cryptocurrency. It is fairly new yet its rewards are plentiful. However, miners these days tend to face higher costs and fewer rewards.

Historically, mining has been a term generally reserved for digging gold and other precious metals. Today, however, mining is also used to search for Bitcoin. Bitcoin miners tend to be equipped with highly advanced computers. They dedicate their computing power to maintain the blockchain as well as verify the transactions that occur each day. They also keep the network safe against hackers and help traders keep track of their trade.

Bitcoin mining refers to the process of making sure that the Bitcoin serves its purpose. It is also the only way to add new supplies to the financial market. Miners are companies or individuals who contribute their computer power to help operate and maintain the blockchain network, which underpins Bitcoin as a digital currency.

Every Bitcoin transaction is tracked by these computers. In return, these computers are able to mine for newly created Bitcoins. Decentralization is actually at the heart of Bitcoin. Then again, even though a universal and fast communication channel has already been created via the Internet, the development of a decentralized system that can operate on a global scale is still being held back.

Since there is practically nobody in control, there is no one to keep a record of every transaction. Likewise, nobody is available to incur the recording costs. There is also no one who can hold such record keepers to account. Furthermore, it may not be possible to incentivize individuals to become record keepers.

Because of these issues, Bitcoin founder Satoshi Nakamoto came up with the idea that miners would deal with such transactions. These people will use their computers to maintain and run the blockchain so that transactions can be organized.

Other miners will then use their own computers to check the work and make sure that it is correct. They will give a public consensus on which transactions need to be confirmed. In the event that an information from an original miner is incorrect or does not match the information of the other miners, then it will be reviewed and corrected.

Miners are paid a fee for every transaction. This is great, considering that the protocol releases a new Bitcoin every few minutes. Such good compensation encourages miners to keep up with their work and address any issues that have brought down the systems in the past.

In essence, being decentralized and incentivized has made mining a great option for many individuals. The ledger isn't under a particular control point and any person may verify and access transactions that have already been recorded. Likewise, since it is incentivized, a lot of people become encouraged to run the blockchain, even if it means using their own equipment. After all, their efforts are rewarded with Bitcoins.

This makes Bitcoin mining quite immune to hacking attacks. It is not powered by a single source, but rather a network of computers. So, even if a hacker was able to get into a computer, it will not take long for his attack to be discovered. No hacker has actually been able to take control of at least fifty percent of the network.

How Bitcoin Mining Actually Works

At present, Bitcoin mining is mostly done using purpose-build and powerful rigs or computer systems that have customize software. These rigs have been set up to mine new Bitcoins. Then again, in order for these new Bitcoins to be mined, miners have to help update the public ledger as well as help validate the work done by other miners who run the blockchain. All the Bitcoins that exist today have been mined. This means that they have been owned by certain individuals at some point until they have been sold to others.

When you decide to mine Bitcoins, you have to first enter the network. Your transaction will then be labeled as "unconfirmed" or "pending". There will also be a constant stream that would need verification by other miners before such transaction will be confirmed.

If this process seems familiar, it is because it works on the same principle as banks that clear payments using debit cards. The transactions have all the necessary data such as transaction codes, messages, reference numbers, dates, and wallet addresses.

Hashes and Nonces

Miners are also commonly called mining nodes. They automatically start to organize data. At first, they reduce the information within a transaction into a hash, which is an alphanumeric string with sixty-four characters. This condenses huge amounts of data into smaller files as well as encrypts the data that the hash currently represents.

When the hash is created, any underlying data it represents may no longer be changed without messing it up. So, if this happens, the other miners who maintain the blockchain will be alerted and prompted to take action immediately.

The blockchain is organized in a chronological order. The mining software automatically begins to gather the latest transactions before going to the second latest transaction. This cycle continues with the latest transactions.

When the transaction is hashed, it is mixed with the data of another transaction so that a new hash is formed. The transactions are continually combined under a hash until a block is formed. These blocks are then used to grow the transaction chain. So, as you may have noticed, this is where the term "blockchain" got its name.

As for nonces and Bitcoin mining, the miners race with one another so that they can seal off the block and insert it into the chain. The miner who successfully beats the others at this race is the one who gets the new Bitcoin.

Then again, sealing off blocks is basically dependent on luck instead of skill. The miners have to compete against each other to search for the random block hash that the Bitcoin protocol looks for. They have to submit nonces, which are random guesses, and hope to strike a match.

This process is random. So, the miners do not really have a pattern to follow. They also do not have a clue on which hash will be necessary to seal off the block. They have to be lucky to earn that new Bitcoin. Nevertheless, they can always maximize their odds of winning by increasing their computing power.

If you notice, this actually has the same principle as with playing the lottery. If you want to increase your chances of hitting the jackpot, you can go ahead and buy as many lottery tickets as you want. However, buying a lot of tickets will not guarantee you the jackpot. You can maximize your odds at winning but you will still have to depend on good luck to get the prize money.

Anyway, when the miner seals off the new block, a block number is created. This number follows the previous block in a sequential manner. These blocks have all been verified by the other miners who run the blockchain. Every new block that is added to this blockchain has to be verified by the miners. A proof-of-work or PoW has to be checked in order to prove that the data submitted is indeed accurate.

Such consensus-based model prevents hackers from tampering with new or old transactions. It also prevents individuals from double spending or spending Bitcoin that they have already spent. The blockchain readily recognizes any new transactions that involve Bitcoins. So, the Bitcoins that have already been spent are tracked.

Bitcoin Mining Equipment

Originally, Bitcoin mining was done using personal computers. Those who want to be miners simply have to download and install the software on their own device. Today, however, serious miners need to use equipment with more computing power in order to keep up with their fellow Bitcoin miners. The first upgrade involved the use of GPUs or graphics cards, which have more computing power than simple CPUs. Eventually, these GPUs have been replaced by bespoke hardware, which is specifically designed for mining. ASICs or application-specific circuit chips have been developed to help Bitcoin miners.

Then again, as the technology evolves, the individuals who use them evolve as well. High tech tools and equipment become more expensive. This makes them harder to afford by regular people. So, large companies that have the money tend to take over the market.

How many Bitcoins a miner earns is basically dependent on his computing power. Even though cryptocurrency enthusiasts are the first ones to mine Bitcoin, they no longer have control of the market. These large companies are now the big players because of their energy-intensive operations.

Cloud Mining and Mining Pools

Fortunately, a new opportunity has opened for Bitcoin miners. So, even if not a lot of people are able to afford high tech mining equipment, they can still earn money from mining through the new models and markets for Bitcoin.

Mining pools have been created to combine the computing power of miners and increase their chances of earning rewards. Then again, since the miners are in a pool, they have to share the rewards that they get. They also have to pay a fee to join.

Aside from mining pools, miners can also opt for cloud mining. Companies or individuals can rent time on another person's rig and earn the rewards that this rig gets during such timeframe.

The businesses that rent out these rigs earn money by charging monthly fees, maintenance fees, and hash rate fees. Even though cloud mining is quite expensive and complex, it still takes out the costs and hassles of setting up and maintaining your own rig.

Bitcoin Mining Alternatives

Mining is not your only option if you want to gain Bitcoin exposure. You can actually buy Bitcoins through cryptocurrency exchanges. They act as the middlemen during these transactions. Then again, you have to take note that these exchanges also bring trading back to centralized control; thus, exposing traders to hackers.

You can also delve into paid email services. Coinbase, a major cryptocurrency exchange, bought a paid email service that lets users earn cryptocurrencies by completing tasks and replying to emails. A lot of companies actually entice people to review products and answer surveys by offering cryptocurrencies.

Likewise, you can earn cryptocurrencies by watching certain videos as well as using ad-supported social media platforms. So, if you are in search of other ways to earn Bitcoins aside from mining and buying them, you can try these alternative options.

Chapter 3: The History of Cryptocurrency

The roots of cryptocurrency can be traced back to the early 1980's. It was invented by David "Schlatt" Chaum, an American computer scientist and cryptographer. Back then, people only used physical money to make purchases and investments. Nobody has ever heard of this 'blinded money'. Chaum created the 'blinding' algorithm that modern Web-based encryption relies on. Because of this algorithm, individuals and businesses were able to exchange information securely online. It laid the foundation of electronic currency transfers.

Chaum eventually persuaded other individuals interested in cryptocurrency to make blinded money known to the public. He moved to the Netherlands, where he started DigiCash, a company that used blinding algorithm to create currency units. He monopolized the market.

At first, DigiCash directly dealt with private individuals. However, the central bank of the Netherlands disapproved of this. So, the company was forced to stop catering to private individuals and only sell to licensed banks instead. This caused it to struggle financially. It was later approached by Microsoft for a partnership, but they were not able to agree on terms.

By the late 1990's, DigiCash went bankrupt. Then, Nick Szabo, one of Chaum's associate created Bit Gold, a cryptocurrency that he eventually released to the public. It became notable for making use of the blockchain system. However, it did not gain popularity. It is also no longer in existence today.

Notable Digital Currencies

A few years after DigiCash was introduced, imitations have been developed. One of these was WebMoney from Russia. Other electronic financial platforms were also established, such as PayPal.

In the United States, a company called e-gold created another digital currency. It was aptly named e-gold, after the name of its maker. Customers sent their coins, jewelry, and trinkets to the company in exchange for this digital currency. They were then able to use their e-gold to trade holdings with other users, exchange it for cash, or acquire physical gold.

By the mid-2000's, the company had millions of users. Sadly, it also attracted lots of scammers and hackers. This caused customers to incur financial losses. In 2009, the company shut down.

At around the same time, the ever popular Bitcoin was introduced by Satoshi Nakamoto. It became a pioneer in using blockhain to combine record-keeping, user anonymity, and decentralized control.

The public introduction of Bitcoin attracted the attention of enthusiasts, who then started to exchange and mine it. In 2010, more alternatives have emerged on the market, including Litecoin. Soon enough, online merchants began accepting cryptocurrencies as payment.

WordPress, a major open-source website creation platform, started to accept Bitcoin payments in 2012. Shortly after, more online retailers such as Microsoft, Newegg, and Expedia recognized Bitcoin as an official mode of payment.

Chapter 4: Benefits and Drawbacks of Cryptocurrency

Cryptocurrency is digital or virtual money. It only exists on digital platforms and can only be stored in digital wallets. When you have digital money, you cannot physically hold it. You cannot touch, feel, and smell it. Nonetheless, you can use it to purchase goods and services just like you would with regular physical money.

But what are the advantages and disadvantages of cryptocurrency? Knowing about its benefits would encourage you to do better at trading while being aware of its drawbacks would make you more cautious with your actions.

The Benefits of Cryptocurrency

Anonymity
The advent of the Internet has opened the doors towards anonymity. With cryptocurrency, you can be private and anonymous. You can limit the amount of digital data that you give out. Hence, you are able to enjoy added security. You no longer have to worry about identity theft.

Transparency
Cryptocurrency transactions are transparent in the sense that they are stored on the blockchain, which is an open ledger. This makes data available for everyone to check out anytime and anywhere. Such transparency improves accountability.

Accessibility
You can check out cryptocurrencies whenever you want to. As long as you have an electronic device that lets you connect to the Internet, you can access your finances instantly. You can buy and sell in real time.

Inflation Protection
Just like with precious metals, you can be protected against inflation with cryptocurrency. This is an advantage you cannot

have with fiat currency. Physical cash is inherently insecure while fiat currencies are naturally prone to inflation. Cryptocurrency are quite scarce in the sense that the number of units produced are predetermined. Actually, certain aspects of cryptocurrency are expected by a lot of political scientists and economists to be incorporated into fiat currencies.

The Drawbacks of Cryptocurrency

Anonymity
The anonymity of cryptocurrencies makes it vulnerable to abuse by criminals. The dark Web and the black market are actually major users of digital money. Criminals from different parts of the world are able to make transactions online.

Complexity
Many people find cryptocurrency easy enough to comprehend. However, there are still those who have a hard time using it. The elderly and people with disabilities, for instance, may not be tech savvy.
Those who do not fully understand blockchains and decentralized financial systems may also be hesitant to use cryptocurrencies for fear of losing money. After all, once your digital money is gone, it may be very difficult or even impossible to recover it.

Safety Risks
As with all kinds of technology, digital currencies are also prone to hacking and online theft. There are lots of scammers, hackers, and criminals out there, so you have to be vigilant at all times.
You should know about the safety risks and security protocols. Treat your cryptocurrency in the same manner as you would treat your cash. Do not readily give personal and financial information to people you do not know well.
Likewise, you should take good care of your electronic devices. Always use a secure Internet connection, especially when logging into your digital wallets. It is not advisable to use public Wi-Fi because it is not very secure.

You should also refrain from using public computers as well as clicking on suspicious links in order to protect yourself against phishing. Refrain from downloading apps that do not come from trusted developers.

It is also not ideal to save passwords on a computer, especially if you are not the only one who uses it. If you are into online casinos, you should be wary of companies with offers that seem too good to be true.

Market Fluctuations

There are numerous ways on how to use cryptocurrencies, including buying goods, online gambling, and investing. If you choose to use your digital money to invest, you should wait for the market to fluctuate in your favor. It is crucial to do your research and stay updated with the latest trends. Otherwise, you may incur huge losses on the digital market.

Chapter 5: The Present and Future of Cryptocurrency Trading

Cryptocurrency is huge now, but what is most likely to happen to it in the future?

Well, cryptocurrencies like Bitcoin are predicted to increase in value over the next few years. Thus, it is advisable for people, especially traders, to invest in it. In fact, now is the best time to buy Bitcoins.

Really? What about the COVID-19 pandemic?

Bitcoin started in 2009 and has risen to popularity ever since. However, when the coronavirus pandemic broke out this year, it also started to go down in value. Fortunately, this setback did not last long. Bitcoin's value rose from $3,000 to $10,000. This made traders and cryptocurrency enthusiasts inspired to invest further in Bitcoin even with the COVID-19 pandemic happening.

Some experts are optimistic that the coronavirus pandemic will only make Bitcoin more valuable. They actually predict that its value will rise up to $100,000 next year. With this being said, it may actually be ideal for you to invest in Bitcoin. The good value of this cryptocurrency shows that investing in it has little risks involved.

Moreover, some experts believe that the COVID-19 pandemic would start a bull market pretty soon. So, aside from Bitcoin, you may also want to consider investing in other cryptocurrencies such as NEO, EOS, and Etherium. Who knows, your $500 may turn into $5,ooo,ooo in just a few months? Don't let the COVID-19 pandemic stop you from making investments.

There are economic analysts who predict that there would be a huge change in cryptocurrency when institutional money comes into the market. Additionally, it is possible that this digital money will be floated on the Nasdaq, which will make the blockchain more credible as well as use it as an alternative to the conventional currencies that we use today.

There are also individuals who say that the cryptocurrency has to have a verified exchange traded fund or ETF. Having this will make it easier for anyone to use Bitcoin for investment opportunities. Nevertheless, there still has to be a demand for cryptocurrency investment, which may not readily be generated with funds.

Bitcoin is referred to as a decentralized currency that makes use of peer-to-peer technology that allows for the issuance, verification, and transaction processing of currency. Such decentralization renders this cryptocurrency protected against the interference or manipulation of the government. However, there is also a downside to this. There is neither any central authority that ensures things flow smoothly nor backs the value of Bitcoin.

Bitcoin is digitally created through mining, which requires high-level computers to deal with complex algorithms. It is presently created at a rate of twenty-five Bitcoins every ten minutes. It is expected to be capped at twenty-one million in 2140.

The characteristics of Bitcoin distinguishes it from fiat currency, which is backed by the government. The issuance of fiat currency is centralized and supervised by the central bank. Then again, even though the bank regulates how much currency is issued according to its monetary policy objectives, there's still no upper limit to how much currency is issued. Additionally, the government typically provides an insurance to local currency deposits so that they can be protected against bank failure. Bitcoin, however, does not have any support mechanism. Its value is completely dependent on how much money investors shell out. Likewise, in the event that a Bitcoin exchange folds, there will be no way for people with balances to get their money back.

The Future Outlook of Bitcoin and Other Cryptocurrencies
What the future holds for Bitcoin is highly debatable. Kenneth Rogoff, a professor at Harvard University, says that cryptocurrency market capitalization may significantly

increase in the next five years. In fact, he predicts it to rise to $5 trillion to $10 trillion.

He further says that the long term value of Bitcoin may actually be just $100 instead of $100,000 as some people believe. After all, the use of Bitcoin is limited to mere transactions; thus, making it prone to a bubble-like collapse. Moreover, the verification process of Bitcoin is not very efficient. Nevertheless, he adds that there isn't any reason to panic despite its historic volatility.

If you still want to invest in Bitcoin and you enjoy its transaction anonymity and decentralization, you should know that government agencies are becoming more and more scrutinizing towards it. This should not be a surprise since criminals prefer to use it for their illegal activities such as drug peddling, money laundering, weapons procurement, and smuggling.

You should also be aware of its limitations such as its vulnerability to computer hacking and crashing. Virtual financial accounts can be hacked and emptied by criminals. Then again, technology tends to improve as time goes by. So, more advanced technology in the future can make virtual financial accounts more secure.

Bitcoin is not the only cryptocurrency you need to watch for. All cryptocurrencies can be vulnerable to attracting more government scrutiny and regulation, which in turn can cease their existence.

In addition, even though more and more merchants have started accepting cryptocurrency as a mode of payment, they are still in the minority. In order for this digital money to be more commonly used, it has to become more popular among customers and clients.

You can say that it is easy for the younger generation to adapt to modern technological advancements. But what about those who are not that tech savvy? Unfortunately, a lot of people still find cryptocurrency confusing and difficult to use. So, they might be discouraged to use it.

Cryptocurrencies that aspire to be included in the mainstream financial system have to fulfill a wide array of criteria. For instance, they have to be complex enough to stay protected against hackers and fraudsters. Conversely, they should be simple enough for users to understand.

Cryptocurrencies should also be decentralized yet with ample protection and security for consumers. They should also be able to preserve the anonymity of users without becoming an outlet for tax evasion and money laundering among other illegal transactions.

Bitcoin Alternatives

Those who know anything about cryptocurrency have certainly heard about Bitcoin. Ever since it was introduced to the public, it has become a widely recognized form of payment. At present, however, companies have started to recognize other cryptocurrencies.

Litecoin, for example, is considered to be the leading rival of Bitcoin today. It was designed to process small transactions faster than the Bitcoin. It was actually called the 'coin that is silver to Bitcoin's gold'.

If you wish to mine Litecoin, you can easily do it on your desktop computer. Yes, that's right! There is no more need for you to acquire heavy computer equipment unlike with Bitcoin. Even better, the maximum limit of Litecoin is eighty-four million while the maximum limit of Bitcoin is only twenty-one million.

You can also check out Ripple. Just like Bitcoin, it is both a payment system and a currency. Its currency component is also akin to that of Bitcoin. In certain ways, you can say that it is better than Bitcoin. For example, its payment mechanism allows fund transfers to be processed in just a few seconds. With Bitcoin, you will have to wait for several minutes for the same kind of service.

There is also MintChip, which is akin to Bitcoin in the sense that both of them do not require personal identification. However, unlike other cryptocurrencies, it was created by a government institution. So, it is backed by physical currency, unlike Bitcoin. It is basically a smartcard that contains electronic value.

How to Find Out Which Cryptocurrencies to Trade

After the Bitcoin was introduced to the public, the cryptocurrency market materialized. That was back in 2009. Cryptocurrencies are encrypted decentralized digital currencies that may be transferred from one person to another.

Ever since the introduction of Bitcoin, a lot of other digital currencies have emerged. So, aside from Bitcoin, traders can also trade Ripple, Ethereum, and Litecoin. With these many different cryptocurrencies available, it became quite hard for traders to select which ones to trade.

So, if you are experiencing difficulty choosing which cryptocurrencies to trade, the following guidelines can help you out:

1. Determine your risk level.

As a trader, it is important for you to know your risk level when trading. This way, you can take calculated risks and minimize your odds of losing money.

There are more than two thousand cryptocurrencies on the market today. Of all these digital currencies, Bitcoin has the highest volatility and stability.

Do not worry about investing in Bitcoin because it is generally safe. After all, it is the oldest cryptocurrency. The other ones are referred to as "altcoins" because they are alternative coins or alternative cryptocurrencies to Bitcoin. Some of the stable and established ones include XRP, ETH, and LTC.

When trading cryptocurrencies, you have to diversify your investment in order to spread out your risk. You may also want to invest in at least one more stable cryptocurrency in order to make your investment portfolio stronger.

Take note that stable currencies mimic the fiat currency and keep the price fluctuations to a minimum. They are also an excellent way to put money in an exchange.

2. Perform independent research.

Even though it is vital to consider the opinions of other people, particularly expert traders, you still have to do your own research. This way, you can gain reliable information first-hand and make good judgment based on your own data.

For example, before you trade ETH/USD vs. BTC/USD, you have to check out their historical charts. See to it that you also pay close attention to the market cap and circulation. Do not merely focus on the price. While it is vital, it is not the only area that you have to consider.

See to it that you also research about the history of the cryptocurrency. You also have to consider stability. Take note that cryptocurrencies do not necessarily have to be old in order for it to show stability. It can still be in the growth stage, but if it shows continuous growth, then it is a good option.

As much as possible, you should avoid cryptocurrencies that have already suffered huge drops in the market cap. Be wary of cryptocurrencies that have a history of huge corrections and peaks. These are indicators of a dying demand.

In addition, you have to learn as much as you can about the companies that offer cryptocurrencies. Learn about the problems they can solve as well as how they intend to solve more problems.

You should search for offerings with a strong idea backing and innovative technology. Do a research on the technical team, leadership, and track record of the company, including its chief executive officer (CEO).

    3. Look for possible ICO offerings.

Digital currency companies that aim to roll out new cryptocurrencies and come up with a working capital tend to go for initial coin offerings or ICOs. This involves making a bet on companies that have the ability to deliver products and yield good returns on investment.

When selecting which cryptocurrencies to invest in, you can gain good opportunities with ICOs. Essentially, you do not have any historical chart to serve as your guide. Hence, you need to depend on your own understanding of the offering. You have to know what makes it stand out as well as what the team behind it is about.

Since you are beginning from scratch, you can invest in a good ICO to achieve your bigger goals. You have to look into successful offerings in the past and keep track of any recent trends so that you can be in the position to see profitable ICOs.

4. Consider unknown cryptocurrency exchanges.

In case you missed out on a particular ICO, do not worry because you still have a chance to purchase cryptocurrencies on the exchanges. However, most of the major exchanges limit the cryptocurrencies they trade. So, you may find better investments if you consider less popular platforms.

In order to keep your investment protected, you should do your research on the cryptocurrency exchange as well as the people who run it.

5. Be vigilant and aware.

It is daunting to choose which altcoins and cryptocurrencies to trade. Hence, you should always stick to the facts. Refrain from making decisions when you feel strong emotions. Always be logical and rational, not emotional. Making this a habit will enable you to choose the right investments.

Once you are done choosing the cryptocurrencies that you want to trade and invest, you have to stay vigilant. You have to closely monitor your portfolio and keep an eye out for news that pertain to your investments. Continue to conduct your research just like you did before you made an investment. Take note that altcoins may not have the same growth rate as Bitcoin. Nevertheless, they can still yield lucrative returns if you know how to handle them properly. At the end of the day, your success will still depend on yourself.

Bitcoin versus Other Cryptocurrencies

You already know that cryptocurrencies are digital currencies that operate independently of governments and banks yet they can be speculated on and exchanged just like any other currencies.

You also know that Bitcoin is the most popular cryptocurrency; but what about altcoins or alternative coins to Bitcoin? What makes them different from the well renowned Bitcoin? They are just as good because of their technological advances, rising demand, and expanded applications.

Bitcoin (BTC)

Bitcoin is regarded as the leader of cryptocurrencies. It is highly popular and valuable. Then again, it also requires specialized mining equipment and has slow transaction speeds.

Bitcoin Cash (BCH)
Although created to serve as an offshoot to Bitcoin, it is still a standalone cryptocurrency that has a faster transaction time than Bitcoin. It has a maximum block size of 8mb, which is much bigger than Bitcoin's maximum block size of only 1mb. It can process more transactions, but it still requires specialized mining equipment, just like Bitcoin.

Ripple (XRP)
This cryptocurrency underpins RippleNet, which is a payment network. It operates differently from other cryptocurrencies. Nevertheless, it has very fast transaction speeds.

Stellar (XLM)
This payment network works the same way as RippleNet. It has the ability to process transactions in multiple currencies. Also, it is underpinned by the cryptocurrency lumens or stellar. Stellar integrates with banks but it is not as widely recognized as the other cryptocurrencies.

NEO (NEO)
It is the cryptocurrency to NEO and is similar to Ethereum in the sense that it allows users to develop dapps or decentralized applications as well as smart contracts. Its network is also tightly controlled by the NEO Team, which requires users to verify their identities on the network. It is compliant with the regulations in most junctions, but it is said that it may not be really decentralized.

Ether (ETH)
This cryptocurrency allows users to code and release their very own dapps or decentralized applications as well as develop smart contracts that enforce clauses automatically. Each time a transaction is processed, a small amount of this cryptocurrency is destroyed. Thus, hackers are prevented from spamming the network. Ether also has fast transaction

speeds. Then again, it also has an uncapped supply, so it can be inflationary.

EOS (EOS)

It is the cryptocurrency of EOS.IO, which is a blockchain platform that replicates the key functionality of the operating system and hardware of a computer. It offers services and tools for developers to create dapps or decentralized applications, including databases, user accounts, and authentication.

EOS is integrated with the EOS.IO network and has fast transaction speeds. Then again, it also has an uncapped supply, so it can also be inflationary.

Litecoin (LTC)

It was created to serve as the silver to the gold of Bitcoin. Its maximum supply is eighty-four million, which is four times greater than the maximum supply of Bitcoin. It has fast transaction speeds. Then again, it also has a low market capitalization as compared to Bitcoin.

Why the Cryptocurrency Differences Matter Greatly to Traders

Non-traders may think that cryptocurrencies are all the same, but traders know the difference. They are aware that the slightest difference can actually make a significant impact on the results of their trade.

These differences provide crucial clues on the supply and demand of cryptocurrencies. They also determine the ways in which cryptocurrencies are traded as well as influence the prices on the financial markets.

The Supply and Demand

The supply of cryptocurrencies play a significant role in determining the prices on the financial markets. In essence, the scarcer a coin is, the higher its value.

Both Bitcoin and Bitcoin Cash have an upper limit of twenty-one million coins each. Ripple and Litecoin have a maximum supply of one hundred billion and eighty-four million, respectively.

Such coins would be deflationary when all the other coins have been released or mined. Coins such as Ether, however, do not have a fixed limit. So, they can be inflationary, depending on how much is lost or burnt.

The supply of cryptocurrencies changes as new ones are released or mined. Mining, as you know, refers to the process in which transaction blocks are verified and new cryptocurrencies are released.

In spite of having just a few applications, the value of Bitcoin continues to rise. It is still the largest cryptocurrency on the market based on capitalization. This shows that reputation is a key component in cryptocurrency valuations.

Because Bitcoin is highly popular, it is also highly valuable. Media coverage can actually affect the popularity and value of a cryptocurrency. For instance, if a major digital wallet hack occurs, the price of the cryptocurrency will be affected. Since it has garnered a negative reputation, its value may also decline.

Although Bitcoin Cash, Litecoin, and Bitcoin are all standalone cryptocurrencies, Ripple and Ether exist as part of bigger networks with expanded applications. So, if the popularity of these networks improved, the demand for their underlying cryptocurrencies may also surge.

As the adoption of cryptocurrencies continue to accelerate, their transaction speeds and ability to deal with huge volumes of transactions also become likely to be under more scrutiny. In addition, scalability may be affected by the security and size of the blockchain. After all, these factors can affect the associated network speed, mining profitability, and the willingness of users to use and purchase coins.

Thus, traders have to pay close attention to forks and software updates in order for them to understand the evolution of scaling technology better.

The Market Hours of Bitcoin
Now that you have are better understanding of Bitcoin, you are probably wondering when you can trade this cryptocurrency.

In terms of market cap, Bitcoin is the biggest cryptocurrency. It is possible to trade Bitcoin on a weekly basis. As a trader, you want to seize every opportunity available for this highly volatile cryptocurrency.

The Bitcoin market is actually open for twenty-four hours per day, seven days per week. This is because cryptocurrencies tend to operate on a decentralized computer network. So, every time you trade, you can speculate on the price movements of Bitcoin from eight o'clock in the morning on a Saturday until ten o'clock in the evening on Friday with the use of CFDs and spread bets.

Through these products, you can attain flexibility and go long if you think that the value of Bitcoin will go up. Conversely, you can go short if you think that the value of Bitcoin will go down. Then again, if you decide that trading is not a good fit for you, you can simply purchase Bitcoins directly from a cryptocurrency exchange. These exchanges operate on a global scale. So, you can purchase Bitcoin at any time of the day and from any location.

Nevertheless, you have to keep in mind that these hours are also subject to exchange maintenance. So, there would be times when they are restricted sporadically. Do not worry because you will be notified of any scheduled exchange maintenance.

The Best Times for Trading Bitcoin

The most ideal time to trade Bitcoin is when the Bitcoin market is most active. However, this may be difficult to predict since the trading volume generally depends on the news and socio-political events of the day.

Nevertheless, you may still find the most liquidity at around eight o'clock in the morning when the European markets are open and at around five o'clock in the afternoon when these European markets are closed.

There are also traders who consider high trading volumes as indicators of increased liquidity. This tends to result in a tighter spread when they open a position.

You may want to trade on a platform in which you can benefit from fixed spreads on the major cryptocurrencies. This way, you will not have to worry about finding the best times to trade Bitcoin since the prices will stay the same regardless of the liquidity and volatility of the market.

Furthermore, you have to keep in mind that even though most of the price movements of Bitcoin are unpredictable, there are still certain events that can greatly affect the price of Bitcoin. For instance, a halving event can cause the value of this cryptocurrency to shirt.

A Bitcoin halving event occurs when the reward for mining Bitcoin transactions is cut in half. It also cuts in half the inflation rate of Bitcoin as well as the rate at which new Bitcoins come into circulation.

A Bitcoin halving event generally occurs about every four years or every 210,000 blocks mined, until all twenty-one million Bitcoins are mined completely.

Chapter 6: Blockchain Technology

Blockchains are lists of records or blocks that are connected by cryptography. Every block has a timestamp, transaction date, and a cryptographic hash of the former block.
Blockchains are also resistant to data modification. The block data can no longer be altered without the alteration of subsequent blocks once it is recorded.
In addition, blockchains are usually managed by peer-to-peer networks that follow a certain protocol for new block validation and inter-node communication. Even though the records in a blockchain can no longer be altered, they are still considered to be secure. A lot of cryptocurrencies also record transactions through blockchain technology. For instance, Ethereum and Bitcoin netwroks are based on blockchains.
Blockchain may seem complicated but its main concept is very simple. It is actually a form of database, which is why you need to know what a database is. Well, it is a collection of data that is electronically stored on a computer system.
Every piece of data or information in a database is in a table form. This way, it can easily be searched and filtered. With this being said, you might wonder what the difference between using a database and a spreadsheet is.
Well, a spreadsheet is designed for only one individual or a small group of individuals. It is used for storing and accessing information of a limited quantity. On the contrary, a database is designed to store large amounts of data, which can be manipulated, accessed, and filtered by any number of users.
While a database or spreadsheet may be accessed by numerous individuals, it is typically managed by an individual and owned by a business that has total control of how much data it has as well as how it functions.
How about a database and a blockchain? What is their difference?
One of the major differences between a blockchain and a database is the structure of their storage. A blockchain generally gathers data in groups that contain sets of data.
A block has a specific storage capacity. Once it is filled, it gets chained on another filled block. This forms a data chain called

a "blockchain". Every new data acquired gets compiled onto a new block, which in turn gets added to the chain.

A database has tables of data while a blockchain has chunks or blocks of data that are chained together. Thus, you can say that all blockchains are databases yet not all databases are blockchains.

In addition, this system results in an irreversible data timeline when it is applied in a decentralized manner. Once a block gets filled, it becomes a set part of such timeline. Every block is also provided with a specific timestamp once it gets added to the chain.

How about decentralization?

To help you understand blockchain better, you can try seeing it in the context of the way Bitcoin is implemented. Bitcoin actually needs to use several computers to store a blockchain, which is a kind of database that keeps all Bitcoin transactions. However, each of these computers is managed by a unique group or person.

Say, one company has a server that consists of ten thousand computers. All of these computers have databases that contain vital client information. The company controls all of these computers, which are stored in a warehouse.

Likewise, Bitcoin consists of many computers, with each one of these computers being in different geographic locations as well as being managed by unique groups or persons. The computers that form the network of Bitcoins are referred to as nodes.

With such model, the blockchain of Bitcoin is decentralized. On the other hand, centralized and private blockchains consist of computers that are managed and owned by just one entity.

All the nodes in a blockchain also has complete records of information stored on their inception. With Bitcoin, such data is the complete history of every transaction. If a node encounters a data error, it may use the other nodes as reference point for correction. This prevents any node within the network to modify the information it holds. In turn, the transaction history of every block becomes irreversible.

In the event that a user tampers with the transaction records, the other nodes will cross-reference one another so that the node that contains the wrong information can be easily determined. Such system allows for the establishment of transparent and exact orders of events. Modifying information and functionality within the system, however, requires an agreement so that any changes that might occur would be in the majority's best interest.

Since Bitcoin's blockchain is transparent, every transaction is transparently viewable to anyone with a personal node. It can also be viewed live by using a blockchain explorer. The nodes have their own chain copy, which is updated every time a fresh block is added and confirmed. This allows investors to track their Bitcoins wherever they go.

So, even though Bitcoin offers anonymity to its users, it can still be traced in case of fraud. For instance, if your account gets hacked and all your Bitcoins are stolen, you will not be able to track the hacker. Fortunately enough, you will still be able to trace the stolen Bitcoins. You will know where they have been spent or moved.

Blockchain Security

In many ways, blockchain technology is responsible for security issues. For starters, new blocks are stored chronologically and linearly. This means that they always get added at the end of the blockchain.

Once the block gets added to this blockchain, you may no longer be able to modify or back up the content. This happens because every block has its own hash and timestamp. So, if a piece of information is modified, the entire has code gets modified as well.

How important is this in the real world?

For example, a hacker modifies the blockchain to steal Bitcoins. If he modifies his own copy, such copy will no longer be similar to other people's copies. In turn, the copies would be cross-referenced and the hacker's copy will be obvious. Perhaps, only an extraordinary hacker will be able to pull off the trick. To succeed, he has to simultaneously control and change most of the copies. This way, this new copy would become the majority.

He also needs to shell out a lot of money to redo the blocks due to the complexity of their hash codes and timestamps. Furthermore, he has to be extremely cautious and stealthy because the members of the network are likely to spot the modifications in the blockchain. Once these modifications are spotted, the members of the network will create a new chain version; thus, making the hacker's version practically worthless.

Blockchain versus Bitcoin

Blockchain's main goal is to let digital data be distributed and recorded while preventing it from being edited. Researchers W. Scott Stornetta and Stuart Haber created the first outline of blockchain technology in 1991. They did this to produce a system that can protect document timestamps from tampering. However, it was only in 2009 when blockchain was actually applied in the real world.

The protocol of the Bitcoin is created on a blockchain. Satoshi Nakamoto, the pseudonymous creator of Bitcoin, called it a peer-to-peer electronic cash system without any trusted third party.

You have to keep in mind that Bitcoin simply uses blockchain as a way to record payments transparently. However, blockchain can also be used to record any amount of data points immutably.

At present, there are lots of blockchain-based projects that aim to use blockchain to improve the society. For example, there are projects that are used during elections. They help reduce the likelihood of fraudulent voting by issuing a single token or cryptocurrency to every citizen.

Let's say that you are a voter. You will be provided with a particular wallet address. You will then be required to send your token or cryptocurrency to the address of the candidate that you want to vote for.

You do not have to worry about your vote being hacked or tampered with. You do not have to use physical ballots either.

The blockchain used is traceable and transparent; thus, significantly reducing the likelihood of human error as well.

Analyzing Market Bias

For many people, the stock market is highly unpredictable. No matter how much you plan your moves, you still cannot be one hundred percent certain of the outcome. Nonetheless, you can still prepare yourself for what might come by following sentiment data and market breadth. Once you familiarize yourself with these indicators, you will be able to understand the unpredictable movements of the market.

Chapter 7: How to Properly Store Cryptocurrencies

Even though cryptocurrencies are digital money, they are still money. They are just as valuable. So, you have to keep them in a safe place just as you would with physical money. After all, you would not just leave your wallet lying around anywhere. So, how can you keep your cryptocurrencies safe and secure?

If you plan to invest in cryptocurrencies, you have to set up a digital wallet. It is pretty much just like the wallet in your pocket, except that it is virtual. It only exists in the digital world. You can link this wallet to a bank account and store it in various devices.

You have to be vigilant because there are a lot of fraudsters and hackers online. If you are not careful, your cryptocurrencies can get stolen. You need to have a secure wallet for your digital money. Cryptocurrency wallets are software programs that store public and private keys as well as interact with a variety of blockchain.

You can send, receive, and track the balance of cryptocurrencies. You can also choose from a variety of wallets. Ideally, you should choose one that best suits your needs. For example, you can choose to be a passive buy and hold investor, an active trader, or a mixture of both. Once you are done setting up your digital wallet, you may start purchasing and exchanging digital currencies on different platforms.

Storing Cryptocurrencies
There are several ways you can store your cryptocurrencies:

Exchange
An exchange is the simplest and easiest way to store digital coins. After all, this is where such money is traded. Then again, if you do choose to store your coins in an exchange, you have to know that it is not regulated. It is not very safe because it is prone to hacking.

In fact, I will not recommend that you use an exchange to store your digital money. Unless, of course, you add more security layers such as a two-factor authentication in addition to a password.

You can also use Google Authentication to ensure that your details are kept safe even if a hacker creates a clone of your mobile device. What's more, you can opt for your coins to be stored in a cold storage for added security.

Hot Wallet or Online Wallet

Storing your digital money in an online wallet is safer than storing it in an exchange. Then again, it is still not the safest way. It can still be prone to hacking. Moreover, it has more requirements. So, if you are a busy person, you may find the processes time-consuming.

However, if you want to keep your digital money safe, you should make time for these processes. Ideally, you have to set up several online wallets. This way, your coins will be distributed to different accounts and will not be likely to get stolen all at once in case a hacker still gets into your wallet. There are a couple of ways on how you can store your coins in an online wallet. First, you can choose a wallet that stores your private and public keys online. Second, you can choose a wallet that stores your private keys on your mobile device or computer.

Say, you choose to store your coins in a cloud wallet. Your coins can remain safe on your personal computer because of your private keys. However, they can be prone to hacking if a virus gets into your computer.

If you prefer to use your smartphone, you can store your coins in a mobile wallet such as Jaxx. This mobile wallet syncs to both your smartphone and personal computer so that you may back up your private keys. It can be used to store various cryptocurrencies such as Bitcoin, Litecoin, and Ethereum among others.

Cold Storage, Hard Storage, or Offline Wallet

It is practically a USB stick where you can keep your private key. It is considered to be very safe since it is offline and not prone to hacking. This is the good thing about old school devices – you get to keep personal information private because you are the only one who has access to it.

Then again, there is also a downside. Since it is offline, you will no longer be able to recover the data once the USB stick gets lost or misplaced. Likewise, you can lose your money if your device gets reformatted.

Paper Wallet

It is what it sounds like – a paper that functions as a wallet. In essence, your private key is written down on a piece of paper. Just like the USB stick, it is offline. So, your sensitive information can be protected from hackers. Then again, also just like the USB stick, you will lose all your vital information once this paper is destroyed, misplaced, or thrown away.

So, how can you make sure that your private key is safe and secure then?

Well, no matter which method you choose to use, you must always have a backup for your vital data. You must also keep your software programs up to date with the latest versions. You must also use as many security layers as possible. Do not merely rely on a password.

Of course, when you choose a password, see to it that it is not easy to guess. Ideally, you should use a combination of uppercase and lowercase letters, numbers, and special characters.

And which one is the best way for you?

It depends on what kind of investor you are as well as what needs you have. For example, if you are more of a trader than an investor, you can keep your digital money in an exchange. After all, the money does not stay there for long since you trade it anyway.

If you plan to hold your money longer, then you may want to store it in a wallet. This way, you can easily check on it every now and then as well as move it whenever you want. If you have large sums of money, then you should probably play it safe and store your money in cold storage to protect it against hackers. Just make sure that your device is locked up in a vault or somewhere safe.

Chapter 8: Tracking and Selling Cryptocurrencies

Once you buy cryptocurrencies, you can track and sell them.

Tracking Cryptocurrencies

You can track your cryptocurrencies using certain websites. You can do this manually or automatically. If you choose the latter, you can simply copy and paste the code you got from the exchange on the website. The process will then be automated. You will be informed of its daily fluctuations. All you have to do is create a portfolio and log in whenever you want to. This is great since you will be able to keep track of your money even though they are kept in different wallets or exchanges. You will also be able to get the average price if you have different positions of a similar coin. What's more, you can have the tax added.

Selling Cryptocurrencies

A trader can be regarded as highly skilled if he knows when he needs to get out of a trade. A lot of traders hold their money because they keep on waiting for the right time to sell. But when is the right time to actually sell?

Well, since cryptocurrencies have just been introduced globally, you may not want to sell them. Unlike stocks and other investments, these digital coins can be used directly just as you would with the United States Dollar. There is no need to sell them in order to gain value.

Then again, merely buying and holding is also not a good move. You do not want to hoard and miss out on making profits. You should try to make profits every now and then to rotate your money and benefit from other cryptocurrencies. Say, you have successfully earned a huge profit and you are thinking of setting a stop loss below it so that you can sell some of your holdings.

You can also earn a profit by watching your money go up and down. If you do not see it hitting a new high, you may trade within such channel of low and high prices. This would allow you to go out near the top and in near the bottom.

Will it ever be too late to invest in cryptocurrencies?
Ideally, you have to invest in cryptocurrencies as soon as possible or prior to the beginning of the adoption. However, it is never too late to start investing in digital money. Someday, there might be new cryptocurrencies and they may have very high rises that you can get into.

Nobody can see the future, so it is best to stay optimistic. Choose to focus on the favorable possibilities that cryptocurrencies may bestow upon you. Research and learn as much as possible on cryptocurrencies. The younger generations are aware of the benefits that cryptocurrencies can give them in the future.

According to Everett Rogers, there are four phases of adoption:

    a. Innovators
    b. Early Adopters
    c. Late Majority
    d. Laggards

The present time may be regarded as the stage of the Early Adopters. Hence, you still have a long way to go with digital money. A lot of people are still unaware of Bitcoins, for example. So, you should take advantage of the situation and invest before everyone else adopts digital money.

BNK to the Future co-founder and CEO Simon Dixon said that cryptocurrencies have five waves:

    a. Bitcoin

This wave had value because it was independent from the central bank.

    b. Altcoins

This wave includes the time when people attempted to copy Bitcoin and produced Dash and Litecoin as a result.

    c. Coinbase and Kraken

These are exchanges that you can have when you have company equities.

    d. ICO's or Tokens

They are produced when companies produce asset classes that trade on secondary markets.

    e. Forks

They are produced when individuals disagree regarding how things have to be split off and done. For instance, Bitcoin Gold is split off from Bitcoin.

Chapter 9: Initial Coin Offering

An Initial Coin Offering (ICO) is a method for fundraising that trades future crypto coins for liquid cryptocurrencies. It is, however, a very risky way to raise funds. It is not advisable to invest in anything that you cannot really afford to lose. Always remember that you can have a hard time getting back the money that you have lost in case you fail.

Anyway, an ICO is basically a crowd sale, which is the cryptocurrency for crowdfunding. It is similar to the Initial Public Offering (IPO), except that instead of selling shares, it sells tokens on the blockchain. It occurs prior to the launch of this blockchain. It also involves a crowdsale or public sale of a coin's initial supply.

An Initial Coin Offering is also sometimes called an Initial Public Coin Offering (ICPO) or Initial Token Offering (ITO). Other people even call it a Crypto Crowdsale. As for the startups, they are referred to as Blockchain Startups.

Most companies that perform ICOs offer tokens instead of coins. You should know the difference between these two. Coins are used to transfer monetary value while tokens are used to store multifaceted and complex data streams.

Likewise, most companies that hold ICOs are built on a blockchain. Hence, they cannot be simply judged based on their monetary value. They have to be assessed according to their solution and business model.

How about the ICO 'white paper'? All ICO's need to have a manifesto or a white paper. It should explain in detail how the technology functions as well as how tokens are designed. It should also explain how users can obtain and use such tokens.

If you want to find out more about certain founders and their work, you can use a white paper. It will tell you whether these founders have actually thought through their project or not. It will also tell you about the problems it can solve as well as how it can be solved.

How ICO's Work

In essence, an ICO works according to the following:

a. The startup releases an advertisement regarding its selling of its new cryptocurrency's initial coin supply.
b. The startup's white paper is read by the investors, who eventually exchange Ether or Bitcoin for new coins.
c. The startup can exchange your Ether or Bitcoin into regular fiat currency to pay for the costs of building out technology.
d. If the project launches successfully, the new currency's value goes up and the investors earn a profit.

ICO is used by companies because it gives them a faster and easier way to perform fundraising for a new blockchain project. Also, it is border-free. So, it is able to connect to all the possible investors worldwide. More often than not, some of the tokens are sold to the participants of ICO while the others are kept for the needs of the company.

What are examples of companies that used ICO for project fundraising? Well, there's Bancor, which raised $150 million in less than three hours. There's also BAT, which raised $34 million in less than one minute. Then, there's Tezos. It raised $232 million in just one month.

ICO truly sounds fascinating. How do investors make money from it? A lot of investors believe that the startup would be successful in launching on an exchange. They anticipate such success, so they can sell coins or tokens as soon as possible to earn a profit. Most of the time, they do not actually believe in the company. They may believe in its idea, but not enough to risk going in for the long haul if earning big is not feasible in the short term.

ICO-Issued Coins and Tokens

Coins and tokens that have been issued in an ICO have three main roles:

a. They represent the product of the company. They can be used as an exchange medium for a specific amount of services or products. They can also be used for project trading.

b. They represent the right to share profits. Just like regular shares, coins can be shared by the company.
c. They represent the product of the company. Coins may be used as a means of exchange for a specific amount of services or products. They can also be used as a means to trade in a project.
d. They represent profit sharing rights. Just like regular shares, coins can be shared at a certain percentage.
e. They represent corporate bonds. Coins can function just like loans. The owner can acquire interest depending on the pre-set rate.

The Disadvantages of ICO Investments

ICO's seem great; but just like everything else, they also have disadvantages. For starters, the concept of the startup is on "white paper". There isn't any evidence of work. Investors mainly rely on this white paper for information. Thus, they become susceptible to fraud.

These fraudsters make people believe that they can become rich if they invest in ICO's. However, they do not follow through their promises. Once they get the money, they go on their way. They do not produce any product.

For example, Mycelium ICO was a huge failure for investors. After acquiring funding, the members of the team just disappeared. It was later discovered that they used the money to have a vacation.

Another disadvantage of ICO's is that some legitimate companies do not have the right technical support and/or knowledge. They may have the intention to produce products, but they lack the necessary knowledge and experience to build a blockchain business.

For example, CoinDash was a disaster for its investors. Millions of dollars were lost when hackers were able to make their way through the company's website. The hackers replaced the ICO wallet address with their own.

How to Invest In ICO
If, after learning about the disadvantages of investing in ICO, you still want to go into this venture, here are the things that you have to keep in mind:

Always do your research.
Staying up to date with the latest trends and news is vital for any business. However, this is especially important for ICO investments. As you know, ICO's are startups that need funding to grow. Without investors, their theories cannot be put into practice. Hence, you should do your research meticulously. Use the Internet to your advantage and learn everything you can about cryptocurrencies and ICO's.
Find out if the team is able to deliver. Read the white paper thoroughly before going to the team members and the founders. Use the Internet to obtain more information. For instance, you can use LinkedIn to learn more about them. Check out what is written on their profiles to know more about their credibility.
Do your research about the team and find out if the members have any experience on cryptocurrency, projects, and ICO's. Learn as much as you can, specifically on their involvement. If you think that they can deliver the results you want, then you can go on with doing more research.
Be careful and meticulous about your research. Make sure that you find out if they are merely scammers or fraudsters. You can join groups or forums for likeminded individuals. You can read their posts or send them questions.

Consider the thoughts of experienced investors.
Ask yourself if their thoughts really do solve problems or if there is any validity in their ideas. Consider if their ideas target a potential market and can lead to success. Ask yourself what values their projects can bring to the society. Are these people offering new concepts or are they merely offering something that has already been developed? Ponder the answers. Do not make an investment unless you fully believe that the team can do things better.

Find out what the tokens are for.
With ICO's, new tokens are created for a project. Every project should state what the tokens are for. For example, ask why Ethereum or Bitcoin are not enough to function as tokens for the project.

Find out how much money is being obtained.
In the past, some ICO's were able to collect an unlimited sum of money. The investors were given open caps that allowed them to send unlimited funding to projects. In general, the more coins circulate, the less unique the tokens become for trading.
In addition, you have to find out what the team uses the money for and how much they allot for development and marketing budgets. Do not forget to find out how much they allot for essential allocations. Remember that a good ICO is transparent and lets investors know where their money goes.

Know the token value.
How much are the tokens currently worth? As an investor, you want to know if your tokens would grow in value over the next few years. You also want to know if there is a chance for the market to be saturated by such tokens. Moreover, you want to know about the incentives involved in these tokens. After all, you can only earn a profit if your tokens grow in value.

Learn how and when tokens are distributed.
If the team members are greedy, more than half of the tokens would be suspiciously distributed. This is why you have to know how and when the tokens would be distributed. Good projects link their token distributions to roadmaps because every milestone requires a specific amount of funding.
See to it that you also monitor the stage when tokens are distributed. Certain projects only release tokens when the ICO has ended. Conversely, certain projects have to have beta versions prior to sending out tokens. Then again, even though learning about these things is helpful, they should still not affect your decision to make an investment.

Exchange Fiat Currency for Cryptocurrency

In order for you to be able to take part in ICO's, you need cryptocurrencies. The most popular ones are Ethereum and Bitcoin. Take note that the startup exchanges investment money for fiat currency in order to pay for costs and developments among others.

ICO Investment

When the startup asks you to send cryptocurrencies to a specific address, keep in mind that many startups do not accept Ether and Bitcoin. There are exchanges that do not send these cryptocurrencies to ICO startups. Usually, they are sent from online wallets.

Follow the Startup Development

Lots of individuals simply leave their money in startups and hope for the best. While there is nothing wrong with doing this, you may want to exert more effort if you wish to get the best results. After all, cryptocurrency investments are a huge deal. Unless you want to lose your hard-earned money, you should not take things lightly.

Cryptocurrency trading is very risky and speculative. So, it is wise to spread out your risks. This way, you can minimize your odds at losing. Moreover, you should exert more effort in knowing more about the startups that you follow. Read the news. Browse the Internet. Communicate with likeminded individuals who may be of help.

You can also go to conferences and meet the team. Talk to them. Send them emails. Find out their reactions. Get acquainted with these people because they may be able to help you out.

Chapter 10: Allocating Your Assets

Allocating your assets is crucial to monitor your finances. You have to know how much money you should invest in cryptocurrencies, especially if you are eyeing startups that have not yet built any products.

It may be a better idea to go for those that have already made themselves public in order to reduce your chances at being scammed. However, it is also not a completely bad idea to invest in ICO's. After all, you may benefit from great returns. How much percentage should you allocate to ICO's then? Well, it all depends on your age, risk level, and preference. For instance, do you want to be aggressive or conservative towards your investments?

For some experts, five percent of your capital is enough to be placed on ICO's. This is because you do not really have any idea on which way the industry is going to and you cannot be truly certain about which ICO's are going to make it.

ICO investments are very speculative. Nevertheless, you may still choose to allocate small amounts of your funds to ICO's on a regular basis. It is really up to you how you would manage your finances.

Say, you can invest less than one percent of your capital in an ICO that is popular and trending. You do not have any guarantee about it, but is what's hot at the moment. You can invest very little money, so in case the ICO does not work out, you will not incur huge losses.

You can invest one to two percent of your capital in an ICO that you like and five percent to an ICO that you like and believe in. It is not advisable to go beyond six percent because this may be too much in terms of allocation.

ICO Investment Risks

As you know, investing in ICO's is very risky. Here are some of the risks that you may want to keep in mind:

a. Unassured Returns

Just like in all other ventures, traders want to have a good return on their investments. ICO trading comes with a huge risk, particularly due to its volatility. Blockchain technology is a relatively new development that is not yet mainstream. A lot of traders are not sure of what to do with this new platform.
As a trader, the only way you can follow is to invest what you can lose. It would be wise to keep the following pointers in mind:

a. The possibility of a scam

ICO's do not have much documentation, unlike IPO's. This is why scams are fairly common. You cannot expect to see a record that you can use to study the performance of the company.
You have to have a lot of faith when investing in ICO's. You can lose a lot of money from your investments. Nevertheless, the Securities and Exchange Commission helps in stopping suspicious offers.
If you want to protect yourself against scams, you need to be very careful. Make sure that you truly understand what is being offered to you. Do not easily believe anything that seems too good to be true. You should also do your research by reading reviews and other helpful materials.

b. Tax issues

When you invest in ICO's, you can experience issues with taxes. Because ICO's are fairly new, many countries have not yet settled on what they can consider as ICO. Some countries see it as an equity while others see it as debt or prepaid goods.
Due to these various classifications, filing returns has become more difficult. You may want to seek help from a tax expert to ease your concerns. If you are not careful, you may encounter issues with taxes and the government. This may cause you to have more problems such as jail time and fines.

c. Security risks

Blockchain is digital, making it highly susceptible to cyber attacks. The digital accounts and tokens of users are at risk of being stolen. Cybercriminals use phishing to steal online. They steal the identity of the users to gain access to their accounts.

When using ICO, see to it that you use online security protocols. Refrain from clicking on links that you do not trust, especially those that are sent via email. In addition, you have to use secure operating platforms. Stick to your personal computer when using your online accounts. Likewise, you should avoid using public Wi-Fi and devices.

d. Regulatory concerns

Sadly, the digital industry is not that regulated. Control measures for returns and security do not exist. Countries are still trying to draft security regulations to provide protection to online users.

ICO Investment Rewards

Even if there are many concerns regarding the use of ICO's, there are still many benefits involved. This is the primary reason why a lot of people are still willing to invest in them in spite of the risks.

So, why do people forego the risks and still invest in ICO's?

a. Ease of investment

The entire process of investing in ICO is easy and straightforward. Unlike IPO's, there aren't a lot of requirements involved. There is no need for you to shell out a certain amount of money for investment. There is also no need for you to show any proof.

It is easy to use digital currencies, especially since they have now become major forms of investments. It is safe to say that blockchain technology has finally become the future of investment.

b. Global access

Traders are free to trade in any token, in any country. All they need is an Internet connection. Once they are able to connect to the Web, they can start to trade. This is what differs ICO investment from IPO investment. Investing in IPO cannot be done anytime, anywhere. IPO trading is reserved for a specific country.

In addition, you need to have a broker to help you invest in IPO. Take note that doing so comes with certain limitations, which may be expensive in the long run. This is why traders tend to resonate with the current global access model. They do not need special training or brokers.

If you wish to diversify your investments, you may benefit from global access.

c. Less competition

Traditional investments are not for everyone. Companies fight for just a handful of investors. These investors also have limited options. Because of this, it becomes very difficult to match companies with the right investors.

Things are different with ICO's. The companies have more options with regard to possible investors. Also, there are more projects available. Each year, millions of ICO's occur.

Investors also have the freedom to choose from different projects. Having a lot of options is helpful in minimizing risks.

d. Openness

ICO's also have more access, unlike IPO's that are mostly just for institutional investors. Early investors are at an advantage because they have a lot of benefits. It is only when more funding is necessary that the shares go to the other regular investors.

With ICO's, preferential treatments do not exist. Any trader who has access to the Internet can benefit from tokens. Such openness gives them complete control over their investments. They also do not risk missing out because of tardiness.

In conclusion, ICO's are reliable fundraising means. In fact, they can beat equity holding and IPO's. Even if a lot of people consider the boom of cryptocurrencies the main event, there is actually more to ICO's.

ICO's come with many advantages. They have opened up investment spaces for everybody. Having assets in any country is so simple and straightforward that anybody can do it. You can invest in USD even though you are not in the United States.

Plus, you get to benefit from reduced competition and openness. Then again, just like any other venture, there are also risks involved. For starters, your account is prone to hacking. You must be very careful. Regulations are also lacking.

So, if you really want to invest in ICO's, you have to do it with due diligence. Make sure that you do your research well and really think of your decisions before acting on them. If you do things the right way, investing in ICO's can be worth your time and efforts.

Chapter 11: Cryptocurrency Trading Strategies

Cryptocurrency investments are, in a way, much better than other investments. Unlike other assets, cryptocurrencies are exciting and new. With the right strategies, you can certainly generate high returns on your investments.

To get started on cryptocurrency investing, you have to select a reliable crypto exchange as well as a currency. A crypto exchange is the one you will use to buy, trade, and sell cryptocurrencies. If you are a beginner, you may want to invest in popular currencies that have a high market cap, like Bitcoin, Bitcoin Cash, Ethereum, and XRP.

Pointers to Remember

When you consider your trading strategy, make sure that you remember the volatility of the market. The financial market is actually highly volatile that it is common to encounter swings of twenty to thirty percent in a coin's value in just a few days. Blockchain technology is fairy new. It is still evolving. As the technology's value to industries outside of cryptocurrency market increases, the currency's value goes up as well.

a. Do not invest money you cannot afford to lose.

The value of currency rises and falls quickly. Cryptocurrencies and blockchains can get affected by bugs and hacks that diminish in value in many ways. Even though the traditional stock market is moody, you can still significantly reduce your odds at major losses if you make good decisions and hold your positions wisely. With cryptocurrencies, your odds at losing money are much higher. Thus, you should always choose to play safe.

b. Do your own research.

Research is vital for every venture, but more so for cryptocurrency investments. You have to research about the currencies you wish to buy to ensure that you meet your goals. Likewise, you have to research about the companies you plan to support. Keep in mind that investing in cryptocurrencies is practically the same as investing in the company that generates them as well as in blockchain technology.

c. Do not give in to FOMO or Fear of Missing Out.
Ever since the Internet and social media have been created, people have become more conscious about the things they may have been missing out on. The generation of today is especially concerned about the things their peers do or do not have. You must not give in to this madness.
You must resist the urge to follow what is trending every time, especially with cryptocurrency investments. Otherwise, you may risk purchasing coins at a very high price and then losing a lot of money when their value goes down. Refrain from investing in currencies just because your peers are investing in them. You have to make your own decisions based on intelligent assumptions.

d. Diversify your portfolio.
There are over a thousand cryptocurrencies on the financial market today. So, you can easily choose which ones to invest in. Just make sure that you do your research beforehand. Just like with stock investments, you need to have safe bets along with any high risk investments you wish to make.

e. Gain profits at intervals.
If you closely observe the cryptocurrency market, you will learn that values can go up and go down at any time. If you engage in short term trading and see a huge increase in value, you may want to know if such value will increase more.
Then again, whatever goes up has to come down. Thus, you can increase your odds of getting steady returns when you set up a strategy where you take profits at regular intervals.

Stop-Loss Usage for Day Trading
You use a stop loss when you set a price at which you will sell a currency in the event that it goes down in value. It is very useful in protecting trades.

Points of Trading

The following points have to be kept in mind when trading:

Long Term Trading

If you use a long term strategy in stock market investments, you may depend on the historical data when making decisions. This does not always happen for cryptocurrency though since only a limited amount of data is available.

Still, those who prefer to engage in long term trading believes that data with currency and recent market activity is useful in forecasting the movements and performance of cryptocurrencies. They think that this strategy is reliable for long term and that it can be beneficial to cryptocurrency investments.

Short Term Trading

This strategy is the opposite of long term trading because its goal is to gain a return on investment in just a short period of time. When you engage in short term trading, you make an investment and wait for the price to go up. Then, you can sell for a profit.

Fundamental Analysis

It aims to determine the currency value based on the project fundamentals. The challenge that comes with it mainly focuses on the fact that cryptocurrencies are not corporations. Hence, they do not have any financial statement. Their viability merely depends on the network community's strength. To start doing fundamental analysis, you have to seek out projects whitepapers that outline the functionality and goals. You may also search for content on the Internet, such as in blogs or community forums wherein you may interact with other users.

Of course, nothing is guaranteed. You should not expect your cryptocurrency investment to generate a profit at all times. You have to stay updated on the changing markets. Likewise, you have to modify your strategy according to the current events. Stay tuned in the news and ensure that you make good decisions based on facts.

Technical Analysis

It refers to the method of analyzing currencies by studying the factors related to the values of similar assets in the current and past marketplace by price data and historical volume. In essence, it is a method built on the notion that the future is predicted by the past. Thus, it makes use of asset performance to predict the future performance of stocks. There are a variety of charting tools that you can use to perform technical analysis on liquid.

Cryptocurrency Trading Indicators

It is not difficult to search for cryptocurrency trading indicators. In fact, you can search for them online. Some of the best ones include Moving Averages, Relative Strength Index, TD Sequential, Williams Alligator, Ichimoku, and Stochastic among others.

You need to learn and master these tools so that you can trade more effectively in the cryptocurrency market. They will help you gain a competitive edge in stocks, commodities, and forex among others. See to it that you also sharpen your knowledge and skills in risk management and trading.

Relative Strength Index Cryptocurrency Trading Strategy

When you trade Bitcoins, you need to learn how relative strength index indicators work. Basically, you get a long signal if your indicator goes below 30 and you get a short signal if it goes above 70. As a trader, you may tweak your indicator depending on your level of comfort. You may modify it if you want to use a looser or stricter approach. Keep in mind that conservative entries generally prevent losses.

The Relative Strength Index is used to measure the speed, change, and strength of price movements. It can top off traders whenever the trends run out of momentum and a reversal may follow. It can also indicate when assets are overbought or oversold.

It is easy to read and use, especially when combined with candlesticks, chart patterns, and other formations. It is actually considered to be very safe since it has fewer disadvantages compared to other strategies. Then again, as a trader, you have to experiment with your sensitivity for what you regard as overbought or oversold. Otherwise, the positions may be taken and you may acquire losses.

The Moving Average Strategy
If you look at charts, you will see that even the most basic ones includes the Moving Average. It is shown in a certain format, such as dynamic, exponential, or simple. When you use these lines, you can benefit from trading setups that are profitable. You can earn money when the prices pass through the moving averages.

How to Use Moving Average to Trade Cryptocurrency
Traders generally use moving averages to smooth the price action over a specific period of time. These lagging indicators are based on past price actions. You have to remember this when you use moving average in your cryptocurrency trading. When you set up a moving average, you may choose the number of periods you wish to take into account. This period pertains to a unit of time that is based on the timeframe that you observe on your chart.
Say, you have a moving average with a period of twenty-one and you are viewing an hourly chart. You will see that the price becomes smoother depending on the last twenty-one hours of data. Then again, if you are viewing a daily chart, you will notice that the price becomes smoother depending on the last twenty-one days of price action.

In essence, there are two classifications of moving averages. These are simple moving average and exponential moving average. The previous is the traditional type while the latter is a weighted moving average that offers more weight to the latest prices.
As for the time period, the length of the moving average you use has to depend on the trading style that you use. For example, if you are a short term trader, you can benefit more from a short moving average. On the other hand, if you are a long term trader or investor, you can benefit more from a long moving average.

Moving averages are expected to serve as a form of resistance and support. Just like many other indicators, you will gain a stronger resistance or support if you use a long time frame.

Slopes and Crosses
On a longer time frame, a moving average's slop may help you define a trend. It is actually very simple. You can confirm that an asset is on the uptrend if the moving average slopes upwards.
Likewise, if the moving average slopes downwards, then the asset that you are assessing is on the downtrend. Keep in mind that moving averages are lagging indicators. Moving average slopes help define trends. It is not possible to use a single moving average to spot a transition from the uptrend to the downtrend.
With regard to crosses, you have to have at least two moving averages on the chart. In order for you to avoid cluttering your chart, you have to only use two. Take note that one of these moving averages should be longer than the other.
When you finally have a long term moving average and a short term moving average switched on, you need to keep an eye out for crosses. Remember that a short moving average cross above a long moving average means that the trading signal is bullish while a short moving average that falls below a long moving average means that the trading signal is bearish.
As a trader, it is necessary for you to include moving averages in your arsenal for trading.

The Advantages and Disadvantages of Moving Average
The Moving Average is simply a mathematical formula designed to study individual data points better. These data tools are placed on a series of time periods to result in visual tools that you may use to signal whether or not you should enter a trade or take a position.
You can also use the Moving Average to set a stop-loss level or plan an exit point. This is particularly useful for traders. It

can result in a winning strategy when used alongside chart patterns.

Moving averages can actually run across various time periods. Thus, you have to be careful when choosing a time frame. 50, 100, and 200 are the most commonly used moving averages.

The MACD Strategy

MACD is short for Moving Average Convergence Divergence. It is a technical analysis indicator that was created in the 1960's by Gerald Appel, a trader and author.

The MACD strategy is popular amongst cryptocurrency traders. It provides an early indication as to whether a reversal may come as the lines start to turn. It later confirms the signal if a crossover happens.

What about the advantages and disadvantages?

Just like every other strategy, the MACD also has its own advantages and disadvantages. It is commonly known as a lagging indicator. In fact, it is one of the most popular technical analysis indicators available today. It can help you predict whether or not trends will change.

In addition, the MACD can provide you with easy to read signals as well as a histogram to further help you with trading. It can show you a visual representation of a trend's strength and clearly defined crossovers.

Then again, this indicator is also lagging. Thus, it can give inaccurate readings that may cause you to take positions earlier than necessary.

The Bollinger Bands Strategy

The Bollinger Bands' midline simple moving average can be used as a trigger for short and long signals. It can be a successful and steady strategy for cryptocurrency traders.

What about the advantages and disadvantages?

John Bollinger, a well-known financial analyst, created the Bollinger Bands in the 1980's. It is used alongside candlesticks, chart patterns, and other technical indicators. You can use it as a part of a profitable and successful strategy in cryptocurrency trading.

There are two standard deviation lines as well as a simple moving average in a technical analysis indicator. These deviation lines narrow or widen based on the significance of volatility of the price action.

Whenever these bands tighten, the volatility drops and signals a volatility surge. A lot of traders tend to make the mistake of trading the band's breakouts. About ninety percent of all the price actions actually takes place within these bands. Hence, any band breakout tends to get rejected back into the bands. You can make a profit by "riding the bands". However, this can only be profitable if the price breaks out of the band with a huge volume surge.

The Parabolic SAR Strategy

The parabolic SAR puts a series of dots below or above the price action. It is when the price comes into contact with these dots that they show on the opposite side of the price action. A signal is then issues.

When you observe weekly price charts of Bitcoins, you will see that short and long signals are issued when the price passes through the dots. This depends on the price action's direction. A lot of traders miss out on gains with this strategy. However, it also allows them to trade more conservatively.

The Advantages and Disadvantages of the Parabolic SAR Strategy

The Parabolic SAR is also known as the Parabolic Stop and Reverse indicator. It is another one of the most commonly used technical analysis indicators for finding potential reversals and gauging the strength of trends. It is also regarded as a lagging indicator.

The Parabolic SAR focuses on the price as well as functions as a useful trading tool. It features visuals signals that are very easy to understand and use. You can use it to confirm signals from indicators as well as a standalone technical analysis indicator. Just like the MACD, however, it can give you late or false signals since it is a lagging indicator.

The TD Sequential "9" Strategy

This strategy is very simply. If you choose to use it, you have to wait until the 9 buy or sell signal becomes perfect. When that happens, you can take out a short or long trade. You can use it on any type of asset and it will give you an accurate prediction.

The Advantages and Disadvantages of the TD Sequential "9" Strategy

This technical analysis indicator created by Thomas Demark, an expert on market timing, is highly popular among cryptocurrency traders. It is useful in calling the bottoms and tops of Bitcoin.

Then again, even though it is useful, it does not have a 100% accuracy. If you want to have a more accurate prediction, you are better off with a visual indicator that is based on moving averages.

Trading Bitcoins Successfully

The top two cryptocurrencies used in trading are Bitcoin and Ethereum, respectively. If you choose to go with Bitcoin, you have to use a strategy that is 15% cryptocurrency trading and 85% price action. You have to use an indicator that works for you.

Ideally, you should use the On Balance Volume indicator. In fact, most experts agree that it is the only indicator that you need. It is specifically recommended for day trading Bitcoins. It can help you analyze the overall money flow in and out of instruments. It makes use of a combination of price activity and volume. It would help you determine how much money goes in and out of the market.

The On Balance Volume indicator can be seen on many different trading platforms. It is also very easy to read. So, even if you are just a beginner trader, you will not have a hard time using it. Theoretically, if Bitcoins trade up at the same time that the On Balance Volume indicator trades down, it means that people sell into this rally. It indicates that the upside move will not be sustained for long. The same thing can be said if Bitcoins trade down at the same time that the On Balance Volume indicator trades up.

As a trader, you want to see the On Balance Volume indicator going in the same direction as the price of the Bitcoin. Keep in mind that trading indicators are not always effective. Hence, you should exercise caution when making trades.

The Rules of Bitcoin Trading

Now that you have learned about cryptocurrency trading strategies, you have to be aware of the unspoken rules of Bitcoin trading. Familiarizing yourself with the rules and following them by heart will do you good in the long run.

Rule #1: Overlay Bitcoin charts with Ethereum charts and OBV indicators.

Basically, your chart setup must consist of three windows to represent each of the three charts. Make the first chart for Bitcoin, the second one for Ethereum, and the last one for OBV indicator.

If you have read and followed the previous strategic guidelines about crypto currency trading, your chart must be similar to the figure above. This should be all for the meantime. Your next step now should focus on creating the best Bitcoin strategy.

Rule #2: Search for Smart Money Divergence between Bitcoin value and Ethereum value

Basically, you should look after and monitor the price variance between Bitcoin and Ethereum. One of the number one reasons why you would want to understand how the smart money operates is because you want to know and manage the proper timing of thins in the market.

Smart money divergence results when one cryptocurrency acts against the other cryptocurrency.

What do we mean by this?

For example, if the Ethereum price break above an important resistance or it has reached the highest peak price before it declines and Bitcoin is not able to get along with it, we will experience smart money divergence. This means that there is an inconsistency between the two crypto currencies or we must say, the other one delivers false results. With this, it is advisable to learn and understand how the crypto currency and Ethereum trading strategies work, so that we could know how to handle such occurrences.

The smart money divergence concept allows us to gain an edge in the financial market. By knowing and understanding how it works, we are able to have a better chance of success than other entities like retail investors.

One of the main reasons why the concept of smart money divergence works is for a fact the crypto currency market moves in the same direction as the trend. We have learned from a lot of sources that this particular idea is also applicable to the three main asset classes (equities or stocks, fixed income or bonds, and cash equivalents). Thus, it shall work too with the crypto currency trading strategy. Before purchasing, we must first need a confirmation from the OBV indicator. Then afterwards, we will push through with the best Bitcoin trading strategy.

Rule #3: Search for the OVB to increase in the trend's direction.

If Bitcoin lags behind the price of Ethereum, it means that Bitcoin has to follow Ethereum sooner or later. It also has to break beyond the resistance.

How can you know this? Well, the OBV is quite remarkable. This technical indicator will show you if real money buys or sells Bitcoin. As a trader, you want to see the OBV increasing in the trend's direction if Bitcoin is not breaking above the level of resistance. You also want it to go beyond its previous level when it was trading at such level of resistance.

Rule #4: Put a Buy Limit Order on the level of resistant to catch possible breakouts.

Once you get a green signal from the OBV indicator, you have to put a buy limit order. You have to put this order at the level of resistant to anticipate any possible breakout.

Rule #5: Put the SL below the breakout candle and then take profit when the OBV reaches 105,000.

You are a smart trader when you put the stop loss below the breakout candle. Also, you want to take profits when the OBV reading is above 105,000. After all, this is an extreme reading that signifies a pause in the trend.

How to Improve Your Bitcoin Day Trading

Just like all kinds of trading, bitcoin day trading comes with risks. Nevertheless, it is possible to reduce these risks. The following are some of the ways you can do to achieve this:

a. Have diverse trades. As much as possible, you have to diversify your trades by combining Ripple, Ethereum, Litecoin, and Bitcoin among other cryptocurrencies so that you can reduce the risks associated with these coins.
b. Reduce trading costs. When you open multiple positions on a daily basis, your daily return on investment will be affected. So, if you want to reduce your costs of trading, you have to go with a trustworthy exchange that does not have high fees.
c. Watch trading times. You have to consider your schedule when planning out trading times. Keep in mind that Bitcoin trades twenty-four hours per day. It is not the same as the 9 AM to 5 PM schedule of the New York Stock Exchange.
d. Follow news reports on Bitcoin. Stay updated on the latest news on cryptocurrencies. Read news on Bitcoin so that you can stay ahead. Set up notifications on your computer and phone so that you can be alerted each time there is a new development or news on the top cryptocurrencies.
e. Use stop losses. You have to set stop loss orders on your trades. You can begin with a profit ratio of 2:1.
f. Use technical analysis. There are great technical indicators that you can use. The OBV, for example, is one of them. These indicators will help you make good decisions on your trades.

At present, the world still relies mainly on fiat currency. Then again, you should never disregard the possibility that cryptocurrencies may, one day, take over the fiat money system. After all, the world continues to change and technological advancements happen on a regular basis. It is best to be prepared when this change happens in the future.

Chapter 12: Cryptocurrency Trading Mistakes to Avoid

Cryptocurrency trading is not just for anyone. It can only be done by individuals who have the knowledge, skills, and attitude for it. It is also impossible to be mastered overnight. It takes practice and perseverance to be able to succeed in this venture.

Even though cryptocurrency trading can earn you a lot of money, it can also overexpose you to digital assets. If you are not careful with your trading, you may also end up lacking balance in your portfolio. This is why you should not only focus on winning strategies. You also have to plan for failures.

The cryptocurrency market has very low entry barriers. This means that anyone who has a computer or a smartphone as well as access to the Internet can start cryptocurrency trading. Then again, as mentioned previously, cryptocurrency trading is more than just having an electronic device, an Internet connection, and starting capital.

If you want to do well with this venture, see to it that you do your research well. Learn about the successful traders who came before you, and find out what made them successful. Likewise, you have to find out about the mistakes they made and how you can avoid making them yourself.

To help you out, here are some of the cryptocurrency trading mistakes that you have to avoid:

Mistake #1: Using real money to trade instead of practicing paper trading as a beginner

Beginner traders should practice before they go out into the financial markets and trade using real money. It is not a good idea to use real money right away if you are just beginning to trade, especially when there are a lot of platforms and resources available for paper trading.

Those who want to become professional traders have to create a system that is based on simple guidelines for risk management, entries, and exits. At first, you have to do paper trading until you are ready to get out into the real financial markets and risk losing real money.

Mistake #2: Trading without any stop loss

Because beginner traders are not used to trading, they are not yet exposed to the ups and downs of the financial markets. Hence, they tend to be emotional when it comes to their trading. They tend to have a hard time accepting losses. You have to understand that traders have to possess an ability to move on and accept losses as quickly as possible. This way, they can go on to the next trade without any heaving feelings. Those who are not able to do this become more prone to losing more money. Yes, that's right. If you are not able to get over your feelings and let go of a loss quickly, you will tend to lose more money in the long run.

Thus, if you want to become a successful trader, you have to know how to regulate your emotions. You need to set a stop loss and refrain from moving it if the trade does not go in your favor. Otherwise, your behavior will become destructive and it will end up blowing your account.

Mistake #3: Not maintaining balance properly

Expert traders know how to maintain their balance properly. In fact, they have balanced portfolios that prevent them from going broke. It is actually up to you how much money you would allot for your trading.

For example, you can allot ten percent of your money in cryptocurrency trading. Within your cryptocurrency portfolio, seventy percent can be your long term holds, fifteen percent can be for trading, and another fifteen percent can be in cash. You can choose to just trade with fifteen percent of your portfolio, with this portfolio being ten percent of your total net worth.

Always consider your investment plan. See if you have outlined your target asset allocation. Rebalancing is actually the process of returning a portfolio to the target asset allocation.

A lot of traders find it difficult due to its tendency to force traders to sell their asset classes that are performing well while also forcing them to purchase more of their asset classes that are performing the worst. Such contrarian action proves to be difficult to comprehend for many beginner investors.

Mistake #4: Adding to losing trades
Do not be confused between trading and investing because they are two different things. Investors generally average down their positions in sound assets that have long time horizons.
Traders, on the other hand, have defined risk levels as well as invalidation for trades. Once their stop loss hits, such trades become invalidated and they have to move on to other assets. If you choose to become a trader, you should never average down.

Mistake #5: Not keeping a journal specifically for trading
Journaling may seem elementary, but it is actually necessary in trading. Expert traders have plans, and they write down these plans on their journals. As a trader, you have to hold yourself accountable for all your actions.
You can only do this by recording the details of your trade on a journal. You can keep a paper journal or a digital journal, although many traders prefer to write down their trades on paper because doing so allows them to understand everything much better.
Keeping a trading journal is actually the best way to avoid making the same mistakes that you have done in the past. It also allows you to learn new things by recalling your past trading styles. Make it a point to always record your emotional state, trade results, and thought process. This will greatly help you succeed at trading.

Mistake #6: Risking more than you can afford to lose
In cryptocurrency trading, people are generally drawn to the idea of making a lot of money if they are at the right place and time. Because of this belief, they tend to go all-in and risk everything they have.
Well, it is a good thing if they end up having great trades. However, this is not always the case. If you are not careful, you can end up losing a lot of money, and you cannot just

blame it on luck. You have to be accountable for your actions, so you need to make calculated risks when it comes to trading.

Mistake #7: Not having enough capital
You do not have to have a huge capital, but you should not be undercapitalized either. Remember the old saying that you need money in order to make more money. So, before you start cryptocurrency trading, see to it that you have enough funding in your account.
A lot of beginner traders think that they can make tons of money even without getting out of the couch. While cryptocurrency trading can be done at home and on your couch, this sole belief is false, unless of course you have a lot of capital to begin with. You still have to get out there and make a living so that you can support your cryptocurrency trading.
If you want to be a professional trader, you have to aim to support your whole life through trading. This means that your profits have to cover your living expenses, without putting a dent on your trading capital. Usually, this means that you have to have $50,000 to $100,000 for trading as well as a regular profit of ten percent every month.
Now, this may be quite hard to achieve if you are just a regular person. So, you really have to prepare yourself before you get into cryptocurrency trading. Beginner traders who look into rose-colored glasses often find themselves getting stressed whenever they fail to have their expectations align with their actual results.

Mistake #8: Using leverage
In cryptocurrency trading, leverage can be a double-edged sword. Hence, you should refrain from using it. Remember that it may increase your returns from a profitable trade and exacerbate your loss on a losing trade.
You should only use leverage if you are confident enough about your skills in trading. Only expert traders who have been trading cryptocurrency for years may use leverage successfully. If you are not yet experienced, using leverage

might just compound your losses rapidly and leave you without any money.

Mistake #9: Acting on trading indicators and patterns that are not very clear to you

When you first started with cryptocurrency trading, it is understandable that you are not yet good with technical analysis. You might identify chart patterns that are not existing or are wrong based on chart placement and context.

So, you have to develop a simple system for your trading as well as refrain from making decisions on indicators or patterns that you do not completely understand. You have to begin with simple resistance and support. You can also begin with clear indicators such as exponential moving averages.

Mistake #10: Going with the herd

Do not be a sheep because you are not one. You are a human being who is capable of thinking on his own. Thus, you have to refrain from merely following the herd. Otherwise, you might end up spending more money than necessary.

Expert traders are used to exiting trades once it gets too crowded. Beginner traders, on the other hand, might stay in a trade longer than necessary, even after the smart money has exited. They may also not be confident enough to be contrarian whenever necessary.

Do not be like the cryptocurrency traders who blindly follow so-called trading gurus. You should also be wary of individuals who might be manipulating you to their own advantage. Always use your common sense and rely on your own abilities.

Mistake #11: Bottom trading

Beginner traders often make the mistake of bottom trading. They monitor a cryptocurrency asset's downturn and aim to purchase at the lowest possible price. If this sounds appealing to you, you have to learn that it is not a good way to trade. If you bottom trade, you can lose all your investments.

Mistake #12: Hodling

Just like bottom trading, you can lose your investments from hodling. Hodling is basically hoarding. It refers to keeping digital assets instead of actively trading them. If you hold onto your cryptocurrencies for far longer than necessary, you can lose money.

Mistake #13: Relying on gut instinct alone
It is not bad to trust your instincts. However, you should not rely on your instincts alone, especially when trading cryptocurrencies. As you know, the price of cryptocurrencies is highly volatile. One minute it can be low, the next minute it can be high. You just can never be too sure about its price. This is why you have to be careful when making trades. Take note that trades can collapse and yield major losses all of a sudden. You need to master your emotions just like fiat brokers. Use logic rather than feeling.

Mistake #14: Trading worthless cryptocurrencies
Bitcoin is the most popular of all cryptocurrencies. Many years ago, it was actually the only cryptocurrency. Today, however, there are more than three thousand known cryptocurrencies. Then again, a lot of these alternative cryptocurrencies or altcoins, as they are more commonly known, do not have much worth. So, you have to do your research well and avoid investing in cryptocurrencies that are not valuable.

Mistake #15: Not having security
Since cryptocurrencies are digital, they are prone to getting hacked. Virtual money, unlike fiat money, cannot be locked up in vaults. So, you should be careful with the exchanges that you use. You should never allow your cryptocurrencies to stay on an exchange if you are not trading actively.
Keep in mind that a lot of exchanges are prone to hacking. In fact, more than one and a half billion cryptocurrencies have been lost due to hacking. This left a lot of traders devastated.

Mistake #16: Anthropomorphizing the market
Keep in mind that the financial markets do not have an agency. You have to understand them well so that you can trade

cryptocurrencies effectively. The market is actually the sum of every economic transaction. It is not a monolithic entity that competes with you. Thus, you have to refrain from anthropomorphizing or personifying it.

Mistake #17: Not diversifying

There is a saying that you should never put all your eggs in a single basket. This saying can be applied to cryptocurrency trading. The concept of diversification has actually been around for centuries. It is true that if you bet everything, you may also lose everything.

So, you have to diversify even if you think you have found a sure thing. It will not hurt you to diversify and have more variety. With diversification, you will be able to keep some money instead of losing it all on a trade.

Mistake #18: Relying on chance instead of skill

Trading is not like playing the lottery. With trading, you can actually increase your odds at winning if you have a good plan and you stick to it. With the lottery, there is nothing you can do except choose a combination of numbers and wait for the results to be released.

If you want to be successful at trading, you have to be knowledgeable and well-read. You should also be updated with the latest trends and news on cryptocurrencies. You should never rely on good luck alone. Expert traders may seem to be lucky, but they actually spent tons of hours researching and practicing.

Mistake #19: Believing other people easily

Simply put, you should not believe just about anyone about just about anything. This is especially true with cryptocurrency trading. Throughout your trading career, you will encounter people who will claim to be experts or gurus.

These people will try to make you watch their webinars or buy something they are selling. They will try to force their beliefs on you. You should not give in to the pressure. Instead, you have to believe in your own self. After all, you are the cryptocurrency trader.

Mistake #20: Panic selling

Traders are a special kind of people because they have iron stomachs. They are able to deal with the financial markets, which are hard to predict. As a beginner trader, you have to refrain from making the mistake of panic selling. You should resist the urge to sell even when things seem to be rough. You need to develop an iron stomach so that you can be like expert traders.

At times, it would be more sensible to cut losses. Then again, remember that they are not losses until you sell. Your investment may go up again if you merely hold onto it. As a trader, you should not merely aim to sell low and buy high. Doing so will just make you lose money. You have to be wise enough to avoid making mistakes. Do not panic easily. Use your logic and reasoning skills.

Mistake #21: Not knowing how to keep the money and then make some more

If you do not know what you have to do after making some money, you will have a tendency to lose what you have. This is why you have to practice staggered selling. You should not hold on too long that you begin to lose money. You should not sell everything at once either. It will only make you miss out on the largest boom. Practicing staggered selling will allow you to make money while possibly making even more.

Mistake #22: Committing the sunk cost fallacy

The sunk cost fallacy is about staying involved in something just because there are a lot of resources invested in it. It does not really matter how major these resources are. You should not risk losing money just because you care too much about the labor, time, emotions, or money that you have already invested.

Mistake #23: Being envious

As you know, being emotional while trading is not a good thing. Even worse, being envious of other people's success will only prevent you from being successful yourself. You have to learn how to appreciate what you have and to always see the bright side. Keep in mind that whenever someone else wins, you win as well. You become a winner when you are able to learn something from such win.

Chapter 13: The Risk to Reward Ratio

As a trader, it is fundamental that you understand the concept of risk. This will give you the foundation for your investment decisions and trading activities. It will also help you grow and protect your trading account.
Aside from risk management, setting stop-loss, and position sizing, you also have to know how much risk you are taking in relation to your potential reward. You have to know how this potential upside compares to the potential downside.
Essentially, you have to know about your risk to reward ratio.

What Is the Risk to Reward Ratio?
The risk to reward ratio calculates the risk a trader takes for a possible reward. Basically, it shows the potential rewards for every one dollar you risk on an investment.
It is easy to calculate the risk to reward ratio. Simply, divide the maximum risk by the net target profit. You can do this by looking at where you want to enter the trade. Next, you have to decide where you want to take the profits in case the trade becomes successful. You also have to decide where you want to put the stop-loss in case the trade is a losing one.
You need to calculate your risk to reward ratio if you wish to properly manage your risk. Expert traders set stop-losses and profit targets before they enter a trade. Once you have both your exit and entry targets, you can start calculating your risk to reward ratio. Just divide the potential risk by the potential reward. Take note that the lower the ratio, the more potential reward you can get for every unit of risk.
To help you understand the concept of risk to reward ratio further, let us consider the following example:
Say, you wish to enter a long position with Bitcoin. You have to perform an analysis and state that your take profit order would be fifteen percent from the entry price. Likewise, you have to find out where your trade idea is invalidated. This is where you have to set the stop-loss based on your market analysis. You will find technical analysis indicators to be greatly helpful throughout your trading career.

If your profit target is fifteen percent and your potential loss is five percent, your risk to reward ratio becomes 0.33 or 1:3 or 5/15. This simply means that for every unit of risk, you are potentially gaining three times the reward. So, for every dollar of risk that you take, you become liable to gain three. If you have a position that costs $100, you become at risk of losing $5 to have a potential profit of $15.

You can move your stop loss closer to your entry to reduce the ratio. Then again, the exit and entry points should not be calculated depending on numbers that are arbitrary. Instead, they have to be calculated depending on your analysis. It may not be worth trying to game the numbers if your trade setup has a high risk to reward ratio. It may be much better to move on and search for another setup that has a better risk to reward ratio.

Keep in mind that positions with varying sizing may have the same risk to reward ratio. Say, if you have a position that costs $10,000, you can risk losing $500 for the possibility of earning a $1,500 profit. This gives you the risk to reward ratio of 1:3. Such ratio only changes when you change the relative position of your stop-loss and target.

In addition, you should take note that a lot of those who perform reverse calculations choose to calculate the reward to risk ratio. Why do they do this? Well, it is merely a matter of choice. Some traders find reverse calculation easier. After all, it is simply the opposite of the risk to reward ratio formula. So, if you use reverse calculation for our example above, you will get a reward to risk ratio of 3 or 15/5. As you can see, a high reward to risk ratio is much better than a low reward to risk ratio.

Risk versus Reward

Imagine that you are in a zoo and you make a bet. Your friend says he will give you one Bitcoin if you approach a parrot and feed it from your hands. As you know, this kind of behavior is not allowed in zoos. So, there is a potential risk involved in this situation. If you get caught feeding the animals, you will be in trouble. Then again, if you do not get caught, you will get one Bitcoin.

Now, let us move on to another scenario. This time, your friend proposes an alternative. He will give you 1.1 Bitcoin if you go near a tiger and give it raw meat using your bare hands. Again, there is a potential risk involved in this situation. In fact, the risk is greater than that of our previous example. If you get caught feeding the tiger, you will be in trouble with the zoo authorities. Furthermore, if the tiger attacks you while you feed it, you might lose your hand or even your life. Then again, if none of these two happens, you will get 1.1 Bitcoin, and this is a better reward than the previous one, which is just one Bitcoin.

So, which of these deals sounds like the better one? Well, both deals are actually bad because they will put you in trouble. Nonetheless, you take on much more risk if you choose the alternative bet, which involves feeding a tiger. Getting in trouble and risking your life is not worth the 1.1 Bitcoin of potential reward. After all, your life is precious. Likewise, a lot of traders will search for trade setups in which they can gain more than they can lose. This is what they referred to as an asymmetric opportunity. It states that the possible upside is better than the possible downside.

In addition, you have to take note of your win rate, which refers to the number of winning trades divided by the number of losing trades. For instance, if you have a sixty percent winning rate, you can earn a profit of sixty percent of your trades. Having this kind of information can help you manage your risks.

Then again, there are traders who can make massive profits from very low winning rates. They are able to do this when the risk to reward ratio on their trade setups are able to accommodate it.

Otherwise, if they merely take setups with a risk to reward ratio of 1:10, they can lose nine trades simultaneously and break-even in a single trade. When this happens, they will only need to win two out of ten trades in order to gain a profit. This shows how the calculation of risk versus reward can benefit you greatly.

Chapter 14: The Best Software for Cryptocurrency Trading

The traders of today are very fortunate because they have a wide array of options to choose from when it comes to trading tools and equipment. They can easily purchase a software program or cryptocurrency trading platform that they can use to improve their trading.

These cryptocurrency trading software, or bots as they are more commonly known, can help you buy and sell cryptocurrency at the right time. Their main objective is to help users increase their revenue while reducing their risks and losses.

Such applications will allow you to manage your cryptocurrency exchange accounts all at the same time. In fact, you can keep them in just one place for ease of access. You can use these software programs to trade Bitcoin, Ethereum, and Litecoin among other digital currencies.

A Guide to Cryptocurrency Trading Bots

Cryptocurrency trading bots are basically automated software programs that allow traders to buy and sell cryptocurrencies with ease and convenience. It helps them make trades during the best possible times so that they can gain maximum profits. The primary goal of these trading bots is to reduce risks and losses while increasing revenue. They enable traders to manage their cryptocurrency exchange accounts in a single place so that they can avoid the hassles of trading.

Trading bots, if executed properly, can perform a variety of functions such as portfolio management, data collection, smart order routing, and rebalancing among others. Then again, there are certain aspects that you have to improve with them.

For instance, repetitive tasks entail a lot of effort and time. An automated cryptocurrency trading bot can help you copy and paste specific tasks so that you can trade without any hassle. Even better, it can help you with periodic rebalances.

If you have to perform such rebalances on an hourly basis, you should either set an alarm for every hour or create a program that would make the trading bot rebalance your portfolio each hour.

Timing is another aspect that you have to consider. As you know, successful trading requires accuracy. You need to place your trades at the right time in order for you to earn a profit.

Your trading bot can help you monitor the market carefully so that you can observe the prices and sell your cryptocurrencies at the right moment. Likewise, you will be able to execute trades at the right time.

Furthermore, all exchange pairs have to be determined carefully as per their trading price and asset quantity. The whole route has to be completed within a certain timeframe as well as market condition. A good trading bot will allow you to automated complex strategies easily and quickly.

How to Choose a Good Cryptocurrency Trading Bot

As you know, there are a variety of cryptocurrency trading software or bots available on the market. Each and every one of them has its own unique features that can help traders improve their trading and earning potential. So, how can you know which trading software or bot to choose?

Well, the following are some of the characteristics that you have to look for in a cryptocurrency trading software or bot:

   a. Free Trial

A lot of trading software or bots are available for free. The ones that come with a price, however, should still offer a free trial version. This way, traders who wish to explore their features will be able to do so. It is always a good idea to experience first-hand what a cryptocurrency trading bot can do before actually buying it.

   b. Backtesting

Cryptocurrency bots that feature backtesting are useful when test trading strategies against historical data. They enable traders to see how their strategies perform under the different conditions of the market.

c. Social Trading

Ideally, you have to learn how to create your own strategies for trading. Nevertheless, it would not hurt to take after the strategies of other successful traders. Having a trading tool that allows for the creation of effective strategies is certainly handy.

d. Indices

A lot of trading bots offer portfolio automation. It is crucial to find out how they create indices. Keep in mind that good trading tools offer information on how the market cap gets weighted in the index as well as which coins are sampled.

e. Server Based or Cloud Based

At present, nearly everything can be stored on the cloud. The files on your smartphone and computer can be backed up to the cloud. The same thing goes with cryptocurrency bots. Modern cryptocurrency bots are usually cloud based. This makes storing and accessing data easy, fast, and convenient. It also ensures that vital information are backed up and safe in case the device gets lost, stolen, or damaged. It is not advisable for traders to use trading tools that require computers or servers to run at all times.

f. Trading Communities

It is nice to be able to compare your trading tools with other traders. More often than not, traders use platforms such as Discord, Reddit, and Telegram to discuss strategies and make trading comparisons.

g. Support and Tutorials

A lot of cryptocurrency traders have created blogs, videos, and modules that aim to help other people learn about trading. If you are a beginner trader, you can use these resources to have a better understanding of concepts, styles, terms, etc. Being able to access tutorials as well as contact customer support is highly beneficial.

h. Cryptocurrency Tax Software Integrations

When you use cryptocurrency bots to trade, it becomes easier for you to earn profits and minimize losses. Likewise, it becomes more convenient to create tax reports. It is essential to consider the cryptocurrency tax software companies that go well with your preferred trading platform.

Here are additional factors that you have to consider when choosing cryptocurrency trading bot software:

i. Team Credibility

Since you are going to entrust your trading portfolio to a cryptocurrency trading bot, you need to make sure that the team behind it is credible and qualified. You can verify their credibility by going through the following checklist:

- Find out about the expertise level of your team members. This would allow you to determine if they truly qualify or not.
- Find out whether they have a good portfolio
- Find out if the bot functionality is documented properly
- Acquire information on how the team raises funding

See to it that the team stays transparent with regard to their development so that they can be held responsible for their actions.

j. Use of Strategy

You have to find out if your trading bot uses the right strategy. Check out the official website and look at the reviews other people have made. Make sure that you also look over the guidelines as well as find out how the trading bot can be configured.

It is alright to have an average know-how on technology, but if you do not think that you are tech savvy enough for a trading bot, then you probably should not get one until you are ready.

k. Strong Team Support

You have to determine how much support the development team is willing to offer. You can do this by following this checklist:

- See if the organization has an active online community.
- Find out if the development team actively communicates with such online community.

- See to it that the developers provide solutions to bugs and other issues on a timely manner.

l. Costs Involved

You need to find out how expensive the cryptocurrency bot is before you get it. Knowing about the costs involved can help you save money and time. You may also want to know if free services are offered, such as a free trial version.

m. Possibility of Adjustment

Find out if it is possible to adjust the cryptocurrency trading bot according to the conditions of the financial markets. Usually, cryptocurrency trading bots perform trading strategies using their own approach. As a trader, you want to see if your bot can adjust well in the changing market conditions.

n. Ease of Use

Of course, ease of use and convenience are excellent qualities to look for in a cryptocurrency trading bot. If you are new to cryptocurrency trading, you may want to consider the following:

- Check for functionality. Your cryptocurrency trading bot should have a user-friendly interface with detailed analytics. This way, you will be able to set up loss targets and profits as you customize trading strategies.
- Find out if there are a variety of tools available. You should be able to use tools that would allow you to analyze, backtest, and create portfolios. You may also choose a trading bot that will let you copy the strategies of successful traders.
- Find out if the cryptocurrency trading bot allows users to establish the prices at which traders have to sell to stop losses or earn a profit.
- See if the cryptocurrency trading bot offers a mobile application that you can download and install on your smartphone. This way, you will be able to trade at any time and from any place.

The Benefits and Drawbacks of Using a Cryptocurrency Trading Bot or Software
Just like any other tool, a cryptocurrency trading bot or software has its own benefits and drawbacks. Of course, such benefits and drawbacks will also depend on the make and model of the bot. Nevertheless, the following are some of the most common benefits and drawbacks traders tend to experience when using cryptocurrency trading bots or software:

The Benefits
      a. Efficiency
Cryptocurrency trading bots have the ability to analyze market conditions and make accurate predictions based on the current state of the financial market.
If you are not that great at multitasking, using a cryptocurrency trading bot can prove to be beneficial for you. It will help you become more efficient at making trades.
      b. Increased Speed
Cryptocurrency trading bots help traders place orders quickly. This makes them more effective and reliable than humans when it comes to placing orders in a timely manner. As you know, delay in trades can result in the loss of value of a cryptocurrency.
      c. Running Period
Unless you do not have a social life or other better things to do than trade cryptocurrencies, being able to get away from the computer screen once in a while is such a wonderful thing. With a cryptocurrency trading bot, you do not have to stay glued on your computer or smartphone for twenty-four hours a day, seven days per week. The bot will take care of the trading for you so that you will not miss out on any opportunities even if you are away from your computer.

The Drawbacks
      a. Not Applicable for Everyone
Cryptocurrency trading bots require the right knowledge and skills. So, if you are a beginner trader who does not have

enough knowledge and experience, you may not be able to maximize your cryptocurrency trading bot.

Likewise, if you are not adept at using even the most basic technology, a cryptocurrency trading bot may not be useful for you. You need to know how to properly configure and use these tools in order to maximize your profits and minimize your losses.

Not knowing how to operate a cryptocurrency trading bot will not just waste your money on its purchase, but you may also lose money during trades. See to it that you are truly ready to use a cryptocurrency trading bot before you even consider getting one.

b. Requires Monitoring

In times of high volatility, a cryptocurrency trading bot may not be the most useful tool for a trader like you. These tools are not attached to money. So, they may only lead to massive losses if not monitored appropriately.

c. Security Concerns

Of course, just like any other thing that is connected to the Internet, cryptocurrency trading bots are susceptible to attacks by hackers. If you are not careful and responsible, you may expose yourself to risks such as theft and phishing. You need to be extra careful when you trade cryptocurrencies.

Are Cryptocurrency Trading Bots Legal and Profitable?

Yes, cryptocurrency trading bots are legal but their profitability does not really have a guarantee. After all, cryptocurrency trading bots are merely software programs. Just like any other software program out there, it will help the user attain success but such success will still ultimately depend on the user's knowledge, skills, and attitude.

In addition, trading bots and automated platforms come with a lot of risks. You also have to remember that trading bots may be beneficial for traders but not for investors and individuals who have just started trading cryptocurrencies.

The Different Types of Trading Bots for Cryptocurrencies

The following are the different types of trading bots that you have to familiarize yourself with if you hope to do well in cryptocurrency trading. Gaining enough knowledge about them will help you make a decision with regard to which type to choose.

d. Arbitrage
Its strategy involves purchasing coins on an exchange and then selling it on another simultaneously. You have to use this strategy if you want to make safe and quick profits.

e. Market Making
Through market making, you can prevent huge swings in prices. It usually involves making buy and sell limit orders close to the present market price. A lot of market making bot traders are connected with their trading project.

f. Momentum Trading
It is also commonly referred to as trend following system. It is recommended for riding positive momentum waves with assets as well as selling them when the momentum of the market reverses. In general, the cost of assets increases beyond the average before going out of momentum and falling down. When this happens, it is necessary to buy and sell.

g. Mean Reversion
It is a type of cryptocurrency trading bot wherein strategies are created on the assumption that if the price of a cryptocurrency differs from the average, it can be reverted back to such average.

h. Copy Trading
It allows traders to automatically copy trades. Usually, it involves a social community and a leaderboard. A lot of cryptocurrency trading bots also allow traders to copy others with just a click of the mouse.

Cryptocurrency Bot Trading and Filing Taxes
You may file taxes for cryptocurrency trading simply by importing trades from an exchange to your tax software. Ideally, you have to know how many trades the trading bot would make. Take note that those that have a high frequency can make multiple trades in a day. This can yield to thousands of transactions. Then again, many of these tools may handle trading on the cryptocurrency tax plan.

Creating Your Own Cryptocurrency Trading Bot
It is possible to create your own cryptocurrency trading bot.
You just have to perform the following steps:

d. Backtesting

Before you even start to trade, you have to backtest your
trading bots against the historical data of the market. See to it
that you backtest as realistically as you can. You can consider
slippage, trading fees, and latency. Do not forget to access
the exchange APIs key to collect high quality data from the
market.

e. Strategy Implementation

In this step, you need to specify calculations that would allow
your bot to determine what and when to trade. When you are
finished creating your strategy, you have to backtest to find
out how it performs.

f. Execution

At this stage, logic may be converted into an API key request
that the cryptocurrency exchange can comprehend. A lot of
bots enable their users to simulate strategies using fake
money.

g. Job Scheduler

Finally, you can automate the whole process by setting up
your job scheduler and executing your trading strategy.

More Cryptocurrency Trading Tips
1. Make the access of your cryptocurrency trading bot limited
to merely writing on selling orders on the exchange. It should
not be able to withdraw your money or have any unauthorized
API access.
2. Have an added layer of security by limiting the IP
addresses of your cryptocurrency trading bot.
3. See to it that you have ample balance on the
cryptocurrency exchanges that you trade on.
4. Choose to deal with reputable cryptocurrency exchanges
that have already been proven to offer excellent security
features. Surely, you do not want the exchange you are using
to be hacked.

5. Keep in mind that cryptocurrency bots do not print money. So, you still have to tweak it constantly so that it will remain in sync with the financial markets.
6. Download and install the mobile application version of your cryptocurrency trading bot. This way, you will be able to monitor your signals and trades even while on the go.

The Best Cryptocurrency Trading Bots and Software Available Today
If you are new to cryptocurrency trading and are wondering which trading software or bots to use, here are some of the best ones available on the market today, in no particular order:

a. Pionex
If you are in search of good yet free trading software, then you have to seriously consider this one. Pionex is actually among the first exchanges to have twelve free trading bots in the world. Its license is also approved by the United States FinCEN Money Services Business (MSB).
You can use it to automate your trading twenty-four hours a day, seven days a week, without having to keep checking on the financial markets. It is also one of the largest Binance brokers, and it aggregates liquidity from Huobi Global and Binance.
Even better, it has notable features that you will surely find handy. Aside from the free trading bots that retail investors like, it also has a very low trading fee. With only 0.05% trading fee for the taker and the maker, it is actually the lowest, considering that major exchanges tend to have high trading fees.
The Leveraged Grid Bot offers up to five times leverage while the Grid Trading Bot lets users sell high and buy low at a specific price range. The Spot-Futures Arbitrage Bot allows retail investors to earn a passive income at a lower risk while the Smart Trade Terminal lets traders set up stop-loss and take profit in a single trade.

b. Cryptohopper

This one is another good yet free cryptocurrency trading bot. It can help you manage all your cryptocurrency exchange accounts and keep them in one place. It will also let you trade Bitcoin, Ethereum, and Litecoin among others.

One of the best things about this trading bot is that it allows users to create their own technical analysis. It also provides templates as well as real time performance reports. You can quickly find strategies and you will not have a hard time using this trading bot because it has a user-friendly interface. So, even if you are not tech savvy, you will be able to get around with ease.

In addition, Cryptohopper has Android and iOS applications. It also features algorithms that support RSI, EMA, and BB among other signals and indicators. What's more, you can rest assured that your account will stay protected by secure protocols and your data will be kept private.

c. Trality

This platform is for users who wish to profit from algorithmic cryptocurrency trading without having to give up their day job. It has high quality tools that can help you create creative and intricate algorithms within a community-driven and educational infrastructure that also promotes development and learning for traders.

The most notable features of Trality include pre-defined and curated strategies, a blazing-fast backtesting module, and a cloud-based live-trading in which algorithms can run for twenty-four hours per day, seven days per week. This will help you monitor your trades and never miss one.

For beginners, they can take advantage of drag and drop graphical interface. For advanced traders who are into Python programming, they can take advantage of the in-browser code editor. Trality is available for free. Its exchanges include Kraken, Binance, Bitpanda, and Coinbase Pro.

d. Quadency

It is an application for managing digital assets. It provides automated trading solutions for retail traders and institutional traders. It also streamlines the process of cryptocurrency investing.

With Quadency, you can easily customize bots. It actually has a variety of trading bots that you can customize according to your preferences. It also has reliable customer support. So, each time you need assistance or guidance, you can simply contact them.

What's more, this application offers an advanced TradingView charting as well as various automated tools. It supports automated trading, and it allows traders to trade on Kucoin, Bittrex, and Binance among other exchanges. It is also available for free, so you do not have to spend extra on this software.

e. 3Commas

For only $14.50, you can gain access to 3Commas, which is among the best cryptocurrency trading bots that allow users to reduce their risks and losses as well as increase their revenue. This application will help you earn huge profits with little effort. It will also help you create good strategies based on its numerous trading indicators.

With this platform, you can buy and sell coins in just one window. You can also trade for twenty-four hours daily. You can even copy the settings of other bots as well as balance your portfolio by maintaining coin ratio.

In addition, it allows you to receive deal notifications on your email, phone, and browser. It is actually available for both Android and iOS. It supports dollar cost averaging, custom TradingView Signal, signals, and backtesting among others.

f. Bitsgap

It is among the best most recommended trading bots for managing cryptocurrency assets. It allows users to analyze over ten thousand cryptocurrency pairs as well as detect coins with the shortest potential. In addition, it allows traders to create their own strategies with ease and convenience.

For $19 per month, you can view your trading on a chart and test settings prior to investing. You can also access this trading software even without downloading it. It is fully automated and works for twenty-four hours per day, seven days per week. It keeps funds on the exchange balance for security purposes. It will also help you maximize your earning potential.

g. Zignaly

This trading platform is free and available for twenty-four hours per day, seven days per week. It has an integrated mining Hamster, which is a cryptocurrency market monitoring service. It also has cryptocurrency quality signals that can greatly help you with trading.

You can use Zignaly for any installation. It will store your coins on the exchange and let you split profit targets. It will also let you check results for every position. Moreover, it will you trade on KuCoin and Binance.

h. Shrimpy

It is a social trading platform specifically created for cryptocurrency. It features automated trading strategies that can help you reduce your risks and improve your performance. It can also help you create effective portfolio strategies, monitor the financial markets, and track your performance. Even better, it is free of charge. So, it is highly recommended to beginner traders who are tight on the budget. It has a securely encrypted API key that is stored using the Federal Information Processing Standards (FIPS) 140-2.

It features a dashboard that shows statistics pertaining to the performance metrics and assets of a portfolio. It will help you simplify portfolio management as well as let you view the live market price.

i. Coinrule

This automated trading platform allows trades to trade via Kraken, Binance, and Coinbase Pro among other exchanges. It offers more than a hundred and thirty templates for creating trading strategies.

It also has real-time customer support, so you can easily acquire information or receive assistance whenever necessary. It will also let you test rule performances on previous data as well as set customized trading rules. In addition, its market indicators will let you allocate funds easily. With Coinrule, you do not have to worry about monthly payments since it is available for free. You can use it for twenty-four hours per day, seven days per week. It also offers military grade encryption, so you can rest assured that your trading will be safe and secure.

j.   Trade Santa

It is another free yet good trading software. This cryptocurrency trading bot will allow you to manage risks with ease. It will let you select which strategies go well with your trading style. This way, you can easily set target profit amounts and close deals at the right time.

With Trade Santa, you can use long and short strategies. You can create your own strategies using their pre-set templates. You can also sell or buy large volumes of cryptocurrencies without any hassle. You can even track your trades in real time.

If you ever need any help, you can contact their customer service for a quick assistance. Customer support is available for twenty-four hours per day, seven days per week. Trade Santa can be used to trade on Huobi, Upbit, HitBTC, Binance, Bittrex, and Bitfinex.

k. Profit Trailer

This trading platform costs $36.46. It allows traders to trade cryptocurrencies with ease. It has an intuitive dashboard that will show you a complete overview of your trading. It will also allow you to customize your strategies when purchasing cryptocurrencies.

With Profit Trailer, you can buy and sell multiple cryptocurrencies. You can rest assured that your liquidity will be protected. You will also be able to view possible trades as well as see your sales with ease. You can use this software to trade on Bittrex, Binance, KuCoin, Bybit, Coinbase, BitMEX, and Huobi among others.

l.   NapBots

It is a cloud-based system that allows traders to use automated trading bots. This way, they can easily buy and sell orders that are automatically executed. It is compatible with a variety of exchanges, such as Binance, Bitmex, and Okex among others.

For $8.51, you can have a safe trading environment with more than fifteen trading strategies. You will be able to manage your savings easily, use your mobile phone to track the output of your investments, and use the API key to keep your money safe.

m. Kryll.io

It is an excellent trading bot that allows traders to develop good strategies even if they are not skilled. It directly connects to the exchanges even without an API approval right. It can also be used on smartphones and tablets, so you can trade at any time and at any place.

With this trading bot, you can do as many backtests as you want. You can quickly and easily set up your trading strategy as well as perform technical analyses. You might also like the drag and drop editor as well as the 24/7 availability of this trading bot. What's more, it is available for free. So, you do not have to worry about additional charges.

n. Mudrex

It is an excellent trading bot that allows traders to create strategies with ease and convenience. It also allows traders to figure out their bad and good investments as well as allow them to choose between the risks and rewards that suit their needs.

Mudrex can be acquired for free. You can use it to trade on Binance, Bybit, Deribit, Coinbase Pro, and OKEX BitMEX. It has an intuitive interface as well as historical data for testing strategy. It can help you maximize your return on investment.

o. Haasonline

This trading platform will let you trade on more than sixteen bots. You can take advantage of the numerous technical indicators, safeties, and insurances, which you can also use to develop complex trading strategies.

This trading platform offers script bots that are programmable and written in C3. It also offers a tutorial for traders so that they can understand the platform better. Plus, it has a dashboard that you can customize. You can also use it to integrate backtesting with Discord and Telegram application.

p. HodlBot

For $3 per month, you can easily create your own custom portfolio with over three hundred and fifty coins using this Bitcoin trading software. It has a user-friendly interface that you will surely find easy to comprehend.

This Binance trading bot actually encrypts data with the use of SHA 256. It allows traders to rebalance their portfolio and to perform marketing indexing with more convenience. It also protects API keys from individuals who do not have authorized access as well as automatically keeps the traders' portfolios on track.

q. Gunbot

This trading bot is customizable and easy to use. It supports more than one hundred exchanges. It also allows traders to customize their trading strategies and develop unlimited bot instances.

You can count on Gunbot to support automated trading and produce consistent results. It provides free updates without the need for a subscription. It also allows traders to generate profits by executing their trading strategies.

You can use this trading bot on Binance, Coinex, Kraken, Bitmex, KuCoin, Coinbase Pro, OK Coin, Huobi Global, and Bitstamp among other cryptocurrency trading exchanges.

Chapter 15: The Best Exchanges for Cryptocurrency Trading

When you first started trading cryptocurrencies, you might be intimidated. You might also be disheartened whenever you see news on failed strategies and scams. Then again, just like any other venture, cryptocurrency trading has its own ups and downs. If you are really determined to succeed at cryptocurrency trading, you should do your best.
This includes doing ample research and learning as much as you can about trading strategies. You also have to stay updated on the most recent trends and news. What's more, you have to keep up with the advancements in technology. After all, technology evolves rapidly.
Anyway, one of the biggest concerns when purchasing and trading cryptocurrencies like Bitcoin is with regard to security and safety. Whether you plan to buy and hold long term, are interested in privacy or anonymity, prefer ease of use, or want to trade more often, you have to consider the best exchanges for cryptocurrency trading.

The Different Types of Cryptocurrency Exchanges
Before you can select the best cryptocurrency exchange for your trading needs, you have to completely understand the different types available. These are the following:

Centralized Exchange
This type of cryptocurrency exchange includes Binance, Gemini, Coinbase, and Kraken, which are private companies that allow traders to engage in cryptocurrency trading. Such exchanges require identification and registration or what is more commonly referred to as the Know Your Client or Know Your Customer rule.
In addition, these exchanges have high volumes, liquidity, and active trading. Then again, centralized exchanges are actually not in line with Bitcoin philosophy. They have their own private servers that create an attack vector. If these servers are compromised, the entire system may be closed for a certain

period of time. Even worse, the sensitive information of users may be released.

For most beginners, the more popular and bigger centralized exchanges are the easiest on-ramp. They also offer an insurance level in case their systems fail. Even though this is true, if the cryptocurrency is bought on one of these exchanges, it does not get stored in your digital wallet. Instead, it is moved to their custodial wallets. This happens even if you have the keys to your wallet.

Such insurance is also applicable only if the exchanges were at fault. So, if your account and your computer get compromised or hacked, then you will not be able to benefit from the insurance. Your funds will be lost and it will be all your responsibility. This is why, you have to withdraw your money if it reaches a large sum. You also have to store your digital money properly.

Decentralized Exchange

This type of cryptocurrency exchange works in the same way as Bitcoin. It does not have any central point of control. You can consider it as akin to a server, except that every computer within this server is spread out all over the world.

Each and every one of these computers is also controlled by a specific person. So, if one of them is turned off, the entire network will not be affected. After all, there are still a lot of other computers that continue to run the network.

This setup is vastly different from one in which a company controls a server in just one location. It is much more difficult to attack something that is decentralized and spread out in this manner. Hence, such attacks are not likely to be realistic and successful.

Because of such decentralization, these exchanges are not subject to the rules of a regulatory body. No specific group or individual runs the systems. Those who even decide to participate merely come and go.

Hence, the regulatory body or government cannot realistically go after a particular group or individual. Those who trade on the platform are not required to state their identification. They are also free to trade whenever and however they want.

The Best Exchanges for Cryptocurrency Trading
Now that you have already learned so much about cryptocurrency and cryptocurrency trading, you are probably wondering which exchanges are best. The following are some of the most recommended exchanges by cryptocurrency traders. They are considered to be safe, secure, high in quality, and user-friendly.

Coinbase and Coinbase Pro
Coinbase is the most popular cryptocurrency exchange in the United States. It is a good buy for under $3. It is licensed and completely regulated. In fact, it is licensed to operate in more than forty states in the country.
Its advantages include high liquidity, user-friendly interface, and many different altcoin choices. Its disadvantages include the lack of control in wallet keys, high fees associated when not using the Pro version, and fewer trading options for altcoins as compared to other cryptocurrency exchanges. Coinbase is very easy to use, making it ideal for traders who wish to enter the financial markets but do not have a lot of funding or experience. It even has insured custodial wallets that traders and investors can use to keep their investments. Then again, Coinbase retains the ownership to the private keys. So, you cannot own the keys that you use.
If you think that you are ready to move on from the standard Coinbase version, you can go with Coinbase Pro. It offers more choices in terms of indicators and charts. It is ideal for traders who want to trade on a more advanced yet still easy to use exchange.

Cash App
It is considered to be the best trading exchange for beginner traders. It is actually a peer-to-peer currency transfer system that allows users to shop online, pay rent, and even split grocery bills. It is very convenient, even allowing users to have a debit card and use it as a bank account.
It charges a service fee, however, for every transaction. Likewise, it charges a fee that is based on price volatility.

Such fees change depending on the activity of the market. You can use it to withdraw Bitcoin, but not any other cryptocurrency. Unfortunately, it only caters to Bitcoins. Also, you can only withdraw up to $5,000 Bitcoins every seven days and $2,000 Bitcoins every twenty-four hours. It also charges three percent for money transfer via linked credit cards.

Binance
This exchange is considered to be the best option for altcoin traders. Its fees are 0.1% for the side of the maker and 0.1% for the side of the taker. So, for both sides, this goes down to 0.02% trade volume. The fees can be lowered by 25% using BNB, the native cryptocurrency of Binance.
With this trading platform, you can choose from more than one hundred trading pairs between various cryptocurrencies. What's more, you can choose from fiat and cryptocurrency pairs as well.
The great thing about this exchange is that it has an advanced charting, low fees, and a wide array of trading pairs.   Then again, this exchange is also more ideal for experienced traders. It also does not support certain states, such as New York.
Nevertheless, Binance can be a good choice if you want to invest or trade in less popular altcoins. It is also ideal if you prefer to use a more advanced charting as compared to that of other exchanges.

Bisq
It is regarded as the most ideal decentralized exchange. Its trading fees can be paid using its own cryptocurrency, which is BSQ, or Bitcoin. If you choose to pay via Bitcoin, 0.70% will be incurred on the side of the taker and 0.10% will be incurred on the side of the maker. If you choose to pay via BSQ, 0.35% will be incurred on the side of the taker and 0.05% will be incurred on the side of the maker.
Some of the benefits of using this exchange include mobile applications for both iOS and Android, thirty different payment options, and a non-KYC (Know Your Customer),

decentralized platform. Conversely, some of the drawbacks of using this exchange include slow transaction speeds and low trading volumes. It is also not made for active trading.

Conclusion

Thank you again for downloading this book!
I hope this book was able to help you learn about cryptocurrencies and cryptocurrency trading. I hope that you were able to learn everything you need to learn as a beginner and that you were able to finally begin trading in the cryptocurrency markets.
2021 is indeed a great year for cryptocurrency trading and investments. In fact, the best time to start cryptocurrency trading is now. Technology continues to advance and the world continues to evolve. So, you should take advantage of the things that you have learned from this book and begin your journey towards a trading career.
The next step is to apply what you have learned from this book. Make sure that you also share your newfound knowledge with the people you care about.
Finally, if you enjoyed this book, please take the time to share your thoughts and post a review.   It'd be greatly appreciated!
Thank you!

Day Trading Beginner Guide + Options:

Trading Strategies to Make Money Online in Cryptocurrency, Forex,Penny Market, Stocks and Futures.Learn Trading Psychology,Money Management & Discipline Tactics.

Table Of Contents

© Copyright 2021 by Ryan Martinez - All rights reserved.
The content contained within this book may not be reproduced,
duplicated or transmitted without direct written permission
from the author or the publisher.
Under no circumstances will any blame or legal responsibility
be held against the publisher, or author, for any damages,
reparation, or monetary loss due to the information contained
within this book. Either directly or indirectly.
Legal Notice:
This book is copyright protected. This book is only for
personal use. You cannot amend, distribute, sell, use, quote
or paraphrase any part, or the content within this book,
without the consent of the author or publisher.
Disclaimer Notice:
Please note the information contained within this document is
for educational and entertainment purposes only. All effort has
been executed to present accurate, up to date, and reliable,
complete information. No warranties of any kind are declared
or implied. Readers acknowledge that the author is not
engaging in the rendering of legal, financial, medical or
professional advice. The content within this book has been
derived from various sources. Please consult a licensed
professional before attempting any techniques outlined in this
book.
By reading this document, the reader agrees that under no
circumstances is the author responsible for any losses, direct
or indirect, which are incurred as a result of the use of
information contained within this document, including, but not
limited to, — errors, omissions, or inaccuracies.

Disclaimer

While the author has exerted the best efforts during the course of preparing and finishing this book, he makes no warranties or representations regarding the accuracy or completeness of the contents of this book. He specifically disclaims any implied warranties of merchantability or fitness for a particular purpose.

The discussions, strategies, and tips given in this book may be not be suitable for your situation.   Therefore, it is best to consult accordingly with a professional as needed. The author shall not be held liable for any loss of profit or damages, including but not limited to special, incidental, or consequential damages.

Introduction

Trading used to be the focus of many corporate and institutional entities, with direct access to closed trading systems. However, the recent technological advances and the boom of the World Wide Web have leveled the walls covering their playing field.

Now, trading, specifically day-trading, is available to everyone, even to you. With the right tools and knowledge, you can capitalize on market crashes. Many are afraid of bubbles and corrections, but after you're done with this book, you can upgrade your standard of living and take advantage of any economic trend.

Today, the markets for stocks, domestic currencies, and other securities are much more accessible than they used to be 20 years ago. Volatility is their key characteristic. Hence, beginners will find it hard to win in zero-sum markets. That's why you need genuine trading skills to generate profit by buying and selling financial instruments. After the 2000 stock market crash, many traders, especially beginners, lost a lot of money.

That's the danger of knowing little in this field. You can lose your hard-winnings and your capital in just one moment. If you're too aggressive, you can even lose everything in your life. But, if you make it big, you can be crazily rich!

You can generate money in your own home, while wearing pajamas, sipping a cup of coffee, and slouching on your sofa. You can be your own boss, with just your pets, serving as your workmate and supervisor.

When you acquire the skills of successful and seasoned day-traders, you can build real wealth and diversify your financial portfolio. So, even if another blanket of a Great Depression covers the world, your money basket won't run out of funds for you and your loved ones.

Containing the essentials and the secrets of day trading, this book will give you the push you need to start in the field. Featuring the rare trading topics below, "Day Trading Options" can definitely make you an instant day trader!

- ➢ Risk management and money management for your capital and future trades
- ➢ Comprehensive guides to fundamental and technical analysis
- ➢ Beginner to advanced day trading tips, strategies, and lessons
- ➢ Learn trading psychology and be able to read market behavior
- ➢ Gain the skill to develop your own trading system
- ➢ Be acquainted with the indicators that can help you come up with profitable predictions

Thanks for downloading this book, I hope you enjoy the journey.

Disclaimer

The data and lessons provided in this book are solely for informational purposes. All information provided by "Day Trading Options" is considered in good faith. However, we have no liability, under any circumstance, to any damage or loss incurred by the reader.

Step 1: Learn How to Trade

Eight years after the first-ever stock market crash of the 21st century, those who came back to the market ran again. They sought safety, trying to take what's left of their wealth. They tried to find ways to manage their portfolio--or the remainder of it. Since the Great Depression, 2008 was considered the worst year for stocks, Forex, and securities trading.

The convention of buying and holding died after the first crash. With the second, traders started looking for ways to trade and invest. Although some still practice meticulous portfolio balancing, with a type of buy and hold strategy, they scrutinized and modified their holdings after the crash. Others successfully got out, completely, but what happened to those who weren't able to? They lost their capital.

Before you try facing the market every morning, why not learn the fundamentals of day trading first. You can't trade efficiently if you've no idea of what close and open positions are? Are they similar to position trading? You must learn the answers to such questions before you actually start trading your money for success.

The Goal of Day Traders

Trading is the act of buying and selling securities (e.g., futures, options, and swaps) based on short-term movement. The goal of day trading is to gain profit from "price movements." When the price of a stock has increased by 10%, then the people who have purchased shares of that stock can make a profit. Active trading, like day-trading, aims to capture market trends and make profits from such events.

The goal of active trading is to "beat the market" through timing and identification of profitable trades. Most times, day-traders resell their stocks hours after they've purchased them. Within day-trading, there are numerous trading strategies that you can employ.

Perhaps, day-trading is the most popular trading style next to position trading. Others consider this style as a methodology since it's a form of speculation in securities. As its name implies, it's the method of buying and selling securities within the day.

Position traders, in contrast to day traders, holds a position in security for a long period. The position could be held for weeks, months, or even years. This is considered the longest holding period among all active trading styles. Position trading greatly considers the long-term performance of an asset.

For example, Company X (a telco company) will officially launch in 2024. The odds, which involve the indicators for the price movement of X's stocks and assets, are in favor of Company X. This implies that, in the long term, the value of Company X and its assets will likely rise before 2024.

Day traders, on the other hand, focuses on the short-term benefits and price movements of financial assets, like currencies, stocks, and options.

Conventionally, professional day-traders are the ones who invest heavily in day trading. Specialists and market makers are what you can call trading experts. However, throughout the years, electronic trading has continuously chipped and destroyed the walls around the playing fields of banks, billionaires, and financial institutions.

Many have now made "trading" as their primary source of income. For such people, it's a medium that allowed them to diversify their portfolio, whether by engaging in active trading or offering their technical know-how and services to others. Many ply their skills in the international markets. Those who like thrills take risks and treat day trading as a full-time job or a business venture. Day-traders, in particular, don't stay in a position overnight. They resell stocks and securities hours after they've purchased them or the day after that. Swing traders, on the other hand, eye opportunities months after the actual purchase. In other words, they hoard securities in the hopes of making huge profits in the future.

This book will be focusing more on day trading, but by the time you're done reading this, you will have the confidence to enter any trading market and engage in any type of online transaction or investment.

This book aims to introduce the world of Forex, futures, options, stocks, and cryptocurrencies, as well as the different trading styles. Although it will be focusing on day-trading, reading this is a great starting point to jump-start your career in any type of electronic trading venture.

Enter Day-Trading!

Day-trading can be a crazy business. Traders, investors, and financial analysts work in front of their personal computer, as they react to blips and patterns. Each blip represents a specific amount of real dollars. Their quick decisions enable them to make real cash by the day, unlike salary people, who only get paid once or twice per month.

Another perk of day trading is its versatility. You can trade any tradable security. In fact, you can day trade two or more securities. What's more, you can take very short positions, while investing or swing trading.

Please recall the example in the previous section. Company X has the potential to grow massively in the next four years. The value of its stocks fluctuates every day. This means it's a good security to day-trade! In chapter 3: A Primer to Fundamental Analysis, you'll learn how to choose the securities that could make you rich. Investing in a dead security won't get you anywhere.

Day-trading can bring in quick profits and quick cash. Some platforms allow for the withdrawal of at least 20 USD. Brokerage platforms, like eToro and IQoption, allow for just a $100 deposit. They also offer a $500 free demo account. When you reach chapter 4: Understanding Technical Analysis, you'll gain insights in choosing the perfect broker for your style and budget. You can use a demo account to practice or test your trading strategy. Chapter 3, 4, and 5 can help you devise a trading system and strategy.

The Golden Rules

Day trading is all about timing, analysis, vigilance, and patience. Does that sound too hard? There are indeed many principles and strategies you can use, but here are some cheats, which are also considered golden rules in the industry:

➢ The larger your capital is, the larger your profit will be. Nevertheless, the ability of day traders to generate large sums depends on their skills in making small profits.

➢ Tim Sykes, Warren Buffet, and other wealthy traders take close positions in futures, options, and stock markets.

> Closing positions every day lowers trading risks: market, country, currency, and interest rate risks. These will be further discussed in chapter 4.
> Don't force your style on stocks that won't make a profit. If you become hasty, you can lose money. In day trading, there are days when nothing seems good to buy, and every trade could be a step closer to bankruptcy.
> Whenever you're day trading, you have to work fast and be vigilant and patient.

As an individual trader, you face against brokers, financial institutions, central banks, and frequency algorithms that could turn the tides to their favor at any given time. Brokerage firms operate frequency algorithms.

They hedge funds objectively, and they can come up with predictions in seconds they have devoured the necessary data. In less than a blink of your eye, they can make trades. You're up against that, so you gotta be the best version of your trader self, once you're on the actual playing field. Beginner day traders possess more advantages than human-generated algorithms and large organizations. Why is this so? You can find the answer after you can actually start practicing and executing "mock" trades. This will be possible after you finish chapter 5.

Why Day Trade?

Making a lot of money is the major reason why many people enter the world of trading, of course. Another is improving potential profits from digital transactions. For those who want to grow their portfolio fast, online investing is a way of life. Trading can bring in money for savings and daily expenses. Regardless of whether you invest through stocks or Forex, a portfolio with securities can give you superior returns. But this will only happen if you're willing to work at it. Those who decide to take the extra mile--to learn anything and everything about trading--do more than just ride the tide of the most recent economic trend. They can also search for loopholes and opportunities during the "best times" and the "bad times." When there's a big bubble that's about to pop or there's a great demand for a specific stock, you must find the best places to be in the market. Your decisions should be based on market cycles and economic conditions. The last chapter of this book "Day Trading Futures, Options, and Cryptocurrencies" is all about getting ahead of other traders. In day trading, the benefit of one opportunity is only limited to one individual or entity.

Those people who take the initiative or make the conscious decision to improve their profit potential--the potential of an account, asset, or product to generate revenue--are the ones who become seasoned and successful traders.

Take Warren Buffet and Paul Tudor Jones as examples. They started small, but look at them now. They're two of world's richest! As of January 2021, Warren is the 3rd richest man in the world while Jones ranked 343rd. These are all according to Forbes, a well-refuted American business magazine owned by the Forbes family and the Integrated Whale Media Investments.

They, along with the other world-renowned traders, watch markets like vultures. They can create an opportunity for profits even when there's an impending recession. They had watched technical signals before the 2000 stock market crash moved into cash positions. After the stocks tumbled, they carefully humped back in the market once the opportunities were evident.

What did they do? While they were waiting, they carefully researched trends and watched indicators. They added new stocks to their watch list and removed those that couldn't rise again. The technical signals from charts told them when to close and open positions, or when to get in and get out.

The Difference Between Short and Long Trades

It's now time to get acquainted with some of the terms and technicalities of day trading. Let's start with the two types of trades.

In stock trading, short and long refers to the first action of the trader. Did he buy first or sell first? Long trades takes place when a market participant purchases shares of an asset with the intention to involve in repurchasing in the future. This is also called hedging or investing. Most swing traders do this. They invest in a low-priced asset today because its value will likely increase at a certain point in the future.

On the other hand, selling initiates a short trade. Investors sell their stocks for short trading. Eventually, when the asset reaches its ceiling price, its value will go down. In this case, the investor will then repurchase the asset at a lower price. That is one-way high-stakes and experienced traders manipulate the market. They make huge profits by selling high. The high price will then attract many fellow traders. This decreases the price of the asset. When the price is lower than the previous noted value, they engage in bulk repurchasing. A short trade, on the one hand, takes place when you sell first. Short traders often repurchase the same stock at a lower price.

When you're "going long," this means you've purchased a security and you're waiting so that you can sell the asset when its price increases. Day traders use the words "long" and "buy" interchangeably. So, please don't be confused about this.

Some apps and web-based brokerage platforms feature entry buttons marked "buy" or "long." Often, the terms are utilized to describe open positions, like "I'm long Sony." This indicates that you own a specific amount of public shares of Sony--the Japanese electronics giant.

-Long Trading Potential

Day traders like to say "go long" or "going long" to show interest in making a purchase for a specific asset. For example, by taking a long position on 100 shares of stock XYX at $5 per unit, the transaction cost will be $5,000. This implies that you bought 100 units of Stock XYX at $5,000. Hence, if you sell all of those shares at $5,200, you're taking a short position because you're actually selling your shares. If there's an opposing trade and you're able to sell those units, then your net profit will be $200.

By going long, the potential for profit is limitless. Why is this so? The selling value of a popular asset can increase continuously. Then, if you invest in one hundred shares of a stock at $2, its value can go up to $10, $12, or $15 over a certain period. The negative side of price increase is a reversal--a sudden gradual or instant price decrease. For example, if you offer your stocks at $10.90 per share, you'll receive $10,900 on your $11,000 trade. In this case, you lose a hundred dollars plus the transaction fee. The largest possible loss in the given situation can occur if the price per share becomes $0.0. This results in a $1 loss per share. Day trading can minimize and prevent such huge losses.

-Short Trades

Taking short positions can be intimidating to most beginner traders. In reality, they need to buy something for them to make a profit. When going short (taking a short position), day traders sell securities before purchasing them.

They do this in the hopes of making a profit from a price decrease. Their trade will only generate profits if the amount they borrowed is lower compared to the selling price of the asset.

Traders utilize the words "short" and "sell" interchangeably. Likewise, some apps and trading platforms feature clickable buttons marked "sell" or "short." The use of the word "short" in the sentence "I'm going short Apple" indicates that you're offering Apple stock.

Day traders who like taking short positions often say "go short" or "going short." This indicates that they're interested in taking a short position in a specific asset. For example, if you take a short position on 500 shares of YYY stock at $9.0, you will receive $4,500 in your account. Your trading account will have -500 shares. In the future, you've to bring the balance to zero by purchasing at least 500 shares of that same stock. Unless you do this, you won't know the odds and the loss or profit of the position you're in.

The Major Markets Available in Electronic Trading

-Forex

In foreign exchanges (Forex markets), the spot exchange FX rate is the current rate of exchange of a currency pair. The market determines the rate of every currency being traded in the exchange. As well, all aspects of trading and converting currencies are determined at current (spot) prices.

The major participants in this exchange are international banks and large financial centers. Day and night, except for Saturdays and Sundays, these financial organizations serve as mediums of exchange for millions of traders.

Also known as the currency market, the Forex market is the largest market in the world. It's also the most liquid and has accounted for billions of trades per day. In 2010, it has accounted for $3 trillion of daily trading. Although it hasn't existed a century ago, it's where the majority of day-traders buy and sell securities.

The Foreign Exchange market facilitates the trades of one currency for another. Even though daily currency trades can be also conducted electronically, like stock trading, the two markets are quite different. Currencies are traded in pairs, while stocks are traded in units.

-The Options Market

The options market is a marketplace that enables participants to take positions in the derivative of an asset\security. Hence, the option--a contract that enables an investor to trade a financial instrument like an index or ETF at a set price over a certain period--is based on specific securities. The value of options and other inputs changes with the value or the lack of that the asset in question provides.

-CFDs

CFD stands for Contract for Difference. This is an arrangement made in derivatives trades, wherein the differences in the given settlement between the first and last trade prices are settled by cash. The settlement leads to a cash payment, rather than settling in bonds, stocks, or commodities.

A settlement, in finance and trading, is a business process, by which securities or interests in securities are physically delivered to fulfill contractual obligations. These days, settlements typically take place in central securities depositories (CSDs).

A CSD is a financial organization that holds securities like shares or stocks in dematerialized or certificated form. With this, ownership can be transferred through a book entry. This allows brokers, electronic platforms, and financial organizations to hold securities at a single location. This makes them available for electronic clearing and settlement--a fast and efficient way.

The Market Conditions

You've just been acquainted with the major markets in electronic trading. It's now time to talk about the market conditions. Keep in mind that they aren't actual marketplaces. Rather, they're like trends that you can use in Forex trading and technical analysis.

-What's a Bull Market?

A bull market isn't actually a type of market, but it's considered as a factor or condition that affects exchanges. In any exchange/market, there are two types of trends. It's either prices are increasing or decreasing. A bull market is like a bull using its horns in an upward motion. Rising prices characterize a bull market.

When market prices are high or an asset's price increases by over 20%, the condition is referred to as a bull market. Usually, a bull market occurs when many traders are optimistic over a particular asset or security.

As mentioned earlier, investors with large investments can manipulate market trends. A bull market can arise when many traders and investors are purchasing a particular asset. Based on the law of supply and demand, which you can learn in chapter 4, the price rises when the demand for the product/asset is high.

The indicators of an impending bullish trend are, at times, unclear. That's why traders utilize technical analysis to recognize signals for a price increase. By researching and studying charts and indicators, you can predict price direction with a certain degree of accuracy. Technical indicators like MAs, RSI, and stochastic are also covered in the said chapter.

-What's a Bear Market?

When the market has experienced a prolonged price decrease, the condition is considered as a bear market. In contrast to bullish trends, a bear market arises when the value of an asset decline by 20%.

Like a bull market, a bear market is a condition. It applies to securities markets and individual assets. Recessions and other economic downturns are often accompanied by bear markets. You can also use the term to refer to any stock index or stock that has experienced a 20% decrease in value for the past 2 months.

Take the Nasdaq Composite bubble in 1999 as an example. Due to the bursting of the dot-com bubble, the value of the public shares being offered by Boo, Webvan, Pets.com, Worldcom, Global Crossing, Northpoint Communications dropped by over 30%. They fell into a bear market territory. Many of the aforementioned entities closed their shutters forever.

Keep in mind that stock market correction and bear market are two different things, even though they're used interchangeably. A stock market correction occurs when a stock's value falls by 10%. A correction is upgraded to a bear market once the price decreases by 20% more.

Here are some factors that can cause corrections and bear markets:

➢ Stock market crash
➢ Recession
➢ Major economic events
➢ Investor fear and uncertainty
➢ A nation's poor credit rating
➢ Widespread investor speculation and irresponsible lending
➢ Over-leveraged investing
➢ Oil price movements

-Invest in a bear market

What's one of the secrets of day-traders? They don't only trade daily, but they also invest for the long-term. Adept day traders also engage in swing trading, especially for volatile assets that have the potential to increase in value in the coming months.

How do they do that? Here are some of their trading secrets and winning characteristics:

1. Thinking outside the box

When the value of a stock seems to decrease infinitely, traders, especially the beginners, tend to take sell positions before things get worse. As soon as they can, they try to get out of the market.

When a bull market arises and the price continues to rise, they often take a buy position. They fear of losing the chance to make a profit.

In electronic trading, many experts, including seasoned traders, like Geroge Soros and Paul Teodore Jones, sell high and buy low.

In chapter 5, it is explained why beginner traders should take advantage of sudden price changes and why they should choose the opposite of what the majority does.

2. Focusing on impactful indicators

Often, a big and influential company may go out of business when a bear market arises. That, in itself, is an indicator. When an economy goes bad, companies, as well as their share prices, are negatively affected.

On the other hand, trending and thriving companies over-perform and outperform their rivals. As a rule of thumb, focus on public shares of companies that are rock solid, well-rooted, and transparent.

The Tools You Need for Trading

Day trading, like swing and position trading, requires tools and services for mitigating risks and improving profitability.

Foremost, you need a smartphone, personal computer, and internet connection.

Depending on your broker, you may also need a telephone and landline. This can come in handy if you have to urgently call your broker. For example, you can contact them if you encounter transaction errors or you need help from a CS representative.

A trading-charting platform showing real-time market data is needed for making highly accurate predictions and for timing your trades. Aside from these, day traders need various tools to support their active trading lifestyles. These can include desk items, software, and hardware:

➢ Day trading charting programs, like Ninja Trader
➢ Laptop or computer
➢ Telephone and landline
➢ Stable internet connection
➢ Backup internet access
➢ Timely market statistics
➢ App or web-based broker or brokerage platform

The items listed above are the most basic tools every day-trader needs. A fast and reliable personal computer or smartphone is a must. A trading charting program is also a necessity. A smartphone with a mobile plan or data can serve as a backup internet source and as a device for mobile charting and trading.

Aside from Ninja Trader, StockCharts and Trading View are also highly-rated charting software, according to Investopedia. Lastly, you need a prominent and trusted broker or brokerage firm. Without either of the two, you can't trade anything electronically.

Chapter Summary

Day trading can be a lucrative business. It can broaden your financial portfolio, keeping you away from bankruptcy. You can also combine it with other types of trading, like swing and position trading. Swing trading is a type of investing. Traders engage in it and take long positions for months at a time. Day traders often opt for short positions, which are also referred to as sell positions. Most day traders exit the market every closing of a trading day. There are many electronic markets out there, namely the stocks exchanges, Forex markets, and options markets. Often, large financial entities can manipulate these markets.

By watching out for reversals, trends, and economic conditions, traders can make accurate predictions and execute profitable trades. In the next chapter, you'll learn how to observe trading markets, as well as the elements that drive them.

Step 2: Observing Market Behavior 101

Inflation, recession, and other adverse economic conditions generate negative news for the industry. This can adversely affect exchange rates and stock prices. However, if you know how to turn the tides in your favor, you can make a profit out of any economic event, whether good or bad.

Governing bodies, such as the US Federal Reserve Board (Fed) and the National Payments System, supervises the US government's executive branches. They're responsible for tax changes and fiscal policy moves. Simply put, they can minimize the detrimental effects of certain business cycles (e.g. expansion and recession) and promote economic growth to raise the value of the domestic currency and local stocks. However, even such an authoritarian organization can't erase economic cycles. Traders and marketers anticipate business cycles with the intention to make profits.

In this chapter, you'll know which indicators affect trading cycles and how to understand economic and market conditions, as well as be able to read market sentiment. The insights you'll gain can help you understand the different strategies and analysis methods employed in day trading.

The Fundamentals of Business Cycles

Foremost, what's a business cycle? The business cycle is the natural fluctuations in economic growth. It occurs over time and is valuable for analyzing trends and making predictions. The business cycle also refers to the upward and downward fluctuations of GDP or gross domestic product over a given time. Its alternate names are "trade cycle" and "economic cycle." Its duration is the period involving a single contraction and boom, in sequence.

The length of a cycle entails the amount of time it takes to complete a sequence. The sequence starts with a boom and ends with a compression. Each cycle has four phases:

. Expansion

The expansion period takes place between the peak and the through. This is when the economy is growing nonstop. The GDP, the monetary measure that determines the economic output of a nation or economy, is steadily increasing. The growth rate of the gross domestic product ranges between 2% and 3%.

The unemployment rate is at its natural rate of 3.5% to 4.5%, while inflation is lesser than 2%. And, the value of most stocks is bullish--in a bull market. For a properly managed economy, it will be in this phase for years.

Expansion transitions to peak when the growth rate is over 3% and when the economy is overheating. In this period, inflation becomes greater than 2%. The inflation rate may also surpass 10%.

In such cases, multiple stock corrections become apparent. Investors and traders become irrationally exuberated, generating asset bubbles. What's this? An asset bubble is created when assets, like gold, stocks, and housing, experience a dramatic rise in value over a very short period. The value of the asset doesn't support the bubble. Irrational exuberance--an economic phenomenon wherein many people are purchasing a specific type of asset--is a hallmark of an asset bubble. After the bubble forms, many even take loans just to invest in the asset. When thousands of investors flock to an asset, like real estate, its price and demand increase.

Peak

This is the second phase. Peak is the month(s) when expansion transitions into the recession or contraction phase. In this phase, the economy, along with the GDP, inflates at full speed.

The GDP, to be more specific, may reach its maximum output. Also, employment levels are also at all-time highs. Investors and businessmen are prospering.

However, inflation nears as salaries and prices increase. In such conditions, inflation may have already set in. High inflation can cause a recession.

Recession/Contraction

During a recession, the economy falls from peak. Employment rate decreases, and unemployment rate increases.

Eventually, output and production decline. Prices and wages stop increasing as well. It may not fall, but if the recession lasts for many years, then employment levels will continue to decline and salary rates start to fall.

. Trough

This is the 4th phase and the month(s) when the country transitions from recession to the recovery phase, which is also considered as the expansion period. The trough is when the economy hits all-time bottom.

If this phase prolongs, it may lead to a depression. Depression, in economics, is a prolonged and severe recession. The trough marks the end of a business cycle. When the economy grows again from rock bottom, output and employment start pick up. This period of recovery and expansion pulls and propels the country in question off the lowest level.

The period pushes the economy towards the next peak, and employment rate increases again. This makes the country's financial situation and credit rating look promising. Improving the economy, investors flock again to the nation to invest.

The Economic Indicators and Their Significance

Any economy goes through the four broad cycles mentioned above. In peak and expansion, the employment rate is high and many are optimistic. Financial prosperity is prevalent.

In the recession and trough phases, things become tougher, economically. Many lose their jobs and numerous businesses close their shutters forever. The end of a business cycle paves the way for a new one.

Economic indicators can help you determine where in the cycle an economy is and in what direction it's moving. Is a contraction near? Does the high employment rate in a country spells an inevitable recession?

With the help of economic indicators, you can find the answer to the questions above and other related inquiries. Most traders, specifically speculators and analysts, those who pore over both economic and financial information to evaluate outcomes and identify opportunities for investment and trading recommendations, tend to observe trends over several releases.

An economic calendar, which is a schedule of dates of significant events that can affect price action of securities and the status of markets, presents economic indicator data.

Some brokers and trading platforms provide regularly updated economic calendars.

Here are the most important economic indicators that you should consider when you're observing market behavior:

- Commodity Price index
- National Employment
- Business Inventories
- Beige Book
- Core Pce Price Index
- Consumer Price Index
- CCI or Conference Board Consumer Confidence Index
- The number of orders for durable goods
- The number of home sales
- Employment Situation Report
- Employment Cost Index
- The number of factory orders
- GDP or Gross Domestic Product
- Housing Starts
- Ivey Purchasing Managers Index
- The results of Ism non-manufacturing and manufacturing surveys
- Initial Jobless Claims
- Industrial Capacity and Production Utilization
- Leaking Indicators
- NFP or Non-Farms Payrolls
- PMI or Purchasing Managers Index
- PPI or Producer Price Index
- Personal Income and Company Spending
- The total number of retail sales of the company in question
- Trade Balance, the net sum of a country's imports and exports of goods
- TIC or Treasury International Capital
- Tankan Survey
- MCSI or University of Michigan Consumer Sentiment
- Unemployment Rate
- The results of the ZEW Financial Market Survey

Please take note that some of the aforementioned indicators are only applicable to businesses/entities in their respective industries.

Indicators reveal important news and data that can affect markets, as well as tradable assets. Depending on the medium and virality of the news, it can impact the performance of stocks, currency prices, and trading volume. As a day trader, you must watch and read economic news relevant to your target security and monitor financial market activities. With help from the right indicators, you can make accurate and profitable predictions. You can utilize an indicator for many sessions, but keep in mind that there are numerous ways of interpretation.

-Interest Rates

Watching the FEDs, as well as the entities, organizations, and authoritative people linked to them must be a daily habit for you. The FOMC or the Federal Open Market Committee includes the following:

➢ Seven members of the Board of Governors
➢ The president of 4 of 11 Federal Reserve Banks (State some names)
➢ The president of the New York Federal Reserve Bank

The FOMC is responsible for monitoring "open market operations." This is the primary tool whereby the FEDs execute US monetary policies. This, in turn, affects federal funds rate, credit conditions, and aggregate demand. In fact, it can affect the whole economy.

You must track what they may or may not do. This is in particular to interest rates since they can manipulate the country's current and future interest rates. The members meet eight times per year, but local newspapers, like the NY Times, and news websites, such as Forbes and Yahoo Finance, publish related stories on a daily or weekly basis.

Every time Ben Bernanke, the chairman of the FEDs, speaks publicly, journalists and various writers listen for indications and plans of the organizations. They also do the same for the other members. Journalists and news writers scrutinize and dissect every information the FEDs share with the public.

Press coverage summarizes the data shared and tell whether the Fed may lower or raise interest rates. Interest rates can significantly impact economies and how trades are made. A rate increase can decrease the spending of a nation. This can lead to an economic slowdown. The FEDs raises interest rates if the economy is overheating.

In such conditions, inflation is imminent. Whether the board fears a downturn to the GDP or they're spurring growth during contraction, they will reduce interest rates to entice foreign investors and promote growth and spending.

Aside from economic news from reliable news outlets, you can also refer to the Beige Book. The US twelve Federal Reserve Banks compiles the data in the Beige Book. This includes the present economic conditions of the twelve districts.

Two weeks before each meeting, wherein monetary policies, which include interest rates, are set. The summaries in the Beige Book are developed through interviews with economists, market experts, business leaders, and other personalities familiar with the economy of the districts.

-Money Supply

An increase in a nation's money supply is a prime indicator of inflation. When this indicator is greater than the supply of goods, the inflation rate and prices go up. Money, stocks, and commodities traders must consider and vigilantly observe the following aggregates:

➤ Inflation
➤ Money Supply
➤ Goods & Services

In particular, the Federal Reserve Bank tracks two aggregates:

1. M1

M1 includes money utilized for payments, such as checking accounts in thrifts and banks and the circulating currency.

2. M2

M2 are the currencies sitting in bank deposits and bank vaults and those being kept in the money market and retail savings account.

At www.federaalresesrve.gov/releases/h6/Current, you can follow the stock measures for M1 and M2.

-Deflation

Deflation is the opposite of inflation. When prices start falling, deflation can take center stage. It typically transpires when there's a prolonged period of a price decrease. The 1930 Great Depression is a classic example of deflation.

As mentioned in the section for "Money Supply," the prices of goods increase when the money supply is greater than goods being produced and circulated. In periods of deflation, improving the money supply won't likely be able to raise an economy in a downturn.

In such cases, adding more money to the economy can be risky. This is especially true when products are in excess and production continues although prices are falling. Japan's economic crisis in 2004 is a good example.

Even though Japan's central bank lowered its interest rates and printed more money to curb the price structure's downturn, the deflation continued until 2007. The 2011 Tohoku earthquake and tsunami have also negatively affected the nation's economy.

Deflation broadly impacted the Japanese economy in the Lost 30 Years, which is referred to as the period between 1991 and 2020. Between the mid-1990s and mid-2000s, Japan's Gross Domestic Product fell from $5.33 trillion to $4.36 trillion and regular wages fell by 5%.

In the last three decades, Japanese policymakers continued to try to curb the consequences. However, their efforts have little economic effect. In the 2000s, the country continued to print money, but the prices kept dropping in a deflationary spiral. Values of stocks, currency exchange rate, and housing and commodity prices continued to fall.

-Jobless Claims

The US Department of Labor reports Jobless claims statistics every week. This includes the number of people applying for unemployment insurance benefits. Jobless Claims are important indicators in knowing the health of an economy or the state of the employment situation of a country.

The report from the BLS or the US Bureau of Labor Statistics compiles the weekly Employment Situation Summary. This report is a critical economic indicator. It determines the expectations for the other statistics for that particular month. Take the scenario below as an example.

A weak labor market, which is usually reported in the summary, can be considered a strong sign of low retail sales and other negative reports. The Employment Situation Summary (ESS) also includes data broken down by industry, like manufacturing and construction.

A notable drop in the employment rate is an indication of a poor labor market. The report for housing starts will be negative. Housing starts is a key economic indicator. It lists new residential construction projects beginning during the given month.

The ESS and housing starts report can shock financial markets. This is particularly true when the numbers released are far from expectations. In this case, the value of some stocks, especially local public shares, could fall or rise. The former can also happen when the employment rate is declining. Consequently, if the report indicates the opposite and reveals numbers better than the expected stats, the value of stocks will rise for a specific period. Remember, nothing is permanent in the markets.

Employment reports can strongly drive markets. Data and statistics reports hold recent assessments of many sectors and industries. The ESS is considered the best indicator for wage pressure and unemployment.

The rise of the unemployment rate is one of the initial signs of impending national inflation. Additionally, the report covers the labor markets of the United States' entire 250 regions and each major industry.

The Labor Department's website (www.bls.gov) releases a report on the first Friday of every month at 8:30 a.m. Four of the most important parts of the report are as follows:

➢ Unemployment rate
➢ Average earnings
➢ Average weekly hours
➢ The number of new jobs created

-Employment Cost Index

The ECI or the Employment Cost Index is also a type of BLS survey of employer payrolls. Every quarter, it measures and presents the changes in total employee compensation in every region. Various employers, investors, economists, and stockholders use the ECI indicator to track the health of the economy in question. The BLS surveys over 3,000 private firms and more than 500 local governments. The report is released every last business day of January, April, July, and October.

-Consumer Confidence

Consumer confidence is defined as the statistical measure of consumer sentiments about the future and current economic conditions. Like the ECI, it's utilized to measure an economy's health. With this indicator, you can take a glimpse at the future of a market.

When the performance is high, spending will increase. The CCI or the Consumer Confidence Index is the best index when monitoring this indicator. The US Conference Board publishes this report by surveying 5,000 households every three to six months.

When confidence is low, the Federal Reserve Banks will lower interest rates. This positively impacts stock markets. High confidence levels, on the other hand, are warning signs of a possible near contraction period. In the early phase of recession or before it, the Feds may raise interest rates in a last-ditch attempt to curb inflation rates. When interest rates are increased, the prices of stocks decrease.

The US Conference Board releases the CCI at 10 a.m. on the last Tuesday of each month. You can track the monthly results at their website www.conference-board.org. Go to the "Economics" section and hover towards the "Consumer Confidence" tab.

How to Use the Data You've Gathered

Indeed, various data is available for both fundamental analysis and technical analysis, which are discussed in the next chapters. However, not every piece of information you've collected is relevant to the type of security you want to trade. Organizing your collection of relevant data for reading charts and tracking trends will allow you to easily analyze phases of the business cycle and wisely choose economic signs.

Now, here are the steps you should take so that your every effort would be fruitful and bear relevant results:

1. Maintain your economic calendar

Above all else, you must maintain your economic calendar for the release dates of relevant indicators. Therefore, always watch trends and the rise and fall of security prices when a key indicator is soon to be released. In chapter 5, you can learn how to read trends and patterns.

2. Determine the industries and parts of the economy that will be impacted by the indicators

The GDP, for example, suggests the future path of economic growth. CPI and PPI, on the other hand, are strong measures of inflation. With these two, you'll have the ability to know the current phase of the business cycle and make accurate predictions about price movements.

3. Scrutinize the crucial parts of your chosen indicators

Like economies, indicators also have parts. Ask yourself, "what part of the index is critical to my future decisions?" For instance, the CPI's energy and food components are often highly volatile. Hence, for stock trading, CPI's core bears the most important numbers.

4. Check for revisions in new indicators

Often, indicators are revised. The changes may be not that significant, but that small modification may reveal a small shift in the cycle. So, always check for revisions and know how the changes impact monthly trends.

5. Watch the trends

On your economic calendar, track the major parts of each indicator you're watching. Monitor the trends of the relevant data components so that you can accurately predict the state of the economy and the current phase of the business cycle. Examples include indices, earnings report, and economic summaries, like industrial production and consumer leverage ratio.

Chapter Summary

Economic indicators, when used properly, provide valuable data for analysis and interpreting future and current trading possibilities. Usually employed in fundamental analysis, economic indicators aid in judging the health of an economy and for determining the phase in a business cycle.

Various indicator data are available online and on economic reports, which are published periodically. You need to be adverse in choosing the right indicators to produce desirable results from your analyses and trades. In the next chapter, you can learn how to do that and conduct fundamental analysis.

Step 3: Getting Acquainted with Fundamental Analysis

It's time for fundamental analysis! FA or fundamental analysis measures an asset's intrinsic value, by examining and observing relevant financial and economic indicators. From macroeconomic factors, like industry conditions to Employment Situation Reports, fundamental analysis involves anything that affects, whether negatively or positively, the value of a security.

The end goal of FA is to come up with a highly accurate figure that a trader can compare with the asset's present price for overvaluation or undervaluation. This stock analysis method is quite the opposite of technical analysis, which is detailed in the next chapter: "Understanding Technical Analysis."

The Importance of Fundamental Analysis

The fundamentals include market and economic conditions that can impact a tradable asset. It also covers the financial data of company activities and information about their failures and successes.

With fundamental analysis, you'll have the ability to know differences in the stock prices of two or more companies using earnings growth, business conditions, and other factors. These are discussed in the succeeding sections.

FA can provide consistent and reliable information. Using this type of analysis, you can evaluate a financial security's intrinsic value. This is the trading price or the net worth of an asset.

For example, the discounted cash flow model is employed when determining a company's weighted average capital and free cash flow. The average capital accounts for the present value of money. The DCF model can determine the present value of a stock by forecasting the cash flow and discounting it. The model employs a discount rate to calculate the DCF.

If the DCF figure is over the present investment cost, then opportunities could give rise to positive returns. Typically, companies employ the capital's weighted average cost. This includes the stockholder's expected rate of return.

The market price (intrinsic value) can be compared to the asset's trading value. If the security being traded is less than its actual book value, you should purchase that asset. This type of trading is called Value Investing.

Benjamin Graham, the late American economist and successful investor, is the father of Value Investing. Warren Buffet, the largest shareholder of Berkshire Hathaway, popularized the said investment strategy, which involves excessive use of fundamental analysis.

That's just one of the significance of FA.

Where to Start

1. To begin, choose a business sector or industry that is relevant to your preferred stock.

2. Research the major players of the company offering the public share. Look at the fundamentals of the sector or industry. For example, the business components of the hospitality industry include safety, sales, finance, maintenance, event management, and office operations.

3. Reduce the list of the firms you want to compare with the company. You should also look at the daily trading volume of the security. If it has a low number of daily trades, then it will be hard for you to get out of a position.

The tools utilized in FA require the comparison of at least two companies within the industry in question.

Here are some of the tools you can use:

➢ EPS or Earnings per Share
➢ (P/E) ratio or price-to-earnings ratio
➢ Return on equity
➢ (P/B) or price-to-book ration
➢ Price-to-sales ratio
➢ Beta
➢ Projected earnings growth
➢ Dividend yield ratio
➢ Dividend payout ratio

For discussion purposes, consider two giant firms in the home improvement sector: Lowe's and Home Depot. After the 2007 stock market crash, both companies experienced a downturn in their public shares.

As a result, they halted expansion, waited for the next phase in the business cycle, and the value of their stocks fell in a spiraling downtrend. That time, before the price gets any worse, many investors and day traders get out of the market. They sold their public shares. Through fundamental analysis, they had predicted that the prices will get worse. They had also taken note of the impending bubble burst. For them to gain such insight, they scrutinized the companies' balance sheets and cash flow statements.

By considering the following section, you will learn how to read critical financial statements that can help determine intrinsic values in an asset. Acquiring such a skill is essential in day trading stocks.

-The income statement

In general, the income statement is a snapshot of the earnings and their impacts on the company's bottom line--the net income after all expenses, which include income taxes, interest charges, and administrative costs, are removed. The income statement is where a public firm states its costs and revenues.

With the income statement (P&L), you can ascertain the effects of taxes, depreciation, and interest of the entity in question and forecast its earnings potential. Every P&L has three important sections: income, revenue, and expenses. The last section (expenses) includes depreciation costs. This is the portion of an asset considered consumed in the present period.

-How to read a financial statement
1. Check all the figures if they're right.
2. Find or calculate the bottom line.
3. Scrutinize the entity's various sources of income.
4. Examine the amounts and determine the biggest expenses.
5. Compare month-over-month and year-over-year numbers
6. Think of the logical relationships between the numbers.

A year's worth of numbers will not reveal much. Hence, it's more effective to look at the trends throughout several years so that you can accurately predict growth potential and assess the current financial state of the company. Doing so also determines how well the entity is doing against its competitors.

Both annual and quarterly reports are important. Differentiating their results on a year-to-year or quarter-to-quarter basis enables you to specify the financial health of the company for every month. In doing so, you can know which dates are the most efficient for day trading.

For example, by examining the reports for Q1 of 2018 versus the results for Q1 2019, you know whether its earnings are decreasing or increasing. For most companies, Q1 is productive, but for others, like retail chains, Q4 brings in a lot of profits. Hence, you may need results for every quarter especially if the asset requires it.

Annual income statements, on the other hand, present a summary of the earnings or losses for a whole year. Public companies, like Lowe's and Tesla, are required to file yearly and quarterly financial reports with the Securities Exchange Commission (SEC).

-Revenues

Sales revenues present the company's overall sales within a specific period before expenses are subtracted. However, some firms, like Nike and Salesforce, only reports net sales on their income statements. From collected figures, you can see growth or decline in revenues.

-Cost of goods sold (COGS)

COGS or cost of services sold is a measure that shows the net costs directly related to the firm's services or products. This includes freight charges, purchase discounts, and other expenses related to the act of selling.

-Expenses

The expenses portion includes the administrative costs, sales costs, and operating costs of the business. Expenses shouldn't be higher than the gross profits. Low expenses figures are good signs, and they could mean excellent growth potential.

-Interest payments

This portion of the income statement presents the short-term financial health of the company. It mainly includes tax-deductible costs. To determine the entity's fiscal health, use the EBIT number or the earnings before interest and taxes, as well as the interest expense number.

Here are some key points for this type of financial statement: o calculate the interest coverage ratio, divide the interest enses with the EBIT number. Those with high coverage ratios can ily meet their loan obligations.

2. By subtracting the tax and interest expenses from the operating income, you can determine the short-term financial health of the company. You can use the result to know whether or not the entity generates enough income to pay its interest payments.

3. Comparing the ratios of different companies within the same sector is an effective way to judge or gauge the ratios' values.

4. Well-refuted analysts, including George Soros and Richard Dennis, consider number 3 as a poor interest coverage ratio. It generally means that the public company is buried in debt or will be in trouble shortly.

-Dividend Payments

Some companies pay dividends. This is a part of a percentage of the profits that the firm makes. The amount depends on the investor's share of common stock. The shareholders receive their dividends once every quarter in a year.

Hence, the shareholders receive dividends at least four times a year. The company needs to have a good cash flow to make dividend payments. Examining its historical and present dividend payouts allows you to gauge its financial strength for fundamental analysis.

-Testing Profitability

Profitability ratios are utilized to assess a business' capability to generate profit relative to its assets, revenues, operating costs, shareholders' equity, or balance sheet assets. Testing profitability can reveal how a firm efficiently generates value and profit for shareholders.

As financial metrics, they can determine whether or not the company can provide dividend payments.

For computation, the net profit margin and operating margin are used. The former looks at earnings less the expenses.

The latter considers profits from operations before tax and interest expenses.

The formula for both metrics are listed below:

Net profit margin = earnings after taxes/net sales or gross profit

Operating margin = operating income/net sales or gross profit

A higher ratio implies that the company has an excellent industry average and historical performance. Like the previous aforementioned metrics, you can also use profitability ratios when comparing two or more companies.

-Cash Flow Statements

A cash flow statement (CFS) is a valuable measure of profitability, strength, and future outlook. It can determine whether or not the business can pay its expenses and loan interests.

Here are the formulas:

Free Cash Flow = Net income + Depreciation/Amortization - Change in Working Capital - Principal Expenditure

Cash Flow Forecast = Beginning Cash + Estimated Inflows - Estimated Outflows = End Cash

Cash Flow from Operations = Operating Income + Depreciation - Tax Payments + Change in Working Capital

-Depreciation

In accounting, depreciation is considered an expense. It relates to an entity's fixed assets. It represents the usage of assets each accounting period, which could either be a fiscal or calendar year. It could also be a week, a quarter, or a month. Various assets incur depreciation. A few examples include equipment, vehicles, and facilities.

When public companies pay for a valuable item or equipment, they record it as an asset, which represents long-term value for a company. Using the asset creates distorted net income. That's why each use is recorded or estimated.

A variety of depreciation formulas are available for accounting and analysis methods. The most relevant to fundamental analysis are listed below:

Unit of Product Method = Asset Cost - Salvage Value/Useful Life in the Form of Units Produced

Depreciation Per Year = Asset Cost - Salvage Value/Asset's Useful Life

Straight Line Depreciation Method = Asset Cost - Residual Value/Asset's Useful Life

Companies, especially those offering public shares, report asset depreciation to stakeholders. It also allows them to cover the asset's net cost over its entire lifespan, rather than immediately recovering the cost of purchase. This enables firms to replace assets with the right amount of revenue.

-Investment activity

This part of the income statement represents how the public company spends its funds for growing and establishing long-term assets, like new buildings and property acquisitions. The investment activity section also covers the sales of large assets and equity investments. By tracking such activities, you can forecast the result of the entity's long-term planning and capital planning activities.

Learning How to Read the Balance Sheet

The balance sheet presents the company's liabilities and assets at a specific period. Unlike the financial statement, which shows a company's operating results, a balance sheet covers the property and liabilities of a public company.

The value that the company takes in is balanced out against its liabilities. Please keep in mind that when liabilities equal assets plus equity, the financial statement is considered *balanced*.

Each balance sheet has three sections:

Assets

This part details everything that the firm owns.

Liabilities

The liabilities section includes the debts and other debtor claims on the company.

Shareholder's equity

Also referred to as owner's equity, this section lists all claims made by investors and owners.

The balance sheet details assets and liabilities according to liquidity, or how easily and quickly you can convert them to cash. The most liquid liabilities and assets are sorted first on the list. The long-term items appear last.

The asset section is divided into two parts:

. Current assets

Current assets are the valuable resources that are exhausted in one year, like accounts receivable, supplies, and inventory.

2. Long-term assets

These have lifespans of more than one year. Fixtures, equipment, and buildings are examples of long-term assets.

The liabilities portion is also divided into two parts:

. Short-term liabilities

Short-term liabilities include customer deposits, dividends payable, taxes payable, accrued expenses, and trade accounts payable.

. Long-term liabilities

Non-current liabilities are due beyond a year. Some examples are deferred revenues, deferred compensation, deferred income taxes, and post-retirement healthcare liabilities.

How to Analyze Assets

When analyzing assets, you've to consider two prime ratios so that you can tell how the company collects accounts receivable (accounts receivable turnover) and how they deplete their inventory (inventory turnover).

For the latter, a two-step process is involved:

1. To know how quickly the entity converts its accounts receivable turnover into cash, use the formula below:

Accounts Receivable Turnover = Sales on Account/Average Accounts

2. Next, you need to determine how quickly the entity collects on its accounts. To do this, divide the quotient of the above formula by 365. Doing this allows you to find the total number of days they take to collect on accounts.

Inventory turnover testing involves a similar process:

1. For a specific year, you can find out the ratio by using the formula below:

Inventory Turnover Ratio = CGS or Cost of Goods Sold/Average Inventory

2. Then, divide the quotient by 365. The result tells the average number of days that the firm turns over its inventory. The quicker the entity finishes its operations or sells its inventory, the better it's handling its assets. By following the aforementioned steps and using the formulas, you can compare the key entities within the industry. This allows you to tell whether the target company is competitive or not.

In contrast, an increasing accounts receivable turnover ratio is considered a red flag. It signals that the entity is facing cash problems. When inventory numbers are increasing or stagnant, that public company isn't selling its products well.

-Considering Debt

Debt is everything that a company owes. It's a type of deferred payment. When planning to make a trade, there are two ratios that you must look at that are directly linked to the company's debt:

-Current Ratio

The current ratio measures the ability of the entity to pay its short-term debts. It tells analysts how the firm can maximize current assets on its balance sheet for satisfying payables, like current debt. The higher the ratio is, the more short-term liquidity the entity has. A value less than 1 may indicate poor liquidity, which suggests an inability to pay short-term liabilities.

By scrutinizing the balance sheet, you can use the formula below to get the current ratio:

Current Ratio = Present Assets/Present Liabilities

-Quick or Acid Ratio

This measure indicates the capacity of the company to pay its present liabilities without having to sell items from its inventory. It also doesn't involve additional financing. The formula to get the acid ratio is listed below:

Quick Ratio = Present Assets - Current Inventory/Current Liabilities

Once you have calculated the two measures above, compare the results of your target company to that of its competitors.

On your list, only include entities that are in the same industry.

When the current ratio is lower than that of other key rivals, then that public company is facing difficulty paying off short-term debts. This is a very strong signal that bankruptcy is near. A higher current ratio is a bad sign as well since it might indicate poor asset utilization.

Hence, day traders positively view companies that have ratios close to the industry average. Some companies release their ratios to the public. Lowe's and Home Depot do this.

For example, 1:1 is a good acid test ratio since it indicates a good credit risk. Any entity that is having difficulty paying short-term liabilities may not meet all of its short-term obligations in the future. When this is fairly obvious, the share price of the company will drop.

How to Employ Fundamental Analysis

You now know all the indicators that will prove beneficial to your trading endeavors. So, it's time to learn how to actually use fundamental analysis using your preferred economic indicators.

1. The very first step to take is to create a list of profitable stocks you can research. You can use a Stock Screener to filter stocks based on dividend ratio, P/E ratio, sector, or earnings per share. Some of the best free web-based stock screeners are listed below:

➢ Yahoo! Finance
➢ Chart Mill
➢ Zacks
➢ StoclFetcher
➢ Google Finance
➢ Stock Rover
➢ FinViz

To limit the results, use the Search option by one criterion at a time.

2. Once you've made a list, research more by examining financial statements. Analyze growth rate, balance sheets, net income, and profit and losses. Several years of growth is a good indicator, while too much debt is a red flag.

3. After that, research their services or products. Do they have something unique? Within the industry, are they competitive enough? If you're aiming to day trade or swing trade using a public share, then consider the future prospects of your target company.

4. Although this step is optional, it can prove to be beneficial especially when there are newly elected executives, managers, or board members. Find the answers to the following questions:

➤ What's their work history?
➤ Do they have a reputation for failure or success with other firms?

When trading stocks, which makes the best use of fundamental analysis, you're putting your hard-earned savings in the hands of executives. So, it's best to consider this step.

When everything is taken into account, you'll probably end up with just a handful of potential candidates for your Mula! From here, you can start devising your trading plan and employing your trading system. These are further discussed in chapter 4.

On Stock Valuations

In this section, let's talk about how to use everything you've calculated and collected. This can help you decide the right price of a share.

Typically, the stock's value is the amount that traders are willing to pay for it. If no one is willing to buy an overpriced stock, many positions taken for that stock will stay open until someone makes a purchase or the owner of the stock voluntarily closes it.

For highly liquid assets, their actual value fluctuates throughout the day. This is especially true when its trading volume is quite high. FA is a tool that day traders utilize to analyze the following:

➤ Future business plans
➤ Market share
➤ Revenue growth
➤ Annual and monthly earnings

Fundamental analysis allows traders and investors to determine the right price for a stock. If it's currently overpriced in the market, then only beginners will be enticed to take the deal.

Likewise, the fair value can be determined with fundamental analysis. Therefore, you can ascertain if an offer is below the average price (fair value). This is a good deal. If you think the trade price won't go any lower, then it's best to grab such a bargain. Basically, FA analyzes financial security to specify its fair value (intrinsic value) by the evaluation of non-financial, financial, and economic factors.

The Six Fundamental Analysis Tools

Aside from the measures and ratios mentioned above, here are more tools that can greatly aid in fundamental analysis. Many trading platforms offer free tools such as EPS and P/E Ratio. You can employ the tools below to maximize the benefits of your economic calendar. With them, you won't be trading blind.

-Earnings Per Share

EPS or earnings per share refers to the profits allotted to each outstanding share. You can use two formulas to compute EPS:

Earnings per Share = Net Income/Total Number of Outstanding Shares

Earnings per Share = Net Income/Weighted Average of Outstanding Shares

-P/E Ratio

P/E ratio stands for price-to-earnings ratio. This tool. enables you to look at the link between EPS and the price of a particular stock. Based on earnings, it presents the entity's value, as well as market expectations. To calculate the P/E ratio, use the formula below:

Price to Earnings Ratio = Market Value or Stock Price/EPS

-PEG Ratio

By using PEG or price-to-growth ratio, you can determine the value of the stock in question while being able to consider earnings growth. The formula of this measure is listed below:

PEG Ratio = P/E Ratio/Earnings Growth Rate

Once you have the P/E Ratio, you can easily compute this measure. Just divide the price-to-earnings ratio by the growth rate of the company's net earnings within a given period.
-P/B Ratio
The P/B Ratio determines the present book value per share relative to the market value of the stock. The book value is the company's total assets less the present liabilities. It serves as an excellent indicator of undervalued stocks.
Here's the formula for the price-to-book ratio:
P/B Ratio = Market Value per Share/Book Value per Share
-Dividend Payout Ratio
This is also referred to as the payout ratio. It can help you know dividends that are issued to shareholders relative to the entity's net income. By calculating the dividend payout ratio, you can figure out how much shareholders receive from their investment.
To be exact, the dividend payout ratio determines how much dividend is paid on a quarterly or annual basis. Unlike other fundamental tools, a low payout rate isn't a red flag. This is especially true if the company is investing retained funds for future growth.
For the formula, please refer to the following equation:
Dividend Payout Ratio = Net Income/Dividends Paid
-Dividends Yield
This the ratio of the yearly dividend relative to the price per share. A high dividend yield ratio may indicate growth and high earnings. To calculate dividend yield, please refer to the formula below:
Dividend Yield = Yearly Dividend/Present Share Price
-Return on Equity
ROE stands for return on equity. It measures an entity's performance base on its shareholder's equity and net income. Using it on fundamental analysis allows you to reveal whether or not a company is using its assets effectively in generating profits. The formula goes like this:
ROE = Net Income/Average Shareholder Equity
When to Use Fundamental Analysis?
With due diligence and intensive research, you can make smart trades, in which you minimize your losses and

maximizes your winnings. Domestic currencies don't have fundamentals. That's why most use technical analysis in Forex trading. In the next chapter "Understanding Technical Analysis," there are many in-depth lessons for the topic. However, if you prefer to trade dividends and company shares, then choose fundamental analysis.

Step 4: Understanding Technical Analysis

Here's a technical analysis! Are you confused about the difference between TA and FA? This chapter is here to clear that up, but it offers more than that. If fundamental analysis deals with intrinsic values, technical analysis is for trends and price action--the changes in the value of a security over time. Those are the focus of technical analysis. As time passes, prices fall and trends become apparent. Patterns can last until they reverse or change due to news or catalyst. In trading, history can also repeat itself. Technical analysis focuses on price action and historical data.

When you finish this chapter, you can be a technician because you will acquire the skills necessary for conducting technical analysis, reading trends in price movements, and making accurate predictions. Technician is another term for technical analyst. You can start with using market statistics and price charts to devise an effective trading plan.

Getting Started

Technical analysis is utilized to identify events that will likely occur. To identify trends, technicians use logical frameworks. They also use logical frameworks to look for breakouts and trading ranges. You'll learn more about these terms in the next sections.

To understand the methods of technicians, you need to be acquainted with the following technical analysis concepts:

➢ Imbalances between demand and supply cause fluctuations in prices.
➢ Price actions aren't always random.
➢ Everything is in the price.

You can Find Everything in the Price

Unlike FA, technical analysis isn't concerned with fundamental indicators, such as the latest financial statements or analyst's report. Hence, the factors integral to FA aren't involved in technical analysis.

Financial analysts scrutinize the present, future, and past prices of securities. They greatly emphasize and scrutinize historical price data.

Technicians, on the other hand, focus on what the price represents. They base their predictions and trades on what they see.

Nevertheless, you can combine TA and FA for optimum strategy. You will learn how to do this in the later sections of this chapter.

Price Actions Aren't Always Random

At times, prices increase, and often, if the indicators are in favor of them, they keep increasing until they reach the ceiling price for the day.

Of course, they can also decrease, and their values fluctuate. When they move in a specific direction over time, you can say that there's a "trend."

Random price actions can appear between trending moments. If you magnify price movements, you can see that trading ranges are formed by several mini trends. The more you zoom in, the more you can see that prices aren't always random.

Looking at Intraday

Basically, TA identifies periods during the occurrence of trends. Generally, technical traders base their trades on trending markets. They try to determine when trends will start or when they'll end. They either focus on mini-trends or long-lasting trends. Others do both.

When observing intraday (i.e., occurring within the day) price charts, you can view examples of trading ranges and mini trends. However, the two aforementioned elements on price-charts are useless for investors and swing traders. They're those who tend to take long positions for months at a time.

To be honest, it's impossible to exactly know, with 100% accuracy, which way a price of a security will move.

Nevertheless, you can make an educated guess with almost a hundred percent certainty. With technical analysis, you can get to that money-making prediction.

Remember, history repeats itself. When stocks make familiar patterns, the same trend, which was notable in the past, could occur again.

In trading, the study of the past can help understand how prices and markets move. Patterns in price fluctuations repeat again and again. As a trader, your main task is to prepare for the next obvious opportunity to make money.

The 3 Most Important Components

Charts, patterns, and indicators are vital to TA. Patterns can't exist without a chart. You can't spot one without a chart. This shows and helps you visualize price movements and the patterns they form. Having a charting platform or application can make trading easier.

Please keep that in mind when you're choosing a broker. In case your preferred platform doesn't have a charting system, then use a real-time securities scanner.

For example, Investagram and StocksToTrade, two real-time stock scanners, can be used for charting and technical analysis. These apps also offer a Paper Trading feature. This allows for trading and pattern spotting simulations. Such features can be valuable to beginner traders.

Technical Analysis: The Complete Step-by-Step Guide

1. Understanding the theories behind TA

Based on Charles Dow's theories about the stock market, technical analysis was conceptualized. For decades, it has guided the approach of technicians towards financial markets. The theories are described below with details of how they're interpreted for technical analysis.

-Market changes reflect all known data

Technicians infer that the price movements of a financial security and its trading volume represent all available information needed to make highly accurate predictions. Hence, price listings can be considered as fair value, a broad measure of an asset's worth.

-Price actions can often be predicted and charted

As mentioned earlier, prices can move randomly. However, there are times when their movements are predictable. With every identified trend, an opportunity to make money arises. There are many trading strategies out there. You may buy low and sell high during a bull market or sell short during a bear market when prices are falling. If you further adjust the duration for analysis, you may spot long- and short-term trends.

-History will repeat itself

According to Investopedia, the majority of traders and investors don't change their trading habits, strategies, and motivations overnight. You can expect that they'll exhibit repetitive behaviors to familiar conditions. Their behaviors can affect the market they're in since they and their motivations can collectively affect future price actions.

You can use this knowledge to profit from every historical trend that repeats itself. It's evident that TA regards market behavior and human actions even though it avoids intrinsic values.

The aforementioned trading principles are not at all times appropriate; however, many traders, including Tim Sykes, Warren Buffet, and Ross Cameron, consider them as their maxims. Look at them now. They're one of the richest people in the world. Buffet, in particular, is in Forbes' top 100 wealthiest men.

2. Look for Instant Results

Unlike FA, which considers financial data and balance sheets, TA focuses on periods as short as few minutes and no longer than four weeks. According to Bloomberg Businessweek, technical analysis is suitable for people who take short positions such as day traders.

3. Spot trends by reading charts

Technicians generally look at graphs and charts of security prices. They try to spot the future direction of the value of their target asset while overlooking individual fluctuations.

Technical analysts classify trends by duration and type:

-Uptrends

Uptrends are characterized by lows and highs that become progressively higher. Like other types of trends, uptrends are also composed of mini trends.

-Downtrends

These are the opposite of uptrends. You can spot mini trends if you use a magnification tool. Successive lows and highs that are progressive lower characterize downtrends.

-Horizontal trends

Horizontal trends have a consistent direction, which is in an almost straight line. These faults change from previous price fluctuations. When the forces of demand and supply are almost equal, horizontal or sideway trends occur. This is common during periods of consolidation.

-Trend lines

Trend lines connect successive maximum highs, point by point. Drawing trend lines streamlines the process of spotting trends. Trend lines are also referred to as "channel lines."

-Intermediates trends

Intermediate trends last for at least 30 days, but they don't last for more than a year. They are consist of near-term trends.

-Near-term trends

Near-term trends last for at least a month. Major trends are comprised of intermediate and near-term trends.

-Major trends

These last longer for more than 12 months. Often, major trends don't have a consistent direction. For example, a two-week-long bull market could suddenly plummet and become a bear market in the 3rd week. This could last for more than 3 weeks. The bull market is a near-term trend, while the bear market is an example of an intermediate trend.

-The four charts

Technicians utilize four types of charts:

a) Line charts are for closing positions over a period.
b) Bar and candlestick charts are used for visualizing low and high prices between periods and for whole trading periods.
c) Point and figure charts show noteworthy price actions over a given time frame.

Over the years, since the conceptualization of technical analysis, technicians and traders have coined the aforementioned phrases for patterns appearing on charts used for TA.

Here are some more noteworthy trends to consider:

- ➤ A pattern or trend that resembles a cup with a handle often indicates that an upward trend may continue after a short correction.
- ➤ A saucer or downward bottom trend indicates a long period of bottoming before a significant uptrend.
- ➤ A double bottom or double top pattern indicates two failed attempts to surpass a low or high price. A reversal trend often follows this.
- ➤ In the same way, a triple bottom or triple top shows three failed attempts. They also precede a reversal.

4. Know support and resistance

Support and resistance are widely used concepts in currency trading. Check out the diagram below. The upward zigzag pattern looks like a bull market. When price reaches a peak and immediately pulls back, the point at the peak is known as the "resistance." The lowest point is called "support." A trend is made up of many supports and resistances. Resistances suggest that there will be a seller surplus. Support levels, on the other hand, indicate an impending buyer surplus. In this regard, resistance and support are continuously formed whether the price generally moves up or down. Hence, this remains true during an uptrend or downtrend.

Traders trade the "bounce." "To buy a bounce" means you're purchasing a financial security after its value has reached a support level. This can bring forth a secondary movement that allows traders to make a profit from the short-term correction. Aside from bounce trading, the following strategies also make use of support and resistance levels:

a) Take a buy position when the price falls or is falling towards the support
b) Take a sell position when the price rises or is rising towards the resistance
c) Sell when the price of the asset breaks up through the support level
d) Make a purchase when the price of the security breaks up through resistance

-How to Plot Support and Resistance

Support and resistance levels aren't exact numbers. Often, you'll see one of them with a figure that appears broken. On candlestick charts, like the example below, tests are represented by shadows that appear like candlesticks.

The shadows tested the support level, which is not a whole number. In such cases, the market is "breaking support," and the market is just testing that level or is being tested.
In TA, a test is when an asset's price nears an established resistance or support. If the price stays within the support and resistance levels, you can say that the test passes. If the price reaches new highs or new lows, then it fails.
What's the purpose of this? The results of such tests determine the accuracy of signals and patterns. These are the distinctive formations in price movements on a chart. Patterns serve as the foundation of technical analysis. They connect common price points, like highs and lows or closing prices, in a given period. In general, traders and analysts utilize tests to confirm support and resistance levels in a stock, currency, or other security.
-Indication of Broken Support and Resistance Levels
There is no definite answer to this. Some traders claim levels are considered broken when the asset's value can close past that level. When plotting levels of supports and resistances, avoid breakouts and decimals. Instead, focus on intentional movements and whole numbers as much as you can.
Please check out the chart below. In the example, it's best to plot the points around areas that form valleys or peaks. These are the lows and the highs respectively.

-Snippets About Support and Resistance
When the asset's price passes through a resistance level or the highest point on the chart, that resistance may become support soon. A breakout is a price moving outside a predefined resistance or support level, with increased volume. Breakout traders take a long position after the price surpasses the resistance level. They take a short position when the price breaks below support.

) MACD and RSI indicators, which are discussed in the following
ections, are used to measure the strength of a breakout.
) When a level is surpassed, the strength of follow-through depends
n how strong the resistance or support break out is.
) The support is the lowest value a financial security attains before
าany buyers take advantage of the situation, come in, and make
urchases. This moves the price upwards.
 Resistance is the highest value a financial instrument reaches
efore traders start selling and cause another price decrease. This is
าore commonly known as the "ceiling price."

In conclusion, the floor price is the bottom line of the given
asset. It's also called the support level, and the ceiling price is
the resistance level. These terms are used for the
confirmation of a pattern or trend and for determining when is
the next reversal.

5. Study the Trading Volume

Once you're done looking at trends, you must consider the
trading volume of the asset in question. Doing so further
validates the existence of the trend and helps in predicting
when is the exact reversal. If the volume rises or falls slightly
as the asset's value goes up, then the trend is valid and may
soon experience a reversal.

-How to measure trading volume with technical analysis?
Trading volume measures how much specific security has
been traded in a given period. For example, the volume of
stocks is measured in the number of public shares traded.
For options and futures, the trading volume is based on how
many contracts or CFDs have changed hands. Indicators and
figures using volume data are provided with online charts.
Observing patterns in trading volume can give you an insight
into the conviction and strength behind the trends in specific
securities and entire markets. The same can be said for
options and futures day trading. The volume in the said
markets serves as an *indicator* of the market sentiment of the
participants.

Volume plays an integral role in TA since it also features
prominent technical indicators:

- Volume can help you measure the number of public shares/futures/options being traded in a stock or contracts.
- Speculators consider volume as an indicator of market strength. Rising markets with increasing volume are viewed as healthy and strong.
- When prices are falling while volume is increasing, the trend on the chart is getting ready for bottoming.
- When prices reach highs while volume is decreasing, a reversal may be taking shape. Watch out for this.
- The Klinger indicator and the on-balance volume are some charting tools based on trading volume.

6. Filter Minor Fluctuations by Using MAs

MAs stand for moving averages. An MA is a series of measured averages. They're calculated over equal periods. The goal of this step is to remove irrelevant lows and highs and to streamline the whole technical analysis process. To be specific, it can help in reading overall patterns/trends.

Plotting prices against MAs makes it easy to spot reversals. You can use many methods for calculating averages to do this:

-Finding the SMA

SMA or simple moving average can be calculated by adding every closing price of a specific period. Then, divide the sum by the total number of addends.

-Finding the LMA

LMA stands for linear weighted average. To calculate LMA, list each price in a given period and multiply them by their position. After that, add all of the plotted prices together. Next, you must divide the sum by the number of addends. For example, over 4 days, the 1st price is multiplied by one, the 2nd is multiplied by two, and so forth.

-Finding the EMA

EMA or exponential moving average can be compared to the LMA. It weighs the latest prices. To calculate EMA, please follow the instructions below:

Calculate the simple moving average

Compute the multiplier for weighting the EMA

Lastly, calculate the present EMA

The calculation for the SMA is similar to computing a mean or average. That is to say, the simple moving average for any time periods is the sum of the closing prices for the time period. The sum is then divided by that same number.

For example, a 5-day SMA is the sum of the closing prices for the last 5 days, divided by 5.

7. Use Oscillators and Indicators to Support Your Findings

In technical analysis, indicators are considered calculations. They support the data collected from trends on a line chart, which are gleaned from the movements of prices. The use of indicators can increase the accuracy of your predictions. The MAs described in the previous step are an indicator. It's possible for indicators to have decimals. Others are limited to a range, like 1 to 100.

To better understand oscillators and indicators, please check out the key points below.

-Indicators may either be lagging or leading. Leading indicators can predict price actions and are useful when reading horizontal trends. They can signal downtrends or uptrends. Whereas, lagging indicators aids in confirming price actions. They're most useful in times of downtrends and uptrends.

-Examples of trend indicators are the ADX and Aroon indicators. The ADX utilizes both negative and positive directional indicators. It can determine the strength of an impending downtrend or uptrend. The scale used is zero to one hundred. If the value is below 20, then the probability of the trend is low. Values above 40 is a sign of a strong trend.

-Aroon indicator, on the other hand, plots the duration of the lowest and highest trading prices. The output data determines the trend's strength and nature. It also helps in predicting when is the emergence of the next trend.

-The OBV is an indicator that relates to trading volume. It encompasses the whole trading volume of a security for a specific period. An OBV with a positive value implies that the asset's price is increasing; a negative value will turn up when the price is decreasing.

-About the RSI and stochastic oscillator

Both the stochastic oscillator and the RSI measures the frequency of the trades for the given security. The index ranges from zero to one hundred. If the value is over seventy, then the asset is being purchased too frequently. A value below thirty indicates that many are selling the asset at a very fast rate.

Typically, RSI is utilized for periods of 2 weeks. This makes it highly liquid. Also, the stochastic oscillator ranges from zero to one hundred and signals frequent purchases at over eighty. Frequent selling is obvious at a value under twenty.

If you trade on margin so that you can resell the security at a higher price at a later date, waiting for the price to reach support provides an opportunity to make money. In the future, you will have to return the money to your broker. Nevertheless, you've already made a profit.

You can also sell at the strength and buy at pullback. A pullback is a reversal of a rising trend. This offers a slim chance to buy at a low price. This is another phrase for "buy low, and sell high." Often, seasoned traders buy assets of any kind when they're being valued at a high price. You can do this at the resistance level or near the peak.

Choosing a Broker, TA Strategy and Trading System

The main focus of this section is to guide you through the process of designing your own trading system. It may not take long to develop one, but testing it and choosing a broker may take some time.

Once you have a trading system and strategy, you know the features, indicators, securities data, and charts you need for technical analysis. Your broker should be able to provide the tools for you. If not, then you can use third-party tools like charting programs and real-time securities scanners.

Choose a strategy for your trading style

Do you prefer trading stocks, Forex, or futures? Which do you prefer, long position or short position? There are no two traders out there, so even if you copy the strategies of the most seasoned traders, it isn't guaranteed that it will work for you.

Do you know what's best? You need to devise your own strategy. It may be a modified version of the trading strategy of your favorite trader. Nevertheless, you've made it your own, making it compatible with your personality and capital. Here's how you can do this:

) Form your market ideology

As a trader, you've to be a reader. That's how you can get through this step. You need to research and research.

Firstly, you must know the indicators that affect your preferred security to trade. Ask yourself, "What are the large entities that can control its value?" "Should you use technical analysis or fundamental analysis?

In this step, avoid get-rich styles. Think about the trading volume and the supply and demand in the market. Your market ideology will help shape the succeeding steps.

) Choose a market

Your future trading platform must have good offers for trading the security. For example, currency trading involves selling with a quote. If you prefer to trade equities, you need options for choosing penny stocks or blue-chips. The golden rule in this step is to understand your preferred market and your chosen trading platform.

) Select a time frame

Should you opt for 5-minute time frames or those that an hour-long? Are you suitable for reading daily charts? The answer to these questions is your availability. If you have free time to watch the market like a prowling vulture, then go for hour-long time frames.

Short ones are best suited for those who treat trading as a sideline. If you have a full-time job, you won't be able to commit to hour-long time frames. In this case, you can work with end-of-day charts Either case, make sure that your broker offers or you have access to the charting tools you need.

) Choose your tools for watching trends

You trade when the asset's price is rising, and you can use a bullish Pin Bar to initiate your trade. Likewise, you won't trade when you see a Gimme Bar.

Rather, the tool is used to confirm whether or not the asset's price is going sideways. It's also utilized to enter the market.

You use tools and programs to watch real-time price statistics and judge market context. Aside from technical indicators, like MAs and MACDs, price movement tools, such as trend lines and swing pivots, can come in handy.

Plan your exit trigger

Similar to entering a trade, your exit should also be planned. This is where stop/loss orders would prove to be beneficial. Remember, the market won't be in your favor forever. If you reach a specific amount of loss, you may be able to get out automatically.

Define risks

In the next chapter, you'll learn more about electronic trading risks and how to mitigate them.

Once you've planned your exit and entry rules with the use of tools and triggers, you can start working on risk management. Position sizing can help you reduce risks and improve accuracy. For any trade setup, position size defines the amount of money you'll put into play. For example, if you triple your trade's size, you're also tripling risks. In chapter?, you can learn how to mitigate trading risks.

List down your trading rules

You can do this step on paper or with the help of your trusty personal computer. By doing this, you have a firm and robust method that promotes consistency and discipline. By creating a record of your strategy and the rules you have for your style, you can reuse it for other types of trades and be able to refine it with ease.

Employ back-testing

Having written your trading rules, you can now proceed to backtesting. To do this, you've to replay market price actions, restudy trends, and record trades manually. Lastly, you need to test your strategy and trades using your chart and past trends.

See and check if you can make a profit with your predictions by playing with your strategy and historical data. Choose a given time frame and start from there.

With your written rules, you can now backtest the strategy. Looking through trades manually is a good method to develop a market instinct, more so than relying on data generators wherein you just input data and have the results on your screen within seconds.

Refining your trading strategy

After backtesting, you can have a general idea of the key areas that need improvement. Does your stop/loss order work for your capital? Were your test predictions accurate? What was the probability of success? Here are tips you can use for this step:

➢ Utilize a demo account for your tests and backtests.
➢ Review your day trades, whether mock or actual.
➢ Adapt your trading plan based on your review.

. Identify securities

Please keep in mind that not all types of financial securities will be suited to your strategy. In this step, you must ask yourself the following questions:

➢ Are my trading rules and system ideal for volatile stocks or stable ones?
➢ Can I get all the resources needed for my analysis?
➢ Do I have the funds to earn a good amount of profit in each trade?
➢ What position will I take?

Different securities also require different parameters. In the aforementioned example, a 15-day and 50-day MA would be suitable.

. Choosing the right broker

Your chosen broker, platform, and trading account must support your preferred security (e.g., options, stock, futures, Forex, options, etc.). Above all, it must offer the necessary functionalities for tracking and observing selected indicators while minimizing costs and maximizing profits. For the example above, a basic trading account with MAs on candlestick charts would be adequate.

➢ Foremost, they must be able to provide a demo account.
➢ Match your style with a broker that charges the least amount of fees
➢ Don't just compare commission. You must also consider other costs, like service charges and margin interest.

- ➤ The broker must be accessible. Also, you need to find out who covers for them if whether or not they're regulated. Only choose brokers that are regulated.
- ➤ You may get referrals. Do you know someone who has been a seasoned trader? Why not ask him/her for advice.
- ➤ Avoid brokers that insist on large investments where they can greatly benefit from. Find out the amount of commissions and how they're determined.
- ➤ Examine their margin rules and the fees for every transaction. Check for additional fees and charges as well.
- ➤ Be careful with deep discount brokers. Their discounts may have hidden charges or high fees.
- ➤ User-friendliness is also another feature to consider. The interface and the responsiveness of the website, as well as the people that run it, must be taken into consideration. When you need help or an inquiry answered, their CS team should be available during trading hours and there must be a section for FAQs and guidelines.
- ➤ The ease of withdrawals and deposits and the margin requirements are also very important. Reliability is what you need to get your profits fast. How many hours pr days does it for them to process your deposit and payment requests? When it comes to taking your profits away and fulfilling options for getting out of the market, they must be reliable.
- ➤ If they don't fulfill regulations, they have to answer to regulators. They'll have their license revoked and face fees and criminal charges if they do something to the funds of traders. That's why you need to choose a licensed broker. The US Securities and Exchange Commission (SEC) and the Financial Regulatory Authority (FINRA) are some examples of such governing bodies.
- ➤ For every broker you review, always consider their reception. Do they have good reviews? Visit websites like brokerchoosers.com and Forexbrokers.com. By doing so, you can have a general idea of the experiences of the majority of their users.

5. Tracking trades and additional tools

Day traders need various functionality levels. What does this mean? For example, you may need a margin account providing access to Level 2 quotes and the feature called "market maker visibility."

You also need additional tools. What are the most important tools in day trading? Here are the tools and services needed for day trading:

➤ Breaking news software
➤ Charting app
➤ Real-time market scanner/market maker
➤ Scanning software

You may need phone and email alerts. This can come in handy when you're margin trading. As well, you must be vigilant of price movements. Letting an opportunity snuck past under your nose would be an opportunity lost forever.

Lastly, an automated trading system could be beneficial to you too, especially if you need someone or something to execute trades on your behalf.

More Tips and Understanding the Risk Factors

Trading is challenging. That's a fact. Day traders have it harder than investors and swing traders. They need to study the market and the charts almost every day. As a day trader, you need to do your homework thoroughly.

Here are some more pointers that you may benefit from:

➤ Backtest your trading strategy. You need to see how your trading style and strategy work. By doing this, you can check the efficacy and accuracy of your predictions with your analysis. Don't cheat. Choose a duration and start and end date, and begin your first trial from there.

➤ There's no need to rush. You must consider practicing using a demo account once you're done reading this book and after devising your trading system and plans. After these, log in to your preferred platform and conduct "mock" trades with a practice account.

➤ Remember, always be flexible especially when you're margin trading. Brokers can change their policies, so you need to be ready with future requirements.

- ➢ Once you've chosen a broker, go for a trial account first before depositing any money or upgrading to a VIP or premium plan.
- ➢ Warren Buffet, one of Forbe's top 10 richest in the world, said, "start small and expand as you improve."

Using TA and FA for Optimum Strategy

Technical analysis evolved from Dow's stock market theories. TA aims to predict future prices of tradable assets, based on performance and historical prices. Meanwhile, the fundamental analysis considers intrinsic values that could determine price action and the future status of an asset. Both FA and TA use the law of supply and demand to identify trends, profit from them, and understand how the markets work.

Many day traders and investors leverage technical and fundamental analysis when formulating trading decisions. TA can fill in gaps of knowledge that FA can't provide. As well, FA can make the results of TA more accurate and easier to implement. By using both, you can improve long-term risk-adjusted returns. In chapter 6, you can gain more knowledge about trading risks.

Chapter Summary

Many traders analyze stocks and other assets based on their fundamentals, like revenue, industry trends, and valuation. However, such intrinsic values aren't reflected in the price of the asset.

Technical analysis, on the other hand, aims to predict price action by examining past price data and historical trading volume. TA helps both investors and speculators diminish the gap between market price and intrinsic value through leveraging trading strategies, such as behavioral economics and statistical analysis.

At its core, TA guides traders to what may happen using past data. For decision-making, most speculators use both fundamental and technical analysis.

Step 5: Knowing More About Day Trading

There are two types of professional traders: hedgers and speculators. Hedgers find protection against price changes. Speculators look to gain profit from price movements--the action of a security's price plotted overtime. Price changes are the basis for all types of technical analysis used in electronic trading. Short-term traders, such as the day traders, rely heavily on price action.

The trends and formations extrapolated from historical data, through analysis, help in formulating successful trading decisions. Hedgers, unlike speculators, make their trading (buy and sell) choices as insurance. Speculators choose their positions to make a profit, offsetting their exposure in other markets.

The Role of Day Trading

To clarify everything that has been said, take a food-processing company for example. The skilled worker, who raises the ingredients required in manufacturing, such as corn and meat, purchases future contracts on those ingredients.

By doing that, if prices go up, the prospected profits of the organization decrease. This could be a compromise to the company. The farmer, on the other hand, benefits if prices increase and suffer if the selling price decrease.

To protect against that, the farmer can sell futures on his commodities. What are futures? Futures are financial contracts. These contracts obligate buyers to buy assets in advance or oblige sellers to sell assets.

Future contracts have predetermined prices and future dates. Futures hedges the price action of underlying assets. This move helps prevent losses from unfavorable price actions. In the example above, the buyer is the company and the farmer is the seller.

The farmer can sell futures on his commodities to protect himself against any price decline. His futures position on the trade will only make money if the price decrease, as it offsets the decrease of prices of his products. Also, with future contracts, he will lose money because of the contracts, but his profits from his harvest offset the loss.

Commodity markets were established to help farmers and agriculturists find buyers and manage risks. The bond and stock markets, in contrast, create incentives for investors and buyers to finance their companies. Speculation, the act of trading that has a high chance of losing value, but also has a high probability for a significant gain, is present in all of these markets. Speculation is also common in Forex, stocks, cryptocurrency, options, and other electronic markets.

Day traders are speculators. They're sophisticated individuals who buy assets for short periods. They employ trading strategies to make profits from price changes. Like hedgers, they are important to markets because they promote liquidity and keep the value of assets active.

Speculators day trade to make money from the current status of markets. Managing risks by allocating money using stop and limit orders, they don't take long positions. Their orders close out as soon as set price levels are reached.

Unlike hedgers, day traders don't manage their risks by offsetting positions. Rather, they employ techniques and strategies that can limit losses. This will be discussed more in the succeeding sections. For example, they employ money management tactics and limit or stop orders. Any electronic market has hedgers and speculators trading in them.

By knowing the various participants and their loss and profit expectations, you can manage day trading and stir away from the turmoils it brings. This is very important since you can only make money from the losses of others in zero-sum markets.

The Zero-sum Markets

The zero-sum markets have as many winners as losers. Stocks, Forex, futures, and options are prominent with day traders. In chapter 8, day trading with the said securities will be further discussed. In such markets, when one makes a profit, someones loses money. That's one notable element in zero-sum markets.

Zero-sum is a situation in game theory, wherein one's gain is equivalent to another's loss. The net equal in benefit or wealth is zero. In trading, futures and options are examples of zero-sum games, excluding the cost of the transaction. As a whole, there's no net loss or net gain.

What does that mean for day traders? Day trading is like a zero-sum game. Most day traders in such markets are also hedgers. They're contented with taking small losses to lower risks in trading, preventing big losses. In specific market conditions, speculators, which are mostly day traders, have a profit advantage. Still, they shouldn't count on those "advantages" at all times.

Who loses and wins in such markets? There are times that the winner depends on luck. But, over the long run, the winners are disciplined traders. The winners in zero-sum markets are those who have a trading plan. Initial losses could just be a part of their strategy.

Some sell a lot to increase the asset's value and reach the ceiling price for the day. That's just one type of tricky trading strategy. Doesn't that peak your interest?

Disciplined traders employ strategies, make use of analyses, set limits, and stick to those limits. They trade based on data rather than emotions, such as greed, fear, and hope. In the next chapter, you'll learn more about trading psychology and the traits needed to develop by traders.

The stock market, however, is not a zero-sum market, although many speculators trade here. As long as the economy improves, the value of the stocks increase. At the end of the day, the number of winners in stock markets is greater than in zero-sum markets. If you know how profits are divided in your preferred market, you will be aware of the risks and what other participants face.

Electronic trading is all about rewards and risks. You don't want others to be making money from your losses. You may be doing what you like, but you will go nowhere if you keep losing.

Closing Your Positions Every Trading Day's End
Day traders start their day fresh because they finish each one with a new beginning--a clean slate. This daily routine decreases risks and forces discipline into people. When there's a possibility for profit, you shouldn't just sit around and watch others take the opportunities. You must refrain from keeping losses longer than one day and always take your

profits at the end of each trading day since winning positions can turn into losing positions overnight.

Doing those decreases risks, and that discipline is important for speculators and day traders. When engaging in day trading, the market doesn't care about your identity or your preferences. You own your time, yet you don't have a boss who can cut you a little slack. You have no coworker who can serve as your substitute, unless you opt for automatic trading or have hired someone to watch the market for you. And lastly, you don't have a client who can drop you hints. Unless you have set rules for yourself and a guide for your trading decisions, you'll be the prey of the Four Horsemen of Trading Ruin--greed, doubt, fear, and hope.

How to discipline yourself? Firstly, you must develop a trading plan and business plan. These two should be different from each other, and they must reflect your personality and goals. After the first step, you've to set your work hours and trading days. These steps are covered in chapter 5.

While thinking about your options, you must test your trading system. This can help you create an effective trading system perfect for your lifestyle and capabilities. By doing so, you can put your strategies and plans into action. Simply put, you need to prepare and create a plan. Whether you're building a new chicken coop, joining a triathlon, or engaging in day trading, those two steps are the basic strategy of winners.

Exploring the Different Kinds of Trading Markets

As trading innovation continues and advents in technology increase, the world of electronic trading keeps expanding, and more financial instruments can be used. Even commodities markers are stealing each other's market share. A company, entity, or product controls the portion of a market.

For example, an individual who needs to purchase gold physically or by a futures contract can now buy an exchange-traded fund (ETF) so that he or she can participate in the price movement of gold.

Since similar scenarios also apply to stocks, commodities, currencies, and other securities, online traders can fine-tune their strategies for different circumstances, like during day- or swing trading.

-What are the financial markets?

Financial and trading markets refer to any market where securities trading occurs. This includes derivatives, Forex, bonds, and stocks. Financial markets are integral to the effective operation of capitalist nations. They create liquidity and allocate resources for entrepreneurs and businesses. The marketplaces facilitate the act of trading for both sellers and buyers. Through electronic trading, they can buy and sell specific securities, which are discussed below, online.

The financial markets allow for the trade of securities products. These offer a return for the people (the traders and investors) who have funds to purchase on a brokerage platform. The buyers, especially the day traders, resell the securities for profit.

For example, the stock market is a type of financial market. Through online brokers and similar platforms, you can trade national and international stocks. However, some local stocks are only available for trading in national financial organizations. In Japan, IC Markets and XTB Online Trading allows for the trading of national-level public shares.

Financial markets are formed by trading many types of financial instruments, which include derivatives, currencies, bonds, and equities. These marketplaces rely heavily on data transparency to ensure that the prices inside the market are appropriate.

The intrinsic value of the securities, like gold, doesn't indicate their market prices. This is because they're also affected by taxes and other macroeconomic factors.

Some markets have little activity. They're small compared to others, such as local stock exchanges. FirstMetroSec in the Philippines is an example of a local stock exchange.

In contrast, the NASDAQ and NYSE experience millions of trades daily and trillions of dollars circulate on these markets, every 24 hours. The equity market or the stock market allows hedgers, investors, and speculators to publicly sell shares of companies they've invested in.

In primary stock markets, new stocks can be issued. Newly-issued stocks are referred to as initial public offers (IPOs). Subsequent stock tradings can also be conducted in secondary markets. This is where investors trade securities that are already known.

The Different Trading Markets

Depending on your experience, you may even be aware of the trading or investment mediums that are available to you with just one click. Even when avoiding illiquid and abstract markets, speculators can find transactions within various markets that are within their budget. Here are the most notable markets and exchanges where you can day trade.

-OTC markets

Over-the-counter markets are decentralized. This means that they don't have physical locations. And, securities trading is conducted online, or electronically. Online, participants in the market include traders and investors.

In the next sections, you will learn how to choose the right platform and method of trading suitable for you. Will you participate in OTC markets? Do you prefer brokers and brokerage platforms?

An OTC market can handle the exchanges of stocks that aren't listed on the NYSE and American Stock Exchange. Generally, financial organizations and entities that trade in OTC and other primary markets require fewer fees and less regulation than secondary markets, which is also called aftermarket in which traders and investors trade financial securities they already own.

Here are more pros and cons of trading in OTC markets:

Pros
➢ High volatility
➢ The ability to stay ahead of inflation
➢ Unmatched liquidity
➢ Flexibility for beginners
➢ Growth opportunities

Cons
➢ Sudden market crashes
➢ Subjection to higher risks

-Stock Market

The stock market is the collection of exchanges and platforms where daily activities of issuance and trading of shares of publicly-held companies occur. These financial activities are executed through OTC marketplaces, brokerage platforms, and institutionalized formal exchanges.

Stock markets, whether they have a physical location or none, operate following set regulations. In any country, region, or state that allows stocks and securities trading, there could be multiple venues for stock and Forex trading. The NASDAQ and NYSE are two of the world's largest securities exchange with physical locations. Major brokerage platforms all offer stock trading.

While the terms stock exchange and stock market can be used interchangeably, the former is just a subset of the latter. If you say you trade in the stock market, this means you trade equities/shares on a stock exchange that is part of the stock market.

The most notable stock exchanges in the world include the NASDAQ, NYSE, and CBOE, or the Chicago Board Options Exchange. These leading national stock exchanges, along with smaller exchanges existing within the country, comprises the US stock market.

A bourse, securities exchange, or stock is a facility or platform where traders and stockbrokers can trade securities, including bonds and shares of stocks. Some also issue issues and allow for the redemption of securities, capital events, and financial instruments, as well as the payment of income and dividends. Dividends are the profit you get from your investments in common shares.

Although most trades in the markets involve public shares, ETF, bonds, and currency trades also transpire in stock markets. The same can be said in Forex markets. This is also true for the US stock markets.

-Bond Markets

What's a bond? A bond is a security in which an investor loans a specific amount of money for a defined period at a pre-established interest rate. Bonds are agreements between the borrower and the lender containing the details of the contract\deal, including the details of the loan and its subsequent payments.

Sovereign governments, as well as states, and municipalities, can issue bonds. The issuance could be for financing operations and projects. The bond market is also referred to as the credit, debit, and fixed-income markets. It involves trades of securities like bills and notes issued by the US Treasury.

How to trade bonds? Understanding bond trading and bond markets are important to proper day trading. The bond market is bigger than the stock market and bond trading occurs thousands, if not millions, of times per day.

When speculators trade bonds, they specify the different types of bonds they're trading. In turn, this sets the credit price in the economy. This is why the bond market affects many economies around the world, both negatively and positively. Unlike stocks, bonds can be traded anywhere that a seller and buyer can conduct a transaction. There is no exchange or central place for bond trading. In fact, this market is a type of over-the-counter market. Nevertheless, convertible bonds, like bond options and bond futures, are traded on formal exchanges, including online brokerage platforms. An in-depth discussion of this topic is included in the last chapter of this book.

-The ETF Market

Funds that represent multiple sectors, industries, and commodities are involved in ETF markets. Like stocks, you can trade such securities daily or hoard them in your account for swing trading.

-The Forex Market

Also known as the currency market, the Forex market is the largest in the world. It's also the most liquid and has accounted for billions of trades per day. In 2010, it has accounted for $3 trillion of daily trading. Although it hasn't existed a century ago, it's where the majority of day-traders buy and sell securities.

Foreign exchange markets facilitate the trades of one currency for another. Even though daily currency trades can be also conducted electronically, stock trading is different from Forex trading. Currencies are traded in pairs, while stocks are traded in units.

-The Options Market

The options market is a marketplace that enables participants to take positions in the derivative of an asset\security. Hence, the option--a contract that enables an investor to trade a financial instrument like an index or ETF at a set price over a certain period--is based on specific securities. The value of options and other inputs changes with the value, or the lack of, that the asset in question provides.

-CFDs

CFD stands for Contract for Difference. This is an arrangement made in derivatives trades, wherein the differences in the given settlement between the first and last trade prices are settled by cash. This is a type of option whereby physical delivery of the security or asset isn't required. The settlement leads to a cash payment, rather than settling in bonds, stocks, or commodities.

A settlement, in finance and trading, is a business process, by which securities or interests in securities are physically delivered to fulfill contractual obligations. These days, settlements typically take place in central securities depositories (CSDs).

A CSD is a financial organization that holds securities like shares or stocks in dematerialized or certificated form. Through a CSD, ownership of a financial security can be transferred. This is executed with a book entry, instead of the transfer of physical certificates. This allows brokers, electronic platforms, and financial organizations to hold securities at a single location. This makes them available for electronic clearing and settlement.

This option type avoids expenses for transaction and transport fees. CFDs don't expire. The CFD market is in fact a hybrid of the Forex, stock, and options market.

Like other markets, the CFD market is accessible anywhere that has an internet connection. All of them have disadvantages and advantages. For this reason, most traders focus on only one type of security to trade. They are afraid to transact in other markets aside from what suits their personality best. This is mainly due to a lack of knowledge.

However, the successful ones do otherwise. Given their trading style, they primarily take advantage of one market and hedge or trade on another as a sideline.

What's the Best Market for You?

You must consider your location, financial resources, and day trading style when choosing which market to participate in. To help you decide on things like that is one of the purposes of this book. It's integral to be aware of other alternatives so that you can easily fine-tune your trades and get profitable results. For a more detailed discussion of this topic, please refer to the next section, chapter 7, and chapter 8.

Alternative Markets for Aspiring Day Traders

Since the 2000 stock market crash, the number of turnovers in the Forex market has increased. In investing, turnover is the percentage of a financial portfolio sold in a specific year or month. A fast turnover rate generates high commissions for transactions placed by a broker.

That implies an increase in the number of new-day traders in the CFD and Forex markets. The greatest lure by brokers is their low initial deposits. Most well-refuted online brokers only require at least $100 to open an account and start trading Forex and stocks.

In the Forex market, the trader exchanges one currency for another. The low commission may sound nice, but in such platforms, a spread must be paid in every transaction.

The bottom line is, you must be aware that multiple markets are out there. Even though it isn't advisable to participate in all of them due to restrictions and time limitations, the use of a combination of markets or the fine-tuning of trading strategies can positively impact results.

For some traders, they need to change markets from time to time since their trading success depends on that. In contrast, entering two or more markets can provide advantages such as risk reduction, capital outlays, and changes in cost. Just remember that becoming familiar with the markets provides more opportunities and increased profits and reduced costs.

-The Stock Exchanges

What's a stock exchange? Stock exchanges are physical and virtual places where stocks can be traded. An exchange of this type is highly regulated, despite being dominated by electronic trading.

How to Day Trade

"Betting against the trend" is an example of a trading strategy. This is also called contrarian investing and is used by many stock traders, including those that manipulate price movements and market volatility. If the market or a stock experiences a downtrend, you buy and trade against the market. You speculate that going up the trend will favor you and your capital.

Highly experienced traders use this strategy. They fully understand the market, and they have profited many times from doing the opposite of what the majority does. Betting against the trend is risky, but it offers high profits.

For example, if the stock market you're participating in is currently bullish, you hedge and take long positions. If you're in a bear market and you take long positions, you're also going against the trend. Your trading success depends on the factors affecting the trend. You need careful and diligent research before employing this money-making tactic.

By simply buying low, you aren't exactly trading in the said fashion. However, it could result in that if effectively done. For example, when day traders predict that a stock will fall low, they may borrow shares and sell them for the purpose of trading at low prices. When they prefer day trading, they will take short positions.

-Short Trades

Taking short positions can be confusing to most traders. In reality, we need to buy something for us to sell it. In short trades, day traders sell securities before purchasing them. They do this to make a profit from a price decrease. Their trade will only generate profits if the amount they borrowed is lower than the selling price of the asset. In financial markets, you can buy and then sell, or sell and then buy.

Day traders utilize the words short and sell interchangeably. Likewise, some programs and trading platforms have a trading button marked short or sell. The use of the word "short" in the sentence "I am short apple" indicates that you're in a short position in Apple stock.

To reiterate, day traders who like taking short positions often say "go short" or "going short." This indicates their interest in taking a short position in a specific asset. Similar to the example in chapter 2, if you go short on 1,000 shares of YYY stock at $9, you receive $9,000 in your account upon completion of the trade. If you can buy 1,000 shares of stock YYY at $10.60 per share, you will have to pay $10,600. If you resell all your purchased shares at $11,000, you receive $11,000 by going short. Hence, your profit will be $400, less commissions.

If the value of stock increases and if you repurchase 1,000 shares at $9.20, then you've to pay $9,200 for the shares. In this situation, you lose $200 aside from the commission.

-Can You Take a Short Position in any Market?

Traders can go short in most financial markets, In the Forex and Futures market, you can always go short. Most public stocks are shortable. The majority of stocks are like this, but not all of them.

In 2010, the SEC imposed an alternative uptick rule. This rule prevents short selling from decreasing the value of a particular stock if its share price has dropped by 10% in just one day.

In margin trading, your broker needs to borrow the shares from an individual or entity that owns the shares. If he can't borrow for you, you can't short the stock. New stocks in the exchange, which are called IPOs, or initial public offerings, aren't shortable.

Better Understanding Stocks and Shares

In financial markets, the distinction between shares and stocks is blurry. As a rule, you can use both words interchangeably when referring to financial equity. This includes securities denoting ownership in a company.

In the olden days of paper transactions, such securities are referred to as "stock certificates." Today, the difference between the two depends on syntax and the context of their usage.

Here are some key points for better understanding:

➢ For all purposes and intents, shares and stocks can refer to the same thing.

- ➢ The distinction is only considered for legal or financial accuracy. That's why traders and investors use the words interchangeably.
- ➢ Specifically, to invest in the shares of a public company's stocks, a trading account is required.
- ➢ Of the two, "stocks" is commonly used, and "shares" has a very specific meaning. The former refers to a slice of ownership of a public company. On the other hand, "shares" describe the ownership of a particular company.
- ➢ Take note that you can own shares of various financial instruments (e.g. ETFs, mutual funds, limited partnerships, etc.) In contrast, stocks refer to corporate equities. These are public shares that can be traded on stock exchanges.
- ➢ What's a preferred stock? Now, two types of equity exist. They are preferred stock and common stock. Preferred shares or preferred stock entitles holders to a fixed dividend. The dividends are paid out to stockholders before the issuance of common stock dividends.

Getting Started

In financial markets, day-traded securities are bought and sold within a single day. That's the maxim of day-trading. Rather than hoarding assets for weeks or months, speculators like day traders purchase securities, such as stocks or Forex, hoping that the value rises within that same day. They take short positions before the day ends and make sure that another market participant will purchase their asset. To get started with day trading, please follow the step-by-step guide below:

Budgeting

This is the very first phase and it is subdivided into three phases:
- a) Decide your capital.
- b) Create a trading account.
- c) Read the rules and regulations and make sure to follow them to the fullest and meet all requirements before trading.
- d) Deposit your preferred amount or at least the minimum capital required by the broker.

Trading through your broker.

As mentioned earlier, it's best to evaluate various brokers and brokerage platforms. If you prefer to request the brokers to make the trades for you, you must tell him/her your preferences, including rules you've set for your strategies and what order will you opt for. You also need to always clarify how much you'll trade.

Lastly, for this step, contact the firm with inquiries about their business practices. Before depositing any amount, don't hesitate to ask questions directly. Inquire about fees, liquidity, and withdrawals. Remember, once you make profits, you will want to withdraw your money. Their modes of payment should be flexible and reliable. PayPal, TransferWise, and Western Union are well-refuted and trusted online payment systems.

Strategizing your online trades

As a beginner trader, avoid trading a significant chunk of your capital. Limit each trade to 1 to 2% of it. If you start by investing 10% or more of your funds, you may exhaust the money you've set aside for trading. For example, if you deposited $1,000 to your account, then it's advised that your first trades should only cost $10 to $20. Likewise, if you start with $15,000, then each of your trades must only amount to $150 to $300 or lesser.

Remember Warren Buffet's words "Start small, and expand as you grow."

The "scalping" method is a favorite of many beginners and professional traders. It allows for quick profits, albeit small. For this strategy to work, you need to sell your purchased securities, as soon as you can make a profit from them. For example, if you purchased 20 shares of stock XXX at $2 per share, and 15 minutes later, the value increased to $2.05 per share, then you can make a quick, small profit. In the scenario above, you have made a dollar in 15 minutes. The higher the number of units of your chosen security you purchase, the higher your profit will be.

The so-called "momentum strategy" involves fundamental analysis and following breaking news about given stocks. It promotes day-trading on 1 to 2 stocks that will do well for the day. For example, if gaming stocks may thrive in the coming week. Purchase 10 to 20 shares of stocks from well-rooted tech companies in the industry. But, before you do that, make sure that that stock is volatile and has been doing well in the

long run. Consider using TA or FA to make value and effective trades. When one or more of the assets wherein you've invested has risen by 20 to 30%, sell your shares/units of the security at high point or near the resistance level.
However, if the value keeps rising, always be vigilant of sudden significant reversals. If the market is gradually entering a bear market, but the asset remains volatile, then take advantage of mini trends. Sell high, and buy low. If the price will likely hit an all-time bottom soon, get out of the market.

Diversify your financial portfolio and improve your trades

Day trading is a great way to diversify markets and improve your financial portfolio. You can invest in a market through swing trading while you're speculating on another. If you have a small capital, you can further subdivide it for two purposes:

➢ Study the markets
➢ Gauge which is the perfect fit for you

Each tradable security offers different opportunities for making a profit. With the data you've gathered through observation and analysis, you can decide, with good judgment, where you can make lots of profits.

Step 6: Speculating in the Forex Market

Does keeping your impulses in check the best way to trade Forex? Like in other markets, do you need a trading strategy to win big in foreign exchanges? What's the best way to read Forex charts? If you're still a beginner in this field, the first trades can be overwhelming

Day trading in the Forex market is harder than speculating in the stocks market. There are a lot of terms to learn before you can day trade effectively! Nevertheless, investing your time and money in the world's largest market can bring in high profits.

Forex trading is also known as currency trading. It's all about profits, rates, trends, and losses. Your losses will be dependent on factors, failed predictions, and trading strategy. Nevertheless, if you employ an effective trading system in every attempt to make money in the market, you can easily gain profits and avoid losses.

In chapter 4, you've learned how to develop a winning trading system. This chapter is all about the world of Forex trading. It holds everything you need to know for day trading currencies.

What's Waiting for You in this Market?

With the advent of IoT (Internet of Things) and the World Wide Web, millions of people around the world, including investors, retirees, solo parents, and young adults are discovering the advantages of Forex Trading. To most of them, trading in Forex markets is their livelihood. Their profits are more than enough to cover their living expenses.

Some have even made a fortune out of Forex trading. With the Foreign exchange market, you can trade for just $20 or $100, but this depends on your broker. You can also leverage for high returns or borrow from a financer.

Forex, or FX, trading is also referred to as currency trading. The Forex market, as a whole, is a decentralized global market, in which many of the world's currencies are traded on a daily basis. It's the largest and most liquid market in the world.

On average, the Forex market's daily trading volume exceeds $5 trillion. Even if all the stock and bond markets are combined, they won't come close to the trading volume in the currency market.

Have you gone abroad? If someone has sent you money from abroad, you may have already made a Forex trade. For instance, you went to Seoul, Korea, and you converted your USD to KRW (Korean Won). The foreign exchange rate between the two aforementioned currencies determines how much KRW you would've gotten with your dollars.

The exchange of a pair, which involves two currencies, is based on the supply and demand in the market. The exchange rates fluctuate continuously. This is because they're affected by many factors, such as terms of trade, fluctuation rates, and political stability and performance.

To reiterate, foreign exchange is quite similar to the stock market. Like stocks, you can trade currencies based on estimates.

The major difference between the two is the fact that you're simultaneously buying one currency and selling another in Forex trading. This is different from stock trading. You either sell your shares or buy more stocks.

Also, you can easily average up or down with Forex.

Averaging up in the currency market is exactly the opposite of averaging down in stock trading. This remains true for the fact that when your trades go in your favor, the best move is to add more positions. In the later sections of this chapter, you'll learn more about this strategy.

In May 2020, Japan devalued its currency to attract more foreign investors and businessmen. If you think that this trend will last for a long time, like a few weeks or several months, then easy opportunities for Forex trading will definitely arise.

In this situation, you can make profitable trades by selling the JPY (Japanese Yen) against the Euro, US dollar, or Australian dollar.

The more the JPY devalues against your preferred currency, the higher your profits will be. If the JPY devalues while you're position is "open," then you'll lose money. In this case, the best position is to "close" your position within the day.

The example above contains several technical terms. What's devaluation? How can this affect exchange rates? What's a currency pair?

How can indicators and economic factors affect the volatility of the Forex market? If you don't know the essential terms in this trade, barriers will face you when trading Forex. This chapter can teach you the principles behind Forex trading, as well as everything there is to know to make it big in this market.

The True Nature of the Forex Market

The FX market trades 24 hours a day and 5 days a week. Greatest volatility transpires during market overlap. This happens when one offers to purchase a security at a high price and sell at a lower price than the highest bid.

currency markets, traders, as well as investors, can exit and enter trades during global business days.

Three trading sessions--Asia, London, and New York--divide the Forex market. This allows you to choose a trading time according to their schedules. Currency trading transpires over the counter. When a region's business hours close, another region will open theirs.

At specific times of the day, the volume of the asset being traded could become high. This depends on the currency pair. Traders can make large profits during times of high liquidity, like the Asian session, New York session, and London session. Volatility is often high during such times and spreads are lower.

In general, traders trade during the London and New York session, and every overlap. Forex traders don't need to observe the market 24 hours a day. They can take advantage of the currency market by trading when the market is highly liquid. A solid and proven trading strategy should also be utilized.

Here are some key tips when day trading in the currency market:

-Watch out for the holidays

You must take note of every holiday in every region. If the USA has a holiday, then the USD market won't be that liquid during that time. Although the FX market doesn't cease, some brokers and platforms are unavailable during public holidays.

-Use different strategies for different trading sessions
Every FX session has various characteristics, which are
detailed in chapter 5. Hence, you must adopt a suitable
trading strategy. During low liquidity, you can employ
range-bound strategies. What's this?

A range-bound strategy is a method wherein traders purchase
a given security at a support level and take a short position at
the resistance level. Traders typically utilize this trading
strategy along with technical indicators like volume to
increase their probability of success.

For example, a trader might have noticed that the given
security is starting to generate a price channel. This transpires
when the price oscillates between two parallel lines, whether
they are descending, ascending, or horizontal. You can sell
when the value nears the channel's upper trend and take a
long position when the lower trendline is being tested.

In the given scenario, the channel in late-August and
early-September formed initial peaks. The trader might have
placed short and long trades in reference to the trendlines. His
market activities totaled two long trades and four short trades.
The asset's breakout from the upper resistance level indicates
the end to the trading following a range-bound strategy.

-The currency pairs
There are many currency pairs. All in all, there are 180
currencies that are circulating throughout the world. Some are
considered "minor," "major," and "exotic." The major pairs
include:

➢ USD/CHF
➢ GBP/JPY
➢ EUR/JPY
➢ GBP/USD
➢ USD/JPY
➢ EUR/USD

Every day, they're traded in high volumes. This implies that
transactions involving the aforementioned currency pairs offer
low costs and reduced spreads for traders.

The Fundamentals of Forex Trading

Forex is a portmanteau of foreign currency and exchange. Forex is the act or process of converting a currency to another.

Therefore, you trade currencies whenever you convert your dollars into another country's currency. According to the BIS (the Bank of International Settlements, roughly $5 trillion is the daily trading volume in the Forex market.

The market establishes the rates for currencies around the world. In trading, the "exchange rate" is the figure at which a specific currency can be traded into another.

The Forex rate of a currency is its value. Foreign exchange is the conversion of one currency into another at a rate known as "the foreign exchange rate." This constantly fluctuates, since the market forces of supply and demand drive the rates for all currencies in the world.

For example, the exchange rate of 100 JPY to 1 USD implies that ¥100 is equivalent to $1. Similarly, 1$ can be exchanged for ¥100. In this case, you can say that the value of 1 USD against the JPY is ¥100. Equivalently, the value of 1 JPY relative to 1 USD is $1/100.

The Forex market determines the exchange rates, which include Foreign and interbank exchange rates. The term "interbank rate" can also refer to the Foreign exchange rates. To reiterate, the market is open 24 hours a day Mondays to Fridays.

Currencies are traded in pairs. What's this? A pair is a quote for two different currencies in a foreign exchange. When you order a currency pair, the first listed currency (the base) is purchased. The quote (the second currency) is sold. In the JPY/USD pair, the Japanese Yen is the base and the USD is the quote.

To date, the EUR\USD currency pair is the most liquid in the whole world. In trading, liquidity refers to how one can quickly convert a specific currency, held in an electronic platform, into hard cash. Liquid assets include cash, checkable account, and savings account.

With regards to the aforementioned currency pair, you can convert your funds into money because of the liquidity of the pair. Since it's the most liquid pair, many are trading and converting the EUR into USD, around the world. Aside from conventional modes of payments, you may be able to withdraw your money in banks or money remittance centers. In foreign exchanges, the spot exchange FX rate is the current rate of exchange of a currency pair. The forward exchange rate, on the other hand, is the exchange rate in contract for the payment for a currency date at a predetermined date. This is usually set 30, 90, or 180 days in the future.

The market determines the rate of every currency being traded in the exchange. As well, all aspects of trading and converting currencies are determined at current (spot) prices. The major participants in this exchange are international banks and large financial centers. Day and night, except for Saturdays and Sundays, these financial organizations serve as mediums between millions of traders.

What's a Forex Market?

The Forex market has different levels, and it involves banking institutions. These are corporations, intermediaries of economic systems. Exchange rates are based on the trades and trading volume in the market. In the following sections, you can learn more about the law of supply and demand. Wherever entities or parties engage in currency exchange, that space, whether physical or virtual, is a market. Hence, a Forex market is just one of the many systems and institutions whereby people can exchange currencies. Brokers, eToro and Ameritrade, run online Forex markets. All Forex markets rely on buyers, sellers, and financial institutions, which are considered "intermediaries."

In Forex markets, brokers and investors can facilitate trades. Although speculators need to adhere to rules and policies in every platform, brokers have streamlined the process of Forex trading, over the years. Specifically, traders must follow proper quoting, competitive pricing, and platform registration.

Things You Need to Know Before Trading Currencies: Pips and Lots

Behind the scenes, banks rely on financial organizations when transacting in the Forex market. These firms are called "dealers." They involve in large currency trades. Most dealers are local, rural, or national banks.

Such organizations operate behind the scenes operate behind-the-scenes and are referred to as the interbank markets. Sometimes, insurance companies and financial firms are also involved.

Trades between two dealers are often large. Each transaction may involve millions of US dollars.

Forex markets serve as a medium for both trades and investments.   Currency conversion is one of their core features. Online brokerage platforms, for example, allows US startups to import products from European Union member states. With Forex markets, business owners that reside in foreign countries can buy goods from EU members in EUR.

-Open position

As the term implies, this is an established trade that has yet to become close with another party's trade. An open position can exist after a short position or a long position. Be that as it may, the position will remain open until there's an opposing trade.

An open position is any trade that a market participant has established; An opposing trade can exist after a buy position or sell position. Be that as it may, the position stays open until an opposing trade transpires.

-What Are Currency Pairs

Foreign exchanges mainly hold currency pair trading. Their names combine the two currencies being traded. To reiterate, the base currency is the first currency. It's the one appearing in the pair quotation and then followed by the quote currency. This determines the value of the base or "the first" currency.

In the Forex market, the unit prices of currencies are represented by currency pairs. The base currency (transaction currency) is the 1st currency in the quotation. The second one is the counter or quote currency.

For accounting reasons, a financial organization can use the base currency and the domestic currency to represent all losses and profits. Fundamentally, it represents the total amount of the quote currency being traded. It represents how much of the quote of to acquire one unit of the base.

For instance, if you're looking at the JPY/USD pair, the Japanese Yen is the base and the US dollar is the quote. The International Organization for Standardization (ISO) set the abbreviations utilized for currency trading. The standard ISO 4217 provides the codes. Three letters represent each currency, as in the example of the JPY, CAD, and USD. The currencies comprising a pair are commonly separated with a slash (/). You can replace the slash with a dash or period. The major codes for currencies include EUR for the euro, the HUSD for the US dollar, the GBP for the British pound, JPY for the Japanese yen. The AUD stands for the Australian dollar, while CAD represents the Canadian dollar.

The Different Parts of a Currency Pair

Currency pairs are written as XXX/YYY or just XXXYYY. In this example, XXX is the base and YYY is the quote. Examples of this format are EURCHF, EURNZD, GBPJPY, etc.

When an exchange rate is added, the pairs indicate how much of the transaction currency is required to purchase one unit of the first currency. For example, the currency pair EUR/USD = 1.26 implies that 1 euro is equivalent to 1.26 USD. This means that you need to pay 1.26 USD to acquire 1 EUR. The quotation is read in the same way when selling the base. Conversely, if you want to sell 1 EUR, you will get 1.26 USD for it.

The reason for this format is because investors and speculators simultaneously buy and sell currencies. For instance, when you buy USD/EUR, this means that you're buying USD and selling EUR at that moment.

Traders, specifically day traders, buy a pair if they predict that the value of the first currency will increase against the quote. Contrastingly, they sell the currency pair if they see that the base will lose value and that the exchange rate for the quote will increase.

What's a Position in Currency Trading?

A position in foreign exchanges is the amount of funds/currency a trader/entity owns in a brokerage platform. Like in stock exchanges, the terms short and long positions are also used in currency trading. Each Forex position has 3 characteristics:

➢ The size of the trade
➢ The direction (short or long)
➢ The underlying currency pair

Traders, as well as entities, can take positions in various currency pairs, such as EUR/JPY or AUD/USD. The position size depends on the margin requirements and the trader's account equity. This refers to the total funds in the trader's account. Equity is their balance plus or minus the loss or profit from open positions.

The margin requirement is the percentage of marginal assets that a trader must pay for with his funds or cash. When he holds the security purchased on margin, the minimum margin at Firstrade for the majority of stocks is lowered to 30%.

Bonds, stocks, futures, and similar assets are marginable securities. This means that the said securities can be traded on margin. Margin trading alludes to trading on money borrowed from a broker to substantially increase market exposure. When engaging in a margin trade, the broker lends a specific amount of money. The loan amount depends on the leverage ratio utilized. (What's this?) A small portion of the trading account is allocated as collateral. The collateral is the margin for that trade.

The act involves purchasing a security where the buyer pays a percentage of the asset's total value. He then has to borrow the rest from the broker. The broker acts as the lender and the securities or funds in the trading account serve as the collateral.

A loan pays for the securities traded on margin, and a broker, brokerage platform, or financial institution facilitates and lends the money for the trade.

Simply put, margin is the amount of funds that the broker will lend to the trader. To calculate margin, subtract the value of securities in the trader's account and the loan amount. Hence, buying on margin is the practice of borrowing money to purchase securities.

Purchasing securities with margin is like using physical assets (e.g. machinery, properties, and other physical properties) as collateral for a bank loan. In trading, the collateralized loan comes with a periodic interest rate. The investor/trader must pay this.

The trader in question is using the leverage or the borrowed money. Hence, both gains and losses are magnified. If the trader can make high profits from a trade, then margin trading is advantageous.

When everything is taken into account, traders can take positions in various currency pairs, as long as they have the funds for it or they can engage in a margin trade. To reiterate, the position size relies on the trader's margin requirements and account equity. The appropriate amount of leverage is important in day trading and trading on margin.

-About Leverage

What's leverage? How much leverage should I use? These are common questions that beginner traders ask.

In trading, leverage is the usage of a loan or borrowed funds to increase one's position size over their trading account's limit. Specifically, Forex traders use leveraging to gain profits from small price movements. Be that as it may, leverage in trading can amplify both losses and profits.

For instance, if you take a loan to buy a house, you're leveraging your balance sheet. The balance sheet shows investors the liabilities and assets owned by the trader. It summarizes what is left when the two are put together. The equation involves the individual's net worth, book value, and shareholder equity.

If you buy a $100,000 house, but you don't have enough savings or on-hand cash, you may have to down 20% of the total price of the property, and then, make regular payments to the seller or bank. In this example, you use your $20,000 cash to control a large asset. With the leverage and existing savings, one can control a large asset.

In the stock market, margin accounts enable traders to leverage their purchases by 2 factors. For example, if you deposit $40,000 into a margin account, then you can control an asset worth no more than $80,000.

-Margin Trading Tutorial

Foremost, margin trading requires a margin account. Based on its definition, this is different from a "trading cash account." The latter is a standard account that beginners can open when they first start trading.

In contrast to a margin account, a normal trading account, or cash account, requires market participants to fund a trade fully before the actual execution. When utilizing cash accounts, debt or margin is unneeded. The trader can't lose more than the funds in his account.

A cash account is different from a margin account. And, some differences exist between the loans a trader can receive for margin trading.

The securities that can exist in a margin account are as follows:

➢ Stocks
➢ Bonds
➢ Futures
➢ Options
➢ Cryptocurrencies
➢ Forex

If one fails to meet the requirements of a margin call, the broker can sell off investments until the equity ratio is restored. This maintenance requirement differs from one broker to another.

The maintenance requirement is the amount you can borrow for every dollar you deposit. The broker, however, can change this and the interest rate at any time.

-An Example of an Actual Margin Trade

A trader deposits $5,000 into an empty margin account. The broker or brokerage platform has a 40% maintenance requirement and charges 5% interest on loans under $20,000.

The investor purchases a public share of company X. In a normal trading account, he can only purchase stocks worth $5,000. In contrast, the investor can invest $9,000 on company X's stocks. At $10 per share, he can buy 900 shares.

But, what if the stock's value fell? The trader will still have to repay $9,000. This is the amount he borrowed through the margin loan.

-The Risks in Margin Trading

All investors and traders must consider the risks that come with trading securities on margin. The risks include the following:

➢ Brokerage firms can increase interest rates and margin requirements at anytime
➢ Failure to avoid losses can result in bankruptcy
➢ You can lose more money than you have invested. And, you're legally responsible for paying outstanding debts.
➢ When the value of the security purchased on margin declines, you will need additional funds to pay off your debt.
➢ They can do it without your notice.
➢ Usually, there's no time extension for new investors.
➢ Under the law, the brokerage platform can sell your securities if the account equity falls below the maintenance requirement.
➢ A short position can cost you. Often, when a stock is halted or delisted stocks, you may still need to pay for interest.
➢ When the price of an asset takes too long to recover, the debt will result in high-interest costs.
➢ Investors often add funds to their accounts to maintain maintenance requirements.

Margin trading can amplify your financial portfolio. It increases both the profit and loss potential of your capital. But ultimately, margin trading can increase the chances of generating more profits.

The Different Types of Forex Trades

Spot trades

Spot contract or spot trading is the most common type of Forex trade. It's quick and simple. Now, what exactly is it? A Forex spot transaction is also known as an FX spot. It's basically an agreement between two market participants to purchase one currency against another at a predetermined price for settlement on a spot date.

An FX spot is a bilateral agreement. This means that two parties are involved in one transaction. The contract is considered an agreement. It's a binding obligation to sell or buy a determined amount of a foreign currency at a spot exchange rate. This is the predetermined price that you must pay on the spot date. Simply put, an FX spot is a binding obligation to buy/sell a specific amount of foreign currency.

rward contracts

Forward contracts can protect you against market volatility. What's so bad about market volatility? Volatility, which is defined as the statistical measure of the price fluctuation of an asset, increases risks and makes it hard for beginner traders to gain profits.

The value of assets can change over time. If a particular currency experiences daily fluctuations, then you can say that it's volatile. By small or large amounts, the prices of assets, including stocks, futures, and currencies, can decrease or increase. The term "market volatility" describes the range of the changes in an asset's price.

For example, if the value of a stock remains consistent for a long time, then it has low volatility. The same can be said when its price experiences minimal price movement.

Generally, high volatility makes a trade or investment risky. It also spells great potential for losses or gains.

indow forward

A window forward trade is a forward contract. However, the settlement in this transaction isn't predetermined. And, it has two agreed dates for future transactions. You can benefit from this type of contract if you desire to secure a currency exchange rate. This allows you to meet a commitment with a flexible date.

Once you know the settlement date, you can settle the contract within the window. If you fail to settle your account within the timeframe, you can settle the contract but the exchange rate may be modified. You, as the trader, may be required to provide a margin or deposit. This happens if the payment has been overdue.

mit order

A limit order, in contrast to an FX spot, is a type of Forex order to trade a stock at a specific price. Two types of this trade exist: buy limit and sell limit. You can execute a buy limit at the predetermined price or lower. On the other hand, you can only carry out a sell limit order. If the asset's market value reaches the limit price, you can fill a limit order.

Stop Loss Order

A stop\loss order specifies that an asset is sold or bought when it reaches the stop price. This is the specific price in a stop order. It generates a market order--an order to buy or sell a security immediately. A market order doesn't guarantee the execution price, but it does ensure the execution of the order. When the stop price is met, the stop order serves as a market order. It is then executed at the soonest available opportunity. Often, a stop/loss order is utilized to avoid losses when the value of an asset drops. You can send an order to brokers if your investment starts to look risky.

Also, with a stop/loss order, you're instructed to purchase if the exchange rate becomes lower than the stop price. Many traders combine a stop/loss and limit order. Doing so protects them from a sudden decrease in the rates.

Aside from making profits, preserving and managing your capital should be your most important task as a trader. Once you lose your trading capital, it will be hard earning back what you've lost.

Every day poses new challenges in trading. Global politics, economic events, and central bank news can affect currency prices, either positively or negatively.

The Risks in Trading Forex

Like other financial markets, the Forex market also has risks that you need to take note of, and they can greatly affect the success of your currency trades.

1) Interest rate risk

Fluctuations in interest rates can impact exchange rates. When the interest rate rises, the foreign exchange rate of a currency increases as well.

A low volatile currency attracts foreign investors. This, in turn, strengthens the value of that currency, making it more stable than before and highly sought after in financial markets.

When the value of the currency weakens, the interest rate decreases too. Interest rates, alone, can cause fluctuations in a domestic currency's value.

-How to mitigate the effects of interest rate risk?

Holding bonds of multiple durations

Hedging fixed income with swaps, options, or derivatives

Purchasing of high-yield or floating-rate currency pairs

2)   Counterparty risk

In FX markets, the counterparty is the platform or entity where you close and open positions. Simply put, a counterparty could be a broker or a dealer.

Counterparty risks encompass platform defaults and broker loopholes. It's defined as the "probability that the other party in a trade may not carry out its part of the deal and neglect contractual obligations.

You should choose a well-reputed and well-established counterparty. It must boast authentic reviews that come from genuine and real people, not from bots or paid reviewers.

You should also care to check the age of the brokerage company and the number of its MAU, or monthly active users.

3)   Country risk

The economic and political status of the issuing country can affect the exchange rate of a domestic currency.

This risk refers to the uncertainty that is associated with trading a currency being issued by a country that has a lot of political turmoil or is economically unstable.

It can arise because of any of the factors below:

Exchange-rate

Economic news and events

Political instability

Exchange rate

Technological influences

-How to mitigate country risk?

Time your investments wisely

Borrow domestically

- ➤ Consider devaluation risks when trading exotic and minor pairs
- ➤ Diverse, disperse, and exit
- ➤ Spreading of buy price if there's an impending devaluation

    4) Liquidity risk

    Liquidity risk is considered a financial risk. For a specific period, a given security or financial asset cannot be traded as swiftly enough without impacting the market price.

    At times, a currency pair or any financial instrument can't be sold due to a lack of liquidity. This can arise from any of the following:

- ➤ Lengthening of the holding period for VaR calculations
- ➤ Creating explicit liquidity reserves
- ➤ Widening of spreads

    -How to mitigate liquidity risks

- ➤ Create a contingency plan
- ➤ Conduct regular stress test
- ➤ Control and monitor liquidity daily
- ➤ Make an effort to identify risks early

    5) Transaction risk

    The time gap between the closing and opening of a transaction creates possible risks. This refers to the negative effect that FX rate fluctuations can have on a completed transaction before settlement. It's actually the currency or rate of exchange risk associated with the time delay between entering and exiting a trade.

    -The factors that contribute to transaction risks

- ➤ Errors in handling and communication
- ➤ Price fluctuations
- ➤ Long time differential between initiation and settlement
- ➤ Volatility
- ➤ Bull and bear markets

    -The best strategies to mitigate currency risks

- ➤ Hedging with ETFs
- ➤ Reducing credit and market risks
- ➤ Engaging in currency swaps, an FX swap involves trading interest and principal in one currency for another
- ➤ Purchase of forward contracts
- ➤ Trading only home currencies

Risk sharing, which involves sharing of exposure risk with mutual understanding

The Best Time Frame for Your Forex Trades

Beginner traders often trade in the wrong time frame. You, as a newbie FX trader, must base your trading time on your capital, availability, and personality.

What's the importance of time-frames in Forex trading? Time frames play critical roles in developing an effective trading system. If you prefer a wide investment, using multiple time frames must be included in your strategy.

As a rule of thumb, three-time frames can be sufficient to give you a detailed and broad market reading of your target currency pair. Lesser than three-time frames leave openings for trading risks. Your trading strategy shall determine the duration for each frame.

Most swing traders have little use for hours or minutes in duration since they often take positions that last for months. The opposite is true for day traders because they tend to cut losses by closing positions before the end of every trading day.

Highly successful traders know how to use time frames to support their trading styles. Day trading in foreign exchanges can be both advantageous and profitable since it's a very volatile market. Hence, the use of multiple time frames is beneficial to day traders.

The use of various FX time frames can help you spot large trades and regular price actions that are still unfolding. You can form different viewpoints while switching between two or more time frames on the same currency pair.

-What are the Major FX Time Frames?

What are they? They're short-term, medium-term, and long-term. You have the option of using all three. Others use one short and one long when considering potential trades. Long time frames are beneficial in determining trade set-ups. In contrast, short time frames can help in timing market entries.

Short-term time frames are used by scalpers and day traders. The trend is usually hourly or 4-hour, but some opt for a minute duration. Trigger time frames usually last for 15 minutes.

Because of the volatility of the currency market, FX day traders chose short terms. In doing so, they can observe meaningful data. Medium-term for an illiquid asset may not provide any valuable data points.

Due to the nature of the Forex Market, switching between various time frames during different sessions (e.g. US, Asian, European) generates various market conditions. These are system and business-related issues that you can use for determining indicators. You can use such indicators to look for trends specific to US, Asia, or European sessions.

-What's a trading session?

A trading session is a period matching the daytime trading for the trading hours in a given region. In general, it's a 24-hour business day in the financial market. The duration between the opening bell and the closing bell is the trading session.

Key Takeaways:

➢ Primary trading hours differ from one country to another. They're dependent on the time zones.
➢ A trading session is the major trading hours for a particular locale or asset.
➢ The sessions vary by country and asset class. For US stocks, the regular trading session starts at 9:30 and closes at 16:00. For the US bond market, the regular weekday trading session starts at 8:00 and ends at 17:00. It closes at 14:00 on six occasions and is unavailable on 10 holidays.
➢ Traders must be aware of the different trading hours for any security that they want to trade.

-What FX Time Frame Should You Choose?

To choose the most optimal time frame for your trades, take into consideration your strategy and trading style. These should be the factors that greatly influence your preferred time frame. Hence, choose a chart that you're comfortable with and execute a very thorough analysis. Also, make sure to establish risk management on your trades.

Day trading forex can be difficult. Beginner traders using a speculating strategy expose themselves to trading decisions that haven't been tested and proven effective for very long.

This deadly combination of frequency and experience paves the way for losses that could be prevented by a different approach like position trading.

Scalpers, as well as day traders, should, at all times, specialize in minuscule price actions. This is why you could trade with just 5-minute or 10-minute time frames. They tend to move quickly in the direction of the price. With this, they are tied to the charts and the trends.

That's what day traders who take hourly positions do. In contrast, those who take a shorter-term approach have a smaller margin of error than its opposite type.

Day traders can evaluate trends on hourly charts and find possible price points. This refers to a point on a graph of possible prices. From given points, some could generate profits.

Entry opportunities are abundant in "minute" time frames like five- or fifteen-minute charts.

Day Trading Forex

Scalpers or day traders need the price of the trading asset to move in favor of their prediction. Hence, they've to practice vigilance when observing charts. Day traders can speculate to evaluate trends on an hourly chart. On minute time frames, like 5-minute charts, they can spot entry points.

An entry point is the price at which a trader sells or buys a security. Usually, it's a component of a specified trading strategy developed for reducing investment risks and removing sentiments from trading decisions. Remember, a good entry point is, oftentimes, a result of a successful trade.

Here are some technical analysis strategies, which you can use to identify any trend:

The use of 200-day MAs for scalpers utilizing daily and hourly trading time frames

Identify and understand Forex trendlines

The use of MACD indicator

A trend line is like a line drawn under pivot lows or pivot thighs to show the current price movement and for predicting future price actions. Trendlines serve as visuals of resistance and support in any trading time frame. They can present the speed

and direction of the price and describe patterns in
compressions.

Aside from those, you can use the following technical analysis
when identifying entry levels, such as the following:

- ➢ MA crossovers
- ➢ The utilization of key levels of resistance and support
- ➢ The use of indicators, including MACD and RSI
- ➢ Candlestick analysis

-Day Trading with Multiple Trading Time Frames
Successful Forex day traders, including George Soros and Bill
Lipschutz, tend to use multiple time frame analysis. This
involves viewing a currency pair at two or more time frames.

Executing Your First Trade

Assuming that you already have a trading account that
enables trading forex, all you have to do is to follow the
straightforward steps below. Also, don't forget to prepare your
trading system for your first-ever currency trade.

Launch the Platform

In Chapter 2, you've learned how to choose the right broker
for your capital and trading strategy. Once you've installed the
platform on your smartphone or personal computer, open the
application to launch it. If you chose a web-based platform,
then you should sign in to your account on your broker's
website.

To finish this step, log in to your trading account by providing
your username and password. Now, take caution when you're
logging in. You must always secure your account credentials,
and remember, it's best to use a trustworthy VPN.

Open the Chart

In this step, you've to choose a currency pair. You must open
a chart and choose a time frame. For instance, you choose a
20-minute time frame. In this case, each candlestick on the
opened chart represents 20 minutes.

Add the Indicators

When you've chosen a currency pair, you need to work on
your chart and add indicators. You can opt for technical
indicators. For example, you may add MACD and a 300
exponential moving average. The basic rule for the use of a
300 EMA is that if the currency's exchange rate is above the

line, then it may increase. If the price is below the 300 EMA line, then it may continue going down.

In the 2nd scenario, it's confirmed that the exchange rate is decreasing unstably. The use of technical indicators can be helpful in this step, in the decision-making process.

However, if you're selling the given currency pair, then it means you're buying JPY and selling AUD. Hence, you need to look at the strengths of the quote currency and the weaknesses of the base, which is the Australian dollar. With the MACD, you can look for signs that AUD's value is indeed going down.

When utilized alone, the MACD indicator isn't always reliable. But, if you use it as an element of a complex trading system, it can accurately pinpoint a possible future price.

In case the price is fighting the downtrend, it's advised to wait for the crossing and heading down of the MACD indicators. You should do this before making a trade.

Calculating profits

Of course, this is also an essential part of forex trading since it's a very different form of trading from the rest. Here are the key points you need to remember when calculating profits in this market:

A pip is used to measure the difference in value between two domestic currencies. A pip is equivalent to 0.0001 of a change in value. For instance, if your EUR/USD Forex trade moves from 1.645 to 1646, then the currency value has increased by ten pips.

Multiply the pips number that your trading account has by the rate of exchange. The product will tell you how much your trading funds have decreased or increased in value.

Place the Order

After studying the charts and rethinking and reconfirming your strategy, preparing to place an order is next. In the example mentioned in the previous section, the price of the currency pair is decreasing, so it's best to go short.

Remember, a short position is a sell position. Traders take this position if they believe that the stock's value will decrease or continue to decrease. If the price indeed drops, you can repurchase the stock at a lower price. By doing so, you can make a profit.

Establish the Levels for Stop/Loss and Take Profit

Step 5 is optional, but this step is highly recommended. Setting a stop/loss order at 1/2 pip can lead to long-term success. Why is this so? With such a setup, you're right 50% of the time, and you can still come out of the trade at the end of the day. However, this is only possible if your risk-reward is indeed favorable.

Setting a stop/loss order can limit losses if the market moves in the predicted direction. Establishing a take profit level ensures that you can exit your trade with profit. Setting these two levels when placing the trade can be advantageous. This is because it is difficult to make decisions once the trade is actually in the market.

Confirm Your Order

When you have set the necessary levels, it's time to submit an order and wait for confirmation. On-screen, it may appear as a dialogue box. Remember, the "confirmation" is important, as well as the ticket number. In case there's something wrong in the execution phase, you can contact the broker and present your ticket number. Doing this can help your broker correct the mistake and refund credits.

The Waiting Period

After order confirmation, the waiting period begins. Many day traders turn off their screen and stay away from the market for some time. Although it's advised to constantly watch the market, you can sit back and relax if you've properly set up your trade, like establishing a take profit or stop loss order before confirmation.

Trade Completion

This is the last step in the Forex trading process. With the given example, the trade could've resulted in a take profit. After this, it's a must to way your losses and profits. Above all, avoid letting your emotions cloud your trading judgments. Just because your winning, don't get carried away by the excitement and start getting careless. You didn't study this book for that.

The foreign exchange market is like the ocean. You'll see a lot of ups and downs and more fluctuations. What matters the most is to continue your analysis of prices, assets, and indicators.

The Law of Supply and Demand

In foreign exchanges, like in floating markets, crowd psychology, as well as the interactions between traders, determine the prices and rates of assets/goods. The buyers in the market represent the demand for a product, security, or commodity.

On the contrary, the sellers and the security they offer represent the supply in the market. If the supply and demand are in balance, the price of the asset in the electronic market will be unchanged for some time.

However, if that becomes imbalanced, then the price of the asset in question will either rise or fall. When demand surpasses supply, the total number of buyers in the market exceeds the number of sellers.

Chapter Summary

Trading Forex on electronic markets or brokerage platforms can be a thrilling hobby and a good source of additional income. To some, profit generation here is slower than stock trading. Still, it offers lower risks since the market is very volatile and highly liquid! Billions of trades are executed per day in Forex marketplaces all over the world. Now that you know all the risks, processes, terminologies, and technicalities in Forex, it's time to execute your first Forex trade.

Step 7: Day Trading Futures and Cryptocurrencies

You've learned how to conduct technical and fundamental analysis, as well as read charts, indicators, and balance sheets. You now know the many ways for day trading Forex and stocks. But, how about the other remaining securities that are also profitable these days? This chapter is all about them. You will finally meet "futures" and "cryptocurrencies."
While employing various strategies and techniques to capitalize on perceived market inefficiencies, day traders take maximum advantage of the fluctuations in the market. They are prevalent in the markets where price actions of securities are volatile and frequent.
Whether you want to supplement your other day trading endeavors or you just prefer straightforward financial securities, you can learn how to make money from other tradable assets, in this chapter.

Cryptocurrency Day Trading: Making $100 per Day

In recent years, crypto trading has boomed. The high trading volume and volatility of the most popular cryptocurrencies (e.g, bitcoin and ethereum) perfectly suit speculators, like day traders.
The rise of bitcoin and other cryptocurrencies has made the market what it is today--a highly volatile electronic market. Remember, volatility and liquidity are what successful speculators, like Warren Buffet and Tim Sykes, highly sought after.
However, you must choose the right coin. As of writing, there are over 1,600 crypto coins out there. Not all of them can give you profit. Yes, millions of trades occur in this market, but they only involve the most popular cryptocurrencies.
The crypto market provides many opportunities for speculators if they do trades right. This section presents a step-by-step guide for the most lucrative type of electronic trading: crypto trading.
Here are the things you need to do to get started:
1. Choose coins that are highly liquid and volatile

Today, bitcoin is the most traded cryptocurrency. Hence, bitcoin is your best choice. The demand for this crypto coin is very high. In February 2021, the price of 1 BTC spiked to In just a month, its value has increased to $20,000, from $32,000 in January 15, 2021 to $5,000 by February 18, 2021. Bitcoin's value is very volatile. What's more, the best part about it is that its price has retained an upward trend in the past years. A sudden significant downtrend will unlikely happen in the coming months.

Ripple, Ethereum, and Litecoin are among the best bitcoin alternatives. You may also opt to day trade minor and exotic coins. However, unlike bitcoin and its alternatives, the price of such crypto coins can plummet as fast as they've risen.

For the full list, please refer below:

-The major cryptocurrencies

➢ Bitcoin
➢ Litecoin
➢ Ethereum
➢ Zcash
➢ Stellar Lumen
➢ Cardano
➢ Polkadot
➢ Stellar
➢ Chainlink
➢ Binance coin
➢ Tether
➢ Monero

2. Apply the money flow index (MFI) indicator on a 5-minute chart

The Money Flow Index indicator is a simple technical indicator. This is utilized to monitor the price movement of e-coins and to gauge when will noteworthy organizations start trading a specific cryptocurrency.

The settings for this indicator should be set at three periods. The default levels for buying and selling must be between the range of 80 to 100 and 20 to 0, respectively. You can learn how to use this indicator in the next step.

3. Use the MFI indicator

A value near 100 indicates the presence of large entities in the market. When big sharks make purchases, they can't hide their digital tracks. They leave evidence of their market activities. The MFI indicator is employed when reading their activities.

To further increase the accuracy of readings and predictions, day traders skip the first two readings even if the result is 100. They do this to fine-tune their strategies and study the reactions of the crypto price. The price must hold up during the 1st and 2nd MFI readings with a value of 100.

If the value of the cryptocurrency is below 100 after the first two readings, then the price may go down throughout the rest of that day. Now, it's time to determine the right marketplace where you can trade cryptocurrencies and satisfy the technical conditions required.

4. Taking a buy position

The subsequent 100 MFI readings present ripe opportunities to make profitable trades. As long as the technical conditions are met, you can treat that result as the right indication.

However, except for the 100 MFI reading, the candlestick needs to be bullish. A candlestick is a price chart displaying the low, high, and open closing prices of a financial security for a given period. The close must be near the upper and its wicks should be small.

When all of that has been taken into account, you need to establish protective stop-loss orders and determine where you can make profits. For this, please refer to the next step.

5. Make your purchase

Eugene Loza (EXCAVO) said, "It's best for crypto day traders to hide their protective stop/loss below the day's low and take profit in the first 60 minutes after opening a trade."

A break below the day's low indicates an impending shift in market sentiment or a reversal day. In such cases, you should get out of the market as soon as possible.

A break can occur as a swift price increase or decrease or as a gap, in which trading transpires at multiple prices along the way. A breakout can occur when the value of the asset breaks above the resistance level or drops below the support level.

In day trading cryptocurrencies, the rule of thumb is to take profit during the 1st hour after you finally make a trade. There's a low success rate in holding trades longer.

Advanced Tips for Crypto Trading

To earn a high return, you must take risks. That's a fact in the electronic trading world. When making money in the short-term, you need to greatly consider the market's volatility. Like in other markets, the prices of the major cryptocurrencies on charts are composed of different types of trends, including mini trends. With FA and TA, you can study the trends to make value predictions.

Short-term trading is also sub-divided into a few different categories. They're based on how quickly you realize days, hours, or weeks.

Crypto day trading is an aggressive form of short-term trading. Your goal as the trader is to sell coins within the trading day and make a profit before going to bed.

In conventional electronic exchanges, a trading day ends at 4:30 pm. The crypto market, however, runs 24/7. Let's start with learning the different crypto trading sessions.

-Defining the crypto trading sessions

Since crypto coins can be traded internationally, disregarding borders, you can opt for the trading sessions of Tokyo, New York, Australia, and the Eurozone. They're considered the financial capitals of the world.

They're quite similar to the sessions in the FX market. Some sessions might provide better opportunities if the coin you plan to trade has a higher volume in that time frame than in others. For example, NEO, a cryptocurrency that is based in China, oftentimes experience its highest trading volume during the Asian session.

The prospect of having the ability to trade night or day can be beneficial for you. Whether you're experiencing a sleepless night or you're having a lunch break, you can just open your trading app or web-based broker and start trading. However, remember that even though you have this flexibility, you mustn't neglect the fundamentals. Always conduct a thorough analysis of the market.

-Secure your crypto wallet

A crypto wallet can either be a device, service, program, or physical medium that allows for the storage of public or private keys. The keys are utilized for cryptocurrency trades and offer data encryption. This is perhaps the most well-known and most valued feature of crypto wallets. A simple crypto wallet can be utilized to receive/spend cryptocurrencies, track ownership, and store digital coins, like BTCs and NEOs.

Contrary to simple wallets that only require one party for transaction confirmation, multi-signature wallets need two or more parties to execute a trade. That's why they're more secured than simple crypto wallets. In the digital currency space. The signing keys for smart contracts are also stored in wallets

-Choosing a crypto wallet

In choosing a digital wallet for your crypto coins, you must consider the people who will have access to your private keys. Remember, those people will be signing capabilities. This means they can access your wallet any time of the day. If you opt for a third-party provider, you have to place your trust in the entity in keeping your coins safe.

In the case of the Mt. Gox exchange scandal, most of their clients lost BTCs. On March 9, 2014, the firm filed for bankruptcy. Many claimed that that bitcoin exchanged is fraudulent. Please keep in mind that downloading a wallet doesn't guarantee that you're the only one who can access it. For getting started, here are some tips for choosing a secured crypto wallet:

➢ Multi-currency enabled
➢ Accessible and user-friendly
➢ Can be accessed offline
➢ It comes from a well-refuted provider with good reviews
➢ Enhanced security
➢ The provider is licensed and regulated and has been around for at least six years

For receiving digital options, you don't need a key for the receiving wallet. You or the sending party just need the destination address. Anyone can send crypto coins to the address. Only the individual or entity who has access to the private key of the corresponding address can utilize the address.

If you're day trading in the crypto market, make sure that you aren't paying for a lot of service and commission fees. Before you engage in any actual short-term trading, consult your broker first and check if their regulations and fees coincide with your trading strategy. Ask yourself, "Can I generate profit in this platform with my trading capital?"

Here's a simple step-by-step strategy you can use for day trading crypto coins:

1) With technical analysis, confirm the existence and the future direction of the trend.
2) Anticipate for a pullback.
3) Purchase at the pullback during an uptrend. To do this, closely watch for mini trends.
4) Take profit at the resistance level. Crypto day trading can be a lucrative business because of the market's high volatility.

Remember, high volatility and liquidity suit day traders very well. Crypto trading could be the environment where you can succeed. If you feel like you aren't into this type of day trading, then do check out the following sections for futures and options.

Everything You Need to Know About Day Trading Futures

What's a future? A futures contract is an agreement to trade a commodity or financial security at a predetermined price and set date.

Major online brokers feature a trading section for futures. You must familiarize yourself with their rules and requirements first before finally choosing any of them.

Investors consider futures trading as a method to broaden their portfolio and maximize profits. Day traders trade futures to earn both instant and gradual income.

-Futures vs. Options

Futures contracts for stocks, bonds, and market indices exist, and they can be considered as cash-settled contracts.

Options contracts, on the other hand, provide traders the right but not the obligation to buy a security. The owner of a call option can buy a given asset at a specific value for a given period. However, the holder of the security has no obligation to purchase the asset.

With a futures contract, both the seller and buyer of the contract are required to transact at a predetermined date and time. In day trading, the trade is often executed the same day that the contract is bought.

Futures also require a daily settling of losses and gains. This means traders must balance their trading accounts when every trading day ends. This may seem like an inconvenience, but depending on the market's flow, you may need to deposit more funds in your trading account until the contract is fulfilled.

With options trading, there are no such daily additions. In the next section, transacting in the options market is further discussed.

-How are Futures Regulated?

Because of the rise of futures trading, tight regulations were established. The regulations ensure that all parties involved in every futures trade are secured. One example is the Commodity Exchange Act, which was passed by the US Congress in 1936. Although the rules have evolved over the years, the framework of the act has remained intact.

In 1974, the Commodity Futures Trading Commission (CFTC) was formed. Five committees comprise the CFTC. The US president appoints the commissioners; they serve 5-year terms and are responsible for setting price fluctuations. The US government regulates futures trading on brokers that are registered in the USA.

Like options and stock traders, futures traders can also use leveraging and margin trading. However, these are dependent on their broker or the platform they're in.

In terms of trading futures, you have to be vigilant, like in any markets. Futures are often traded during after hours and outside traditional trading hours. With this, when the market reopens, you'll have a good idea of the status of the asset due to the overnight changes evident on your chart.

-Where to trade

Major online brokers have a trading section specially dedicated to this financial instrument. Before choosing a broker and settling for it, you must familiarize yourself with their rules and requirements.

In terms of margin trading futures, brokers only provide a margin account to users they certify that can pay back the loan and interest. Accessibility to margin usually requires a specific amount of funds in your original trading account. Some brokers, like TD Ameritrade, require passing a test or class before one can begin margin trading. TradeStation, Interactive Brokers, and TD Ameritrade are some brokerage platforms that allow for margin trading futures.

-The risks in futures trading

Ben Fitzsimmons, an algorithmic trader, says, "Unlike stocks and equities, futures don't pay dividends or provide incentives that investors can gain over time." Futures are quite different from other financial instruments. They're a 100% zero-sum game. When one trader losses, another one makes a profit. Barry Johnson, one of the UK's top financial analysts and equities trader, says, "The futures market doesn't represent any ownership to anything." Futures are just side bets and have no economic value. Nevertheless, each part of a trade pays commissions and other service costs.

Nevertheless, futures trading paves the way for traders to hedge investments and engage in daily scalping.

-Choosing a future

Once you've selected a broker and have set up your trading account, you must then choose a futures contract. For this step, you've to consider several factors, including the indicators below:

➤ Volume

Choose contracts that have a trading volume of 300,000 trades per day. Doing this allows you to trade on the levels you want. And, due to such liquidity, another trader will always want to take your offer as long as it's reasonable. A few of the most traded contracts are listed below:

a) Crude oil WTI
b) 10-year treasury note
c) GE or Eurodollar
d) ES or E-mini S&P 500

Once you've selected a profitable futures contract, you must next consider its price movements and the margins that fit your style of trading. The available margin depends on the amount and agreements your broker offers. For example, margin trading of crude oil contracts often demands high account deposits.

➢ Movement

To establish price movement, you need to consider two factors. The first one is point value and the number of points the contract moves within 24 hours. By calculating the simple average true range (ATR), you can get the data you need to enter a profitable position in this market.

For the formula, please refer to the image below:

$$TR = \text{Max}[(H - L), \text{Abs}(H - C_P), \text{Abs}(L - C_P)]$$

$$ATR = \left(\frac{1}{n}\right) \sum_{(i=1)}^{(n)} TR_i$$

where:

TR_i = A particular true range

n = The time period employed

To calculate the range, look at the difference between the low and the high prices of the future in the present day.

Remember, "true high" is yesterday's close and today's high. "True low" represents yesterday's close and today's low. Meanwhile, "true range" refers to the true high less the true low.

To better understand this concept, take the following scenario as an example. If the future closes in the day at ninety, then gaps will open at ninety-one and may reach an intraday high at ninety-two. In this case, the true range is 90 to 92 since yesterday's close is at 90 and the true high is 92.

-Using the factors and indicators

Today, you can confidently choose the type of futures contract to trade especially that you now know how to read the market. Will you choose equities contracts related to commodities or crude oil?

The E-Mini futures is a good starting point for beginner day traders. You can avail of margins that are as low as $600. This futures market is more volatile than that of crude oil's. With the E-Mini S&P 500, you can start trading with just a $3,000 trading account.

Conclusion

The journey has been long, hasn't it? There have been ups and downs, like the fluctuations on price charts. Trends are there, and like a startup business, you need to watch their performance. Will the price continue to go up? Will the trends experience a sudden reversal? TA and FA are your go-to tools for analyzing the trends and the factors that affect price movement.

Indicators, such as the EPS, volume, and P/E ratio, are the main ingredients for technical and fundamental analysis. Even the classic strategy "buy low and sell high" strategy makes use of such indicators. After that, you need to determine support and resistance levels to come up with profitable trading plans.

Once you have all the elements in place, you need to set up orders and parameters for your trades. If you can't watch the markets that closely, consider using a stop/loss order. In doing so, even if the price of the security keeps decreasing, you can get out of the market before it hits all-time bottom. In their respective chapters, all of these methods, techniques, and strategies have been covered.

Day trading is all about dealing with volatile assets. As a day trader, you won't profit from stagnation. You can only increase your savings and capital if you buy/sell financial instruments that exhibit price fluctuations. Your profit will depend on the success of your trades and how you efficiently read indicators and market sentiment. There's no shortcut to day trading. It's a step-by-step process, but by following the teachings in this book, you can start making a profit from tradable securities and grow your wealth every day.

Book Description

In this fast-paced digital world, people often forget how to live. You wake up, get ready, and go to work, or you just watch another day pass by from the shutters at your home, office, or business establishment, while worrying about what tomorrow will bring.

When was the last time you actually enjoy living? Have you given up your passions so that you can make ends meet? After working for years, can you say that you've enough savings to cover the needs of your family in the future?

Only a handful of businesses can give you the freedom to actually "live" your short life. Day trading may just give you the key to that door to freedom. As a day trader, you're your own boss. You can trade today and cherish a memorable family time tomorrow.

That's the undeniable life of a day trader. "Day Trading Options" offers everything you need to know about day trading, from setting up your devices, choosing the right brokerage platform, to reading MACD indicators for technical analysis. This book also features several sections dedicated for the best tradable assets for scalpers, speculators, and day traders. What's more, there are also bonus sections for swing trading and profiting from long trades, on top of the rare topics below:

- ➤ Risk management and money management for your capital and future trades
- ➤ Comprehensive guides to fundamental and technical analysis
- ➤ Beginner to advanced day trading tips, strategies, and lessons
- ➤ Trading psychology and market behavior
- ➤ Developing your own trading system
- ➤ The indicators that can help you strategize   profitable trades

Aiming to help beginners succeed and for advanced traders to gain industry secrets and rare day trading insights, this book won't only give you the confidence to start day trading, but it will also help you become an advanced trader.

Options Trading Crash Course

The #1 Beginner's Investing Guide to Create Passive Income. Market Evaluation Techniques and the Most Effective Strategies Available Now! Learn How to Trade for a Living

All rights reserved. No part of this publication may be reproduced, stored in a retrieval system, copied in any form or by any means, electronic, mechanical, photocopying, recording or otherwise transmitted without written permission from the publisher. Please do not participate in or encourage piracy of this material in any way. You must not circulate this book in any format. Chana Cohn does not control or direct users' actions and is not responsible for the information or content shared, harm and/or actions of the book readers.

In accordance with the U.S. Copyright Act of 1976, the scanning, uploading and electronic sharing of any part of this book without the permission of the publisher constitute unlawful piracy and theft of the author's intellectual property. If you would like to use material from the book (other than just simply for reviewing the book), prior permission must be obtained by contacting the author at
Thank you for your support of the author's rights.

Table of Contents

© Copyright 2021 by Ryan Martinez - All rights reserved.
The content contained within this book may not be reproduced,
duplicated or transmitted without direct written permission
from the author or the publisher.
Under no circumstances will any blame or legal responsibility
be held against the publisher, or author, for any damages,
reparation, or monetary loss due to the information contained
within this book. Either directly or indirectly.
Legal Notice:
This book is copyright protected. This book is only for
personal use. You cannot amend, distribute, sell, use, quote
or paraphrase any part, or the content within this book,
without the consent of the author or publisher.
Disclaimer Notice:
Please note the information contained within this document is
for educational and entertainment purposes only. All effort has
been executed to present accurate, up to date, and reliable,
complete information. No warranties of any kind are declared
or implied. Readers acknowledge that the author is not
engaging in the rendering of legal, financial, medical or
professional advice. The content within this book has been
derived from various sources. Please consult a licensed
professional before attempting any techniques outlined in this
book.
By reading this document, the reader agrees that under no
circumstances is the author responsible for any losses, direct
or indirect, which are incurred as a result of the use of
information contained within this document, including, but not
limited to, — errors, omissions, or inaccuracies.

Introduction

I want to thank you and congratulate you for downloading the book, *"Options Trading Crash Course: The #1 Beginner's Investing Guide to Create Passive Income. Market Evaluation Techniques and the Most Effective Strategies Available Now! Learn How to Trade for A Living"*.

Options trading has been doubted for such a long time that a lot of people still think of it as a risky endeavor. So, how can you reduce your risks and maximize your returns? Likewise, how can you improve your knowledge and skills?

This book is going to be your guide in fulfilling all your options trading objectives.

Options are highly popular among economic markets, particularly in the United States. In fact, it is the preferred trading type of the general public, being economically friendly to traders from diverse backgrounds.

Then again, even though a lot of people have already succeeded in options trading, some are still doubtful and hesitant towards it. They do not feel safe and confident that their money will grow.

The truth of the matter is that options trading is good to those who truly understand it. So, if you want to succeed in this endeavor, you have to have a practical trading plan that suits you. You should aim to maximize gains and reduce risks. Your trading plan should be well-structured but simple enough to be followed on a regular basis.

In addition, you need to have the right attitude for trading. Learning about the terms and techniques is great, but developing the right attitude for trading is even better. You need to train yourself so that you can be a smart and disciplined trader.

In this book, you will learn everything you need as a beginner, including terms, strategies, current events related to options trading, as well as the traits that you have to develop if you truly want to succeed.

You will learn about the financial markets and how you can analyze them effectively. You will learn about risks and rewards, and how important practicing is. You will know what paper trading is and why you should do it before you start actual trading.

In addition, you will learn about trading plans, how you can create a good one, and how you can successfully follow it throughout your trading career. You will learn about options and futures, and what their differences and similarities are. Furthermore, you will learn about the trading platforms that novice and advanced traders use. In the last chapter of this book, you will read about the best trading platforms recommended by experts. You will learn about their features, advantages, and disadvantages. You will also learn how you can effectively choose a trading platform that suits your needs, trading style, and budget.

Indeed, this book has everything you need to know as a beginner options trader. The basics are covered, so you can go from zero to knowledgeable. There are also examples that can help you understand concepts better. Hopefully, you will find this book informative and interesting at the same time. Thanks again for downloading this book, I hope you enjoy it!

Chapter 1: Introduction to Options Trading

What is trading?

Trading refers to the economic concept that involves the buying and selling of assets, including services and goods. During the transaction, the buyer has to pay the seller his compensation. In some cases, such transactions may also involve an exchange of services and goods between trading parties.

The assets traded in financial markets are called financial instruments, which include stocks, futures, bonds, cryptocurrency, Forex currency pairs, margin products, and options.

What about options trading then?

Well, if you are familiar with stocks and are already comfortable trading them, you will also do well with options. When it comes to options trading, you have a right to either buy or sell assets at fixed prices prior to their predetermined dates but you are not obligated. Options have values and you should find out more about them.

So, when you buy an option put or call, you are not in any way obligated to sell or buy its underlying instrument. Nonetheless, you have a right to sell or buy at a fixed price. The only risk involved when buying options is related to their price.

Selling imposes an obligation but selling options make you obligated to buy or deliver to the buyer if he exercises the option. When you sell options naked, you may have a risk profile without limits.

However, this may not be ideal for you if you are obligated to do something. Unless you are an advanced trader, you should refrain from selling naked options. You should also have a good strategy for covering downsides.

What should you know about options?

Options are contracts that give buyers a right, but not an obligation, to purchase or sell underlying assets at a certain price on or before a specific date. Just like bonds or stocks, they are securities. They are binding contracts that have strict properties and terms.

Even if you are just a beginner trader who does not know a lot about options, you will be able to understand it better by looking at ordinary day-to-day situations. For instance, if you found a house that you like, you have to have the money to purchase it.

You have to talk to the seller and enter a deal that would benefit you. Negotiate if possible. Say, your money is not enough. You will not have enough money to purchase it for the next three months. You speak with the owner and agree to purchase the house for $200,000 in three months. The owner agrees, yet for this option, you pay $3,000. This scenario would give you two theories:

a. You found out that the house is, in fact, the real birthplace of Albert Einstein. Because of this, its market value goes up to $1M. Since the owner gave you such an option, he becomes obligated to sell the house for $200,000. As a result, you can earn a profit of $797,000.

b. As you tour around the house, you find out that the walls are filled with asbestos and a ghost haunts the bedrooms. Also, you discover a whole family of rats in the basement. Even though you initially thought that you finally found your dream house, you slowly realize that it is the opposite. The house is a disaster! On the bright side, however, since you purchased the option, you no longer become obligated to continue the sale. Then again, you still lose $3,000.

The above-given example shows two focal points: One, if you purchase an option, you gain the right but not the obligation. Two, the option is just a contract that deals with the underlying asset.

So, you may allow the date of expiration to go by and make the option lose its value. Options are also referred to as derivatives. They derive their value from other things. In this example, the underlying asset is the house. Oftentimes, the underlying asset serves as an index or a stock.

Puts and Calls

Puts and calls are types of options. Calls provide the holders a right to purchase assets at a specific price within a certain period of time. Just the same, calls can be compared to long positions on stocks. The buyers of calls usually wish that the stock would substantially increase before the expiration date of the option.

Puts provide the holders a right to sell assets at a specific price within a certain period of time. They are the same as maintaining a short position on stocks. The buyers of puts usually wish that the stock price would go down before the date of expiration.

Options Market Participants

Options markets involve four kinds of participants. These participants depend on the positions that they take. They are the:
   a. Buyers of calls
   b. Sellers of calls
   c. Buyers of puts
   d. Sellers of puts

Those who purchase options are known as holders while those who sell options are known as writers. Moreover, sellers tend to have short positions while buyers tend to have long positions.

Take note that sellers and buyers have this vital distinction: the put holders and the call holders are neither obligated to sell nor buy. Instead, they have the option to exert their rights if they want.

Sellers may be required to buy or sell. Selling options is actually more complicated than you may have thought. It can even be much riskier. Thus, you have to learn about the two sides of a contract on options.

The Language or Lingo

In order for you to successfully trade options, you have to learn about the language or lingo involved. There are plenty of terms that traders use when trading. These terms will be discussed later in this book.

The price at which underlying stocks may be sold or bought is known as the strike price. This refers to the price a stock price has to go below for puts or go above for calls before positions can be exercised for profits. This should occur prior to the date of expiration.

Options that are traded on national options exchange are called listed options. You can find examples of these options on the Chicago Board Options Exchange. They have fixed expiration dates and strike prices. Every listed option represents one hundred shares of contract or company stock. When it comes to call options, the options are claimed to be in-the-money when the share price is beyond the strike price. Put options are in-the-money if the share price is less than the strike price.

Amounts by which options are in-the-money are known as intrinsic values. The overall cost of the option is known as the premium. Such price is based on factors like the strike price, stock price, volatility, and remaining time until expiration. As a beginner, you may not be able to determine the premiums of options right away as this is such a complicated thing to do. As you continue to practice trading, however, you will eventually learn everything about it.

Why Should You Use Options?

Investors generally use options because of two reasons: for speculating and for hedging.

Some people view speculation as betting on security movement. A benefit of options is that it does not limit you to just earning a profit when the market rises. It offers a variety of options, so you can also earn a profit when the market falls or goes sideways.

The territory wherein big money is either made or lost is called speculation. Options use in such manner is the reason why options are said to be risky. When you purchase options, you need to be right in identifying the direction of the movement of the stock as well as the timing and magnitude of this movement.

To achieve success, you have to accurately predict if the stock would rise or fall. You also have to accurately estimate the price change. Your instincts should be reliable enough so that you can know how much money and time you will need for all of this to take place. Do not forget to factor in the commissions. When these factors are combined, you might feel that the odds are up against you.

This sounds tricky; but why do a lot of people still speculate with options. Well, other than versatility, it is all about taking advantage of leverage. If you control a hundred shares with a single contract, it will not take much of a movement in pricing to generate enough profits.

Hedging is another function of options. You can view it as your insurance plan. Houses and cars are not the only ones that have to have an insurance policy. If you want to protect your investments, you have to use options correctly. When used the right way, they would protect you in times of economic downturns.

Those who criticize option claim that if you are not sure about your stock pick and you had to have a hedge, then you should not make any investments. Then again, you can rest assured that hedging strategies are helpful, especially for major institutions.

Even individual investors can find it beneficial. Say, you wished to benefit from the technology stocks as well as their upside, yet you also hoped to limit your losses. You can use options to restrict the downside while still being able to enjoy the full upside. Now, this is cost-effective.

Stock Options

Employee stock options are not available to just about anyone. It is a type of option that can be regarded as a third reason for going with options. A lot of companies use it to attract and keep good employees, particularly the management team.

It is similar to a regular stock option in the sense that its holder has a right yet not an obligation to buy company stocks. However, the contract is between the company and the holder. Normal options, on the other hand, involve contracts between two parties that are not related to the company.

Options in the Real World

Simply learning about the theories on options trading is not enough. You have to put these theories into practice. However, before you set out into the world of trading, it would be wise to learn more from examples.

Let's say, we have a company called Company X. On April 1, its stock price is $67 while its premium is $3.15 for a June 70 Call. This means that its date of expiration is on the third Friday of June while its strike price is $70. The contract's total price now becomes $3.15 x 100 = $315. Then again, in the real world, you also have to consider the commissions. This would give you an amount close to, but not exactly $315. Keep in mind that stock option contracts are the options to purchase a hundred shares. This is why you have to multiply this contract by one hundred in order to obtain the total price. Thus, a strike price of $70 means that the stock price has to go over $70 before a call option can be worth something. Also, since the contract costs $3.15 for every share, the price of breakeven becomes $73.15.

If the price of the stock is $67, that would be less than the strike price of $70. Hence, the option is useless. Then again, you should remember that you paid $315 for the option. This is why you are down by this much money.

Three weeks after this, the stock price becomes $78. The options contract has gone up together with the stock price. It is now $825. If you subtract the amount that you paid for in your contract, you will earn a profit of $510. This shows you that your money has been doubled. You can sell your options or close your position when you get your profits. You can do this unless the price of stock continues to go up.

Anyway, let's say that the price goes down to $62. Since this is less than the $70 strike price, the option contract becomes useless. So, you go down to $315, which is your original amount. The price swing for the duration of this contract was $825, which would've given you more than double your original investment. Now, you see how leverage works.

Trading Out versus Exercising

You have learned that options are all about having the right to buy or sell the underlying. In reality, however, a lot of options are not exercised.

Going back to our example, you can earn a profit when you exercise or buy or sell the underlying at $70 before selling your stock back at $78 in the market for a profit of $8 per share. You can also retain the stock since you know that you can purchase it at a discounted amount.

Then again, a lot of time holders opt to close out or trade out their positions. The holders choose to sell their options while the writers buy the positions back to close them.

Time Value and Intrinsic Value

Let us learn more about options pricing. Going back to our example, the premium of the option went to $8.25 from $3.15. What happened here is related to time value and intrinsic value.

In essence, the premium of an option is the sum of its time value and intrinsic value. Keep in mind that the intrinsic value refers to the amount-in-the-money. With call options, this means that the stock price is equivalent to the strike price. The time value represents the probability of the option going up in value. Thus, the option price in our previous example can be said as the premium is equal to the sum of the time value and the intrinsic value. So, $0.25 and $8 combined equals $8.25.

The Options Used by Traders

In general, traders use two types of options: European Options and American Options. American options are exercised any time between the expiration date and purchase date. Our previous example showed this type of option. A lot of exchange-traded options are actually of this type.

On the other hand, European options are exercised only at the end of life. Take note that your geographical location does not have anything to do with the differences between these two types of options.

Long Term and Exotic Options

Long-term investors may prefer holding times of multiple years. These options are referred to as long-term equity anticipation securities. By giving opportunities to manage and control risks, they are basically the same as regular options. Then again, long-term equity anticipation securities provide opportunities for a much longer period of time. Even though they are not available on stocks, these options are still available on many issues.

Exotic Options

Plain vanilla options are known as the simple puts and calls. Although options may be quite hard to understand in the beginning, these simple puts and calls are actually very easy to grasp.

Due to the option versatility, there are a lot of variations and types of options. Those that are not standard are known as exotic options. These are either variations on the plain vanilla payoff profiles or are completely different products that have optionality.

Reading Options Tables

As a trader, the more you learn about the advantages of options, the more encouraged you will be to engage in trading. It is a well-known fact that the trading volume of options has grown over the years. Such a trend has been driven by the introduction of data dissemination and electronic trading as well.

There are traders who use options to make speculations on price direction. There are also those who hedge anticipated or existing positions. In addition, there are those who craft unique positions that provide benefits that are not available routinely to traders of only the underlying stocks, futures, or index contracts.

Regardless of the objectives of these traders, the key to success is to choose the right option or option combination necessary to create a position with the preferred risk to reward tradeoffs. With this being said, the savvy option traders of today are usually searching for more complicated sets of data with regard to options than traders of past years.

Option Price Reporting in the Past
Many years ago, newspapers feature rows of option price data that are quite indecipherable. These data can be found deep within the financial sections. Today, the Wall Street Journal and Investor's Business Daily still have a partial listing of options data for active optionable stocks.
These old newspapers mostly included just the basics such as a C or P to indicate calls and puts. They also included the strike price, open interest figures, and the last trade price.
This worked for traders in the past decades. Today, however, option traders know more about the variables that work for options trading. Some of these variables include Greek values that have been derived from option pricing models, implied option volatility, and vital bid or ask spreads.
Because of this, more traders have started to find option data through online sources. Even though every source has its own format for data presentation, the key variables mostly include the following:

a. OpSym – it designates the strike price, the contract year and month, whether it is a put or call option, and the underlying stock symbol.
b. Bid – the bid price is the most recent price offered by the market maker to purchase a specific option. So, if you enter a market order to sell an option, you will be able to see its bid price.
c. Ask – it refers to the most recent price offered by the market maker to sell certain options. So, if you enter a market order to purchase an option, you will be able to purchase it at its ask price.

Keep in mind that selling at the ask and purchasing at the bid is how market makers earn money. It is crucial for options traders to take note of the differences between the ask and bid prices whenever they consider option trades.

In essence, the more active the option is, the tighter the bid or the ask spread. Wide spreads can be a problem for traders, especially those who are short-term. For example, if a bid is $3.40 and an ask is $3.50, you can lose -2.85% on your trade if you buy the option and then sold it later. You will lose this much even if the option price stays the same.

    d. Extrinsic Bid/Ask – it refers to how much time premium is built into the price of every option. This is vital to keep in mind because every option loses its premium by the time of expiration. Hence, such value reflects the whole amount of time premium currently built into the option price.

    e. Implied Volatility Bid/Ask – it is computed by an option pricing model like the Black – Scholes model. It also represents the expected future volatility level based on the present price of the option as well as other known variables for option pricing. This includes the amount of time until expiration, the risk-free rate of interest, and the difference between the actual stock price and the strike price.

In essence, the higher the implied volatility bid/ask, the more time the premium is built into the option price and vice versa. If you can access the historical range of implied volatility values for security, you will be able to tell if the present extrinsic value level is on the low end or high end. The previous is ideal for buying options while the latter is ideal for writing options.

    f. Delta Bid/Ask – Delta refers to the Greek value that has been derived from an option pricing model. It also represents a stock equivalent position for the option. A call option's delta may range from zero to one hundred. The current risk and reward characteristics linked to holding call options with a 50 delta are basically the same as holding fifty stock shares.

In case this stock goes up by one whole point, the option would gain about half a point. In essence, as the delta approaches a hundred, the option trades more and more like an underlying stock. For example, an option with a 100 delta will lose or gain one whole point for every dollar loss or gain in an underlying stock price.

   g. Gamma Bid/As – Gamma refers to the Greek value that has been derived from an option pricing model. It also tells you the amount of deltas an option would lose or gain in case the underlying stock goes up by one whole point. For instance, if you purchased March 2010 125 call at $3.50, you will have a 58.20 delta.

In essence, if the IBM stock goes up by one dollar, such option would gain about $0.5820 in value. What's more, in case the stock goes up in price at the present day by one whole point, such option would gain 5.65 deltas as well as would have a 63.85 delta. From here, another point gain the stock price will lead to a price gain for an estimated $0.6385 option.

   h. Vega Bid/Ask – Vega refers to the Greek value that signifies the amount by which the option price will be expected to fall or rise based only on a point increase in implied volatility. Hence, if you consider the March 2010 125 call once more, the option price will gain $0.141 if the implied volatility goes up by one point.

This shows you why it is ideal to purchase options when the implied volatility is low. You will pay a much less time premium as well as a rise in the implied volatility will inflate the option price. You will also write the options when the implied volatility is high.

   i. Theta Bid/Ask – Keep in mind that options lose the all-time premium by the expiration. Additionally, the time decay accelerates as the expiration date comes nearer. Theta is actually the Greek value that signifies the amount that an option loses with the passage of a day's time.

j. Volume – it merely tells you the number of contracts a certain option has traded during the most recent session. Even though this does not happen all the time, the options that have huge volumes tend to have much tighter bid or ask spreads because there is such a great competition to sell and buy options.

k. Open Interest – it signifies the total number of contracts a certain option has opened but not yet offset.

l. Strike – it refers to the strike price of an option. It is practically the price that the option buyer can buy the underlying security at in case he opts to exercise his option. In addition, it is the price at which the option writer has to sell the underlying security in case the option gets exercised against him.

With regard to puts and options, see to it that you take note of the following:

1. In general, call options become more expensive when their strike price becomes lower. Conversely, put options become more expensive when their strike price becomes higher. With calls, however, the lower strike prices tend to have very high option prices.

The option prices decline at every higher striker level. This happens because every successive strike price is more out of the money or less in the money. Hence, every one of them has less intrinsic value as compared to the option at the next lower strike price.

The opposite thing happens with puts. The higher the strike prices go, the more in the money or less out of the money the put options become. This, in turn, results in a more intrinsic value.

2. With call options, the values of delta are positive and are actually higher at a lower strike price. With put options, the values of delta are negative and are actually higher at a higher strike price.

Such negative values of the put options are derived from the fact that they indicate a stock equivalent position. Purchasing a put option is the same as entering a short stock position. This results in the negative value of the delta.

Option trading as well as the level of sophistication of an average options trader have greatly evolved since this venture started many years ago. The option quote screen of the present time actually reflects these innovations.

It is wise to keep in mind that options trading is not for every person. Not all investors would succeed in this venture. Options can be regarded as complicated trading tools that may be dangerous if you are not educated enough prior to using them. Nevertheless, they can prove to be fruitful if used the correct way.

Basic Pointers to Remember:
- Options are contracts that give buyers a right but not an obligation to either sell or buy an underlying asset at a particular price on or before a specific date.
- Also, options are regarded as derivatives since they derive values from underlying assets.
- Calls give holders a right to purchase assets at a specific price within a certain timeframe.
- Puts give holders a right to sell assets at a specific price within a certain timeframe.
- In essence, there are four kinds of options market participants. These are calls buyers, calls sellers, puts buyers, and puts sellers.
- The buyers are generally called holders while the sellers are frequently called writers.
- Premium refers to the total cost of an option. It is determined by certain factors such as the strike price, the stock price, and the time that remains until the expiration date.
- The price at which underlying stocks may be sold or bought is known as the strike price.
- A contract of a stock option represents one hundred shares of an underlying stock.

- The investors usually use options to hedge and speculate risk.
- The employee stock options are not the same as the listed options since they are actually a contract between the holder and the company. They also do not involve third parties.
- European and American are the two major classifications of options.
- LEAPS are more commonly referred to as long-term options.

Traits You Need to Develop In Order to Be a Successful Options Trader

Generating income from this venture involves good luck, effort, and attitude.

Patience

Patience is a virtue that can serve you long term. Those who have the capacity to stay calm as they wait are able to reap rewards. In the world of trading, patience is something that you need to have if you want to succeed. After all, good things come to those who wait.

As a beginner, you may find yourself wishing for good luck each time you make a trade. As time goes by, however, you will notice your skills improving. You will begin to develop an intuition. It will become much easier for you to make a decision and trade.

If you still think that patience is not necessary, then ponder this: would a person fly an airplane after just a single training session? Would a doctor perform surgery after reading just one book?

Professionals who do well in their career have had years of studying and training. They have gathered enough experience for them to be efficient. You, too, as a trader need the same amount of patience to succeed.

You should refrain from jumping into investments if you are not completely sure about them. You should always think twice, even thrice before making a move. Review your trading plan each time. Think of the possible consequences of your decisions.

For example, if you are just making one percent each week, you should not be disheartened. Do not rush into anything. Instead, you should think of compounding interest. Let your returns accumulate. If you stay patient with trading, your efforts will be rewarded.

Furthermore, you should choose a strategy that allows you to make the most of your time as well as covers your downside. Later in this book, you will be given more information regarding the options trading strategies that you can use. Nevertheless, no matter which strategy you decide to go for, always keep in mind that patience will bring you to the right opportunity. Do not trade if you are not a hundred percent sure that it is what you have to do. Learn how to wait. Stay patient. Soon enough, you will succeed and acquire wealth.

Perseverance

Successful traders come from different backgrounds and have different trading styles yet they all have a thing in common: perseverance. None of them gave up when things looked bleak. They kept going.

As a trader, it is crucial for you to hold on even when things start to look difficult. Nobody, not even the best trader in the world, can predict what will happen exactly in the future. So, you have to sit tight and keep doing what you are doing in order to achieve your goal.

Once you reach this goal, you should not be complacent and stop. You have to have another goal and keep moving forward. Do not worry if you are not the brightest trader. As long as you have a positive attitude and maintain a desire for learning, you will surely succeed.

A lot of successful traders actually come from humble beginnings. These people were not the most remarkable students. Many others were more intelligent and talented. Nevertheless, they persevered. That's why they were able to attain their trading objectives.

You should create attainable goals and stick to the timeframe. The more you succeed in attaining these goals, the more confidence you build. In turn, you become more experienced and better at making decisions.

Knowledge

You cannot delve into trading blindly. You need to possess the necessary knowledge in order for you to use trading strategies efficiently. Fortunately, there are plenty of tools that you can use. Lots of information are available on the Internet as well as written in books.

You should learn how to create plans for minimizing risks and maximizing profits. You should also learn about entry, exit, and breakeven points. You have to know how to stop losses and generate profits.

Then again, you also have to remember that knowledge is not merely theoretical. It is not enough to simply study trading. Reading books and watching tutorials are helpful, but you also need to gain experience and wisdom.

Smart traders know all about the best strategies. They know when to buy and when to sell. They are aware of the latest trends on the market. However, they also know how to manage themselves, including their emotions.

Remember that emotions are a natural part of being human. There will be times when you will feel emotional towards your options. You might feel scared, happy, or sad with trading. This is why you have to learn how to work around your emotions instead of ignoring or giving in to them. You have to be objective at all times.

Being in the right state of mind is crucial. Use your experiences to your advantage. Each time you trade, see to it that you find the lesson that comes with it. So, next time you find yourself in a similar situation, you will know what to do.

Honesty and Accountability

Every decision you make is your responsibility. This is why you need to be careful with every step you take. You roll the dice. So, you have to live with the consequences.

Pre-Planning

Every trade you make should be pre-planned. This means that you have to be aware of your maximum reward and risk as well as your breakeven points. In addition, you should plan both your entry and exit points whether you want to gain profits or stop losses.

For example, you may base your stop loss on the underlying stock, which is generally more liquid than the options. Hence, it is much easier to make a decision based on stock, future, and other underlying asset prices.

When pre-planning, you should study your chart pattern. This way, you can create your trading plan. You need to be disciplined enough to stick to your plans. Pre-plan before trading and use your experience to do better each time. You can also seek guidance and inspiration from other people's trading experiences. Learn from their mistakes and follow their successful moves.

Resist the urge to change your plan, even though you have had a last-minute idea that you think might benefit you. Always aim to be methodical. Remember that discipline is key to becoming a successful trader.

If you do not know how to manage your finances wisely, no trading system will work for you, not even the best ones. When you stick to good principles on managing money, you will be able to minimize your losses and maximize your gains. What's more, you will be able to avoid risk profiles that are suicidal. Be wary of unhelpful risk profile curves. Always study these curves so that you can achieve success at options trading.

Chapter 2: Trading Strategies

In order for you to survive the intense competition in the financial markets, you need to use successful and properly tested trading strategies. Keep in mind that if you use a trading style that is based on chaotic cross-betting, you will surely fail. You need to have systematic trading.

The Importance of Using Good Trading Strategies
Systematic trading is vital for long-term success. When you stick to a strategy that lets you stay focus in spite of the huge inflow of economic data and news, you will be able to remain rational. Your analysis process will not be negatively affected by these factors.
In addition, profound knowledge is necessary for the pricing characteristics of certain asset classes or assets. Aside from profound knowledge, you also need technical analysis to set the exit and entry points. Beginner traders tend to fail due to the lack of these analyses.
Take note that you may still profit from merely using a predetermined strategy based on price action. You can measure and improve your own performance. Be careful not to trade chaotically. You should always have a good trading plan so that you can evaluate your performance and have a constant basis for comparison.
When you use a trading system for a long time, you can create a statistical database that would allow you to evaluate its performance. Once you are done with the evaluation, you can start to improve it. Do not forget to change the necessary parameters and compare the new results with your historical data. This would allow you to find out if the upgrade is a success.
Another reason why trading strategies are important is that they help you regulate your emotions. It is natural for humans to be emotional because it is part of their nature. So, when it comes to putting your money at stake, you might become

emotional at certain times. After all, you work hard to earn your money. You certainly do not want to lose it.

A lot of traders have a problem with controlling their emotions. They tend to be overcome by greed, fear, and sometimes anger. Do not be like these traders. You should always be calm and collected. Winning and losing come with trading. There are days when you would lose and there are days when you would win. Even the best traders have experienced defeat at some point in their lives. Thus, you should not be carried away by your emotions when you win and especially when you lose.

Do not allow greed to overcome you when you win. Otherwise, you will start to bet too much than you need to. Do not allow fear to overcome you when you have experienced losses. Remember that the best traders are courageous. They do not avoid entering good positions because they know that they can gain huge profits.

Do not allow anger to overcome you when you do not get the outcome that you expected. Nobody can make exact predictions about the future. Nevertheless, you can make intelligent guesses and study your strategies carefully. A good trading strategy can help you disregard any volatility in your performance. This, in turn, can help you manage your emotions well and concentrate on achieving success. Furthermore, you should be careful not to overtrade. It is important for you to have a trading system with well-defined exit and entry rules. Otherwise, you can slip into a position opening frenzy. You may overtrade and hurt your chances at achieving success. Always watch your actions. Do not make trades more than you can actually handle.

Selecting the Trading Strategies for You
Every trader is unique. So, you should not expect one trader's strategy to work for everyone else. Different traders follow different strategies as well as make different analyses. There is not a single strategy that works for all. The financial markets continue to change. Thus, you need to grow, change, and evolve with them.

It is wise to study different strategies in order to find out which ones work well for you. Here are some of the trading strategy characteristics that you have to keep in mind:

a. Profitable and effective strategies are simple.

Professional traders use advanced techniques to increase their chances of success. However, using more techniques than necessary can also be harmful to your success rate. Complex trading strategies can be difficult to use and earn money from. This is especially true if you are a beginner trader without much trading experience.

b. Every strategy needs sufficient testing prior to employment.

You need demo accounts to survive in trading. Traders have to use them, regardless of their experience. After all, these are great for testing new ideas free of charge. Do not forget that various assets have various trading specifications. Hence, you need to study the different strategies carefully.

Remember that a certain strategy may work well for a certain type of investment but not for another. So, a strategy that works great with stocks may not work well with cryptocurrencies. You need to use a demo account to find out about things like this.

c. The strategies used in trading can become obsolete.

Nothing lasts forever, including trading strategies. Those that are effective now may no longer be effective in the future. After all, the development pace of the financial markets continues to evolve. The performance of a trading strategy is expected to diminish at some point. This requires monitoring. When the trading strategy starts to underperform, you can either abandon or fine-tune it.

d. Every strategy is subject to drawdowns.

Take note that even the most successful trading strategies can fail at some point. So, if the strategy that you are using has a 60% success rate, it is possible for your binary option to end up as "out of money". Since losing positions is unavoidable, all you can do is accept losses and follow your trading plan.

Combining Trading Strategies
In order for profits to be gained, trading strategy diversification is necessary. Expert traders do not rely on a single strategy because they know market conditions are diverse. Hence, they need to use a variety of trading strategies to succeed. Using more than one trading strategy allows you to easily digest the inevitable losses that one strategy can cause. Once these losses start to diminish your confidence, it would be difficult for you to perform at your best. However, once you are able to reap profits, your morale will be improved.
Also, as the financial markets evolve, some strategies start to die down. They are no longer able to keep up with the latest trends. They start to lose their relevance. This is why you should always be prepared to switch to an alternative strategy. Remember that trying to mend a previous strategy can actually do more harm than good. For instance, it may cause you to lose more money in the long run.
Furthermore, asset diversification is a vital hedge against drawdowns. If certain asset classes or assets defy your expectations, specifically after you bought options with a longer maturity, having positions that are opened in other asset classes or assets can offset such losses and keep you at or beyond breakeven.
Then again, since different assets and asset classes tend to have different trading specifics, you have to use different optimized trading strategies. This, of course, calls for a system of strategies used for trading.

Different Options Trading Strategies
The following are some of the strategies that you can use for options trading:

Covered Call
If you wish to buy a naked call option, you need to use buy-write, also known as covered call. This strategy is highly popular amongst traders due to its ability to reduce the risk involved in staying long on stocks while generating income. However, you may have to sell your shares at a short strike price, which is a set price.

Covered call is actually a strategy used by investors who feel that their underlying position is quite bullish in the near term although good for medium to long term. In order for you to be able to use this strategy successfully, you have to buy an underlying stock while simultaneously writing or selling a call option on such shares.

You have to sell a call option on one of your stocks so that you can have a premium inflow. When the underlying increases, so does the profit. However, this profit is capped once it reaches the strike price.

Also, if such underlying crosses this strike price, the payoff will get capped because the call option will incur losses. Nevertheless, you can still generate good income using this strategy if the market is neutral.

What does this mean exactly?

Say, an investor uses a call option on a particular stock that represents one hundred shares of stocks per call option. When this investor buys shares of stock, he has to sell a call option simultaneously. In essence, every one hundred shares of stocks require one call option.

This example illustrates the covered call. If ever the stock price increases, the long stock position covers the short call. As an investor, you may go for this strategy if you have a short-term position in stock as well as a neutral opinion. You may be protected against a decline in the value of the underlying stock or earn an income from the call premium sale.

With the covered call strategy, both your risks and rewards are limited.

Buy Call

This strategy is ideal if you are bullish on the direction of the market going up short term. Also known as Going Long on a Call, Buying Call is the easiest way to make a profit if you think that the market will go up. It is also the most commonly used strategy by beginners.

When you go long on a call option, you can enjoy gains if the underlying stock or index rallies. Then again, if this stock or index makes a correction, you can have risks.

In essence, this strategy comes with unlimited rewards and risks that are limited to your paid premium.

Buy Put

The buy put, also known as go long on a put, occurs when investors become bearish on the direction of the market going down in the short term.

The put option allows the put buyer to sell a stock at a pre-determined price in order to limit his risks. With this strategy, you can be at an advantage if the underlying stock or index goes down. Nevertheless, there are limited risks on the upside when the underlying stock or index rallies.

Sell Call

The sell call, also known as go short on a call, occurs when investors are not bullish on the market. With this strategy, you can gain a premium from the call buyer.

There is limited profit potential in this position. There is also a possibility for huge losses on large advances in the underlying prices. Even though this strategy is fairly simple, it is still risky because the call seller becomes exposed to unlimited risk.

Sell Put

The sell put, also known as go short on a put, occurs when investors are bullish on the direction of the market and they expect the prices of stocks to increase or remain sideways at a minimum.

If you sell a put, you can earn a premium from the put buyer. When the underlying price goes higher than the strike price, the position of the short put allows the seller to earn a profit depending on the premium amount. However, if the price goes lower than the strike price, particularly if such price goes lower than the premium amount, the seller of the put loses money.

Married Put

With this strategy, you can buy assets while simultaneously buying put options for the same number of shares. The put option holder can sell stocks at the strike price. As an investor, you can use this strategy to protect your downside risk as you hold a stock. It works the same way as an insurance policy since it establishes the price floor in case the price of the stock goes down.

Let's say, you buy a hundred shares of stocks as well as a put option. The married put strategy may appeal to you since you get to be protected against the downside in case a negative change occurs in the stock price. Likewise, you can take part in upside opportunities in case the value of the stock increases.

Then again, in the event that the stock does not decrease in value, you lose the amount that you paid in premium for the put option.

Bull Call Spread

With this strategy, you can buy calls at a certain strike price simultaneously while selling the same amount of calls at a higher price. These two call options would have the same underlying asset and date of expiration.

You can use this vertical spread strategy when you are bullish on an underlying asset and you expect a slight increase in asset price. If you use the bull call spread, you can limit your upside on a trade as you reduce your net premium spent.

You can use this strategy if you are moderately bullish on the direction of the market going up in the short term. It actually occurs when an in-the-money call option is bought and an out-of-the-money call option is sold. These two call options should have a similar month of expiration and underlying security.

This strategy's net effect is to pull down the cost as well as breakeven on a long call or buy call. As an investor, you can benefit from this strategy if your underlying stock or index rallies. Then again, you can have limited risk if a correction is made on the underlying stock or index.

Bull Put Spread

This strategy should be used if you are moderately bullish on the direction of the market going up in the short term. It occurs when an out-of-the-money put option is bought and an in-the-money-put-option is sold. These two options should have a similar month of expiration and underlying security. The idea is to buy a lower strike put in order to protect or provide insurance to the put sold.

Bear Call Spread

This strategy is ideal if you are moderately bearish on the direction of the market as well as expecting the underlying to go down in the short term. It occurs when an out-of-the-money call option is bought and an in-the-money call option is sold. These call options should have a similar month of expiration and underlying security. As an investor, you will receive a net credit since the purchased call has a higher strike price than the sold call.

Bear Put Spread

This vertical spread strategy is preferable if you simultaneously buy put options at a certain strike price while you sell the same amount of puts at a lower price. These options will have the same underlying asset and date of expiration as well.

You can also use this strategy if you have a bearish sentiment with regards to the underlying asset as well as when you expect the price of this asset to decrease. You can expect limited gains and limited losses from the bear put spread. This strategy should be used if you are moderately bearish on the direction of the market as well as expecting the underlying to go down in the short term. It occurs when an in-the-money put option is bought and an out-of-the-money put option is sold.

These put options should have a similar month of expiration and underlying security. As an investor, you have to pay a net premium since the purchased put has a higher strike price than the sold put.

Protective Collar
When you use this strategy, you have to buy an out-of-the-money put option while you write an out-of-the-money call option. Also, you have to ensure that both the date of expiration and the underlying asset is the same.

You can use the protective collar strategy after experiencing substantial gains from a long position in a stock. It will give you downside protection since the long put locks in the possible sale price. Then again, you may be obliged to sell your shares at a higher price. Hence, you may not be able to gain additional profits.

Say, an investor goes long on a hundred shares of Company X at $50. Supposedly, Company X increases in value to $100 by January. You may sell a Company X March 105 call and buy a Company X March 95 put to gain a protective collar. Remember that until the date of expiration is reached, the trader gets protected below $95. As for the trade-off, you may be obligated to sell your shares at $105 if Company X trades at such a rate before the date of expiration.

Long Straddle
If you simultaneously buy a call and put option on a similar underlying asset with a similar strike price as well as the date of expiration, the long straddle occurs. You may use this

strategy if you think that the price of an underlying asset might significantly move out of a certain range yet you are not sure of which direction such a move would take.

In theory, the long straddle allows investors to have a chance at unlimited gains. Likewise, these investors may suffer from a maximum loss that is nevertheless limited to the cost of the two options contractors combined.

Long Strangle

If you buy a put option and a call option that is out-of-the-money on a similar underlying asset with a similar date of expiration, this strategy will occur. With a long strangle, the investor believes that the price of the underlying asset would have a huge movement yet he is not sure about the direction that the move would take.

Long Call Butterfly Spread

With this strategy, you get to combine the bear spread and the bull spread strategies. You also have to use three various strike prices. Plus, every option is for the same expiration date and underlying asset.

You may actually construct a long butterfly spread when you buy an in-the-money call option for a low strike price. At the same time, you can sell two at-the-money call options as well as buy an out-of-the money call option.

The wing widths of a balanced butterfly spread are the same. When you attain a call fly, you can expect a net debit as result. You will then go into a long butterfly call spread if you believe that the stock would not move a lot prior to the expiration date.

Iron Condor

With this strategy, you can hold a bear call spread and a bull put spread simultaneously. It is basically constructed when you sell an out-of-the money put and buy an out-of-the-money put with a lower strike.

The expiration date as well as the underlying asset for every option are the same. The call and put sides also have a similar spread width. If you use this strategy, you can earn a net premium. In fact, a lot of traders rely on it to attain a high probability of generating a small premium amount.

Iron Butterfly

With this strategy, you buy out-of-the-money put and sell at-the-money put. You also buy out-of-the-money call and sell at-the-money call. Every option is on a similar underlying asset and has a similar expiration date. Even though the iron butterfly is quite similar to the butterfly spread, it actually uses both puts and calls whereas the butterfly spread only uses one of the two.

The iron butterfly also combines purchasing protective wings and selling at-the-money straddle. Profits and losses are limited to a certain range. This strategy may work well for you if you typically aim for high income and small gains with non-volatile stocks.

Buy Straddle

The buy straddle, also known as the long straddle, is a non-directional strategy. It is typically used when the investor expects the underlying to show big movements in any direction.

It also involves purchasing a put-and-call on a similar underlying for a similar strike price and maturity. Through this strategy, you can choose to move in either plummeting or soaring direction, giving you a great advantage.

You can earn a profit if there is volatility in the underlying to cover the trade costs. Your loss is also limited to how much premium you had paid when you bought the options. As an investor, all you have to do is to find out if the underlying exponentially breaks out in either direction.

Sell Straddle

The sell straddle, also known as the short straddle, is actually the opposite of the buy straddle. This strategy is used when investors expect the underlying not to show any big movements. Instead, they expect the underlying to show some downside or upside volatility.

With this strategy, a call and a put are sold on the same underlying for a similar strike price and maturity. It also gives you a net income. In the event that the underlying doesn't move in either direction, you get to retain the premium since the call and the put will not be exercised. Then again, if the underlying moves down or up, you may be at risk of unlimited losses.

Long Synthetic
This strategy can be used if you are bullish on the direction of the market. It involves selling put options and buying call options at a similar strike price. These options, however, should have a similar month of expiration and security.
You can say that using the long synthetic strategy is akin to being long on an underlying security. If you go long for this strategy, you can expect to see payoff traits that are the same as holding a features contract or stock. It also has the advantage of being less expensive than purchasing an underlying outright.

Short Synthetic
This strategy can be used if you are bearish on the direction of the market and you expect it to go down soon. This strategy also involves purchasing put options and selling call options at a similar strike price. These two options should have a similar month of expiration and underlying security.
You can expect this strategy to behave exactly like being short on an underlying security. You can also use this strategy when you expect the payoff traits to be the same as being short on a future contract or stock. As for the rewards and risks, you can expect them to be unlimited.

Call Backspread
It is ideal to be used if you are bullish on the direction and volatility of the market. It can be effective if you are both bearish and bullish on the market with a bias to the upside. It involves buying two Out of the Money Call Option lots and

selling one In the Money Call Option. These call options should have a similar expiration month and underlying security.

Chapter 3: Advantages and Disadvantages of Options Trading

There are many advantages and disadvantages to options trading that you have to learn about if you wish to be successful in this venture.

The Advantages of Options Trading

Cost Efficiency
With options, you get to enjoy lots of leveraging power. You may actually have an options position that is equivalent to a stock position at a lower margin.
Stock trading requires a higher upfront financial commitment than options trading. The cost of purchasing an option, which includes both the trading commission and the premium, is much less than the cost of purchasing shares.

High Returns
You get to have a better chance at yielding high returns with options trading than with using cash to buy shares. If you are able to choose the correct strike, you can gain an equal profit from the option as you would when you buy stocks. Hence, you can enjoy higher returns since you get to acquire options at a lower margin.

Low Risks
While it is true that options are riskier than equities, they are still more widely used for hedging positions. Take note that the risks involved with options are predefined since the maximum losses may be the premiums paid to purchase such options.

Strategy Availability

There are many different trading strategies that you can use to buy and sell options. Even better, these strategies may be combined to give you more flexibility as well as allow you to develop a strategic position.

Limited Downsides

If you buy a call or put option, you are not obligated in any way to follow through on a trade. In case your predictions on the direction and timeframe of the stock's trajectory goes wrong, you do not get to suffer huge losses. Instead, your losses are merely limited to the amount you paid for the trading fees and contract. Then again, the same thing cannot be said for those who sell options.

More Flexibility

With options trading, you can enjoy more flexibility. After all, before your contract expires, you can execute several strategies that include buying shares and exercising an option to add to your portfolio, selling shares and options, and selling in the money options contracts.

Fix Stock Prices

You can freeze a stock price at a strike price or a particular amount for a certain period of time. This will guarantee that you will be able to sell or buy such stock at such strike price at any time prior to the expiration date of the contract.

The Disadvantages of Options Trading

Less Liquidity

Certain stock options can be highly difficult to trade due to their low liquidity.

High Commissions

Compared to stock or future trading, options trading is more expensive. Then again, there are still discount brokers who can let you trade at a lower commission. Nevertheless, the majority of the full-service brokers charge high fees for options trading.

Time Decay
When time decay occurs, your options premium's value decreases. It continues to decrease each day regardless of the underlying movement.

Non-Availability
Stocks that have been registered with exchanges don't have any options contracts. Because of this, traders often experience difficulty in hedging their positions with their strategies.

Chapter 4: Analyzing the Market

When it comes to stock trading, it is imperative for you to study the market. You need to find out if it has a momentum that can be sustained. You also have to determine whether or not you need to use sentiment analysis and breadth tools. Keep in mind that the market can be quite unpredictable. The advances on the market also tend to be better when more stocks advance. You can use the options market as a reference when determining the status of the stock market. You can monitor options to determine whether the stocks are advancing or declining.

Pointers to Remember
Before you focus on the market, you may want to learn about interest rates and global economic trends first.
In general, falling or low-interest rates are considered to be bullish for stocks while rising or high-interest rates are negative. Take note that interest rate trends may affect the prices of underlying stocks. This, in turn, can affect the prices of options.
With this being said, it is only sensible to watch for global interest rates. All the markets in the world are linked together, so you have to understand how they move. According to experts, there would be a market inflection point someday. This would cause the stock prices to decline, making stocks unattractive investments.
As for global economic trends, you have to realize that the global economy was generally synchronized until the United Kingdom exited from the European Union and Donald Trump was elected as the United States president. These events have majorly affected the trends in the market.

Identifying Movement Strengths
Every decline and advance on the market is unique. For instance, a moderate advance may occur with a lot of sectors

going up together in frenzy. It may also go up with certain sectors and stocks outperforming the others.

If this happens, you should not waste your time trying to figure out what the market would do at any time. You should, instead, focus on analyzing the chances of trend direction continuing. As an investor, you want to trade in the direction of the currently dominant trend on the market.

You may find it quite difficult to have a new position if you think that you have missed a move. Nonetheless, you can still look at the breadth of the market so that you can decide with more certainty if the advance conditions are improving or not. You will also be able to predict downsides better in case the market appears to deteriorate.

Do not forget to use various tools for confirming market assessments. You should also use strategies that would allow you to stay consistent with these assessments. Keep in mind that gaining profits and being successful in trading requires patience, vigilance, and smart use of trading strategies. Whenever you see a possible change in trend, make sure to create a plan as soon as possible so that you can follow the new trend accordingly.

The Market Breadth

The breadth of the market is the heartbeat of the market. It is the one that offers an in-depth look at the market's internal components, which make it rise or fall. If you observe how much stocks advance and decline for a particular index, you will be able to predict the health of its move.

When it comes to markets that rise, you should observe if the gains are spread out amongst major companies. When it comes to markets that decline, you should observe if the bear gets exhausted due to too much participation.

The indicators of breadth include the following:
  a. Volume and number for declining and advancing issues
  b. The up and the down volumes
  c. Number of issues that reach new lows or new highs
  d. Issues that trade below or above moving average lines

You can say that an advancing market is bearish if its declining stocks outnumber the advancing stocks in both volume and number. When this happens, the stocks may do well even if the overall market is unhealthy. We call this the bearish divergence.

Conversely, market advances with stocks from various sectors that trade above the moving average is bullish and suggest a healthy increase.

You can use the advance-decline, also commonly referred to as A-D line and Adv-Dec, line breadth indicator. There is no need for you to search for a certain bearish or bullish number. You can simply use it as a tool for diverging or confirming. The most vital aspect of this breadth indicator is its line because it tells whether the direction of the market is going sideways, up, or down. You can construct this line by maintaining a regular cumulative total of: advance-decline line = number of advancing issues − number of declining issues. Take note that an index can rise even if the advance-decline line goes down. This can occur when a small number of stocks advance yet the value of the gains from the advancing stocks is higher than that of the losses from the decliners. It can also occur if the component stocks that have a lot of influence on the index increase despite the decrease of most of the component stocks.

If you wish to calculate the advance-decline line as a ratio instead of a cumulative value, remember that the ratio becomes greater than one if there are more advancers and that the ratio moves between one and zero if there are more decliners.

Do not forget to monitor the divergent movements, movements into extreme ranges for possible turns, and the center line's oscillator crosses. The indicators of the advance-decline line may be calculated on any ETF or index that offers regular declining and advancing statistics.

Whenever you monitor the advance-decline line, see to it that you search for advancers that would outpace the decliners in markets that rise as well as declines that would outpace the advancers in markets that fall. This would confirm the index changes. Also, whenever the indicator diverges from the index action, the present trend can be problematic.

As for analyzing such indicators, it would be in your best interest to keep track of their long-term record or history. Consider their twenty-day moving average, the rate of change indicator, and the relative strength index indicator among others. You can stay up to date with the trend once you understand the tops and bottoms of the market. In general, the more information you have, the more successful you can become.

Analyzing the Market Psychologically

It is great to be able to assess the market based on actual facts. However, aside from looking at the physical aspect of the market, should you also analyze it from a psychological perspective?

Well, some people believe that in order for you to be able to understand the market better, you have to know why it does what it does. But are these people correct?

Essentially, it is actually much better to focus on staying on the right side of the trend rather than trying to comprehend why the market does what it does. After all, the market acts on whatever data it receives.

It gives a response based on this data, regardless of whether it is wrong or right. Such response comes from the opinion of the majority. The market basically goes in the direction of the money flow.

Then again, this does not mean that the movement of the market is predictable. People are naturally drawn to fulfilling their self-interest and preserving themselves. Since selling and buying securities means losing or making money, you need to understand that the participants are typically influenced by their own desires. They can be irrational.

Hence, you should learn about the different ways on how you can monitor the conditions of the market as well as the behavior of the crowd. This would allow you to better understand the reasons behind the actions of the market. You can use market sentiment analysis, which can help you determine the human emotion that drives the reaction of the market.

What is sentiment?
Sentiment generally refers to the market's overriding bias. This can either mean bearish or bullish. The human emotion fear coupled with greed can result in a bullish market while fear can be associated with the market's decline.
Regardless of the changes in the economy, greed and fear will surely occur. They will continue the pattern for as long as possible.
You can imagine the market as a very wavy ocean. The undulation of these waves is the sentiments. The waves will continue to show up. However, they can show up in variations. The same thing goes with the market. It would be fueled by greed and fear over and over again. Nevertheless, it would have variations with regard to the period of time in which such emotions rule the underlying dynamics.
Options and stock statistics can be used as sentiment tools. These would give you the data you need about crowd activities in times of declines and advances. You can search for such information on charting packages and exchange websites.
When using sentiment analysis, see to it that you determine the times when fear has become exhausted or when greed is no longer sustainable. At a certain point in time, a major change can happen and you need to be prepared for it. This way, you will be able to quickly respond to the change in direction.
Keep in mind that trading is actually a balancing act. So, you have to focus on the market sentiment. Always remember that whatever happens in the market may not be the same as what you expect. So, you should always be prepared.

Measuring the Actions of Investors
Most of those who use sentiment analysis become doubtful of the trade because it tries to measure bearish and bullish actions as opposed to what is being said about the market or its direction.

As a trader, you need to be mindful of the following factors:
  a. A bullish commentary that is contradicted by an unusually high put volume
  b. An economic report that yields an enormous swing in the market
  c. A huge change in the Federal Reserve's interest rate policy that results in an unexpected reaction
  d. Whether or not the traders are bullish or buying calls and selling puts
  e. Whether or not the traders are bearish or buying puts and selling calls

The data obtained from options trading usually makes traders doubtful and fearful. Volume and historical volatility let them know how emotions affected previous decisions. Implied volatility, on the other hand, let them know what they can anticipate for the future.

Watching Put and Call Activities
Traders and other investors are mostly optimistic. They often think of the market as bullish. Fortunately enough, the market has a tendency to go up than down. This shows that the trends on the market are generally reflected by the positive disposition of traders and investors.
Keep in mind that observing the bullishness of the market is advantageous. This is because the call volume typically exceeds the put volume, which in turn reflects the market's tendency to advance. It gives you an option activity baseline. What happens when people get nervous? The put volume goes up.
When you observe the relationship between puts and calls, you will be able to see the extreme levels that correspond with the market reversals. Put volume, whether alone or along with call volume, can be used to measure the complacency or fear that people have towards the market.

The Put-to-Call Ratio
The put-to-call ratio is derived by dividing the volume of the put contract by the volume of the call contract. Its creator,

Martin Zweig, predicted that the stock market would crash in 1987. He was able to make this accurate prediction by using such ratio. Today, there are various ratios that you can use to guide you in trading.

The put-to-call ratio focuses on bearish and bullish actions by considering the different participants on the market. Be mindful of the contrarian measures as well. When people become overly bearish, the conditions become right for an upside reversal. When people become exuberant on prospects, the chances of having a decline become higher. In essence, you can interpret the put-to-call ratio according to the following:

    a. Very high readings are considered to be bullish
    b. Very low readings are considered to be bearish

How about some good news? You can count on the following for information regarding the readings and indicator construction:

    a. CBOE equity P:C ratio
    b. CBOE index only P:C ratio
    c. ISE Sentiment Index
    d. ISE Index and ETF put/call ratio

How can you maximize the sentiment tools available? First, you have to have knowledge of basic indicator construction information. Next, you have to understand the implications and historical extremes of this tool. Finally, you have to recognize the changes in the market as well as the impact on the indicator data.

See to it that you also get the data from every exchange that performs options trading for the underlying in case you want to zero in on sentiment for individual security. Note that indicators can also exhibit different behaviors during bear and bull markets, as well as during various bear or bull market stages. If you want to use a new indicator, do not forget to verify its performance with the use of a new indicator.

Chapter 5: Fundamental and Technical Sector Analysis

A market that functions properly involves broad advances such as stocks and sectors. At times when broad averages strongly go up, stocks and sectors follow. In a downtrend, the reverse is also true. Stocks, indexes, and sectors usually fall during such times.

Then again, there are always exceptions. In some instances, the market's general trend is not followed by certain sectors. This happens when economic conditions are favorable towards a particular group for a particular timeframe. As the conditions change, however, the sectors that display weaknesses or strengths also change.

When you focus on weak and strong sectors, you are able to customize your trading strategies according to the conditions of the market. Just make sure that you are able to find these sectors. You can use technical analysis such as those geared towards determining relative weaknesses and strengths.

Chart Analysis

Chart analysis focuses on the visual cues that determine volume and price information, which may lead you towards useful market trends. There are actually a variety of data displays and charts that you can choose from. All of these can provide you with a long list of analysis tools. Just make sure that you go for the one that fits your needs best.

Chart Fundamentals

Charts are also commonly referred to as price charts. They are essentially visual price activity records or pictures that are formed from price data plotting. They allow users to see their trading activities over time. Some of the charts that you may encounter are:

   a. Line Chart

They are charts that document the movements of prices versus time. A line is used to connect the price data point for every period. These charts also plot the most significant value for the week, day, or any period of time. In essence, they plot the closing price value.

As a trader, you will not have a hard time interpreting line charts since they are fairly easy to understand. You will be able to see the data you need for the trends and price movements when you filter out the noise from the minor movements.

However, even though line charts seem to be great, they also come with certain disadvantages. For example, they do not give any information on day trading strength as well as on price gaps.

Price gaps are made when trading for a period is totally below or above trading for a previous period. This occurs when the market is closed and there is news that affects the company.

b. Open High Low Close Bar Chart

This chart shows the price versus the time. The trading range of the period is shown using a vertical line. The opening prices are shown using a horizontal tab on the left side of the range bar while the closing prices are shown using a horizontal tab on the right side of the range bar.
Every bar is constructed using four price points. The open high low close bar chart is also regarded as more useful over different timeframes since it provides data on both the price gaps and the strength of the trading period.

c. Candlestick Chart

This is perhaps the most popular chart amongst professional traders. It shows the price versus the time and is quite similar to the open high low close bar chart in the sense that the price range between the close and the open for the period is highlighted with a thick bar.

The candlestick chart also shows the gaps and ranges of prices. It also has unique patterns that can help improve your daily analysis. It also has distinct pattern interpretations that describe the differences between bears and bulls. Ideally, you should apply this to your daily chart.

Time Horizon Adjustment
Before you focus on a certain chart interval, it would be best to consider your trading or investment horizon. You have to determine your timeframe and objective for trading options. You can use technical analysis to help you with your timeframe. In general, long-term trends are stronger than short-term trends. Whenever you look for trends, you should analyze the charts carefully so that you can effectively depict the price action over several time intervals.
The daily chart is generally the chart default. You can use it to plot the price action daily. You can also use a chart that measures minutes, years, weeks, and months. Furthermore, when you complete a market analysis to find good sectors, see to it that you evaluate the following:
   a. Long term trends with the use of monthly charts on sectors and indexes
   b. Intermediate-term minor and major trends with the use of weekly charts on sectors and indexes
   c. Short term minor trends with the use of daily charts

When you recognize the intermediate and major trends first, you will be less likely to make irrational decisions. You will not get caught up in the emotions related to short-term moves. You can draw a horizontal support line after the price goes down twice for the price level. This line will be confirmed if the third touch of such price level finally holds as well as if the buying demand goes back to the security and makes the price go up.

Supply and Demand Visualization

Surely, you are familiar with the supply and demand on the market. You can count on a chart to display this data. In essence, purchasing demand makes prices go up. The supply creates a selling pressure that makes prices go down. In addition, the volume shows the magnitude of either the supply or demand.

The market does not simply move up or down. The variations in its price are a result of dynamic and constant battles between the bears and the bulls. In this case, the bears are the supply while the bulls are the demand.

There can be a horizontal resistance line and the price can go up to reach a price level two times. This line will be confirmed once the third touch of this price level is able to hold and the selling demand goes back to the security; thus, making the price go down.

Resistance and Support Areas

The resistance and support of the price can stop the current trend. Support is actually a chart area in which buyers go into a trend that falls. It represents the transition from the declining prices, which are driven by the supply to the climbing prices whenever a renewed demand starts at such price level.

On the other hand, resistance is a chart area in which sellers go into a trend that rises. It represents the transition from the climbing prices that are driven by a strong demand to the declining prices whenever a pressure starts at such price level.

Each time you trade, make sure that you observe these transitions. They tend to line up and create sideways trading channels whenever the price moves between them. Just like with every price trend, the longer a price functions as a resistance or a support, the stronger it becomes.

Resistance and support levels are not merely chart points. They are actually areas that you can use when you need to act. For instance, resistance and support levels are helpful in determining the trading positions at exit and entry points. You can also use them during price projections to determine the profit-taking and the stop-loss exits as well as the calculating risk-reward ratios. More often than not, the price areas that formerly functioned as support function as resistance areas in the future and vice versa. Every time the prices go above the resistance or go below the support, a new price trend tends to occur.

Analyzing Trends

As a trader, you surely know about upward and downward trends. With upward trends, the prices go up and down in a way that rising lines can be drawn under the pullbacks that show higher lows. Upward trends also have higher highs. With downward trends, the prices tend to fall and retrace in a way that declining lines can be drawn over the retracement peaks, which show the lower highs. Downward trends also have lower lows.

Chapter 6: Risks and Rewards

Risk is a natural part of life. Nobody, not even the so-called psychics, can see the future. So, you can expect trading to be risky as well. Options trading is actually a very risky endeavor. No matter how hard you research and study the market, you still cannot be 100% certain of the outcome. If you are not careful with your actions, you can lose a lot of money. Experienced traders are generally adept at making decisions regarding their exit position. Before opening a trade, they either go to the exit position through a profit objective achievement or a stop loss. If you want to be a successful trader, you should not merely be good at making decisions. You should also be good at executing your strategies and creating trading plans.

Take note that whether you manually execute your exit or you use an advanced automated order design, there is a tendency for the stocks to gap down below your expected exit level; thus, making you incur much bigger losses. These stocks can be open for trading at a closing price that is way below the previous one.

What's more, if you want to have a manual exit, your position may suffer a much greater hit. The mechanical trading increase by means of preconceived algorithms has caused trading to be more challenging for traders.

In other words, a stock trade's maximum risk can be an entire initial investment. You may lose more money if you use a margin. If you want to avoid such huge losses, you must understand that you can incur major losses. You have to be aware of the reasons why you may end up this way. With enough knowledge, you can reduce your chances of losing a great deal of money.

The Risks of Trading

With risks, there comes rewards. This is the good thing about trading. You can expose yourself to great losses, but you can also expose yourself to great gains. Then again, you have to play the cards wisely. With options trading, risks and rewards can be lopsided. You may find risk-reward profiles to be different even though they seem to be similar at face value. In fact, when presented with two different trades, you can have more risks in a single trade as compared to the other. This is even if both of these trades have the same reward potential. However, the final outcome would depend on the risk characteristics of your traded security.

Before you start trading, see to it that you fully understand the risk involved. Here are some pointers to keep in mind:

    a. Probability of sustaining a loss
    b. Maximum amount of possible loss

If you wish to be a professional trader, you need to spend enough time learning about possible risks. You have to prioritize this more than knowing about possible rewards. More importantly, you have to learn how you can manage your risks by creating strategies that can limit or decrease your risks while maximizing your profits.

There are two main types of risk: lack of gains and potential for losses. When investments are not able to keep up with inflation or the increasing costs of living, they may be reduced or depleted.

Risking Funds with Stocks

The moment you became a trader was the moment you exposed yourself to risks. Involving yourself in options trading means potentially losing all your investments, regardless of how careful you become.

Take note that there are a couple of ways on how you can establish a long stock position. You can buy the stock on margin with even just 50% percent cash or you can buy the stock with 100% cash.

Even if you may limit how much margin is used to a number below 50%, this ½ of the amount is still the maximum amount that you can use for an initial position. As you know, the prices on the market continue to fluctuate. Thus, when you purchase a particular stock at a particular price, this price can go up, down, or sideways.

Perhaps, the worst thing that can happen is when the price falls and the losses add up. Also, even if the stock price goes up and down, you may still buy-in on a bad day when your particular stock begins on a prolonged downward trend. What's more, if this particular stock stops trading for any reason, you may no longer be able to exit at any level. Although you may also exit a trade at a certain point, the stock may also go downward to zero. In turn, this would result in a total loss of investment. Thus, your maximum risk when purchasing a stock becomes:

Number of Shares x Stock Price = Risk

The margin has both pluses and minuses. It is also not recommended by most experts. When you buy a stock on a margin, you get to have leverage. This allows you to have more stock for an initial investment. However, this also magnifies your losses and gains.

Say, you bought a particular stock on margin instead of using 100% cash. This doubles your risk by one divided by the initial cash percentage. This is your leverage.

If you want to compute for the maximum risk of purchasing a stock on margin, you may begin by multiplying your initial investment by one divided by the initial margin percentage. After that, you may add the cost of using the margin or the margin interest rate for the holding period of the stock. When you use a margin to buy a stock, your maximum risk becomes:

Risk = (Number of Shares x Stock Price) x (1 / Initial Cash %)

Make sure that you add the margin interest to your equation. It is computed based on how much money you wish to borrow to purchase the stock. Say, you wish to borrow $10,000 with a 5% margin interest. You can then borrow $500 when you borrow the money for one year. Interest is usually calculated based on 360 days, which is equivalent to one year. So, if you borrow the money for twenty days, you have to divide $500 by twenty. You will then get $25 and your margin cost will be $25.

How about shorting a stock?

Those who do this usually hope that the price of the stock will go down. So, they reverse the order of the stock transaction. Instead of purchasing first and then selling, they sell first and then purchase the stock.

If you wish to sell a stock that is not yours, you have to borrow shares. However, these shares may not be available for selling short if the conditions of the market are not right. Hence, you must always check the short sale list or your broker or directly communicate with them to find out if you can go on with the transaction depending on share availability. Traders who have brokers with active trading accounts usually have smooth transactions.

You may also use the Internet for short selling. When you become an online broker, you can indicate your trading type in the drop-down menu. Your trade will push through when there are available shares for short selling. However, if there aren't any shares, the trade will not push through. You will be given a notification.

When you do brokerage account paperwork, you may provide authorization to lend out the shares in your account, which will then be available to the short-sellers. You may only hold short stock positions in margin accounts.

Take note that stock short selling cannot be done in retirement accounts like the Individual Retirement Arrangement (IRA). Credits may be received for stock sales. However, there may still be margin issues. So, you have to ensure that you truly know about the process before you make any trades.

What about your risks? Shorting a stock can put you in a highly risky position because there's no limit to how high stocks can go upwards. Shorting stocks basically involves unlimited risks.

On the other hand, long stocks represent limited yet high-risk positions. They are limited because stocks may only go down to zero. They cannot go down further. Because of this, the risks stay high. They increase when the margin is used and you are put in a situation in which you may lose more money than your initial investment.

Option Risks, Call Options and Put Options
When you buy both put and call options, you become exposed to risks that are limited to your initial investment. When you sell options, you expose yourself to more risks and greater losses than your initial investment. Such initial investment may differ in size. Nevertheless, whether you buy or sell options, this initial investment is still less than the required investment for controlling the same amount of underlying stock shares.

In dollars, the risk is quite smaller. However, it is vital to recognize that the odds of the purchased options going to zero is very high due to their limited life security. Once the option expires, its value becomes zero unless it is in-the-money.

Call options give buyers rights to buy underlying stocks at the strike price of the contract by its date of expiration. As this expiration nears, the call option loses time value; thus, resulting in losses when the stock trades above the option strike price.

Let's say the stock's price level stays the same. When there is time decay, you can gain losses as a trader. These losses, however, are limited since the option retains its intrinsic value. When the stock trades below the strike price, the value of the option is all time value. Let's say the stock's price level stays the same. The time value would diminish when you get closer to the expiration date. There can also be a total initial investment loss when this manner continues.

More often than not, stocks fluctuate. You cannot expect them to stand still. So, even though there is a likelihood for the underlying stock to rise in value as it goes above the call strike price, it can still decline in value as well as go below the strike price. When this happens, you may lose all your investments as the expiration date approaches.

With regard to put options, they give the buyer rights to sell underlying stocks at the strike price of the contract by its date of expiration. These options lose their time value as the date of expiration approaches. This, in turn, typically results in losses for the traders when the stocks trade above the option strike price.

When you trade below the strike price, your losses are limited due to the options retaining the intrinsic value. Then again, when stocks trade above the strike price, the value of the option becomes the all-time value. Let's say that the stock stays at the same price level, the time value decreases when the expiration date approaches.

Going on in this manner would lead to a complete loss of the initial investment. Since the price of the stock has a possibility to either fall or rise, there is a likelihood that the underlying stock would rise in value going above the put strike price. When this happens, you may also lose all your investment when the expiration date approaches.

Reaping Rewards

You already know the risks, so why should you still bother to make trades? For starters, investments can beat inflation. Traditional savings may become unreliable. After all, even though their interest rates go up, the rate of return is still going to be likely below the inflation rate.

Hence, if you plan to use the money for more than a sport, you have to assume the risk of trading. If you are willing to take on higher risks, you have to expect rewards that are much better than the money at market rate. Both options and stocks actually give such potential.

Stock Benefits

When you become a stockholder, you may benefit from the gains and dividends of the stock. These gains tend to increase whenever the profits or sales of the company increase as well as whenever there are new technologies or products introduced among other reasons. You can also benefit from the approaches that let you download moves in these stocks.

Chapter 7: Practice, Practice, Practice!

It is imperative for beginner traders to practice. You have to test the water before you dive deeply into it.

Have you ever wondered why professional athletes are so good at what they do? It is because they devote countless hours into practice. They dedicate years of their life into mastering the sports that they are in.

So, even though nothing is truly perfect, there is some truth to the saying that practice makes perfect. Repetition is the key to rewire your brain. When you do something repeatedly, you get used to it.

The same principle works in trading. When you practice using strategies, you get better at them. As a beginner, you can start with paper trading. It is a form of practice trading in which you do not have to use actual money.

Before you shell out any money, you have to try out strategies and do some practice runs. You need to be adequately prepared before you trade in real terms. Likewise, before you use a new trading strategy, you have to understand the rewards and risks of security. You have to practice the trading strategies that you plan to use and you have to thoroughly analyze trades before you execute them.

As a trader, you have to start with paper trading and then transition into active trading through learning and analysis. In essence, you have to move from using concepts into taking actions.

How can you do this exactly?

First, you have to monitor the different components of option pricing as well as paper trading. You have to simulate the live conditions and begin rewiring your brain. You have to do this so that you can get used to dealing with real-time situations. This would give you better intuitions as well as prevent you from making expensive mistakes.

When you develop your skills in backtesting, you implement the best methods and allow yourself to remain in the game long enough to acquire valuable experience. You will eventually reach strategy mastery through experience and practice.

Monitor Option Greek Changes

It is important for you to recognize the right options pricing in strategies. However, it may be more important for you to understand the basic options strategies since they can help you learn more quickly. As a beginner, you have to know how to monitor Greek and price changes under various conditions.

Track Premium Measures

Once you develop your skills with options strategies, you will understand how options premiums get affected by changes in the expiration time and the underlying price.

You have to be active. An ideal way to have a better intuitive feel for the effects from these factors is by tracking the changes in the various components of options prices on a daily basis. You need to gain access to the market prices as well as have a spreadsheet program and an options calculator.

Once you monitor several different options, you will be able to learn about the effects of changing conditions on prices. When you include Greeks in this process, you will be able to understand the factors that play vital roles at various times.

As much as possible, you have to aim to review the tracking prices and markets when the prices move around. This would help emphasize the effects of theta, delta, and gamma on the prices. Make sure that you also learn about Rho, which refers to the measure of influence on interest rates, and Vega, which refers to the measure of volatility.

In addition, before you shell out dollars, see to it that you use a spreadsheet to keep track of the underlying stock price, the in-the-money prices, and the out-of-the-money and at-the-money puts and calls with different expiration dates. You should also keep track of the option intrinsic value, theta, gamma, delta, and options time value.

When you keep track of these values, you will be able to determine the measures that have major effects on options strategies.

Prices of Options and Volatility

The prices of options can be affected by volatility. This can actually be quite difficult to handle because implied volatility is an expression of the expected volatility of options in the future.

Traders, especially beginners, often get confused with the terminologies related to volatility. So, here is a great way to remember things: Past or Historical Volatility refers to the measure of the actual price movement of the underlying stock. Future or Implied Volatility refers to the measure of the price movement of the underlying stock and is derived from the prices of options.

Having a Volatility Grip

A stock's historical volatility can effectively predict implied or future volatility in the same price of the stock in the future. In addition, a primary factor in a stock's actual volatility is the way the options price affects it.

Implied Volatility

It refers to the volatility in the price of stock implied by the price of the option. Since it is also a critical factor in pricing options, it is ideal to study it to the best of your abilities. You see, in terms of implied volatility and trading, you have to remember that high readings can accurately predict major future price movements. Low readings, on the other hand, can accurately predict minor future price movements.

Likewise, when low implied volatility periods are combined with event timing and technical analysis, they can offer good entry points while extended high volatility periods can offer good exit points.

Basically, a 30% volatility for a stock that costs $100 can give you a chance to trade between $70 and $130 in the coming year. The price movement is actually dependent on one standard deviation of the price of a stock, which is typically distributed at 68.2%.

Consider the rules as your guidelines so that you can be guided accordingly. Knowing these rules by heart will allow you to apply them to your trading strategies with ease. You will be able to trade options or stocks naturally.

Say, when you hold a long-term position that you want to be protected, you have to be very careful. Do not allow yourself to be carefree because a huge amount of your money is at stake. Do not be tempted to give in to a burst of emotions just because the implied volatility is high. You have to evaluate the strike prices and months of expiration.

If the implied volatility is high and suddenly it drops, an implied volatility crash occurs. This occurrence is event-driven and basically a response to news such as product launches, earnings reports, and a major change in leadership of a company.

When such an event turns into a reality, it no longer remains an uncertainty. This diminishes the effects on the price of the options. However, since there isn't any guarantee in trading, you have to remember that the news may have caused a price move in the stock. Thus, selling high implied volatility options while hoping for an implied volatility crush is not a good strategy because the value of the option is not able to move. This is because of the movement of the stock price in spite of the implied volatility declining after the news happened.

Take note that implied volatility can vary in certain ways, such as the following:

    a. By time to expiration

It is a factor that occurs in real-time trading and affects the option values of various strike prices. Generally, a higher implied volatility in an expiration means that the stock might move by a higher percentage during this particular expiration compared to others.

    b. By strike price

The at-the-money implied volatility is usually the lowest. The price of an option may be broken into two separate components: extrinsic and intrinsic value. The intrinsic value depends on the option moneyness, the difference between the current stock price and the strike price.

Nevertheless, implied volatility does not have anything to do with this value. So, the deeper the in-the-money option is, the lesser the impact of implied volatility on the overall option premium. This happens because the implied volatility is the main determining factor of time value, which determines the price of the option along with the intrinsic value.

With regard to short option strategies, the time-value can work in your favor since the deep-in-the-money options do not have a lot of time value. The selling options that have thirty to forty-five days to expire accelerate the time-value decay. This is what you call the sweet spot of the time-value decay since it combines the accelerating decay rate with how much time value is left and has not yet decayed. In addition, the time-value decay isn't a linear constant. So, the closer you approach the expiration, the quicker it would drop.

Paper Trading the Trading Strategy
You can develop your skills in trading further when you continue to seek and implement new strategies. Through paper trading, you can make progress without much risk. Then again, when you make use of paper trading, you have to make sure that you incorporate the trading costs associated with the position in order for you to obtain the best strategy profitability value.

The Pros and Cons of Trading on Paper
Options traders practice trading constantly. When you use paper trading on a regular basis, you will be able to improve your skills in record keeping, market response, and method of analysis.
Your goal should be to learn about new strategy mechanics as well as how to reduce losses. It is also less painful to watch long out-of-the-money options go down in value as the implied volatility goes down when it is on paper.
Even though paper trading is not really trading and it does not completely prepare you for the trading world, it is still helpful in the sense that it encourages you to address your situation

before you shell out money. It lays down mental grooves that help your brain rewire quickly.

So, what are the advantages of paper trading?

Well, it gives you feedback through the profits and losses that you acquire. It lets you incorporate the costs of trade as well as determines issues that you may not have thought of. It also helps you avoid any account loss.

How about the disadvantages?

As for the disadvantages, paper trading doesn't prepare you emotionally for financial losses. It also doesn't help you understand trade execution. There aren't any assignments and it doesn't address possible margin problems.

Electronic Paper Trading

In this day and age, nearly everything is done digitally. So, you can also practice paper trading using spreadsheets and other electronic platforms. According to scientific studies, you can maximize the rewiring of your brain if you write on paper. So, even though nearly everything, including paper trading, is done digitally, it is still more beneficial to do paper trading the old-fashioned way.

A lot of financial websites let traders enter various positions in a portfolio tracker that makes updates by the end of the day. Sadly, not every tracker accepts option symbols. Basic trackers can give position details that include price changes with losses and profits. More advanced platforms may include risk chart displays as well as other tools for managing a trade.

Trading Systems

Trading systems are methods that have certain rules for exit and entry. So, even though you use systematic approaches to strategies, trading systems are still more rigidly defined. Keep in mind that in terms of system usage, you have to do these:

    a. Create a position for every buy signal that is generated by the rules.

    b. Exit every position once an exit signal gets generated.

Make it a habit to do the above-given procedures. Once you get used to them, you will be able to trade more frequently, especially when the market is volatile. See to it that you also consider your time commitments as well as any other potential changes. Incorporate all these factors into your everyday routine.

Of course, you must also know what you are getting. Trading systems are actually mechanical. So, there isn't any decision-making when it comes to system implementation. This is especially after they have been tested and designed. You do not think of accepting entry or exit signals. You have to stop the system completely if the system produces losses frequently or if something seems awry.

Formal systems are good in the sense that they minimize trading emotions and they allow for backtesting in order to have a sense of expected performance. When you begin to use discretion or when you decide to take on a specific trade, you will no longer be able to enjoy these benefits.

Your emotions will surface and you might give in to them. This would, then, affect the results of your trading. Hence, just like with any other trading strategy, you need to work with a system that suits your trading style as well as the size of your account. It should also be able to produce the results that you desire.

It is also true that the system rules are rigid and that it is common to build in flexibility. Filters can be added. They can serve as additional rules for trade exit or entry. Indicators can also be used since they serve as system parameters.

You can say that a trading system is good if it has the following characteristics:

    a. Profitability across various markets, market conditions, and securities
    b. Ability to outperform buy and sell methods
    c. Ability to diversify trading tools
    d. Suits your time availability and style
    e. Stability with drawdowns that are manageable

You must be very careful when setting up a system and leaving it to go on autopilot. You must monitor the trades at all times. Likewise, you must make the necessary adjustments based on system performance reviews.

Doing a Backtest

Backtests rely on past data to identify whether systems generate stable profits or not. You can do a complete backtest by downloading data or mechanically tracking trades. However, if you really want an effective way to do it, you should use a software application specially made for backtesting. Just make sure that you actually test what you think you test.

When doing system backtests, you have to include the time periods that are long enough to capture bearish, sideways, and bullish markets so that you can acquire results from worst-case scenarios. This would allow you to experience realistic drawdowns. Drawdowns refer to the cumulative account losses that stem from losing trades consecutively. Nevertheless, you can always manage your risks by evaluating drawdowns.

Robust trading systems work well in various markets, including commodities and stocks among others. They also work well under various conditions, including bullish and bearish markets. See to it that you backtest the system in every individual environment prior to using it.

Also, when you review backtest results, you should look for stability and profitability. Stability actually refers to result consistency. As a trader, you have to know if your trades are spread over different trades or if they generate profits.

Take note that stable systems have average system profits that are close to median system profits. Their average profits also exceed the average losses of losing trades. They are able to sustain manageable drawdowns and they do not depend on certain trades for profit.

Systems also do not need to have more winning trades as compared to losing trades. A lot of trending systems depend on allowing profits to run for a smaller number of trades as losses are quickly cut on losing trades. In other words, you have to look for consistency. Do not allow yourself to be fooled into believing that you have a good system when you actually do not. You may get lucky at times, but this does not mean that your system is good.

If you want to design a good system, you have to consider the common characteristics of your best trades. Once you are able to create a system that performs well in backtests, you can move on to forward testing and run the rules in a shorter timeframe. In general, you can begin the test at the latest date of backtesting and then run it sometime before you implement it.

During the forward testing process, you can expect your returns to diminish. System trading is actually not the solution to profitability. It is simply a way that you can use to reduce the harmful trading emotions that you may have. It can help you achieve results that are more consistent.

How to Backtest Systems

In order to successfully backtest a system, you have to follow these steps:

1. Determine your basis of strategy. For instance, you may choose to capture conditions that are currently trending.
2. Determine your rules for entering and exiting a trade.
3. Determine period and market traded backtests.
4. Determine account assumptions.
5. Test your system and assess the results.
6. Determine any reasonable filters in order to reduce your odds of losing trades.
7. Add a filter depending on what you got for Step #6. Test the system and then assess the results.
8. Include a component that can help manage risks.
9. Test your system and assess the results.

Furthermore, if you want to determine whether a system is suitable or not, you have to evaluate the average value of losing trades and the consecutive and maximum losses.

System Result Review

When reviewing or designing systems, it is much more ideal to work backward. This way, you can manage risks more effectively. Evaluating systems that do not have any stops may appear to be counter-intuitive.

If you think about it, such stop levels are quite arbitrary. Whatever position you enter, the market will not care. You have to let the system determine viable stop-loss points during the backtesting process and then make up your mind if you think it is a good risk.

In the first run, the system results can seem favorable. Hence, filters are no longer necessary. The Max Adverse Excursion percentage was reevaluated to identify if the stop level is reasonable and may be added. If the results do not prove to be highly favorable, a stop loss will be incorporated.

For an indicator, different calculations may be used by charting packages. When you change systems, however, see to it that you compare the indicator values that give off the signals. This way, you will be trading the same system tested. You should always try to retest the system on a new platform.

Backtesting with Risk Management

Every trade approach has to consider risk management. You have to focus on the biggest adverse moves for strategies whenever you attempt to determine stops that allow for strategies to function correctly. You may implement the system or strategy if including this stop would maintain the stability and profitability of the system as well as if it remains consistent with risk tolerance.

About Cutting Losses and Taking Profits

It is possible to use a systematic yet not mechanical approach and also backtest it. Then again, the method you use in doing this backtest does not really matter. You have to watch for the major moves that happen on the generated trades. This would let you determine systematic and reasonable filters as well as help you minimize your losses.

Take note that stop-loss orders may lead to bigger percentage losses if the trade gets executed. Worst-case scenarios may happen if signals are generated at the close of trading one day while the security has a price gap at the open the following day.

Once you get used to trading, it would be easy for you to identify stop-loss points that manage risks. Nevertheless, you may still think about what if you had a trade that started moving the other way? It may have started to move when you realized that you do not have a good exit plan for gaining profits.

At times, traders tend to focus too much on the risks that they forget to determine good price targets. You have to be very careful with your moves. There are also traders who determine profitable exit points yet the conditions begin to deteriorate even before they reach the price level.

If this happens to you, what can you do to protect yourself? Well, you have to determine the stop–loss level. You also have to determine a trailing stop percentage or a dollar amount in order to reduce the amount of profitable trades that result in losses.

Such trailing stop has to be incorporated into the strategy or system that you use. You also have to test it. If you wish your system to produce the trailing amount, you have to assess the trades with huge favorable moves that yielded way less in the way of profits. Once you are done with your review, you can do the following:

    a. Add a filter that can accelerate your exit.
    b. Generate a trailing percentage with the use of favorable excursion percentage data.

Allowing Profits to Run

Effective trading strategies do not always need to have fewer losing trades than winning trades. All it needs is to outpace declines with profits. This is actually what happens with a lot of trend-oriented systems. Even if you get more losing trades, the average loss value is still much smaller than the average gaining trade value. Just as expert traders would say, see to it that you cut your losses as you allow profits to run.

When you sort trades by the greatest loss to the greatest profit, you will be able to review their statistics more easily. Even if you have to determine a strategy for gaining profits, you should also avoid cutting your levels of profits in a way that they do not outpace your losses anymore.

If you want to trade successfully, you have to have some pre-work. Make sure that you focus on these three things: cutting losses, preventing profits from becoming losses, and allowing profits to run.

When you trade options, you can set a dollar or percentage gain for a target area wherein you would take profits. You can benefit from this the most if you own more than a single contract. If every contract reaches the target gain, then you may be able to sell more than one contract while letting the others ride.

Being Simply Knowledgeable to Mastering Trading

Mastering trading strategies does not mean that you have to gain a profit from every strategy you use. It simply means that you are able to trade at appropriate conditions. It means that you are able to put the odds in your favor so that you can have a profitable trade.

Correctly managing positions is another component that shows discipline. You have to know when to exit a trade once the conditions change. This may sound easy, but it is actually not. You have to spend years of learning and training to become a master trader. Your goal should not be limited to simply knowing how to trade. Instead, your goal should be to become a master trader. You have to adjust your system constantly based on your past successes and mistakes.

Take note that the best trades are actually the ones that take the longest to find. When you evaluate individual and market stocks, you have to search for the proper set of conditions or setup.

This is more important than just finding the right trade. So, you may have to spend a few hours or even a few days trying to search for the right opportunity. Just like every other profession, trading may be described as one that is made up of minutes of sheer pleasure or panic combined with hours of boredom.

If you focus on the basic mechanics and concepts, you will be able to come up with a good foundation that lets you grasp advanced techniques quickly. You will be able to apply new strategies through paper trading so that you can avoid expensive mistakes.

Once you are prepared to take this new strategy live, you may reduce the costs of mistakes further by remembering to gain profits and reducing position sizes. Such a strategy keeps you in the market longer, letting you develop and search for strategies that would suit your needs and preferences.

Setting the Correct Pace

Beginner traders are often advised by more experienced traders to start out with paper trading. If you have just started options trading, you can gain more knowledge and experience by using straightforward strategies with paper trading such as purchasing calls and puts before transitioning to live trading. Then again, there is no guarantee that the conditions of the market would be conducive to this strategy. Hence, you may prolong paper-trading for a few more days until you are ready to use another strategy or until the market changes. Always keep in mind that you have to focus on the strategies that seem sensible to you. This would enable you to develop mastery ultimately.

Beginning with Certain Strategies

If learning new methods and strategies is something that you like, then you will surely find a lot of opportunities in the financial market. Then again, you have to bear in mind that not every strategy works well in every market condition. Even more, not every strategy will fit your risk tolerance and style. If you are a beginner, you are better off sticking to just one or two basic strategies to have a very good understanding of the premium mechanics and changes.

Different strategies are available and you can choose the ones that would let you earn a profit. Just like the methods of analysis that you prefer, you will realize that you have a list of preferred strategies as well.

More experienced option traders are advised to determine the current conditions of the market before exploring them. This way, they can arm themselves with the right information. You can begin with paper trading and then move from there.

In case you are fond of a certain strategy but you do not find the conditions to be right, it is recommended that you simply paper trade it. After all, it is much better to concentrate on the approaches that seem sensible to you.

Adapting to the Changes of Market Conditions

Traders cannot expect the market to be the same every single day. The financial market is constantly changing. Even if there is a continuous cycle of bearish and bullish phases, the financial market never stays the same. This is why you have to adapt your strategies to the changes in the conditions of the market.

You have to perform a strategy checkup when things do not seem to follow the norm. If the strategies that tend to work well for you begin to take a step back, then you have to do some thinking over the weekend. Perform a comprehensive assessment of the market. You may be able to detect signs of change in the conditions of the market early on.

Options trading lets you use strategies that may be profitable regardless of the conditions of the financial market.

For example, a bullish market with low volatility involves married puts and basic long calls. You can buy an at-the-money call option, an out-of-the-money married put, and an at-the-money call debit spread.

A bullish market with high volatility involves credit spreads and covered calls. You can buy an at-the-money call option, an out-of-the-money married put, and an at-the-money call debit spread.

A bearish market with low volatility involves debit spreads and basic long put. You can buy an at-the-money put option, an out-of-the-money put calendar spread, and an at-the-money put debit spread. A bearish market with high volatility involves credit spreads. You can sell an at-the-money-call credit spread and an out-of-the-money naked call.

A range-bound market can have high volatility. It involves a condor and a butterfly. You can sell two short options that are of the same kind together with a long higher strike price option and a long lower strike price option. A range-bound market can also have low volatility. You can trade at the money calendar spreads and at the money diagonal spreads.

You can have great options with the combination of options with options and stock with options. However, you have to remember that every approach requires mastery. You cannot just wing it. You have to actually know what you are doing.

You have to be thorough when you check out strategies. See to it that you also consider the circumstances of the present market as well as the kind of security that you used in your chosen strategy prior to discarding it just because it did not work the way you wanted it to.

It is highly possible that you will not be able to use all the available trading strategies. A lot of traders use different approaches along the way before mastering some of them. Your financial goal is the largest influence on the strategy that you choose. There are strategies that are more suitable for income while others are much better for capital gains. There are also those that hedge the risk of ETF portfolios and stocks.

When you gain experience from trying various approaches, you are able to maximize your profits using the strategies that you prefer. You are able to determine when you should hold your options, for example. Likewise, you are able to minimize your losses. For instance, you are able to tell when you have to fold.

Deciding on the options strategies you have to use is similar to market analysis. There are many different ways on how you can approach it. However, none of these ways would represent the single correct way. You have to go with the one that ultimately makes the most sense. Use your instinct. This way, you will be able to stick with your plan confidently in case the conditions change and you find yourself in hot waters.

Using Longevity to Achieve Mastery

Longevity is actually about having patience as well as staying power. It is about showing up for work every single day, no matter how hard things seem to be. Then again, in order for you to be able to do this, you need to stay on top of everything. You need to create a routine that you can consistently follow. It has to allow for the inevitable changes in market trends and volatility.

Take note that the bull market may run for many years. Volatility conditions may stay stable. Nevertheless, things may change instantly. In order to prevent heartburn and burnout, you have to be able to incur added losses in the event of market transitions as well as whenever new strategies are implemented. You will be able to achieve longevity when you are able to manage risks through strategies that yield unlimited gains and limited losses.

With paper trading, you can use techniques that would minimize your learning curve losses. Then again, there is another method you can use that can also have positive results. This method is known as proper position sizing. It is about starting out with a small initial position so that you can manage your losses. It also includes rules that would help you gain profits.

Of course, just like any other venture, trading is not a guarantee of success. You can never be too sure of the outcome. You need to work hard in order to increase your chances of winning. There is no such thing as an overnight success. Every successful person knows that. You have to spend enough time observing the different conditions of the market, having different emotions, developing trading skills, and making low-cost mistakes.

Identifying the Appropriate Trade Sizes

You can find a variety of techniques for identifying the proper trade sizes. They will help you identify the maximum dollar amount that is allocated for every trade as well as identify the maximum percentage amount that is allocated for every trade. As the size of your account changes, the maximum percentage amount that is allocated for every trade changes as well. Conversely, there are certain markets that are best traded using the first approach. You have to determine how much money is allocated for every trade to increase your chances of earning a profit.

See to it that you always have a variety of options. This is especially true whenever you experience difficulty with the strategies that you use. Since options represent leveraged options, there is no need for you to allocate the same amount of money to the options position as you do for the stocks. Actually, it may not be a good idea to do this at all.

You can use your stock allocation plan as your base. You can assume an initial allocation amount by determining an options position that has control over the same amount of stock. See to it that you test and review your starting point.

You must establish your trade allocation amounts before you even analyze a particular trade. You have to know the maximum amount that is available for trading beforehand. This way, you can minimize the account risk.

After doing paper trading, you will use a new strategy. Make sure that you reduce the trade sizes further so that you can reduce your mistakes as well. Keep in mind that your main goal is to earn a profit in the financial markets, not to impress anyone with your trade sizes.

The more you develop your skills, the more you have to increase your position sizes to the tested allocations. This way, you can improve your gains. After all, the costs of options trading tend to be higher than the costs of trading stocks based on a percentage standpoint.

If you have prepared adequately and you continue to apply risk management in your trading, you will be able to increase your position sizes effectively. You will be able to realize the economies of scale with the costs of trading and your results will improve.

Taking Profits

As you may have already learned by now, one of the keys to succeeding at options trading is learning how to manage risk. Then again, you should also focus on taking profits. It is not enough to just have high numbers of profitable trades, you also have to gain a profit. In fact, your profits should exceed the trading costs, your losses, and conservative investment approaches.

You need to create a plan that involves reviewing trade results and strategies in order to benefit greatly. You will be able to reduce the number of profitable trades that become losses as well as let the profits run. You can say that you have evolved as a trader once you finally developed these skills.

Chapter 8: Creating a Trading Plan

Trading options can be regarded as a unique situation that needs a specific language and management style.

Regardless of what you trade, you need to know how to run your business properly. You need to understand the costs that are associated with your business so that you can stick to your budget.

At first, some costs may be lower while others may be higher. You may even be likely to pay more for your learning curve and education. Nevertheless, as you go on with trading, you will notice these costs going down while your subscriptions to data services and analysis platforms are going up.

You should always remember that operating expenses involve losses. So, your goal should be to manage and minimize your risks. You can do this by identifying proper trade allocation amounts as well as the maximum loss for every trade. In addition, even though executing trades effectively is another step that you can take towards reducing your losses, you should still make sure that you come up with a good trading plan.

Having a Good Trading Plan

As you know, having a good trading plan is one of the keys to trading success. However, before you execute such a plan, you have to take certain steps into consideration.

For starters, the actual development of this plan is vital. You need to have a good picture of your goals. It is not enough to have a vague understanding of what you want to accomplish. You need to have all the details.

Nevertheless, development can be as basic as guiding statements such as "I would like to earn a lot of money" or "I want to have a consistent source of income". Once you get this big picture, you will be able to have more details.

A good strategy is to design a trading plan and have it revolve around just one purpose. This way, you can think that if you accomplish this goal, you are successful. Otherwise, you can think that your expectations may have been lofty. You may also think that your trading is not really compatible with your goals.

You have to have a quantifiable and reliable way to measure your failure and success beyond traditional methods such as annual percentage losses or gains.

The following are some of the guidelines that may be able to help you out:

    a. Write down your proposed trading plan.

Simply thinking or talking about your proposed trading plan is not enough. Just doing this can make you easily forget details. It can even make you forget about trading and important schedules.

So, you have to write down your plans on paper or type them out on your computer. The important thing is that you are able to see them. This would encourage you to do better with your trading since it would remind you of your purpose.

    b. Set goals that are realistic. Having goals is good, but make sure that your goals are something that you can actually accomplish. For instance, if your account is small, you have to refrain from setting goals that are too high. This way, you will not be pressured or overwhelmed.

In addition, it is wise to break one big goal into several smaller goals. This way, you can accomplish every goal in a reasonable timeframe. You will not feel overwhelmed because the goal is small enough for you to achieve easily.

    c. Use your goals as your measuring stick. Although meeting your goals is a good thing, you should not obsess about it. Remember that there will be days when you will not be able to reach your target goal. Nevertheless, you should not be disheartened because this can still be regarded as a good thing.

For example, if you are still able to gain a profit even if you do not reach your target objective, you can still say that you are on the right track. After all, you were able to gain something positive out of the trade. So, you have to search for ways on how you can improve your strategy. Just refrain from making so many changes without giving yourself a chance to prove whether you are right or wrong.

d. Keep records of your trades, expenses, and results. The results and trades will guide you as your plan evolves. The expenses will prove to be handy when the time comes for you to pay your taxes. In fact, you may use some of your losses and expenses to reduce your taxes. Having these records will allow you to manage your finances better.

e. Allow your goals and your plan to evolve. As time passes by, you may or may not become an expert trader who earns huge profits. If you are diligent and fortunate enough, you may make a lot of money from this venture. If this happens, you have to consider going full-time. Otherwise, you should still consider allotting more time for trading.

Managing Expenses
With trading, there are various costs that you have to consider. Some of them may be higher at the beginning of your career as an options trader and may even continue for the years to come.
You have to consider trading as a business. See to it that you manage your expenses wisely so that you can reduce them as well as their effects on the amount of money that you can earn when your business goes into maturity.
The following are the expense categories that you have to take note of since you will continue to encounter them throughout your career in options trading:

a. Education

The expenses associated with education include courses, materials, and learning curve expenses for new strategies and markets. As time goes by, however, these costs would decrease yet they will continue as you remain current with the market conditions. You need to spend on periodicals and books, after all. You will also spend money when you continue to learn new strategies.

Your learning curve is actually among your biggest education costs. This would begin to decline, however, once you find out how to trade under the best conditions for every individual strategy as well as how to use options with the right liquidity. It would also decline when you learn how to develop skills in paper trading, enter orders effectively for the best exit, gain profits, and allocate the right amount to trading.

b. Cost of Analysis

The more your skills improve and your trading yields profits on a regular basis, the more costs you may incur with regard to analysis. You may also include analytical tools in your expenses.

A great way to begin is to talk to other traders who use these analytical tools. You should also find out which ones offer free trial versions that you can use for a spin. These costs represent among the few that can increase as time goes by. See to it that you merely subscribe to a limited amount of services. You should also get to know them better so that you can maximize their usage.

c. Trading Costs

Do not just account for the commission. You also have to account for the slippage, which refers to the cost associated with a market spread. It is basically the difference between the ask and the bid.

You can compute for the slippage and commission percentage for the various size option positions established at various price points. This would be an ideal exercise for you as a trader.

    d. Taxes

You have to determine the kinds of trading that are completed in your various account types. You can defer these taxes if you use the limited options trading that is permitted in retirement accounts. The complete details regarding the kind of options trading permitted in retirement accounts can be acquired from the Internal Revenue Service or IRS.

Additionally, when you establish some option positions when you have a position in the underlying, you can trigger a tax event. See to it that you contact your account regarding the tax considerations related to options trading. In the long run, the cumulative costs have to outpace the buy and hold approach.

So, when you borrow from your broker by trading on margin, you have to add a monthly margin interest charge to the trading cost. Take note that short option positions tend to have margin requirements that are complicated. You have to consider if the option is naked or covered for such margin.

If you want to use the strategies that require a margin in the long run, you have to make sure that you contact your broker so that you can completely understand each and every one of the account requirements and calculations involved. Then, you have to add the costs to the expenses.

e. Losses

In every business, losses will be encountered. There is no single business owner or trader, for that matter, who has achieved massive success without experiencing failure at some point in their career. So, if you want to become a successful trader, you have to prepare yourself for losses.

In the beginning, your losses may tend to be higher. Nevertheless, you will see them go down with experience and time. If you develop a good trading plan and stick to it, you can significantly reduce your losses.

Trading Plan Guidelines
Speaking of following a good trading plan to significantly reduce losses, the following are some tips that you have to keep in mind in order for you to maximize your chances of earning a profit and minimizing your odds of suffering losses:

a. Determine your trading allocations.
It is crucial for you to determine both your maximum allocations and total trading assets for your different strategies and assets. ETF and stock trading generally require bigger allocations as compared to option positions. If you wish to include a maximum allocation amount for your new strategies based on the results of paper trading, you should break this down even further.
b. Calculate the size of a trade.
You should also know the guidelines of maximum position sizes before you enter any trade. When you are done setting these guidelines, you will be able to identify the maximum amount of contracts you may allocate to a position more easily. To finish it off, you have to divide the options price by the allocation amount below the maximum. Refrain from using the maximum allocation to make assumptions.
c. Identify the maximum acceptable loss on the trade.
You may define the maximum acceptable loss as a dollar percentage or value. Since a fixed dollar value may be

significant with a small trade or if the trading asset decreases, you may find the previous option to be more preferable.

You also have to perform trade result analyses on a periodic basis so that you can identify if your losses stay at sustainable and reasonable levels. You should be able to see how much money gets left on your account as well as whether or not it is sensible to go on with your present method.

    d. Focus on exit and entry rules.

Oftentimes, the option entries are driven by trending and volatility conditions. However, they may also be time-oriented in which the positions have been created before a particular scheduled event.

The option exits may also be time-driven, such as pre-expiration or post-event. They may also be triggered by a movement in the underlying security. These methods have to be focused on supporting risk management as well as the maximum allowable loss.

Using technical indicators to exit usually does not give you any price for use with the risk calculations. Of course, you should not forget to identify the maximum loss price. You have to consider setting up another brokerage account that you can allot for options trading along. This would make record-keeping much easier and simpler for you.

Optimizing the Execution of Orders

Trading options successfully means having proficiency with the execution of orders. There are various factors that you have to keep in mind with this.

You have to understand the rules of order placement that are unique to options trading. You have to know how the different order types work. You have to learn how to do combination orders for positions that are multi-legged. You have to gain skills as you use the underlying to determine option exits. You also have to recognize the role of your broker in the quality of execution.

Take note that a learning curve exists for performing options trading. However, these are usually mechanical steps that you can easily master with continuous practice. You may do paper trading to improve your skills. However, nothing will beat real time action. You have to experience trading in real time to really know how things work. The experience will enable you to devise strategies that work for you.

Furthermore, you have to know that the offer is actually the best price or the ask available from the sellers.

Learning About Option Orders

Stock is actually constrained by its float. Options are not like this. They are not limited to a specific number of contracts, which are created by the marketplace and have unique considerations when it comes to placing orders.

Options are created when a couple of traders open a trade or create a new position. This increases the open interest for such an option. The open interest decreases when the trader closes the positions that exist. Floats refer to the number of shares available for stock trading as well as the outstanding number of shares.

Open interest is not updated on a basis of trade by trade. It is more of an end-of-day reconciliation via the Options Clearing Corporation. This explains why the option orders get placed in a particular manner. The Options Clearing Corporation has to maintain a straight accounting. This means that you also have to communicate more information when you place your option orders.

The Fundamental Rules of Option Orders

Selling or buying options may be done at any order. Opting to go short or long on a contract depends on your account's option approval level as well as the strategy that you use. You cannot go out there developing short option positions with unlimited risks until your broker allows you to.

The current market refers to the asking price and current bid for a security. Since contracts are retired and created based on the demands of the market, you have to enter an order in a manner that supports this options markets' end-of-day reconciliation. You have to use a certain language.

Say, the new position that you create is an opening order or the existing position that you exist is a closing order.

Chapter 9: Options and Futures

As a trader, it is crucial for you to know all about options and futures. You already know that options contracts give investors a right, but not an obligation to purchase shares at a certain price at any period of time during the effectivity of the contract.
What about futures? What about futures contracts?
Well, futures contracts are practically the opposite of options contracts. They require the buyer to buy shares and they require the seller to sell them at a certain date in the future, unless the position of the holder gets closed prior to the date of expiration.
Options and futures are financial products that you can use to earn money as well as to hedge present investments. They will both allow you to purchase investments at a certain price by a certain date. However, the markets for these products are actually different in the way they work. They are also different in terms of the risks involved.
Options are based on the underlying security's value. Stocks are an example of an underlying security. Investors do not have to buy or sell assets if they do not want to. After all, they have a right but not an obligation to do so.
Options are also derivative forms of investments. They can be offers to sell or buy shares but they do not represent the actual ownership of underlying investments until there is a finalized agreement.
Buyers usually pay premiums for an options contract, which reflects a hundred shares of an underlying asset. In general, a premium represents the strike price of an asset, which is the rate to sell or buy it until the expiration date of the contract. Such data shows the day by which this contract has to be used.
Put options and call options are the only two types of options. Put options are offers to sell stocks at a particular price while call options are offers to purchase stocks at the strike price prior to the expiration of the agreement.
To help you understand call options better, let us take this example: say, there is an investor who opened a call option to

purchase stock ABC at the strike price of $50 for the next three months. Currently, the stock trades at $49. When the stock goes up to $60, the call buyer may exercise his right to purchase this stock at $50. He can also sell the stock immediately for $60; thus, earning a profit of $10 for every share.

Alternatively, the options buyer may opt to just sell the call and take in the profit. After all, the call option costs $10 per share. In the event that the option trades below $50 during the expiration period of the contract, the option loses its value. The call buyer will then lose his upfront payment for this option, which is known as the premium.

On the other hand, if this investor owns a put option and you want to sell ABC at $100 but the price of ABC goes down to $80 prior to the date of expiration, you will earn $20 for every share minus the premium cost.

Then again, if the price of ABC goes above $100 during the period of expiration, the option loses its value and you lose the premium you paid upfront. The writer or the put buyer may close out the option position in order to lock in a loss or profit at any time prior to the expiration date.

The writer can buy the option while the buyer can sell the option. In addition, the put buyer can opt to exercise his right to sell it at the strike price.

Futures

As you have read earlier, futures contracts refer to the obligation to buy or sell assets at an agreed-upon price at a later date. They are real hedge investments. In fact, you can compare them to commodities such as oil and corn.

For example, a farmer might want to ask for a reasonable upfront payment for his crops in the event that the market price goes down before they can be delivered. Then again, the buyer may also want to ask for a reasonable upfront payment in case the prices go up by the time the crops get delivered.

To help you understand futures better, let us consider this example: say, there are two traders who agree to pay $50 for every bushel price on a certain corn futures contract. When the price of corn goes up to $55, the buyer can earn $5 for every barrel. On the other hand, the seller can lose out.

Then again, the futures market has greatly expanded beyond just corn and oil. At present, stock futures may be bought on an index or on individual stocks. Those who buy futures contracts are not obligated to pay upfront for the contract's full amount. Instead, they can pay an initial margin, which is merely a price percentage.

Futures were actually made for institutional buyers who wanted to buy crude oil barrels and sell them to refiners. They also wanted to buy corn and sell them to supermarket distributors. Once a price is established in advance, the two businesses are able to avoid huge price swings.

However, retail buyers sell and buy futures contracts as a bet on the underlying security's price direction. They hope to earn a profit from the changes in the price of futures. They do not wish to take possession of products.

In addition, aside from the above-mentioned differences, there are many other things that set futures and options apart. Also, investors have to be wary about the risks associated with both futures and options.

Options contracts come with a lot of risks since they are quite complex. Both put and call options typically have the same amount of risks. When investors buy stock options, the sole financial liability they have is the premium cost during the period at which the contract is bought.

Then again, when sellers open put options, they become exposed to the maximum liability of the underlying price of a stock. If buyers have a right to sell a stock at $50 per share because of a put option, the individual who started the contract has to agree to buy the stock for $50 per share, which is the contract's value if the stock goes down to $10. The risk to the call option buyer is limited to the premium that is paid upfront. Such premium falls and rises all throughout the duration of the contract. It is based on various factors, such as the distance between the strike price and the price of the underlying security. It is also based on the time remaining on the contract. The premium gets paid to the investor who has opened the put option. He is referred to as the option writer.

Option writers are on the trade's other side. They have unlimited risks. Still using our previous example, if the stock rises to $100, an option writer will have no other choice but to purchase the shares at $100 per share. This way, he can sell them to a call buyer for $50 per share. The option writer will then lose $50 per share in return for a small premium.

The writer or the buyer of the option may close their position at any time by purchasing a call option. This takes them to a flat. The difference between the cost to purchase back the option and the premium received is the loss or the profit.

It is true that options come with a lot of risks. However, futures are actually much riskier for individual investors. The futures contracts have a maximum liability to the seller and the buyer. When the price of the underlying stock moves, anyone involved in the agreement can put more money into their trading account in order to fulfill their daily obligation.

The gains on a futures position is instantly marked to the market on a daily basis. This means that the change in the value of the positions, whether upward or downward, gets moved to the futures accounts of the individuals at the end of the day.

Futures Contracts versus Futures Options

The short answer is that it actually depends on your time horizon and risk profile.

Among the initial decisions, new commodity traders tend to face is having to choose between futures options or futures contracts. Then again, even expert commodity traders sometimes experience this dilemma. Which one is indeed the better choice for trading?

Options and contracts have their own advantages and disadvantages. As you go farther into your trading career, your instinct will be more developed. Hence, you will be able to use your present situation to your advantage. You will be able to tell which one is more suitable for the time being.

Of course, there are also traders who choose to focus on just one. You can also opt for this method. Just make sure that you completely understand the characteristics of both options and contracts.

Futures contracts are regarded as the smoothest means to trade commodities. Compared to options contracts, they are more liquid. They also move faster than options contracts since options tend to solely move in correlation to futures contract.

Futures contracts are more ideal for day trading. They have less slippage and they are easier to get in and out since they move quickly. A lot of traders prefer to use spread strategies, particularly in the grain markets. They find it easier to trade calendar spreads as well as spread various commodities.

A lot of new commodity traders begin with options contracts. For most people, the primary attraction with options is that it is not possible to lose more than the investment. It is very unlikely to have a negative balance since the risk involved is small.

Options trading can be regarded as a conservative approach, particularly if option spread strategies are used. Bear put spreads and bull call spreads may increase your chances of success if you purchase for a long-term trade and your spread's first leg is in the money.

On the other hand, futures options are said to be wasting assets. Options can lose value each day. Their decay increases as they come nearer their expiration date. You may find it frustrating to be in the direction of the trade. However, your options will still expire worthless since the market did not go far enough to offset time decay.

Well, this time decay can actually work for you or work against you, depending on the circumstances. For instance, it can be advantageous if you use an options selling strategy. There are traders who sell options just because a huge percentage of options expire worthlessly. There can be an unlimited amount of risks if you sell options. Nevertheless, the chances of winning on every trade are better compared to purchasing options.

There are also options traders who like the fact that options are not as fast-moving as futures contracts. It is possible for you to quickly get stopped out of futures trades with just a single wild swing. With options, your risks are limited. So, you may ride out most of the wild swings in futures prices. You may find options to be the safer bet as long as the financial market reaches your goal within the set timeframe.

Chapter 10: The Best Platforms for Options Trading

Compared to stock trades, options traders offer higher profit margins to online brokers. Because of this, the competition in attracting clients is fierce. Nonetheless, such a market atmosphere is good for traders. After all, healthy competition is key to product innovation.

In order for you to succeed in options trading, you need to learn the theoretical aspects as well as put your knowledge into practice. Aside from knowledge and skills, however, you also have to have the right equipment. The following are some of the best platforms for options trading that experts recommend. It is ideal for you to learn about each and every one of them so that you can choose accordingly.

E*TRADE

According to many expert traders, it is the best overall options trading platform. It features $0 trades, the Power E*TRADE platform, and two mobile applications, which are highly recommended to beginner traders. It is easy to use and has a straightforward commission structure.

a. Stock Trades

Every trade is a flat rate of $0. $25 is added for trades that are assisted by a broker. Another $0.005 is added per share to the regular commission rate if you will trade during pre-market and post-market hours. Moreover, $6.95 is added if you will buy OTCBB or Pink Sheet stocks as well as penny stocks. Limit orders can only be used for placing trades for stocks that are under $1 per share.

b. Options Trades

Each contract costs $0 to $0.65 and is reduced further to $0 to $0.50 when making at least thirty trades for every quarter.

c. Mutual Funds

Every mutual fund costs $19.99 per trade. Depending on the funds, additional fees may be applied.

E*TRADE does not require a fee for streaming quotes in real-time. However, it requires a minimum balance of $1,000 before streaming quotes can be enabled.

Tools and Platforms

It delivers and innovates the ease, speed, and tools necessary for traders to achieve success. It features a charting engine that is powered by Chart IQ, which is a great third-party HTML 5 chart provider.

The highlights of this platform include integrated Trading Central technical analysis, smooth zooming and panning, thirty-two drawing tools, and a hundred and fourteen optional technical indicators.

The Power E*TRADE has an amazing blend of tools, position management, and usability. Hence, it is perfect for active and casual options traders. In fact, Power E*TRADE is the top choice of new investors.

It also offers an excellent experience for futures trading. It allows for the running of multiple futures ladders all at once. The orders can also be fired off easily using the Quick Trade widget. Furthermore, it allows for managing positions with the utmost ease.

E*TRADE also ranks highly in terms of research. It gives daily investors everything they need to perform in-depth market analysis across bonds, mutual funds, stocks, and ETF's among others. With this being said, this platform trails in web design areas as well as in-house market commentaries.

With E*TRADE, you can benefit from consensus ratings from third-parties and charting websites. It also has an in-house staff. Then again, the quote and screening of this platform could do better. It also does not feature live broadcasting. Nevertheless, E*TRADE ranks highly in terms of mobile trading. Its mobile apps are rich in features and easy to use, even for those who are not that tech-savvy. It is recommended for those who are into options, futures, and stock trading.

It focuses on portfolio management, market research, trading, quotes, and watch lists. Its watch lists are actually streaming and customizable. Its quotes include advanced and basic charts, news, price alerts, and even added research like third-party reports. It even offers Bloomberg TV as well as basic trade idea screeners for mutual funds, stocks, and ETF's.

Young traders are especially impressed with the modern layout and design of the Power E*TRADE Mobile. You can actually switch between the advanced multi-legged options trading and their various pre-defined strategies to futures trading and Bloomberg TV. You can also use advanced tools such as Live Action to help you search for investment opportunities that have pre-defined options screeners. Power E*TRADE also has ChartIQ, which can give you a unique charting experience. In addition, you can take advantage of the user-friendly indicators for panning, conducting high-level analysis, and zooming.

Furthermore, E*TRADE ranks highly in terms of investment offers, education, and banking. It has everything you may need, including a full-service brokerage. It also has a variety of investment vehicles, from options to stocks to bonds. It also offers financial planning services via its Capital Management. Then again, this platform does not offer forex trading and international trading.

If you visit its official website, you can find lots of educational content. Helpful topics on investing, including retirement and stock trading, are available. You can read articles and attend webinars to help you broaden your knowledge and skills.

TradeStation

This one has been renowned as the best desktop options platform. Casual traders can benefit from the web-based platform while active traders can benefit from its desktop platform. Both platforms have $0 stock and ETF trades. According to experts, TradeStation has highly robust desktop platforms. It is among the best in terms of technological advancements. In fact, it is highly recommended for mobile trading, options trading, day trading, professional trading, and futures trading.

With this platform, you can take advantage of various commission structures. Its most popular pricing plans, TS Go and TS Select, offer $0 trades and are very easy to comprehend. It also does not incur any monthly charges as well as includes free market data.

TS Select is the most popular pricing structure of TradeStation. It requires a minimum deposit of $2,000. It also includes access to the three trading platforms. These are TradeStation desktop, TS Crypto, and Web Trading. The first is the flagship product of the company. The second is a platform solely dedicated to cryptocurrency trading, and the third is a browser-based platform that was made for traders who prefer simplicity.

TS Go, on the other hand, does not require any minimum deposit. It offers unlimited $0 stock as well as ETF trades along with futures trades for only $0.85 per contract and options trades for only $0.50 per contract. Then again, even though it will give you access to all the platforms, you will need to pay $10 for the trades you place.

Under TS Go and TS Select, penny stock trades cost $0 for the first ten thousand shares. After this, however, you will need to pay $0.005 for every share. If you wish to direct the order to a particular venue, you will have to pay an additional $0.005 for every share.

With TradeStation, you can choose from two commission structures: unbundled and per share. If you are an active military personnel, first responder, or veteran, you can register for the Salutes program and enjoy free stocks, options trades, and ETF's.

If you wish to invest in cryptocurrencies, such as Bitcoins, you can start with just 0.5% for every trade. The commission rate will drop once your account balance goes beyond $100,000. In addition, you will have the opportunity to earn interest when you hold specific cryptocurrencies.

The functionality in the desktop platform is filled with dept. The tools include Scanner for custom screening, Radar Screen for real-time streaming watch lists, Walk Forward Optimizer for advanced strategy testing, and Matrix for ladder trading. Its coding language also allows traders to code applications and upload them on the TradingApp Store.

As for the desktop charting, there are over forty years of historical data available for stock charts. In addition, more than two hundred studies or indicators are available. They can be adjusted or reworked to your preferences with the use of EasyLanguage.

Then again, you may be displeased with the minor flaws in charting. It is not possible to plot y-axis markets for corporate events like splits, earnings, and dividends. Automated technical analysis is also lacking.

You will find TradeStation Web Trading simple and easy to comprehend. You can use it to manage your active positions, watch lists, perform stock chart analysis, place trades, and open orders. Compared to other flagship platforms, its chart-trading functionality is superb.

If you are into options trading, the OptionStation Pro will prove to be handy. It is a built-in tool that is designed for robust analysis and streamlined trading. Some of the options tool functionalities include streaming real-time Greeks, advanced position analysis, and grouping current positions.

Conversely, if you are into futures trading, you will like the TradeStation desktop. It features advanced tools that you can use to trade equities as well as perform futures trading smoothly.

You can also use TradeStation to screen options and full stocks, backtest equity, and stream forex and futures data. However, you may not use it to do traditional research for stocks. It is also not ideal for fixed income or mutual fund research as well as ETF research.

In addition, the depth and range of research available are limited. The market research is a combination of video and written content for both fundamental and technical analysis. You can also use the mobile application, which is designed meticulously and offers functionality for professional and active traders.

With regard to charting, the charting on the TradeStation mobile is clean and robust. It is everything you could ever want if you are demanding with your trades. You will benefit from the after-hours visibility, date range flexibility, full chart type, optional indicators, and filled order visibility. You will also benefit from the drawing tools.

If you are into trading options on futures, you can also use the standalone application. It is called the FuturesPlus, which offers various advanced tools that you can use for price visualization, advanced contract analysis, risk management through the Greeks, custom and predefined strategy builders, and real-time sales.

With TradeStation, you can have access to a variety of trading products. You will have full access to ETF's, stocks, options, and futures trading, including direct market routing, IPO access, and advanced order types.

As for the disadvantages, there is no international trading available with this platform. Also, the dividend reinvestment plans are not provided and every order for mutual funds has to be phoned in.

With TradeStation, you can also take advantage of educational materials. These materials will help and guide you through the desktop platform. You can access help guides, videos, and private learning sessions.

TD Ameritrade

This platform is considered to be one of the best tools for options trading by many experienced traders. It delivers $0 trades, outstanding market research, great trading platforms, reliable customer service, and industry-leading education for novice traders.

You can use TD Ameritrade on both your desktop computer and mobile phone. The mobile app is handy and ideal for daily investors. The platform is actually recommended for every active trader. So, whether you are into day trading, futures trading, or options trading, you will surely like TD Ameritrade. What's more, TD Ameritrade is known for its artificial intelligence and advanced technology. It can be accessed via

Facebook, Apple Messages, Twitter, Alexa, Apple CarPlay, and Android Auto.

In October 2019, a pricing war ensued. Thus, TD Ameritrade brought down the cost of its stock trades from $6.95 to $0. The options trades were brought down to only $0.65 per contract. Then again, even though ETF and stock trades are at $0, penny stocks are still at $6.95.

TD Ameritrade's thinkorswim is regarded as a top trading tool and platform. It is a desktop-based tool that is preferred by day traders, futures traders, and options traders. It is actually a favorite amongst casual investors.

This trading tool is also highly advanced in that it is able to stream dozens of charts in real-time. It also features more than four hundred technical studies available, making it favorable to the pickiest traders. Even better, all studies are customizable via the proprietary coding language of thinkorswim.

With thinkorswim, you can use fake money for virtual trading, plot economic data, chart social sentiment, perform backtesting, replay historical markets, and perform advanced earnings or options analysis. You can also conduct and create real-time stock scans, workspace layouts, and share charts.

If you prefer to use your mobile device for trading, you can install the TD Ameritrade Mobile or the thinkorswim mobile. The previous is ideal for daily investors who like customizable dashboards. It is easy to navigate. It is also filled with features that will allow you to sync lists, receive price alerts, read the news, and place trades.

The latter is just as great. Upon logging in, it will take you to your watch lists. It actually mirrors its desktop counterpart. You can use the indicators for charting as well as access Trader TV.

In 2017, TD Ameritrade was regarded as the first-ever broker to integrate with Facebook Messenger. It was also amongst the first brokers that offered Alexa Skill. In 2018, it also integrated with Apple Business Chat. Eventually, in 2019, it integrated with Android Auto and Apple CarPlay. Indeed this platform is the best choice for traders who are into advanced technological innovations.

Charles Schwab

With over $6 trillion assets, it is a unique order type for options trading and is one of the most valuable tools you can have as a trader. Its highlights include outstanding stock research, vast trading tool selection, industry-leading financial planning services offers, and $0 trades.

Charles Schwab is a full-service brokerage with an amazing, varied offering of investments that will surely satisfy you. It even has an excellent phone service. In fact, it is a top choice for IRA accounts due to its excellent stock market research offering. It also has robust tools that are great for traders who are into options trading, stock trading, and day trading.

Both ETF and stock trades are $0 while options trades are $0.65 per contract at Charles Schwab, which also lists the price improvements received on eligible orders. This makes it highly recommended for anyone who appreciates order execution quality transparency.

As for the fractional shares, you can buy a minimum of $5 from any company. If you are into penny stock trading, you can buy stocks and OTCBB companies for less than $1 per share. Every transaction fee related to mutual funds is $49.95 per trade. Take note that unlike other brokers, this one merely charges for original purchases. It does not have additional charges for selling.

Aside from the website, you can also access two other platforms: the StreetSmart Edge, which is a desktop-based platform for active traders, and the StreetSmart Central, which is a web-based platform for futures traders. Even though each platform has its own lowlights and highlights, both of them certainly satisfy a lot of traders.

The StreetSmart Edge is the flagship of Charles Schwab. It can be downloaded to any trading platform. It offers most of the whistles and bells that day traders and options traders need in their trading career.

The Trade Source is great for casual traders who are in search of simple tools that feature clean charting and streaming quotes. Then again, even though this platform offers futures trading, you should only trade on the

StreetSmart Central platform. You are not permitted to use the website or StreetSmart Edge if you want to place futures trades.

According to experts, Charles Schwab offers one of the best quality research. It has a terrific in-house and market commentary. Aside from traditional third-party ratings, it also offers proprietary equity ratings that make the research experience more valuable. You can find these ratings throughout your platform experience. Furthermore, you can use the new Beta Research to research stocks, mutual funds, and ETF's all at once.

Interactive Brokers

This one is ideal for professional options traders due to its institutional-grade desktop platform as well as very low margin rates. Then again, it is not only attractive to professional traders. It is also preferred by many casual investors due to its user-friendly web-based platform and $0 trades.

Interactive Brokers is actually well known for giving traders access to more than one hundred market centers all over the world. It also offers professional traders industry-leading commissions. New users are even offered special margin rates.

In addition, there are two main pricing plans you can choose from. These are the IBKR Lite, which is recommended for casual investors, and the IBKR Pro, which is ideal for professionals.

With the IBKR Lite, you will not incur any data fees or inactivity fees. All ETF and US stock trades are $0. The options trade also have the same pricing as IBKR Pro. The primary caveat to this pricing plan, however, is that its order executions are of lower quality. Just like other brokers at $0, it earns profits from the order flow.

A lot of experienced traders go for Interactive Brokers because of its Trader Workstation. This desktop-based platform supports all forms of trading. If you are a seasoned trader, you will surely like the Options Strategy Lab, Algo trading, Risk Navigator, Volatility Lab, Strategy Builder, Portfolio Builder, and Market Scanner.

You can also benefit from the watch lists, which typically include equities, options contracts, forex, warrants, and futures among others. You will also benefit from the IBot, which uses artificial intelligence to respond to clients via voice or chat.

Then again, in spite of these amazing advantages, Interactive Brokers is not perfect. You may find pulling up stocks to trade a bit tricky because of the wide array of securities. You may also not like the fact that automated technical analysis tools like the Trading Central are only available as paid subscription add-ons.

If you prefer to use your mobile device for trading, you can perform charting on your phone with ease and convenience. There are seventy optional indicators available. Then again, stock and index comparisons are not available for the mobile version of Interactive Brokers. It is also not possible to deliver stock alerts via push notifications. You can only receive these alerts through your email.

As for banking, Interactive brokers offer bill pay, a debit card, and the option to earn interest on cash that you did not invest. It does not offer traditional banking services though.

How to Choose a Trading Platform

Trading platforms are tools that allow traders to buy and sell assets on the financial markets at any time of the day. Now that you have learned about the best platforms for options trading, you have to figure out which one you will use.

Ideally, you have to go for the one that makes trading simple and straightforward for you. This way, you can focus better on your strategies instead of getting distracted by the platform. The interface should be user-friendly and easy to navigate. It is great if you are tech-savvy; you will find it easy to use almost any trading platform. However, if you are not that adept with gadgets and software programs, you should go for a trading platform that is simple and easy to understand.

Trading platforms with complex interfaces are not recommended for beginners. You may only waste hours trying to figure out buttons instead of focusing on your trades. You will get distracted and you might even lose money if you use the platform incorrectly.

Account minimums are another thing to consider when choosing a trading platform. Be wary of brokers that require a minimum investment. Furthermore, you have to consider the broker's fees as well as your trading needs and style.

You want a trading platform that gives you flexibility and convenience. Go for something that is reliable and simple enough to be used on a regular basis. In addition, it has to offer paper trading so that you can practice at first. After all, it is not wise to start trading in real-time using real money without any real trading experience.

Conclusion

Thank you again for downloading this book!
I hope this book was able to help you learn about options trading so that you can become a successful trader.
As you know, nothing good in life comes easy. You need to be diligent, smart, and dedicated to succeed. You need to possess the right knowledge and skills. You also need to have the right character for trading.
Through this book, I hope that I was able to give you an overview of everything you need to know about options trading. I hope that the examples are easy and practical enough for you to understand. I also hope that the lessons are complete yet brief enough for you to absorb with ease.
The next step is to apply what you have learned from this book.
Finally, if you enjoyed this book, please take the time to share your thoughts and post a review.   It'd be greatly appreciated!
Thank you!

Swing Trading for Beginners:

The #1 Step by Step Guide to Create Passive Income in The Stock Market Trading Options. Real Strategies to Create $10 000/Month Machine. Money Management & Trading Psychology

© Copyright 2021 by Ryan Martinez - All rights reserved.
The content contained within this book may not be reproduced,
duplicated or transmitted without direct written permission
from the author or the publisher.

Under no circumstances will any blame or legal responsibility
be held against the publisher, or author, for any damages,
reparation, or monetary loss due to the information contained
within this book. Either directly or indirectly.

Legal Notice:

This book is copyright protected. This book is only for
personal use. You cannot amend, distribute, sell, use, quote
or paraphrase any part, or the content within this book,
without the consent of the author or publisher.

Disclaimer Notice:

Please note the information contained within this document is
for educational and entertainment purposes only. All effort has
been executed to present accurate, up to date, and reliable,
complete information. No warranties of any kind are declared
or implied. Readers acknowledge that the author is not
engaging in the rendering of legal, financial, medical or
professional advice. The content within this book has been
derived from various sources. Please consult a licensed
professional before attempting any techniques outlined in this
book.

By reading this document, the reader agrees that under no
circumstances is the author responsible for any losses, direct
or indirect, which are incurred as a result of the use of
information contained within this document, including, but not
limited to, — errors, omissions, or inaccuracies.

Disclaimer

While the author has exerted the best efforts during the course of preparing and finishing this book, he makes no warranties or representations regarding the accuracy or completeness of the contents of this book. He specifically disclaims any implied warranties of merchantability or fitness for a particular purpose.

The discussions, strategies, and tips given in this book may be not be suitable for your situation.   Therefore, it is best to consult accordingly with a professional as needed. The author shall not be held liable for any loss of profit or damages, including but not limited to special, incidental, or consequential damages.

Table of Contents

Chapter 1: Brief Introduction to Swing Trading

Earning profit in the stock market may be done through various means. As such, no matter what your appetite for risk and financial goals are, you would likely find one that suits you. This book primarily discusses one of these methods: swing trading.

What exactly is it?

To begin, check out the primary characteristics of swing trading:

a. Accessible

Whether you are doing this on your own or as part of an institution, swing trading could be a profitable way to invest in the stock market.

b. Short-term

On average, swing traders monitor the price movements of securities within a period ranging from a few days up to two months.

c. Low-risk

Those who engage in swing trading tend to be quite sensitive about the overall condition of the market. They prefer to capitalize on low-risk opportunities, and just try to get the most out of them whenever there is a favorable movement.

d. Adaptive

If the market is strong, swing traders either buy more or go long. However, if the market takes a downturn, they go short instead. In case the overall market is stagnant, swing traders have no problem with having to wait patiently by the sidelines.

Next, let's go over the differences between swing trading, day trading, and buy-and-hold investing. Learning how swing trading differs from other approaches would help you gain a better understanding and set more realistic expectations about investing in the stock market.

- Swing Trading vs. Day Trading

Speed best encapsulates the practice of day trading. Those who engage in this don't hold their positions overnight. Otherwise, they would put themselves at a serious risk of getting a significant portion of their accounts wiped out when the price of securities increases or decreases. As such, they monitor price movements every minute, thereby allowing them to quickly enter or exit as needed.

Day traders specialize in feeling out the volatile parts of the market. Fundamental data doesn't matter to them as much as investor psychology, which enables them to keep track of security price movements of other buyers and sellers.

Though the idea of earning profit quickly appeals to many, take note that the profit gained through this approach would be significantly reduced after taxes, commissions, and other operational costs have been deducted.

Commissions faced by swing traders tend to be high too but not as high as day trading. The longer holding period allows the fundamentals of a company to influence price movements. As such, you would have a higher potential to earn more profits by doing swing trading rather than day trading.

•Swing Trading vs.
Buy-and-Hold Investing

Warren Buffett famously built his wealth through this strategy. Rather than fussing about the tiny movements in market prices, he focused on studying and analyzing how things would appreciate in the years to come.

In this type of trading approach, small changes in prices are regarded as opportunities to either pick up or exit securities instead of indicators of their actual value. Because of this, buy-and-hold investors—or also known as position traders—tend to have a low annual turnover rate, averaging at 30%.

Given these passive qualities, this approach is suitable for those who aim to build or grow their wealth. Profit would take a longer time to be gained due to the nature of the investments, hence investors know that this cannot be used to generate their current income. In comparison, the more flexible swing trading approach may be a source of current income if you have enough dedication and discipline in trading stocks.

As you may have noticed, swing trading falls somewhere in the middle of buy-and-hold investing and day trading. Those who engage in it should be able to develop skills, harness techniques, and follow strategies that would allow them to grab opportunities whenever there is optimal movement in the market. They must learn how to balance being quick enough to buy or exit, thereby keeping themselves from becoming too idle while waiting for that moment.

Many investors opt for swing trading over day trading or buy-and-hold investing because it allows them to use their capital in a more efficient way and get more chances of earning higher returns along the way. However, it also opens them to costlier commissions as well as to increased volatility and risk.

Looking at the similarities and differences among the different types of stock trading approaches, you might have begun analyzing which one would suit you the best. Determining the answer to this question is one of the most important steps you need to clear in order to achieve success and maximize your profits as a stock trader. The next chapters will help you figure out if swing trading is the right fit for you.

Chapter 2: Committing to Swing Trading

Swing trading can be quite appealing for many because of the wider earning opportunities and flexible holding period that it offers to traders. However, it also requires a high degree of discipline and work ethic, as well as a moderate appetite for risk, in order to make it a rewarding venture.

Therefore, in order to assure your success, you must ask yourself first about how much of your time you could commit to swing trading. You don't necessarily have to devote your entire working day.

While many do this as their full-time occupation, there are also swing traders who only engage in this to supplement their income. Some only do this to experience the rush that you would feel while dealing with the stock market, while others start small to give themselves time to learn the ropes before committing themselves fully to the trade.

Which one of these types of swing traders do you think you would be?

Let's go over the different levels of commitment that you could give to swing trading to help you figure this one out.

•Full-Time Swing Trader

Those who intend to make swing trading their main source of income need to devote their full workday to this. However, it is not as simple as it may sound.

More often than not, people spend several months learning the ins and outs of the trade while still maintaining their current job. This involves a lot of research work to better understand what happens before, during, and after the market hours. During the course of gaining more experience, they also become more capable to monitor price movements and get their timings right.

Much of the pressure felt by full-time swing traders could be felt from the need to produce steady profits from their trades. If not handled well, some give in to the temptation of taking the risk and gambling with securities that normally wouldn't be touched by swing traders.

As a result, they experience one loss after another. Less experienced traders would react to this by countering with more trades. However, the better response would be to take a pause, reevaluate the situation, and form your next move.

• Part-Time Swing Trader

The majority of swing traders fall under this category. They engage in this either to supplement their current income or to increase the returns on their investments. Since they are still retaining their primary job, part-time swing traders experience less stress compared to their full-time counterparts.

Given that they dedicate fewer hours of their day to swing trading, part-timers conduct their research and analysis after their regular work hours. Their trades would then be placed on the following day. Though they may not be able to keep track of market movements throughout the day, part-time swing traders are still able to protect their investments by entering stop-loss orders as needed.

Experts recommend going through a part-time phase first before committing fully to swing trading. Furthermore, it is highly advised to start out with a tiny part of your current portfolio. After all, you would likely make mistakes during your first few attempts. Putting a lot of capital right from the start would just make your mistakes more expensive than you could probably afford.

There are a small fraction of part-time swing traders who do it for fun. They are really not in this for the money-making potential, but rather for the "high" of making successful moves on the stock market. As such, they are more likely to ignore the established rules and strategies of swing trading, which then opens them up to more and costlier mistakes.

If you think you belong to this type of swing trader and you insist upon doing so despite the risks associated with it, then I advise you to minimize your probable losses by putting up limits upon yourself. Use only a tiny portion of your investment portfolio, and avoid tapping into your retirement funds.

Keep in mind that you would be interacting with other swing traders whose main goal is to earn a profit. That alone could put you out of the "game" faster than you are expecting.

To better set your expectations about swing trading, take a look at how a typical workday goes for Sean, a full-time retail swing trader.

A. Pre-Market

Sean starts his day early, usually at around six in the morning. This allows him to prepare himself before the opening bell, which signifies the beginning of the trading session at an exchange.

During this period, he first makes it a point to get an overview of the market. This means catching up with the most recent development and news that may affect the market. To do this, he tunes in to a reputable news television channel, and then check out the posts on websites dedicated to monitoring the stock market, such as MarketWatch.com.

From these sources, Sean takes note of the following points:

1. The general sentiment of the market

This covers but is not limited to the important economic reports from within and outside the country, inflation, as well as currency developments.

2. The sentiment of the sector

Sean tries to identify the hot and growing sectors that he needs to put on his list of priorities for the day.

3. Current holdings

Updates, such as SEC filings and company earnings, are helpful when analyzing the market and making decisions later on.

Once Sean has gotten a better feel of the market, his next step is to look for potential trades for the day. Normally, a fundamental catalyst would prompt him to enter a position. In order to find one, he would employ the following methods:

a. Search for special opportunities.
These may usually be found by looking at the SEC filings, and sometimes, by reading through the news headlines. To make things easier for him, Sean makes use of websites such as SECFilings.com to set up alerts for him whenever there is an SEC filing for him to check out.

Common examples of special opportunities for swing traders include mergers, acquisitions, IPOs (initial public offerings), takeovers, buyouts, corporate restructuring, and bankruptcies.

Special opportunities are attractive to swing traders because of their high profit-earning potential. However, take note that they are also quite risky so dealing with them would require a lot of careful research on your part.

If Sean is certain about a particularly special opportunity, his go-to strategy is to either buy when the majority are selling or sell when most are buying. Doing so allows him to fade the market, and capitalize when there is a reversal of the prevailing trends in the market.

b. Analyze sector plays.
Sean takes the time to seek out financial information about sectors with good performance recently. Usually, these sectors are the ones that are most popular among other traders.

However, for bigger rewards albeit higher risks, Sean would also take a look at less known sectors that are performing well. For example, compared to the fuel sector, the titanium sector may be considered as an obscure part of the industry.

In order to maximize the profits from sector plays, Sean's objective is to get his timing right and buy into the current trends, and then exit once he notices signs that the said trends are dying down.

c. Look for chart breaks.

This involves going after popular stocks that traded a lot but are almost reaching a critical support level or resistance level.

With the use of predictive techniques, like the Gann levels, triangles, or Wolfe Waves, Sean would be able to spot a pattern, and then buy after a breakout has occurred. However, he would then sell it again as soon as the stock reaches another resistance level.

After gathering critical pieces of information for the day, Sean would then create a watch list. Basically, the list serves as a reference about the stocks that have good potential and a fundamental catalyst.

Sean writes down his watch list on a whiteboard beside his workstation. It includes concise but important details such as the entry prices and stop-loss prices.

As a final preparatory step before the market hours begin, Sean checks his existing positions for any changes that could have happened overnight. This could easily be done by simply tapping into financial news websites that report about the stock market as well.

If there are, this might have an effect on his trading plan so he would have to take the time to analyze and adjust his strategies and priorities accordingly.

    B. Market Hours

In the US, market hours begin at 9:30 AM and last up to 4:00 PM. This may vary depending on your location though, so be sure to double-check the actual market hours in your country.

Like many stock traders, Sean takes a look first at the Level II quotes in order to get a clearer idea of the price action of the stocks. In Level II, you would be able to find out the Nasdaq stocks that is sold or bought by different types of traders. You may also be able to obtain information about the direction of a particular stock that has piqued your interest.

Once Sean has found and entered a viable trade, he would start doing technical analysis in order to find an exit. His go-to technique is the Fibonacci extensions, which would be further explained later on in this book. He also tends to analyze by looking at the price by volume and the resistance levels.

Take note, however, that Sean has already done an analysis earlier during the pre-market hours so he is just confirming again his observations based on the actual trading activities of the day. Doing so prevents him from placing trades that would be a loss or too risky for him.

Speaking of risks, one of Sean's trading rules for himself is to avoid adjusting his position just to be able to accept more risks. He would only do so if adjusting his stop-loss levels is going to lock in profits, or if the overall feel of the trading has become bullish.

C. After-Hours Market

Swing traders rarely place trades during the after-hours. After all, stocks at this point tend to be harder to sell quickly and easily without incurring a substantial loss.

As such, Sean uses this time to evaluate his performance for the day. He takes the time to carefully document his trades as well as ideas. Aside from tax purposes, doing so would allow him to reflect on the points that could be further improved upon.

To close his day, Sean reviews his open positions for the final time. He would check to significant events that may affect impact holdings, and the earning announcements made after-hours.

As you may have noticed from the above-given account of a swing trader's regular workday, it involves careful planning and thorough preparation in order to achieve success and healthy returns.

Given these, do you think you have what it takes to commit yourself to swing trading? Is this the right path for you to earn passive income and build your wealth?

If you have answered "yes" to these questions, then you have made the right decision to pick this book as your guide and companion for this particular endeavor.

There are a lot of skills involved to be a successful swing trader. However, things would be made easier if have a solid foundation for your growth and development. Learn more about the basic but important principles and terms used in swing trading.

Chapter 3: Planning Your Trade

Much like starting your own business, trading must begin with a strategic plan. This serves as both your foundation and guide to keep you from making rash decisions and costly mistakes along the way.

Failing to make a plan before engaging in swing trading would also hinder you from learning from your experiences. As a result, the progress of your growth as a trader as well as the increase of your earnings would likely not meet your expectations in the long run.

The succeeding chapters of this book shall cover how to develop and implement a trading plan. But for now, let's go over the important parts that must be included and specified clearly in your trading plan.

A. What to Trade

The first thing to do when making a plan is to determine the type of securities that you could trade. There is a wide range to choose from, but the decision on which to select depends on various factors, including your interest, financial goals, appetite for risk, to name a few.

To help you through this step of preparing your trading plan, I'll go over the definitions, advantages, and risks associated with the different types of securities that are popular among swing   traders:

- Public Equity

Most swing traders, especially beginners, prefer public equity—or more commonly known as stocks—because it is more familiar and easier to trade. For example, in the US, ADRs (American depository receipts) and ETFs (exchange traded funds) can be categorized under this type of securities.

As a general rule, swing traders go after stocks that have met a particular level of volume. Doing so would keep you from making the expensive mistake of selling shares of a stock that falls below the ongoing level of volume.

Another great thing about trading stocks is that it increases the probability of being exposed to other classes of assets. For example, you may be able to learn more about commodity gold if you are trading ETFs that are associated with gold bullion as part of its assets.

While it is recommended for people to stick with their area of expertise in order to continually build up their skills as a trader, there is no harm in widening your knowledge about other positions that you could take.

- Commodities

Nowadays, more and more traders are paying attention to commodities. This is brought about by their rising prices, may it be energy commodities like crude oil, or precious metals like gold.

Profiting from commodities may be achieved by monitoring the price movements of similar stocks or ETFs. Take for example how the prices of gold bullion can be tracked by looking at the price movements of gold shares. More and more websites, such as SPDRGoldShares.com, make this easier to accomplish.

A word of caution though. The risks and issues associated with commodities differ from stocks. Compared to equities, commodities are more volatile in terms of price and margin—among other types of risks. Therefore, take the time to research and learn more about them first before trying out your luck at trading commodities.

- Closed End Funds

These refer to mutual funds that are mainly traded on a secondary exchange. Their prices are based on the degree of supply and demand for their shares. In comparison, open end funds have prices that are based on their net asset value, which pertains to the fund's value after the liabilities have been deducted from the assets.

Because of its nature, closed end funds may sometimes be traded for higher or lower than their net asset value.

- Fixed-Income Markets

Securities that are issued by different levels of government fall under this type of securities. Their values are normally dependent on the ongoing interest rates, inflation, as well as the creditworthiness of the issuing party.

Because of the relative stability of their prices, experienced swing traders tend to avoid them. After all, they would have a higher chance of earning more profits by going after more volatile stocks or commodities.

- Currency Market

Often referred to as the foreign exchange market or simply the forex market, this is considered as the biggest global financial market. As of 2020, its overall worth is at $1.93 quadrillion. Every day, around $5.3 trillion is being traded there, making it also one of the most active financial markets in the world.

However, despite its size and volume, one limiting factor about the forex market is that it focuses on only a handful of currencies—the US dollar, the British pound sterling, the Euro, the Swiss franc, and the Japanese yen.

Beginner swing traders should also note that aside from learning how to complement the technical analysis with fundamental analysis, they must also understand how various factors—such as political stability, economic growth, and inflation—could influence the value of currencies.

- Futures Contracts

This involves buying or selling an underlying asset with a predetermined price at a particular date in the future. There is no exchange of money between the two parties until the contract has reached its expiration. Furthermore, a margin ranging from 5% to 10% of the total value of the contract must be posted by the traders.

Given this, extreme leverage may be imposed if the traders would like to do so. However, I discourage you from doing so because it would expose you to the risk of losing most—if not all—of your assets in the case that there is an unexpected movement in security.

B. Where to Trade

Equities, commodities, currencies, and other types of securities are traded in different financial markets. Therefore, what you decided to trade would determine where you should trade.

Financial markets can be categorized in various ways. For example, if it is based on the kinds of assets that are being traded, the markets would be classified as either traditional or alternative. Traditional markets are where financial assets like stocks and bonds are traded, while alternative markets deal with venture capital funds, fiduciary rights of real estate, investment projects, and portfolio investments—just to name a few.

Markets may also be categorized according to the phase of negotiation. Financial assets are created in the primary market, wherein the issuer could transmit them directly to traders. On the other hand, the exchange of existing financial assets that have already been issued before occurs in the secondary market.

If markets are categorized based on the assets transferred, then the sub-types would be the money market and the capital market. Assets with a term that does not exceed one year belong to the money market. Aside from money, these can be traded with any financial assets that are highly liquid and have a short-term maturity. Any asset that has medium-term or long-term maturity is traded in the capital market.

The US in particular is home to various types of financial markets that could attract all kinds of traders. For instance, stocks, ETFs, and other asset classes that are based in the US and other countries can be found in the lists of NASDAQ Exchange, NYSE (New York Stock Exchange, and AMEX (American Stock Exchange). For commodities, the CBOT (Chicago Board of Trade) is a good place to trade precious metals and major agricultural commodities like rice, corn, and wheat. Those who want to engage with crude oil, gas, and coal should check out the NYMEX (New Your Mercantile Exchange) list.

Take note, however, that stock trades are not limited to just these markets. With the rise of ECNs (electronic communication networks), traders may be able to match with big brokerage companies. Many consider this as a more efficient way to buy and sell, and sometimes, ECNs could even provide higher prices compared to ones offered by brokers.

C. When to Trade

As discussed in the previous chapter, swing traders may be classified as either full-time or part-time traders depending on their degree of commitment. This affects the timing of entering orders, which would then serve as one of the bases of the entry and exit strategies.

How exactly so?

As illustrated earlier, full-time swing traders have more time to spend researching opportunities and sector plays that are critical for analyzing the positions that they would make later on. They can also make their entries and exits at any point of the day, and take into account any changes in the price movements that have not been foreseen during the pre-market hours.

In comparison, part-time swing traders usually have other affairs to focus on during the market hours so entering orders can only be done after the market has already been closed for the day. As such, they tend to focus more on stop losses in order and limit in order to keep themselves from losing their investment.

D. How to Trade

Your game plan for the trading opportunities you have identified is composed of various strategies for different phases of the trade.

- Analysis

There two primary analysis techniques employed by swing traders:

- Technical Analysis

Using this would enable you to analyze chart patterns, as well as apply mathematical formulas to the prices and volume of securities.

The main advantage of this technique is that its applicability to any type of security or market. For instance, Sean uses technical analysis to quickly identify chart patterns, which would then serve as the basis for his decision on whether to buy or sell. Whether it is for stocks, commodities, bonds, or currencies, he could apply the technique as long as he could interpret the information that it would yield.

Compared to the other analysis technique—fundamental analysis—this is much quicker because you do not need to go over the details about the company's business and earnings before reaching a decision.

- Fundamental Analysis

If you want to understand why particular security is having price movements, you should use the fundamental analysis technique. This covers the fundamentals of a security or a company, including its sales and earnings.

By applying this, you would be able to determine whether the price movement is caused by fundamentals or just events in the market like the liquidation of a large mutual fund. The latter tends to be less profitable to trade in the long run, so traders want rallies and declines that are driven by the underlying fundamentals of security or a company.

Take for example the price increase of crude oil commodity. Technical analysis would likely tell you that the movement is caused by a bullish formation that has developed in the chart. When compared to fundamental analysis, this would appear like a superficial analysis of the situation, especially when the price increase is actually caused by the scarcity of the supply of crude oil in the market.

Swing traders who don't like doing fundamental analysis say that the process takes too long and may sometimes lead to inaccurate decisions. Yes, this would require you a lot of reading and research work. However, if you seek to improve your skills as a swing trader in a more holistic manner, then doing fundamental analysis could be well worth your time and effort.

As you may have noticed, technical analysis is useful when you need to determine the optimal timings for your entries and exits. Fundamental analysis, on the other hand, would help you be more prepared by telling you which direction a security or company is heading to.

- Identification and Entry

Securities that worth pursuing may be identified through either of the following approaches:

  o Top-Down

In this approach, the identification of opportunities starts at the market level. This would then proceed down to the industry level before ending at the company level.

Choosing this method would influence how you enter positions. Basically, you would have to survey the general market first, then go over the industries that belong to the strongest or weakest sectors.

Ranking of securities using either technical or fundamental analysis would follow. The final step is to identify the securities that match well with your entry strategy.

o Bottom-Up

This approach involves looking for strong securities to serve as a starting point for your analysis. The ones that belong to rising or good sectors or industries would then be chosen for entry.

People who use this approach establish a quantitative filter that shall be used to screen the securities. Usually, the screen would be based on the value or growth of the stocks at that particular time.

The securities that passed the screen would be compared against the value or growth indices of the market in order to rank them from highest to lowest value or growth. If the top ranking securities meet your entry strategy, the industries or sectors where they belong would be checked to determine if they are doing well or not. The final choice would then depend on whether you want to buy or short.

- Exit

Inexperienced swing traders tend to focus more on their entry strategy. However, experts know that having the right exit strategy would influence when you would earn profits or losses, and when you need to redeploy your capital to a better position.

Your exit strategy must cover the following three points:
o When to exit to gain profit

Since exit strategies should be based on technical data such as a trigger or catalyst, it is never recommended to listen to your gut feel even if it tells you that you are going to profit.

A common example of a data-driven exit strategy is a stipulation wherein an exit would be appropriate only if the price has reached a certain point on a chart pattern.

o When to exit to limit a loss

This part of the exit strategy should be based on either movement of price zones or a form of moving average. Price zones where securities have ceased falling are known as support levels. On the other hand, price zones where security prices have stopped increasing are referred to as resistance levels. Recognizing these points would be quite helpful in limiting your losses to a particular quantity only.

o When to exit if there is neither profit nor loss
If the trade has become essentially a dead weight, many swing traders would opt to exit the position as soon as possible. Still, there are some who would wait it out first before making a decision. For example, Sean makes it a rule for him to exit only if there has not been any indication of either a profit or loss after ten days.

- Shorting
In case of a price decline, a swing trader may still profit from this by shorting securities. Therefore, it is wise to include this in your trading strategy.

There are two ways to go about this—either you will net long or net short. Net long means that most of the assets that you have invested into belong to the long side of the market. Conversely, net short means that the majority of your assets are on the short side instead. If there is an even quantity of long and short assets, then it is considered market neutral.

So, how exactly do you make this decision?

The answer depends on the current state of the major market index. For example, if the S&P Market Index is rising, then the majority of the swing traders are net-long. However, if it is falling, then several swing traders are net short. Market neutral swing traders can only be possible if the index says that the market is in a trading range.

- Risk Management

Expert traders consider this as the most vital part of a trading plan. After all, a rather weak entry or exit strategy could still lead you to earning profits if the risk management part of your plan restricts your losses while allowing your profits to run.

Managing risk should be planned from the investment portfolio down to the individual securities. Here are the critical points that must be addressed in the risk management portion of your trading plan:

o Acceptable risk on an individual position
This means you have to clarify in your plan the amount you plan to allocate for each position.

o The acceptable risk for the total portfolio
In general, swing traders set this at 0.5 to 2 percent.

o Achievement of proper diversification
As you expose yourself to various types of asset classes and sectors, the more securities are going to be added to your portfolio. This means that you would also be exposed to more and different kinds of risks along the way.

o Long and short positions
By combining long and short positions, you would be able to ensure that your overall portfolio would still gain something regardless of an up or down market.

o The 7 percent rule
This trading rule states that total risk for individual positions and your portfolio should not exceed 7 percent.

o Establishment of Exit Points
As explained earlier, exits due to profit, loss, or lack of significant market movement must be determined by technical indicators such as price zones and profit targets.

o Management Over Emotions
Since no human being is completely devoid of emotions, a good risk management strategy must take this factor into

account. Your emotions would likely be affected by the good and bad experiences as a swing trader. In turn, they would influence how you execute your trade plan.

Those who cannot control their emotions well may find themselves ignoring or completely going against the rules that they have established for themselves. That could only lead to disastrous results.

Fortunately, emotions can be managed, and you can get better at this over time. You will find more tips on how to achieve this later on in this book.

As you may have noticed, managing risks associated with trading involves minimizing your losses at the individual and portfolio level. While you might be thinking that individual losses wouldn't hurt that much, there are certain scenarios that could significantly affect your investment.

Trading master Alexander Elder best explains this through the shark and piranha analogy. First, he described a single major loss that could inflict a "shark bite" damage to your entire portfolio. When this occurs, the value of your account would likely be significantly wiped out just because of that one particular loss.

In comparison, "piranha bites" damages happen when you encounter several small losses in a short period of time. If you would think about it, the prey of this tiny but aggressive fish would likely not die if there is only one of it. However, when a group of them attacked, then their attack tends to be quite fatal.

Applying this to your portfolio, an individual loss might not pose a serious risk to your total portfolio. Unfortunately, if you continually experience one loss after another, then they could eventually build up and cause a massive loss to you.

Given these, don't you think that spending time coming up with a solid risk management system for your trading plan is well worth your time and energy?

Now that you have a sneak peek of what is ahead of your path towards becoming a swing trader, I hope that this chapter has strengthened your resolve to pursue this endeavor.

As committed earlier, this book shall delve deeper into the concepts that you have learned so far. However, before getting into the nitty-gritty parts, it's best to familiarize yourself with the most important tips that you should keep in mind, as well as the critical mistakes that a trader might commit. Check out the next two chapters for the top 10 things to remember and top 10 things to avoid in swing trading.

Chapter 4: Top 10 Swing Trading Tips to Remember

As mentioned in an earlier chapter, swing trading can both be a profitable and exciting way to earn money. Many regard it as a game of survival, but actually, it is more like a balancing act where you have to follow your own rules, control your emotions, and manage the risks.

To guide you on how to successfully pull this off, I'll share with you ten simple but helpful tips about swing trading. Though they may sound rather straightforward and even boring at times, these rules would keep you from losing your balance and falling off the proverbial tightrope.

Tip No. 1: Stick to your trading plan.

A trading plan serves as a general guide on how you should go about your trades. It must cover every phase of swing trading, from the research and preparation part up to your exit strategies.

However, no matter how well thought out a trading plan is, it would not be of any to use to you if you do not write it down. Traditional swing traders make sure to have a printed copy of their trading plan nearby whenever they engage with their trades.

However, more and more swing traders are opting to have a digital copy in their work computers instead. Since electronic means of trading are becoming more popular these days, this practice has proven to be more efficient and convenient for many.

A great way to ensure that you are following your trading plan is by condensing its most important points into a questionnaire form. Answering this before entering a position would allow you to analyze first in a more organized manner. It would also prevent you from giving in to temptations or your emotions, thus keeping you from making decisions that would harm your earnings or total portfolio.

For your reference, here is a sample trading questionnaire from Sean, the full-time swing trader:

- In the case of long positions, does this security belong to an industry group that is ranked within the upper 20% of the market?
- In the case of short positions, does this security belong to an industry group that is ranked within the lower 20% of the market?
- Did the volume increase according to the direction of the trade within the past few days?
- Is the direction of the overall market trends the same as the direction of the trade?
- Has there been any buy signal given for it within the past few days?
- Is the company going to announce its earnings within the next 14 days?

Sean's questionnaire may seem quite simple to answer since it only requires him to respond with either yes or no. However, each point would force him to analyze the information he has gathered so far vis-à-vis his own trading plan. In case he could not give a definitive answer, the questionnaire shall also serve as a reminder for him to conduct more research work.

Tip No. 2: Maintain a trading journal.
A trading journal is not just simply a record of all the trades you have executed. It also serves as your coach.
Since it contains important information about your trades, you can review its contents and learn more about your assumptions that have turned out well, your trading tendencies that need to either be reinforced into habits or be dropped as soon as possible and the patterns in the good and bad trades that you have entered.
By getting this general overview of your trading profile, wins, and losses, you would be able to gain self-awareness and use that accordingly to make the necessary adjustments in the way you trade. It opens up an opportunity to replicate your previous successes and points out the things you should avoid to prevent the recurrence of your mistakes.
To maintain a trading journal, you must build the habit of recording information into it after a trade has been entered.

Failing to do this would likely overwhelm you later on when the data that you need to write down piles up. In the end, you might even completely give up updating your trading journal. In general, the more details you record in the trading journal, the more useful it would be for you. The suggested content of your trading journal will be discussed further in BALIKAN Chapter _____ of this book.

Take note, however, that this also means that you need to spend more time to update it every time you make a trade. What many swing traders do to save time is to take screenshots of the trades, and add those images into the primary document or spreadsheet of their trading journal. From there, they write down other important pieces of information to complete the journal entry.

Tip No. 3: Take control of your emotions.

Emotions can ruin even the most hardworking swing traders. More often than not, those who try to make up for their losses by making more trades are not being guided by their rules but rather by their emotions. As such, what should have been just a small loss becomes bigger and bigger, some of which end up as billion-dollar mistakes.

One of the best qualities that a swing trader can have is emotional stability. Professional traders do not associate their profits or losses with their emotions. After all, whether you gain or lose is a matter of your skills and experience as a trader. They should not be regarded as a source of your happiness or a trigger for your despair.

Having control over your emotions would also help you keep your trades close to your chest. Some swing traders make the mistake of announcing the trades that they currently have, or the profits they have earned. Telling others would put you at the risk of becoming too attached to your positions. As a result, you would find it harder to make urgent but hard decisions when push comes to shove.

Emotional control is something that you have to develop over time. Don't feel frustrated if you still sometimes find yourself being subjected to the whims of your emotions. The important thing is to catch this moment as soon as possible, take a pause, and reflect on these emotions that are likely influencing your trade.

Once you become more aware of how and why your emotions are affecting your trading, you would be able to keep better track and exert more control over the emotional side of yourself.

Tip No. 4: Diversify your portfolio.

As a general rule, swing traders should have at least ten positions in different sectors in order to have a diversified portfolio. Better yet, add other asset classes as well, such as REITs (real estate investment trusts), commodities, and ETFs into the mix.

You might be wondering though why this is important in the first place.

Portfolio diversification would allow you to benefit from any kind of movement in the market. If some of your positions have become losses, you would still have the chance to offset that when your other positions earn you profits instead.

Otherwise, you are going to be more exposed to the so-called idiosyncratic risk, which is brought about by having only one position from a single company.

Tip No. 5: Enter trades on a limit order.

Experts suggest entering a trade through a limit order instead of a market order. Why? Because upon execution, the price of limit orders remains the same as what you have specified. On the other hand, you do not have as much control over the price of a market order.

Limit orders also help effect the cost of market impact on you. Basically, if the order size is larger than the average volume order for the day, then your buy or sell order would have a higher chance of significantly increasing or decreasing the price of the security. In comparison, the execution of a market order might just be 2% to 5% more than the original price of the security when you made the said order.

As long as it is near the level where shares are being traded, placing a limit order may be done at any price level. It is better though to place them at a slightly lower level if you are buying, or at a slightly higher level if you are shorting.

Tip No. 6: Make use of stop-loss orders.
Some swing traders consider stop-loss orders as unnecessary once they got the hang of things. They assume that they would be able to exit a trade as soon as they observe a weak point.
However, more often than not, this is not the case for most swing traders. Because they do not recognize the purpose and importance of stop-loss orders, they end up with losses that could have been avoided in the first place.
Why are stop loss orders essential in swing trading? Basically, they reduce the risks and protect your investments in various ways, such as:
- Limiting your downside
In the absence of a stop loss order, all of your capital would likely be your downside. To keep this from happening to you, impose an upper limit for the losses that you may encounter by placing stop loss orders.

- Helping you stay objective
There are some traders who only make use of stop loss orders in their minds. As such, nothing or no one else could stop them from changing their predetermined stop loss order if the market begins moving against them.

For example, your imaginary stop loss order is at $99.50. However, when the trade price dropped down to $99, you try to justify holding on to that position by telling yourself that $98.50 should be your exit point instead given the recent movements in the market. As a result of this rather impulsive change of mind, your losses would accumulate.

- Dealing with sudden, unexpected movements in the market
There are times when you need to act fast in order to save your account. If you have a diversified portfolio, that means you would have to handle around 10 different positions in a

brief period of time. Without stop loss orders, you would have to do this completely on your own.

With stop loss orders in place, you may be able to take a break from swing trading whenever you need one. May it be for a vacation or to recover from an illness, you would have more peace of mind that you something would act on your positions in case the market starts acting up while you are away.

Tip No. 7: Establish your risk level.
Stop loss level is not enough to completely protect you from the volatility and unpredictability of the market. As such, all swing traders must set their acceptable risk levels for their trades.
Risk levels serve as signals for traders when the original assumptions about a particular security have turned out to be wrong. Beginner traders benefit greatly from them because having risk levels would force them to admit the mistake early on, and thus prevent them from incurring even bigger losses. Some swing traders set the risk levels based on a certain percentage level from the entry order. However, this kind of strategy might cause automatic exits that are based on a non-existent reality on the market. For instance, if your risk level is set at 5%, then you would automatically exit a trade as soon as this level has been reached regardless of the actual daily volatility is only at 4%.
Therefore, the smarter strategy for establishing your risk levels is to base them on either the support levels or resistance levels. For example, if the support level of a stock is usually at $25, then you may assign your risk level to be $24.93. Avoid using a whole number because that would increase the likelihood of your stop loss order—which should be set at your established risk level—being the same as many others who have also placed their respective orders.
If you are not comfortable with the conspicuousness of a support level, then you could use a moving average as a basis instead. However, take note that doing so would require you

more work because you need to regularly adjust because as its name implies, a moving average is in constant motion. Swing traders who prefer trading ranges can easily identify their risk levels since all they have to identify is the continuation of an already existing trading range. Therefore, any breakout above or below the support level or resistance level indicates that it is the end of a trading range.

Tip No. 8: Assign a profit target or technical exit for your trades.
A large portion of swing traders bases their profit targets on the previous support level or resistance level. For example, they will sell 50% of a position once it has gained 5% upon its entry, and sell the remaining 50% once a 10% gain has been reached.
Another way is to base it on a technical indicator, such as a moving average or a sell signal. Doing this could be useful in generating more profits from securities that tend to trend for longer than initially expected.

Tip No. 9: Pay attention to what the overall market and industry group leads are saying.
As a general rule of stock trading, trades should match the current direction of the overall market to ensure maximum profitability. Swing traders know that if the market is in bull mode, most of their trades are in long positions. However, once it turns into the bear mode, traders switch the majority of their portfolio into short positions.
However, experienced swing traders understand that paying attention to the overall market is not enough. The performance of industry groups influences the probable returns that you could from securities.
Securities from high-performing industry groups would rise, while those from troubled industry groups would also fall. That is why when the homebuilding group was on the down back in 2007, traders had greatly profited from homebuilding companies, such as Beazer Homes USA, through shorting.

Tip No. 10: Make swing trading a rewarding experience for you.

While all traders are advised to never mix their emotions—whether positive or negative—with their business, how you feel about trading still matters in your long-term success. At the very least, you should find some form of pleasure in swing trading.

Remember, you would be spending not just your money, but also your time and energy. If you are just forcing yourself to go through it, then there is a high chance that swing trading would not be a successful venture for you. If you have realized along the way that swing trading does not exactly match your personality or goals, then you are better off trying other means of building your wealth.

Chapter 5: Top 10 Swing Trading Mistakes to Avoid

Making mistakes in swing trading is an inevitable part of the process. Even experienced traders still commit them every now and then, only to realize where they went wrong after everything has been said and done.

However, just because you didn't suffer from any consequences this time does not automatically mean that you would always be safe from loss or harm. While one or two mistakes will not lead to losing your account value, recurring mistakes would eventually catch up to you and bring significant losses to your entire portfolio.

To keep yourself from the common pitfalls of swing trading, here are 10 of the most critical mistakes that you need to avoid, and how you could arm yourself against them.

Mistake No. 1: Having insufficient capital at the start

Much like starting your own business, you need to have starting capital as part of your investment. Honestly speaking, this has to be a substantial amount because of the various costs associated with swing trading. Otherwise, your initial run would be quite hard because of the following factors:

- Trading Cost

There is a round-trip commission charge for every security you trade. This could be quite expensive if your trading increment is relatively small as well. For example, if your trading increment is $500 and the commission charge is $20, then you need to wait for the position to increase by more than 4% to actually earn from your trade.

- Portfolio Diversification

If you are aiming to diversify your portfolio by having at least 10 positions, then spreading a small amount of capital would make trading a lot harder for you. For instance, if your total capital is only $5,000, the average size of your trades would be only $500. That would likely not be enough to cover the amount needed to buy the shares that you are eyeing.

Moreover, because of this, you would be forced to limit yourself to only a few positions, which in turn increases your overall risk.

Given these, how much starting capital do you actually need for swing trading? While there is no set amount that would apply for everyone, here are my suggested capital amounts for different types of swing traders:

a. For those trading for a living

If you plan to make swing trading your primary source of income, then you need to have a large starting point, not only to use for trading but also to cover your current living expenses.

Take for example Carla, who is switching from being a part-time swing trader into full-time. On average, a swing trader could make around 10% to 20% per year. Since her total monthly expenses are at about $5,000, her account value must not fall below $300,000—provided that she could achieve a 20% annual return. However, to be safe, she needs an account value of $600,000. With this, her living expenses per month would still be covered even if her annual returns are just at 10%.

To find out how much you need for yourself, take inventory of your personal expenses, and then use that as the basis for your computation about your target account value.

b. For those trading as a hobby

Normally, people who treat swing trading as a hobby have the majority of their other assets invested in a professional and diversified manner. As such, they may be able to trade about 10% to 20% of their total assets—as long as that amount is not lower than $10,000. Anything below would likely not be enough to cover the expenses associated with swing trading.

c. For those trading for their retirement fund

Building up your retirement fund usually means that you have other means of earning your current income. Given this, you could probably set your starting capital of $10,000 at a minimum—much better if you could increase it up to $20,000. With this amount, you could hold around 12 positions.

If you do not fit exactly into any of these categories, the suggested minimum capital remains to be $10,000. This amount would be sufficient to cover the swing trading costs, such as taxes, slippages, and commissions.

Mistake No. 2: Trading before earnings dates
Ideally, swing trading must be done after the company has already announced its earnings. That is why trading stocks at least one week before their earnings dates is considered a reckless move.

Earnings dates can rarely be accurately predicted. Furthermore, it is quite hard to guess whether the company has good or bad earnings for that period. Of course, you may try to gather information from the clients and suppliers of the company. Some even try to fish for information based on how the competitors of the company are doing.

Such research work normally takes a lot of time—more than what swing traders have at their disposal. Therefore, those who have a high appetite for risk tend to gamble with earnings dates especially when their gut feel tells them to do so.

This could easily be a fatal mistake for your account value. While the payout for a successful gamble is tempting, the possibility that you would encounter a major loss should be enough to dissuade you from trading before earnings dates. Yes, there are websites now—like MarketWatch.com—which list down the upcoming earnings dates of several companies. However, such resources cannot be used to determine the companies' actual earnings.

Mistake No. 3: Trading penny stocks
Penny stocks refer to any type of US-based stocks that are traded for a cheap price—usually less than a dollar but it can go up to $5. It attracts beginner traders because, at first glance, trading penny stocks would give you higher than

average returns even if there have only been small movements in the value of the stocks.

In reality, however, penny stocks can be one of the worst addition to your portfolio. Studies show that companies that offer penny stocks are suffering from bad financial health. They could be experiencing massive losses or are burdened with so much debt that they could not afford to pay them off. Because of the state of the companies offering them, penny stocks tend to have low liquidity. They are also highly susceptible to have price fluctuations out of the blue. Moreover, there are days when penny stocks cannot be traded at all. This would seriously hamper your ability to profit from them.

You might be thinking that penny stocks could be easily avoided since they are associated only with small or unknown companies. However, big companies like Blockbuster Inc. and Vonage Holdings had also offered them when they were in the midst of an internal financial crisis.

Mistake No. 4: Changing your reason for trading a stock

Losses are difficult to accept because it is essentially admitting that you have made a mistake. In trading, this means that rather than sell a poorly performing security, you would keep it in hopes that your initial expectations for it would be met eventually. Having this kind of mindset ignores your original objective of earning as much profit as possible from the trade while limiting the risks that you are putting yourself in.

Sean has committed this mistake during his early days as a swing trader. He bought stocks of a reputable company that is on the long side. However, shortly after this, the company has experienced a financial mishap, which resulted in a 15% decrease in the price of their stocks.

At first, Sean thought that the company would recover soon, and the price of its stocks would surely be back to 20% again. So, rather than sell the stocks, he opted to wait it out instead, even if it takes weeks, months, or even years.

Beginners tend to overlook the effect of keeping a poor-performing stock in their portfolio. Much like pruning a plant to make it grow healthier and more aesthetically pleasing, removing the problematic parts of your portfolio should be part of your strategies as you continue to diversify. This would allow you to focus more of your time, effort, and resources on trades with higher earning potential instead of being weighed down by the wrong decisions that you have made.

Mistake No. 5: Doubling down on a bad trade
Doubling down in swing trading means doubling the investment you have initially made because the trade has gone against you. This may sound counterintuitive at first, but some swing traders find this as an appealing move despite being highly risky.
Why?
Most believe that by doubling down on that particular share, you would have a chance to earn a lot more profit in case that the trade begins to move in your direction. The thing is, this strategy works a lot better for those who have long-term time horizons. They do not care much about short-term losses because they can afford to wait things out until the market conditions have become favorable for them.
In comparison, most swing traders cannot wait for years just to make a decision on whether to exit and find something else to invest in. That's why doubling down is not really recommended for those engaged in swing trading. More often than not, the risks far outweigh the expected rewards. If you have noticed that things aren't going your way within the first few days, then it is best to sell as soon as you can and minimize your losses.
Furthermore, doubling down in swing trading usually indicates that you are reacting emotionally to a probable loss. Instead of acknowledging that you have made a mistake that led to a loss, you are essentially putting more of your money into that bad trade, thinking that doing so would make things right. That is almost never the case. As discussed earlier, don't forget your original reason for trading stock.

Mistake No. 6: Going for option securities

Option securities and swing trading has never been compatible with one another. Even most professional swing traders tend to miscalculate them, thus exposing them to more risks than they can actually afford.

Why?

Because options are best left for those who need to hedge risk for speculators. They give the right to trade for a particular price at a certain time in the future. Swing traders do not benefit from this because it is nearly impossible to short-term trade options securities. You have to get the timing, direction, and magnitude of the price movements in order to be successful at it—a feat that is not achievable or realistic for most swing traders.

Furthermore, options tend to be quite expensive regardless of whether you are planning to buy or sell them. Since their spread is also wide, you would likely encounter a 5% to 10% loss in your investment if you bought them at the asking price without having the opportunity to sell them immediately.

Mistake No. 7: Being overconfident

In swing trading, too much confidence about your skills and luck often leads to arrogance. Yes, you might have gotten one win after another lately. That is certainly worthy of a celebration. However, this does not guarantee that you would always be on the winning side of things.

Believing that you would always gain from your trades would lead you to accept more and bigger risks along the way. It would also blindside you from other swing traders who may have done a more thorough prep work than you.

Such poor development leaves you open to more probable losses. Worse, rather than admitting that you have made a bad trade, you would begin making excuses, such as the marking being in the wrong instead.

Another complication of being overconfident is stunting your own growth. Some swing traders think that learning and mastering the core principles of the trade are enough to keep on achieving their targets. However, the market continuously changes so traders must keep themselves up-to-date with the latest news, theories, platforms, and techniques.

Mistake No. 8: Failing to Properly Diversify the Portfolio
There is a psychological phenomenon called familiarity bias that affects many traders. This may be observed among those who tend to invest only in companies that they have already traded with before. They get a sense of comfort and security that things would go well again because of their prior experience.

Unfortunately, familiarity bias could be quite dangerous for swing traders. This reduces the chances of diversifying your portfolio with new but promising trades. For example, you are more familiar with the technology sector so you opted to invest in different tech companies rather than branch out to other sectors.

So while you have a portfolio of 10 stocks in your account, all of them belong to the same sector. Any rise or fall in the sector would affect your entire portfolio because you have failed to completely diversify your investments. Keep in mind that the right way to diversify is to have long and short positions in various sectors and for different asset classes. One well-known example of how this bias puts traders and investors at risk is the Enron retirement assets, which occurred in the 1990s. At that time, a large portion of their employees decided to invest their retirement assets in the energy stocks of the company. Since many opted to put everything or a majority of their retirement assets in just one place, they had placed themselves at a high risk of losing everything after the company's rapid decline.

Mistake No. 9: Placing too many trades
As described earlier in this book, swing trading falls in between buy-and-hold investment and day trading. It involves far fewer trades than day trading since it isn't concerned with every tiny movement in the stock prices. Conversely, it requires more dedication and focus than buy-and-hold investing since your sights are more on the short-term gains rather than ones that pay off after months or even years of waiting.

Achieving this balance is one of the key components to become a true and successful swing trader. While you may be tempted to keep making as many trades as you can, remember that each trade also means that you have to also invest more time, money, and effort to enter, monitor, and exit your trades. Eventually, you would also realize that you are trading stocks that move due to non-fundamental reasons, which do not lead to substantial returns.

There is no universal rule about the optimal number of trades that you could place. However, on average, swing traders hold positions for multiple days up to a few weeks.

If you notice that your holding periods is less than the average, take the time to reflect why you feel the need to make more trades than usual. Is it caused by certain events in the market, or are you becoming more impatient with your current progress? Once you have identified the probable cause, you would be able to formulate a plan to address whatever issues are affecting you.

Mistake No. 10: Failing to Follow the Trading Plan

A good trading plan is the professional swing trader's constant guide in every trade they enter, monitor, and exit. It contains the strategies and risk management measures that you have formulated for yourself. As such, it does not only lead you to gain profits but it also safeguards your capital from the ever-changing market.

Failing to follow your trading plan is tantamount to disobeying your boss at work—which in the case of swing trading: yourself. Ignoring what you have set out to do in favor of your whims at the moment would most likely hurt you in the end.

Don't think that trading plans are completely cast in stone, however. You can always make revisions to it as needed, provided that you do them after the market hours for the day has ended and only if you have good reason to do so.

In this way, you are not violating the trading plan. Instead, you are just improving upon your strategies and system based on the evaluation of your actual performance.

Chapter 6: Recommended Tools, Platforms, and Other Resources for Swing Traders

Before beginning to trade in the market, swing traders need to secure these three components: brokers, service providers, and a trading journal.

Choosing the right type of broker who is compatible with their trading plan is critical for swing traders to achieve their goals. They also need the help of certain service providers to carry out key administrative activities, such as conducting screens and analyzing charts. Meanwhile, in terms of performance evaluation and skills development, a trading journal is an indispensable tool for swing traders.

All of these points will be discussed in this chapter to give you a head-start in swing trading.

A. Brokers

Every swing trader needs to have a broker, but not every type of broker can be helpful in executing your trades. That's why, as a beginner, you need to learn how to find and how to deal with a broker.

First, let's go over the two major classes of brokers that swing traders tend to choose:

o Discount Brokers

This type specializes in executing trades. All you have to do is relay to them what you want to buy or sell, and they would do it for you. Nowadays, this is normally via the Internet rather than over the phone. Take note that most discount brokers offer limited services only though some do provide free services to their clients, such as bank-related services and research work.

o Direct Access Firms

If you want to have more control and trade directly with the market, you should consider hooking up with a direct access firm. Through this, you would be able to see the shares of a security that are being offered, as well as the bids for the said shares. Choosing which exchange or market maker you wish to trade with is also possible with the help of a direct access firm.

As you can see, selecting which type suits you best depends on the kind of services that you are expecting from a broker, as well as the acceptable cost of broker's commissions for you.

Full-service brokers, such as Merrill Lynch Wealth Management and Morgan Stanley, are not exactly recommended for swing traders, such as. Yes, they are more involved with their clients, and their wide range of services can be quite appealing, especially for beginners. However, all of that comes with a hefty price tag.

Furthermore, swing traders who are heavily reliant on the advice of others about which securities to trade are not exactly doing swing trading the right way. After all, having the capacity to be independent is one of the qualities of a good swing trader.

To help you find a suitable broker for you, consider looking for one at these online resources:

- o Charles Schwab
www.schwab.com

- o E*TRADE Financial
www.etrade.com

- o Fidelity Active Trader
www.fidelity.com

- o Interactive Brokers
www.interactivebrokers.com

- o TD Ameritrade
www.tdameritrade.com

In order to evaluate your prospects for a broker, consider the following factors before making your choice:

- o Commission Rate

As a personal rule, the commission rate of a broker should not exceed a $10 flat fee. If the rate is per share, it should not be more than 1 to 2 cents. Anything higher than these caps would increase your target returns as well.

- Range

For the purpose of diversifying your portfolio, look for a broker who can handle multiple types of asset classes. Take note, however, that the wider range comes with a higher price tag so keep in mind what you plan to trade and try to stick to those asset classes.

- User-Friendliness

This refers to how easy it is to use the broker's trading website or software interface. The best way to determine this is to actually try using the website or the demo version of the software yourself.

Ask yourself if entering orders can be done without much fuss. If market data gathering is one of the services of your broker, check if watching the market could be done without having to go through hoops.

- Customer Service

The broker's responsiveness to the query and concerns of the clients should be one of the most important evaluation points for you. After all, when things don't go your way in the market, you would want to have someone to help you as soon as possible.

Though you can only truly verify the quality of customer service by opening an account with the broker, you can read through the broker rankings compiled by reliable sources, such as StockBrokers.com and Kiplinger.com, to get an idea of how well their customer service is rated by the actual clients and trading experts.

- Bank-Related Services

These usually include the provision of a dedicated ATM card for your portfolio, online transfer of assets, and writing of checks from your account. If such services are vital to you, then your ideal broker should be able to them as well.

○ Documentation and Analysis

A broker who can handle these for you would be a great time-saver, especially for tax-related paperwork. Beginners would also benefit from portfolio analysis done by professional brokers, especially since it usually takes some time to understand the various indices that are used to compare your performance.

○ Amenities

Common amenities offered by brokers to their clients are research services, stock reports, and charting programs. With regards to research, swing traders don't really avail them because those are generally about long-term trading opportunities, which are not really that useful for swing trading.

Once you have chosen your broker, your next step is to open an account. There are 4 major types to choose from: cash account, margin account, traditional brokerage account, and retirement account.

Which one should you choose?

Basically, your choice depends on what you intend to do. For example, do you plan to borrow your trading money from the broker?

Cash accounts will limit you to the amount of cash that you currently have in your account. On the other hand, margin accounts enable traders to borrow money to invest from the brokers.

Take note, however, that the amount of money you could borrow cannot exceed the amount of cash you have in your margin account. That means if you have $20,000 in your margin account, the most you could borrow from the broker for your trade is $20,000 as well.

Beginner traders should avoid opening margin accounts. Investing the money that is technically not yours tends to lead to gambling with riskier securities and strategies. As much as possible, stick with trading the current assets that you own rather than exploring the market with money that isn't yours. If you are after a convenient access to your money, then traditional brokerage accounts would give this to you. However, particularly in the US, choosing this type would turn your profits into taxable income unless the IRS (Internal Revenue Service) officially classifies you as a full-time trader. You may be able to avoid taxes by opening a retirement account, but that would seriously limit the amount of money you could deposit into the account per year, as well as the amount of money that you could withdraw without triggering the penalties.

B. Service Providers

Traders rely on various types of service providers, especially those that offer access to a key database or charting. Here are some of the most useful ones that you should do business with as a swing trader:

o Technical Software

Good charting software is an essential companion of every swing trader.

If you plan to trade intraday, then the software should be able to incorporate quotes and charts that are updated on a real-time basis. However, if you are a part-time swing trader who only enters orders after the market has closed for the day, then a real-time chart is not important to have.

To guide you on finding a technical software that is easy to use, check out the charting services offered by the following popular service providers:

- Active Trade Pro

www.fidelity.com

- E*Trade Pro

www.etrade.com

- TradeStation

www.tradestation.com

○ Database

The newspaper "Investor's Business Daily" is a great resource for those seeking fundamental data about a large collection of stocks. The finance section of Reuters.com also offers data about the overall market, as well as comparisons between one company to another.

Staying up-to-date with the latest financial and market news may also be possible through the help of news-focused service providers. While you can set alerts in the trading software you are using to inform you of the changes happening in securities, keeping tabs on what is occurring in the market is essential for making smart trading decisions. Here are a couple of recommended sources of financial and market news:

○ MarketWatch

Introduced by the Dow Jones & Company, this website is useful in monitoring the pulse of various markets. Aside from the latest news about the stock market, financial updates, and business developments, it also offers financial advice to its users, as well as stock market quotes.

○ Investing.com

For real-time news, charts, and an economic calendar, visit this website on a regular basis. It is also known among traders for its various tools and calculators, as well as in-depth posts about commodities, currencies, futures, and options, just to name a few.

○ Real Vision TV

First things first: to get full access to information from this source, you need to pay for a subscription. It does offer a free 1-week trial for only $1 so that you can decide if this is their content that is useful for you as a swing trader.

To give you a better idea of what to expect, here is a quick rundown of what to expect from this website:

- Videos of talks and interviews done by experts in trading, investments, and economics
- Popular topics covered include interest rates, currencies, and equity markets.
- Provides access to debates among experts regarding new issues or innovations in the trading world
- Offers content for any type of trader

For traders who want to engage with the forex market, there are plenty of dedicated resources that you can tap into in order to get a better idea of what's going on there. Here are some of the most recommended resources for both beginners and more experienced traders alike:

- FXStreet

A large portion of forex traders considers this as the top resource when it comes to reliable news and updates. This website covers a wide range of topics and currencies, including controversial cryptocurrencies.

Much of the articles posted here are from the FXStreet team itself. However, you may also find every now and then some content made by trading brokers and even banks every now and then.

- Forex Factory

This website provides real-time forex news that is aggregated from other news sites. As such, you may expect to get more comprehensive updates about foreign currencies from their posts.

The tagging system of Forex Factory is also incredibly useful, especially for swing traders. High-impact news posts are marked in red, the medium-impact ones are in orange, while the low-impact updates bear the color yellow.

- o DailyFX

This is one of the most popular websites among forex traders because of its excellent posts about market analysis. Furthermore, they are known for supporting their posts with a technical analysis, which you could use as reference points for your trading strategies.

DailyFX also touches on whether the forex market is in bull or bear mode. They do this by sharing the percentage of traders who are either buying or selling on certain currency pairs.

- o BabyPips

Beginners would benefit greatly from this website since they are more known for producing educational posts about the forex market. They also provide a forum so that traders could interact and exchange their opinions and advice with one another.

Aside from educational materials, BabyPips also post forex articles, though the majority of what they release are based on the US dollar. Aside from articles, the website also posts a forecast for the week every Monday, while their Fridays are reserved for the weekly review of various currencies.

A word of caution though. Not all service providers for traders can be beneficial for you. Some may even cause havoc in your portfolio and prevent you from making good trades. For example, avoid checking message boards about stock investments, such as those found in Reddit forums. While it is tempting to connect with other traders, the information available there is unreliable and often based on subjective experiences that would likely not apply to you as well. Newsletters that give out recommendations on which stocks to buy or sell are not exactly helpful for traders in general. Yes, they might be market experts who really do know what's going on. However, simply listening to their suggestions and acting upon them might cause you to follow blindly a piece of advice that will ultimately be bad for you.

In the long run, it is better for traders should learn how to think independently. You may refer to newsletters if their content deals more with the overall picture of the market or an industry-level analysis. That could actually serve as your guide when making your trades later on.

   C. Trading Journal
Continual improvement is one of the keys to becoming a successful swing trader. However, honing your skills without basing them on your previous performance is like going on a journey without any map or guide. You would likely make the same mistakes over and over again, and as the saying goes, that's insanity.

One of the best tools a trader should have in order to achieve continually is a trading journal. It is basically a record of every single trade that you have made.

A good journal entry is concise but meaningful in the sense that by just reading through it, you would be able to understand the following:
- how you found the trade in the first place
- the name and a brief description of the position that you have traded
- triggers that made you enter that trade
- technical indicators that you have gotten from the charts that you have reviewed before making your entry
- the reason for your exit, preferably accompanied by a relevant chart of the given security
- the return rate after you have made your exit

You are free to add more elements to your trading journal, as long as you could commit to updating your entries in a timely manner. For example, some traders prefer to add the size of the position and chart of the overall market so that they could refer back to these data points before making decisions about entering a trade. However, that would naturally increase the amount of time and effort that you need to exert in order to create a journal entry.

Therefore, the key to successfully keeping a trading journal is to balance between being informative and being convenient. During your first days as a swing trader, try out different formats for your journal entries until you find one that would be useful and sustainable for you.

Chapter 7: Developing Your Trading Approach, Style, and Strategy

Your approach, style, and strategy as a trader would influence how you find and handle promising trading opportunities. In this chapter, you will learn about the two general scope approaches—top-down and bottom-up, the two main trading styles—discretionary and mechanical, and the two primary trading strategies—technical analysis and fundamental analysis. Your main goal at this point is to determine which of these would suit your interests, preferences, and skill level.

    A. Top-Down Approach vs. Bottom-Up Approach
If you plan to follow the top-down approach, you need to find securities with good earning potential by starting at the macro level and industry group level and then narrowing it down to the company level.

However, if you look for promising securities first before screening them according to the performance of the respective industry groups where they belong to and macro-level fundamentals, you are doing the bottom-up approach.

You might be wondering if one of these approaches is better than the other. Most trading experts say no, but you do have to select only one of the two instead of trying to do both. Since either approach is useful for swing trading, your choice would all boil down to your personal preferences and skill level as a trader.

Take note that you have to combine a top-down approach or bottom-up approach with any trading strategy that you would decide on for yourself. For example, those who choose the top-down approach should analyze industry chart patterns to recognize which of the stocks are strong. Further investigation about the companies' fundamentals must then be conducted to determine which one of them must be bought or shorted.

On the other hand, a bottom-up trader would greatly benefit from fundamental screens to find undervalued securities. Once found, they can then analyze chart patterns to verify if those securities are strong or weak.

B. Discretionary Style vs. Mechanical Style

Traders who evaluate the potential of trade against their trading plan follow the discretionary style. Whether they use technical analysis or fundamental analysis to do so isn't the main point. Discretionary swing traders could use either or both strategies as long as their evaluation criteria are based on the predetermined trading plan.

However, swing traders following this style are not exactly bound by the rules that are set in the trading plan. They still factor in their previous experiences and gut feel at times to finalize their decision about a particular trade.

Because of this, the main advantage of the discretionary trading style arises when analyzing a set of data from another perspective that could not be captured by most trading software programs. This is a double-edged sword though.

Since traders themselves decide on whether to take or pass on trades, there is a chance that emotions might come into play, thus violating one of the most important rules of trading. Those who succumb to this and become emotionally attached to their trades usually end up ignoring their trade plan altogether.

To avoid such shortcomings, consider following the mechanical trading style instead. To do this, you have to use strategies that could be executed by a trading software program. These may include technical indicators, as well as fundamental data points, such as the company's rate of sales growth.

Once the information has been inputted, the software would process it based on other historical market data. The output will then be analyzed by the swing trader to determine if the strategy that has been tested by the software is worth pursuing.

As you can see, the mechanical trading style removes as much human interference as possible. The trader's inputs will be limited to the capital allocation for the positions, the signals for entry, and the rules for an exit. As for the rest of the analysis, the computer program shall handle them on its own.

Unfortunately, there is no trading software that has been proven to capture all the events or conditions that could arise from the trades. Furthermore, a lot of swing traders do not like relying completely on computer programs to evaluate their trades. As such, the majority still prefer using the discretionary style to evaluate the potential of trades.

No matter which approach or style you decide to follow, the two main trading strategies may be used to examine securities. Swing traders, especially beginners, mostly lean towards technical analysis than fundamental analysis. Why?

The answer can be summed up in two words: "convenience" and "objectivity".

Technical analysis does not require as much effort as fundamental analysis, wherein you would have to consider the companies' industry dynamics, management structures, competitors, just to name a few. All these pieces of information, however, can still lead to an inaccurate conclusion because they are less subjective compared to chart patterns and technical indicators.

Fundamental analysis is far more popular among buy-and-hold investors, too. After all, there is no assurance that the shares of an undervalued company would rise in value within the next few days. In some cases, it can take up to months or even years before a reasonable return can be achieved.

Still, some trading experts recommend combining the two strategies in order to come up with a more holistic understanding of the trade. Each method has its own drawbacks that may be addressed by the other. Fundamentals could also provide more context to technical indicators, thereby allowing traders to understand what is driving the price movements in the market.

You don't necessarily have to integrate technical analysis with fundamental analysis though, especially if you are just doing it for the sake of it. Remember, you should base your decision about your trading strategy on your personal preference and skills.

To help you determine if technical analysis or fundamental analysis is suitable for you, let's go over each strategy in greater detail.

- Technical Analysis

Though its name may sound intimidating for beginner traders, this strategy can actually be as simple as interpreting chart patterns to identify the direction of securities. If you could learn how to do this, then you may be able to work up your way to more complex analysis, like Intermarket evaluations, later on.

In general, traders use technical analysis to determine the following points:

- o If the security is trending or in a trading range
- o If the market will be in a bull or bear mode and how that would affect the security
- o If the buyers or sellers are in control of the market
- o If the controlling party's strength is increasing or decreasing
- o If a reversal or failure is imminent
- o The entry and exit signals to watch out for

Given these, here are the main advantages of technical analysis:

- o Can be used to quickly analyze an individual security
- o It may be applied in a consistent manner across different markets and time
- o Can indicate the level of rationality of buyers and sellers

- It may be used to determine the support levels and resistance levels that would signal entries and exits
- Minimizes the subjectivity of the traders when analyzing charts

On the flip side, here are the drawbacks of technical analysis:
- Always assumes that the market is right
- Does not factor in the fundamentals of security and major events of the company
- Includes irrational traders in the analysis

Despite these shortcomings, technical analysis remains to be the preferred choice of a large majority of swing traders. It has been proven to be effective in providing insights about how prices would move in the future.

But how does this strategy actually work? In general, the technical analysis relies on two components: charts and technical indicators.

Analyzing securities using chart patterns is appealing for many because it is relatively easy to do. Many traders, even those who primarily rely on fundamentals, refer to stock charts before buying. There are several types of charts that swing traders can use, but the most popular ones are the bar charts, candlestick charts, and line charts.

Technical indicators, on the other hand, are primarily used by traders to determine the right direction for them to take. To use them, you must first apply them to security prices before analyzing the strength of particular security against the overall market.

These two aspects of technical analysis will be discussed further in later chapters of the book.

- Fundamental Analysis

This strategy is mostly concerned about the value of the company compared to its peers, as well as the company's growth rate and returns. If traders know these data points, they would be able to have a better idea about the reasonable prices for the shares of a particular company.

For instance, traders are more willing to pay more for the shares of a company that has higher earnings. They rationalize this by expecting that the company's future earnings would also be good.

Swing traders don't usually use this strategy because such expectations may take a long period of time to be realized. Still, this method does have its own merits—some of which address the shortcomings of technical analysis.

- o Provides an estimate of a company's intrinsic value instead of just its market value
- o Takes into account the effects of industry and market events that could affect security prices
- o Allows assumptions that the market could be wrong sometimes

As you can see, most of the advantages of fundamental analysis revolve around its ability to determine the actual worth of a company. That could be quite useful for swing traders because, as explained earlier in this book, it tells them if the price movements in the market are actually driven by the company's fundamentals rather than just by mere market noise.

On the other hand, the drawbacks of fundamental analysis are mostly due to its nature as a trading strategy.

- o More subjective because it hinges upon the ability of the trader to interpret the information at hand
- o Cannot be used to determine where assumptions went wrong upon exiting a trade
- o Tends to be less accurate when used for short-term analysis

About the last point, swing traders who use fundamental analysis make up for this by analyzing catalysts—or the internal or external events that could influence the short-term price movements as well as the market value of a company's shares. Examples of catalysts are corporate mergers, earnings dates, acquisitions, and the release of new products. Given what you have learned in this chapter, start reflecting on which of the various types of trading approaches, styles, and strategies. Don't worry though if you cannot make up your mind yet. The next chapters shall continue the discussion about how they work as a means of analyzing the market.

Chapter 8: Getting to Know Stock Charts

Traders use charts to study the relationship between the price and volume. Though the price is usually considered more important when making a decision, the volume demonstrates the commitment of buyers and sellers. As such, understanding how each chart component affects one another could tell you when to enter or exit a trade.

While reading charts is an easy skill to gain, it does require you to learn not just one type of chart but at least the four main types: bar chart, candlestick chart, line chart, and P&F (point and figure) chart.

A lot of swing traders favor using the candlestick chart because they find it to be the most informative type. They show patterns that can be used to determine your entries and exits. However, line charts and bar charts are considered as the most commonly used ones, while the less common P&F charts can be quite useful in filtering out unnecessary data points.

It is never wise to just rely on a single type so let's go over each type of chart and how they are used in technical analysis. Discussions of how to interpret the chart patterns shall be covered in the next few chapters of this book.

- Bar Chart

Bar charts show a security's open, high, low, and close. As such, it is also known as the OHLC bar chart. It may be used to showcase information on an hourly, daily, weekly, or monthly basis.

A standard bar chart is composed of two horizontal lines that protrude from the bar signals. The one on the left is the opening price of the security, while the one on the right indicates the closing price. Meanwhile, the top and bottom of the bar show the highs and lows of the period.

- Candlestick Chart

Just like a bar chart, this type also indicates the open, high, low, and close of securities, but because of its two components—the real body and the shadows—it presents information in a clearer manner. The real body is the range that exists between the open and close, while the shadows demonstrate the price movements.

If the closing of security is higher than its opening during that particular period, the real body tends to be light in color. On the other hand, the body becomes dark in color if the closing is lower than the opening. In case that the security opens and closes at the same level, the body becomes a horizontal line only, though shadows in the upper and lower parts remain.

- o Line Chart

The lines in this chart show the connections of closes from a certain period to the next. While many use this because it is simple to understand, a line chart does not actually say much even though it does highlight the closing price for the day—which, for many, is one of the most important pieces of information to remember.

First, it cannot be used to find out where the security has opened for the given day since its focus is on the closes. The highs and lows of each period cannot also be determined by looking at a line chart.

- o P&F Chart

This chart type can filter out market noise—which refers to price movements that are not really important for traders. However, their main drawback can be seen when the given security did not have any significant price movements for several days.

A P&F chart is composed of Xs and Os. Rising price movements are indicated by a column of X's, while O's show falling price movements. Its ability to screen information is possible because new X's and O's can only be added to the chart if the price movement meets a pre-determined amount. As mentioned earlier, charts depict the relationship between price and volume. However, rather than just showing a single point, charts can actually showcase the four different phases of the natural cycle of securities.

Learning how this cycle goes is important because the different phases denote the need for a different trading strategy. Therefore, let's take the time to discuss each phase and how you could recognize them in charts.

A. Accumulation Phase

This is normally the longest phase-out of the four. At this point, there is no meaningful movement in the price of a security. As such, you will not see any significant rise or fall, just sideway movements through time.

During this phase, a balance between the supply and demand is being maintained most of the time. Smart money—which pertains to money that is being invested by people who have extensive knowledge about the industry—tend to gather more shares of undervalued security.

Because almost everyone in the market agrees that the price of the security is accurate, the volume during the accumulation phase is typically light. Prices cannot be pushed further than a ceiling—or a resistance level—by the buyers, and cannot be pushed lower than a floor—or a support level.

Ceilings and floors cannot be predicted accurately, but they can be easily spotted in price charts, where they are shown as price levels that securities couldn't rise above or fall below.

B. Expansion Phase

Also referred to as the markup phase, this is best described as a period where prices begin to increase. Because of this, swing traders who trade trends take long positions as soon as securities reach this phase. This can last for multiple days or even weeks, so the earlier you buy the more opportunities to profit you will get.

Stocks usually expand when the outlook for the earnings of a company is expected to improve. For example, the successful launch of new iPhones of Apple has led to a steady rise in their share prices.

You can easily see in a chart if security has truly reached the expansion phase—that is the volume becomes strong. If the volume is weak, that means that the increase will be short-lived due to the lack of conviction from the buyers. This indicates that the security will likely fall back to its price when it was in the accumulation phase.

C. Distribution Phase

This phase indicates that the share prices have started to even out again. Experienced traders know that this is a signal to either exit their long positions or enter short positions.

On the other hand, beginner traders are often fooled into buying during the distribution phase because they have mistaken it for the accumulation phase. This usually occurs when the news of a good investment opportunity only reached them after everyone else also knew about it. In reality, the expansion phase is already nearing its end, and share prices are about to drop again instead of continually rise.

To differentiate the accumulation phase from the distribution phase, you must:

- Observe if there is mark-up or mark-down before the phase that you are looking at. The former denotes a distribution phase, while the latter indicates that it is an accumulation phase.
- Check out the fundamentals of security. Normally, if the fundamentals are on the strong side, then that is an accumulation phase.

Other signs of a distribution phase may be given by the companies themselves. For example, if they know that their shares are overpriced, they tend to open to the public a secondary offering of new stocks.

D. Contraction Phase

A security's natural cycle ends with the contraction phase, or also known as the markdown phase. This is depicted in charts as a series of highs and lows that are lower than the other three phases. As such, sellers who short benefit the most at this time.

Be extra cautious with securities that have entered this phase. Many traders, especially beginners, make the mistake of buying securities that have fallen in price but have not yet reached their true bottom.

The price decline does not happen in a steady fashion. You might be thinking that security has already hit its lowest point, only to realize later on that it could drop to a new low.

Why would buyers even consider such securities in the first place?

Known by many as "bottom fishing", this phenomenon stems from the idea that you will be profiting from the all-time-low prices, especially once the cycle renews itself. Plus, there is a certain psychological pleasure experienced when you buy something that used to be more expensive for a much lower price now.

Unfortunately, the rise of securities happens at a slower rate than their fall. A security may lose its gains for the past months in just a matter of days, but as discussed earlier, the accumulation phase lasts for a long period of time.

Remember as well that security prices rise due to the greed of buyers, but they decline when fear starts to set in. Since fear tends to be stronger than feelings of want, it affects traders at a much faster pace. As a result, fear-stricken traders sell as fast as they could.

Security rallies during the contraction phase is a normal movement, but it is not a sign for traders to buy. Instead, they are signs for the short sellers' entry points.

The best way to go about the contraction phase is to wait until it is over. Better yet, before making your move, wait until the security is either in its accumulation phase again or is about to enter the expansion phase. By doing so, you would be able to ensure that your next trades will go along the direction of the overall market.

Now that you have a better idea of what charts are in the world of trading, let's proceed to the next chapter and discuss how to make sense of chart patterns.

Chapter 9: Understanding Chart Patterns and Trendlines

To be perfectly honest, chart patterns have received skepticism from the academic side of trading. After all, seeing shapes and sequences can be a subjective observation, especially when the reader isn't even quite sure if the pattern actually exists or if it is just a product of one's overactive imagination.

Nonetheless, many trading experts consider the skill of reading chart patterns as essential to be successful in whichever type of trading you plan to engage in.

While computer programs may be created to look out for patterns, it is quite difficult to establish systematic and consistent rules for them to follow. Therefore, experienced traders know that to reduce the probability of making a purely subjective reading of a chart, they only seek out the five major patterns: cup and handle, Darvas box, gaps, head and shoulders, and triangles.

Yes, other chart patterns exist, but these five types are the most commonly seen and used by traders. To better understand how they could help you interpret a chart, let's go over each major type of pattern.

A. Cup and Handle Pattern

This chart pattern indicates that the security is on the verge of a rising movement as the shares continue to accumulate. Since it is technically a continuation formation, it must be followed immediately by an uptrend.

The formation of this pattern happens once the shares start to rally to form a peak. Then, shares will be brought down by 10% to 20% from the peak by sellers either due to a fundamental or technical reason.

Inexperienced traders who bought shares during this time would think they have made a mistake. As such, they usually want to sell as soon as they have reached a breakeven.

The thing is, the shares they bought near the peak would give them the opportunity to do so once the said shares begin to rally again back to the peak. After the mass selling of the inexperienced traders, a resistance level will be created, thus preventing the shares to go higher than the current peak.

Still, the shares do not drop down to the previous low because smart money would start to accumulate at a small discount. At most, the fall of shares is going to be around 5%.

The shares will then have a second attempt to break through and surpass the peak. If the volume is sufficiently heavy, the full cup and handle pattern would be realized.
Take note that the cup and handle pattern is not considered to be as reliable as the head and shoulders pattern. There are times when it would show a false breakout instead.
To keep yourself from falling into this trap, double-check the current performance of the overall market and industry group to where the security belongs to. If the overall market and industry group is strong, then the breakout is more likely to be genuine. Otherwise, there is a high probability that cup and pattern formation will fail.
    B. Darvas Box
This chart pattern is introduced by Nicholas Darvas, a professional ballroom dancer who developed his personal trading system by reading investment books during his spare time. His development as a trader over the years allowed him to turn $25,000 to over $2.2 million within a span of 18 months.

As the name implies, the Darvas box is used to show that the price of securities usually trades between the support level and resistance level before passing through a certain price level and then either rallying or falling from then on. If you would remember from the previous chapter, this indicates the securities are in their accumulation phase.

Through this rectangular-shaped pattern, Darvas highlighted the following observations. A support level indicates the price point wherein buyers decided to buy shares, thus keeping the price of the security from decreasing. On other hand, a resistance level shows where sellers started to sell shares, thereby preventing the security price from increasing. In line with these rules, any security that doesn't follow this would be automatically ignored by Darvas.

Once a security has been identified to be trading between the support level and resistance level, the waiting game would commence for Darvas. He would bide his time until the security had breached through the upper band with a heavy volume.

At that point, Darvas would buy the security. A stop-loss order will be placed under the support level of the rectangle. In case that a new rectangle would appear because the security had risen, the stop loss level will be adjusted accordingly to the new support level indicated by the rectangular pattern.

The Darvas box may be useful for short sellers, too. Basically, all they have to do is reverse the original rules for this chart pattern. If a security that has been trading between the two levels breaks through and goes below the support level, then it is time to short.

A stop loss level will be established on top of the said support level, but if a Darvas box forms below that, they would also move the stop loss to the upper part of the new resistance level.

C. Gaps
Breaks in price continuity may be represented by gaps in the chart. For instance, the trading range of a particular security is in the $24 to $25 range, but with a gap up to $30.

There are four types of gaps to look out for:
a. Common Gaps
These are gaps up or down in prices that appear and then disappear when the gap becomes filled in after a few days.

When this occurs, the price just returns to its original level before the gap has appeared.

Common gaps are essentially meaningless to traders, and therefore should not be used as a signal to trade. Their volume is normally light, so they do not reflect the convictions of either buyers or sellers.

b. Breakaway Gaps

If there are major changes happening in the security, a breakaway gap will appear. You can easily spot them because their volume is so heavy that it is usually twice the average daily volume. The percentage also increases or decreases significantly.

A congestion period precedes the occurrence of a breakaway gap. During that time, the price level where the security has been trading at for weeks or months suddenly shoots up or down in just one day. This rather violent movement reflects how the value of a security has changed among investors.

Swing traders should still exercise caution when it comes to breakaway gaps. After all, many things could still happen after it has occurred. However, once you have confirmed that the breakaway gap is true, you should try to buy or sell as soon as you can.

c. Continuation Gaps

As the name suggests, this type of gap indicates the continuation of the previous trend while security is in either an uptrend or a downtrend.

Some swing traders use continuation gaps as a reference point in estimating how far the price levels of a security will move. By looking at how much the price has appreciated or depreciated prior to the continuation gap, they try to project how far the trend will go from then on.

Unfortunately, experts say that doing so could be somewhat subjective. So rather than this, they suggest analyzing what will happen if you buy or sell depending on the direction of the gap.

Then, check if whether or not shares will return to fill that gap after you have placed a protective stop loss within the said gap. If they did not, then what you have there is a true continuation gap.

d. Exhaustion Gaps
This gap signals the end of a trend. Some mistake this for a continuation gap. However, as explained earlier, shares do not fill a continuation gap, but they do for an exhaustion gap. Ultimately, this type of gap does not prompt any action from a swing trader.

D. Head and Shoulders Pattern
This is widely considered as one of the most reliable chart patterns among traders. Even the Federal Reserve Bank of New York agrees with this observation. In one of their articles entitled "Head and Shoulders: Not Just a Flaky Pattern", they stated that this pattern has repeatedly shown a certain level of being predictive, thereby allowing its users to earn profits in some markets.

The head and shoulders pattern signals the end of an uptrend. It is characterized by three "hills". The left and right sides are almost of the same height, while the middle hill is the tallest, thus giving the pattern its recognizable head-and-shoulder shape.

E. Triangle patterns
This chart pattern demonstrates the competing relationship between the buyers and sellers. Depending on the situation in the market, one party would have the upper hand over the other—though there are still times when both are in a stalemate.

Given this, triangle patterns highlight the so-called measurement movements in the market. This may be used by traders to gain an estimate of how far the current trend will go after it has broken out of the triangle formation. Let's discuss how you could do that by going over the three main types of triangles:

a. Ascending

This triangle pattern forms when the buyers are strong and steady while the sellers continually get weaker.

In this scenario, the buyers push the shares back every time the sellers try to bring the prices down. This attempt to push back the prices, however, always ends up higher than the previous one. If the buyers continue to overwhelm the sellers, the security will then break in an upward manner.

To measure how far the prices will move upon breaking out, add the height of the triangle—or the vertical part that exists between the support levels and the resistance levels—to the breakout price level of the security.

b. Descending

As its name implies, this is basically the direct inverse of the ascending triangle. Sellers are able to maintain their strength as buyers grow steadily weaker.

In charts, you will see these dynamics as a series of falling prices that are followed by rallies that end in lower peaks than the previous one. At some point, the buying pressure will lose power, thereby giving way to a downward break of prices.

Price movements after this breakout may be determined by deducting the height of the triangle from the breakout price level.

c. Symmetrical

This pattern appears if the buyers and sellers are evenly matched. The rallies end at a lower point than the previous one, while the declines stop higher than their past troughs.

In such cases, there is no easy way to tell which party will win. However, you may expect the price movement to continue along the direction that the trend has taken before the symmetrical triangle has appeared.

Estimating the price movement may be done by either adding to or subtracting from—depending on how the prices break—the height of the triangle from the breakout level. Regardless of which type of triangle pattern appears on the chart, keep your eye on the actual volume of the breakout to determine if the breakout is true or false.

In terms of trading, it is best to stick with either ascending or descending patterns since you are certain about which direction the breakout will be taking. Symmetrical triangles are riskier, so avoid them as much as possible.

The patterns that appear in candlestick charts are quite distinctive so they deserve a separate section. There are several variations to look out for, but the following four pattern formations are the ones considered by many traders as the easiest to recognize and the most accurate in terms of signaling changes or continuation of trends.

   1. Hammer

This signifies the bottom of a given trend because it appears at the of a downtrend. This means that after a security price has been opened, the sellers in the market have brought it down. Buyers, on the other hand, should have recouped a large portion of their losses by the end of the day.

The real bodies of the hammer are small in the upper part of a candlestick bar. Meanwhile, their lowers shadows are long, and if they have any, their upper shadows are small.

Hammers must always have a confirmation. It is better to see one that goes even lower than the latest price action. Otherwise, you may disregard that hammer for being an unreliable indicator of the trend's bottom.

Another way to confirm hammers is through volume. True hammers are formed on heavy volume. Those that don't, cannot be considered genuine.

2. The Hanging Man

Though the name sounds intimidating, this chart pattern is quite bland. Though it looks similar to a hammer, it appears at the end of an uptrend instead of a downtrend.

To confirm if what you are seeing is a genuine one, check if it emerged on heavy volume and if it's high will not be breached through by the subsequent price action. If these conditions are not met, then the signal you have observed is false.

3. Bullish Engulfing Pattern

This chart pattern involves two candlestick bars each. A bullish engulfing pattern may be observed if the opening of a candlestick bar is lower than the closing of the previous candlestick bar and if the closing of that same candlestick bar is higher than the opening of the previous candlestick bar.

Looking at this in a chart, you will notice how it starts with a candlestick bar with a small real body. This is then followed by another candlestick bar that has a body that engulfs the real body of the previous candlestick bar.

What does this pattern exactly mean though?

A bullish engulfing pattern signifies a big "defeat" for the bears. By the time the second candlestick bar opens, sellers are already attempting to push down the prices until they become lower than how much they were when they closed the previous day.

However, this is thwarted when the buyers start buying in large quantities. As a result, the buyers manage to change the direction of the trend, they are able to increase the prices even higher compared to the previous day. All in all, it's an overwhelming victory for the buyers that day.

4. Bearing Engulfing Pattern

Like its counterpart, this pattern also involves two candlestick formations. The difference is that it occurs at the end of uptrends, thus indicating where important reversals happen.

The real body of the first candlestick bar is smaller than the second one. This reflects how the opening of the second candlestick is higher than the closing of the first candlestick, and how the closing of the second candlestick is lower than the opening of the first candlestick.

As always, remember to wait for confirmation first before proceeding with your plan to short a bearish engulfing pattern. There are some cases wherein this formation does not lead to decreased prices. You will know that you are dealing with a true bearish engulfing pattern if the prices declined after it occurred and it didn't surpass the bearish engulfing bar's high.

5. Morning Stars and Evening Stars

Both of these chart patterns are comprised of three candlestick bars. What distinguishes them from one another is where they can occur.

Basically, a morning star signals the end of a downtrend and the start of an uptrend. This reflects how the bears are in force before the reversal happened. Meanwhile, an evening star represents the end of an uptrend and the beginning of a downtrend. This demonstrates the last moments of the bulls before the change in trend has taken place.

How does each of these patterns appear on charts?

A morning star is made of the following:
- First Candlestick Bar

Has a long, dark body that pushes the downtrend to a lower point
- Second Candlestick Bar

Has a small body that gaps lower at the open

o Third Candlestick Bar

Has a white body that gaps higher than the second candlestick bar and closes near the upper part of the first candlestick bar

On the other hand, an evening star consists of:

o First Candlestick Bar

Has a long, white body that pushes the uptrend to a higher point

o Second Candlestick Bar

Has a small body that gaps higher at the open

o Third Candlestick Bar

Has a dark body that gaps lower than the second candlestick bar and closes near the lower part of the first candlestick bar

While these chart patterns could give you an insight into trends, they do not necessarily show the strength of the said trends. To measure this, traders make use of trendlines to analyze how different price points relate to one another depending on which kind of line will be formed: uptrend line, downtrend line, or horizontal line.

Take note that the conclusions that can be drawn through the use of trendlines are 100% accurate all the time. After all, there are plenty of gray areas in the market that could affect the validity of trendlines.

As a guide on how to tell if a trendline is valid or not, here are the three general rules about drawing trendlines:

1. A trendline must consist of three different price points. Going below this number would mean that you could basically draw a trendline anywhere in the chart.

2. The strength of the support or resistance of a particular trendline increases the more it gets touched.

If a break of a trendline has been tested multiple times, then it can be said that there is a major shift in the trend.

3. A trendline becomes more meaningful the longer it gets.

The length of a trendline is measured by time. This means that the true staying power of a trend is reflected by how long that trend has been going on.

Now, let's go over how you could use trendlines to enhance your ability to make successful trades.

A. Uptrend Lines

An uptrend line is drawn by connecting multiple lows, thus forming a support area for the buyers. It tells the rate of ascent—measured in dollars per period of time—that has been maintained by the buyers for a particular duration. As such, some swing traders use uptrend lines to determine their entry points for long positions.

While uptrend lines should be drawn through the lows, remember not to overdo this. It is okay if some prices have slightly intersected with the line, as long as the majority stays above the trendline.

B. Downtrend Lines

A series of peaks may be connected together by a downtrend line to mark the resistance area for sellers. Much like uptrend lines, a downtrend line offers more meaningful insight the longer it is and the more prices have touched it.

Be cautious when interpreting this though because a trendline break does not automatically means that a new trend will begin. Therefore, you should not immediately buy or short just because you have noticed a break in the trendline.

C. Horizontal Lines

These lines occur when the support level or resistance level has no or little movement. More often than not, only when these levels are breached could a new trend be developed.

In swing trading, you will encounter horizontal lines in certain chart patterns, such as the horizontal resistance level of ascending triangles, and the horizontal trendlines of support or resistance in a Darvas box.

As you have learned in this chapter, charting the market requires you to learn how to recognize patterns and examine if the said patterns are valid or not. These patterns are useful in guiding how you swing trade, but in order to come up with a well-rounded analysis of the market, you must also apply technical indicators and use them along with the chart patterns.

The next chapter covers the various technical indicators that every swing trader should know.

Chapter 10: Applying Technical Indicators

Back before the introduction of trading software programs and websites that could calculate technical indicators, traders would try to figure them out through manual calculation. Fortunately, there are several resources now that offer this service, many of which are free to use.

Given this, the aim of this chapter is not to teach you how to calculate technical indicators. Instead, we are going to discuss the right inputs that you need to get the technical indicator that you need, as well as how you could apply that technical indicator to market charts. The succeeding chapter to this one will cover how to analyze charts by combining these elements.

Before going through the nitty-gritty parts of understanding technical indicators, here are seven important reminders that you should remember throughout this chapter:

1. Technical indicators cannot be simply applied to every type of price charts.

For example, many amateur traders have a tendency of applying trending indicators to price charts even if they do not even know yet if the market is in a trend. As a result, they would get false signals about price movements towards either a support level or resistance level.

In reality, those movements are just fluctuations in prices. They are not signaling the start of a new trend.

Applying non-trending indicators can also lead to disastrous results when they are applied to a chart depicting a market in a trend. Traders would get false signals indicating either extreme levels of shares being overbought or oversold in the market.

How could one differentiate a trending market from its non-trending counterpart?

There are two ways you could go about this—either eyeball the chart or apply a technical indicator, such as the ADX (average directional index).

Eyeballing a chart requires you to go through the series of highs and lows, and check out if a pattern exists. To spot an uptrend, there must be a series of higher highs and higher lows. Conversely, a downtrend is characterized by a series of lower highs and lower lows.

If you do not see either of these patterns, check if there is a clear support area or resistance area. In case you find one, then you are dealing with a non-trending chart or a security that is in a trading range.

If you cannot recognize either the series or the areas, then it is best to avoid dealing further with that chart or security.

Going to the ADX, this indicator is used by many to determine the strength of a trend. Here are the probable readings that you could get by applying this indicator using a 14-day duration:
- 20 or below

The given security is in a trading range.
- Between 20 and 30

This is an ambiguous reading so you should examine further the direction of the ADX to figure out if the security is in a trend or not. If it is rising, then it means that the security is trending, but if it is falling, then the security is likely entering or is already in a trading range.
- 30 or higher

The security is trending.

2. Be careful when analyzing price swings.
There are instances wherein technical indicators fail to recognize significant price swings, thus rendering them essentially meaningless. There are also times when a price swing is just reflecting a data error or an unverified rumor.

Given these, traders should learn how to properly examine and judge price swings. You may also be able to better protect yourself from making mistakes by choosing indicators that do not incorporate data errors, as well as by using other technical tools such as chart patterns when making your analysis.

3. Take into account the volume as well.
While it is alright to use price as a sole basis of an indicator, doing so would not tell you about the commitment of other traders. To determine more accurately whether a movement is meaningful or not, consider the volume of security rises or falls as well.

Given this, experts recommend using at least one technical indicator that incorporates volume. Aside from commitment, analyzing the volume would also tell you more about the staying power of a particular trend.

4. The accuracy of a technical indicator does not reflect its value.
As discussed earlier, there is no technical indicator that can be accurate all the time. There are certain occurrences that could completely throw them off, thus giving traders a false signal instead.

A good example of this is a whipsaw. This pertains to violent price movements that inevitably happen every now and then.

With that said, don't judge a technical indicator based on its accuracy alone. Instead of focusing on the fruitless task of finding the perfect indicator, improve your risk management system instead so that you would be better protected when you receive false signals.

5. Try to limit yourself to two to three indicators per chart.
When using a trading software or website, you might be tempted to add as many indicators as you think you need because doing so can be done with just a click of the mouse. It may look like it would make things a lot easier for you, but

overdoing this could amplify the noise that could drown out the important pieces of information that you should be paying more attention to instead.

Furthermore, adding more indicators would reduce your chances of getting consistent signals. As a result, you might be led to think that you should not make any trades at all during that time.

Experts suggest limiting the number of indicators to three. Any more than that would not provide you insightful results.

   6. Your inputs should match your time horizon.
The time settings of almost all technical indicators may be adjusted according to the information you need out of them. For example, you can set the duration of a moving average to see changes in price within a short period of time. However, take note that the shorter the duration is, the more likely you would encounter whipsaws.

On the other hand, setting a longer duration for the moving average might turn it to become unresponsive. Yes, it may produce around two to three signals for a given year, but that would not be useful for swing traders who need to make trades within the following week.

   7. Look for divergences when doing technical analysis.
Divergences occur when the crowd in the market believes one side has the upper hand when, in reality, the opposite is true. As such, they can be used by traders to signify entry or entry points with lower risks than usual.

Using divergences leads to getting more accurate signals compared to most indicators. Even renowned technical analyst John Murphy declared that they can produce the strongest signals for traders.

However, divergences can be quite hard to spot, even for trading software programs. After all, recognizing one would require the keen eyes and interpretative mind of an experienced trader.

With these reminders under your belt, let's proceed to the ways on how you could recognize major trending technical indicators.

There are so many trending indicators to choose from, but I personally recommend the following three because of how useful they are for swing traders: DMI (Directional Movement Index), Moving Averages, and MACD (Moving Average Convergence/Divergence).

A. Directional Movement Index

This indicator is used to determine if a security is in a trend and if it is, the direction of the said trend. There are three DMI plots:

o +DMI (Positive Directional Movement Index)

This is used to indicate the effectiveness of buyers in pushing the prices beyond the high of the previous day. A high reading means that the buyers are strong.

o –DMI (Negative Directional Movement Index)

This shows the efficiency of sellers in pushing down the prices until they are under the low of the previous day. If you get a high reading, then it means that the sellers are strong.

o ADX (Average Directional Index)

Traders use this to measure the strength of a trend by highlighting the difference between the +DMI and –DMI. Swing traders analyze the crossovers between the +DMI and –DMI and use those as signals for trading. For example, the control of shares belongs to the bulls if the +DMI crosses above the –DMI. But if the –DMI crosses above the +DMI, it means that the bears have gotten the control. If the +DMI and –DMI frequently cross over one another, then you may say that neither the bulls nor the bears have the upper hand.

To maximize what you could get in return for using DMI, follow these steps:

1. Use an ADX plot to confirm if a trend is already in place.

2. In case a trend exists, use either moving averages or MACD to make an entry to a trade.
3. Incorporate the direction of +DMI or –DMI.
4. When the +DMI or –DMI crosses over the other, exit that trade.

B. Moving Averages

This is one of the most often used indicators by swing traders. Basically, it is designed to find out the underlying trend in a set of price data. There are two types of moving averages that you could choose from: simple moving averages, and EMA (exponential moving averages)

o Simple Moving Averages

This shows the consensus price agreement within the predetermined length of the moving average. For example, if prices increase more than their 14-day average, then you may say that traders and other market participants believe that the value of a particular security is going above the average within the 14-day period.

o Exponential Moving Averages

While this also indicates the consensus price agreement within a particular period of time, EMA weighs historical prices in a different manner—that is, more recent price action has a heavier weight than the older ones. Given this, EMA is more responsive than the simple moving averages. Unfortunately, this also increases the likelihood of getting false signals.

No matter which type of moving averages you use, the most important thing to look out for is the slope. If the moving average is rising, then the slope is positive. Conversely, the slope is negative if the moving average is falling. In case that the moving average is flat, then the slope is zero.

Traders should always make trades according to the direction of the slope. You should buy a security if the slope of the said security is positive. However, if you want to short security, then its slope must be negative.

Take note that completely basing your trades on a moving average would not be enough to ensure success. In general, a moving average tells you if it is time to make an entry. It won't tell you how much you should invest in a particular position, nor will it tell you where your stop loss should be or where you will take profits.

To guide beginners like you on how to use moving averages for swing trading, here are two strategies that you should try doing:

       o Using Slope Changes

          1. Set your moving average length.

If you are using a daily chart, a length of 18 days or lower is advisable.

          2. Look for a security that in a trend using the ADX indicator.

Go for one that is trending upwards.

          3. Buy the security once the flat or negative slope of the moving average becomes positive.

It is better to wait until the last 30 minutes of the market hours before doing this so that you would be sure that there won't any reversal in the slope change. If you are not watching the market intraday, then buy the security on the days after the slope change has occurred instead.

          4. Place your stop loss under the low of the day.

          5. When the moving average becomes flat or negative again, exit that trade.

       o Using Moving Averages Crossovers

          1. Use the eyeball method or ADX to check if a trend exists.

          2. If there is, use either of the same methods to confirm if a moving average crossover is aligned with the direction of that trend.

3. Once the short-term moving average crosses over the long-term moving average, buy the security.

4. Place your stop loss level below a recent low.

5. When the short-term moving average crosses under the long-term moving average, exit that security.

Using moving average crossovers allow swing traders to make earlier entries or exits compared to when they use slope changes. However, this added speed would open you up to more frequent occurrences of whipsaws so be extra careful when following this strategy.

C. Moving Average Convergence/Divergence

This bears similarities with the previous tending indicator. However, MACD has the added function of being able to tell not only the direction but also the intensity and strength of the buyers and sellers.

Generally speaking, MACD lines move according to the difference between the 12-day EMA and the 26-day EMA.
- The MACD line crosses above 0 if the shorter EMA crosses above the longer EMA.
- The MACD line crosses under 0 if the longer EMA crosses above the shorter EMA.

A moving average is also directly applied to the MACD, thus making it like the average of an average. A histogram is used to show the difference between the two.
- The strength of buyers is increasing if the histogram is rising.
- If the histogram is falling, then the sellers are becoming stronger.

Let's now discuss the three different trading signals that could be generated through the MACD:

a. Positive and Negative Divergences

If a security reached a new low but this movement is not reflected in the MACD histogram, then a positive divergence has occurred. This means that the strength of sellers is decreasing, and you may expect a change in trend soon.

Similarly, if the MACD histogram did not reflect a security's new high, then a negative divergence has developed. In this case, the buyers are losing their strength, and a trend change will happen in the near future.

      b. MACD Crossing Over Its Nine-Day Moving Average
Assuming that the market is in a trend, a buying signal is produced when the MACD Line crosses above the moving average. However, if the crossover happens below the moving average, then a selling signal will be generated.

      c. MACD Line Crossing on Top or Under the 0 Line
The results you will generate from this is just similar to what you get by basing your trades on the crossover of the 12-day EMA and 26-day EMA. This means that you would not exactly benefit from the advantages of MACD, so it is better to refer to the previous two trading signals.

Now, let's move on to the major non-trending indicators. Also known as oscillators, these are used to monitor the price swings in trading ranges.

More often than not, securities are in trading ranges. At this point, neither buyers nor sellers can make significant moves to push the prices. Buyers are in their support area, while sellers are in the resistance area, so a party's attempts to push prices to their favor are frequently rebuffed by the other party.

The non-trending indicators are grouped between the overbought and the oversold securities. Of these, there are two that are quite popular among swing traders: stochastics, and RSI (Relative Strength Index).

    A. Stochastics
This indicator is designed to compute the position of the day's close relative to a particular range that has been established over the specified period of time by the user. Basically, a

security is overbought if the day's close is higher than the range.

If a security is overbought, then there is a bigger chance that it will revert to its mean. Keep in mind that this does not mean that this expected change will occur immediately.

Stochastics are composed of the following:
- %K Plot

This is used to show where the current close is in relation to the highest high and lowest of a security's price within a specified period. Most swing traders use a 14-day period for stochastics.

- %D Plot

This indicates the average of the %K plot for the past three days.

Stochastics primarily generates two types of signals:

a. Positive and Negative Divergences

If the price of security falls to a new low but the stochastics indicator follows a higher trough, then a positive divergence has formed. This indicates that buyers are getting ready to push the prices while the sellers are exhausted.

On the other hand, a negative divergence occurs when the security prices have reached a new high but the stochastics indicator is found tracing a lower high. In this scenario, the buyers are the ones who are exhausted, and the sellers are preparing to push down the prices.

To use stochastics, follow these steps:

1. Check if there is an existing trading range with the use of either the eyeball approach or the ADX.

2. If there is, buy after a positive divergence has occurred—or shortly after a negative divergence has formed.

If you are entering a long position, do it only when the %K turns up above the %D. In case of the %D has turned up above the %K, enter a short position instead.

   b. Crossovers from above the overbought level or under the oversold level

Usually, charting programs measure overbought and oversold levels on an 80-20 basis. This means that if a price makes a move towards an extreme—whether it is the upper 20% or the lower % of the boundaries of the past price range—traders may expect this extreme to be reversed.

Inexperienced traders tend to buy securities that are in a trading range just because the stochastics is either overbought or oversold. Unfortunately, doing so would increase the occurrence of whipsaws.

The better trading strategy is to wait for the stochastics to exit the overbought or oversold level. More often than not, the stochastics will remain overbought or oversold for a longer period of time.

To use the overbought and oversold levels in trading, follow these steps:

   1. Confirm the existence of a trading range through the use of the eyeball approach or the ADX.

   2. Wait until %K has entered either the overbought or oversold level.

If it is through the overbought zone, short the security, but if it through the oversold zone, buy that security.

   3. Make your exit once stochastics has reached the opposite level, or after a certain number of days have passed, or after you have achieved your return target.

   B. Relative Strength Index

This oscillator is designed to compare a security unto itself. Through this, you would be able to determine if the price of a security is overbought or oversold. RSI can also create chart patterns that may be used to predict the direction of a breakout.

RSI works by examining a security's price history within a specified period—usually within 14 days. A comparison will be drawn between the average gain that has been achieved during the up days and the average loss experienced during the down days. The indicator will then be determined through the ratio between the average gains and the average losses.

RSI readings range from 0 to 100. Anything that is higher than 70 signals an overbought territory, while anything below 30 indicates an oversold area.

Let's go over how you could use the RSI indicator for swing trading:
  a. Positive and Negative Divergences
Divergences in RSI happens when there is a failure to confirm the new high or new low of a security's price.

As a rule, positive divergences should only be traded when RSI turns up. Conversely, if the RSI turns down, then negative divergences can be traded. Remember to check first if the trading range exists though.

  b. RSI-Developed Chart Patterns
Compared to trading based on overbought or oversold areas, referring to the RSI is considered to be the more reliable approach.

  c. Turning Down or Turning Up
This bears similarities with the process of using stochastics to trade overbought or oversold territories. Here are the steps on how to use these signals:
      1. Verify the existence of a trading range using the eyeball technique or the ADX.

2. Wait for the RSI indicator to breach through either the overbought or oversold area.

If the RSI enters the oversold area, you should buy the security. However, you should short instead if the RSI enters the overbought area.

3. Make your exit once the return target has been achieved, or after the RSI has reached the zone on the opposite side, or after a predetermined number of days have passed.

Combining these technical indicators with chart patterns help enhance the accuracy of your swing trades. To do this, you must evaluate trades according to what the charts and the indicators are saying. Only when both charts and indicators are saying the same thing should you take a trade.

A more thorough discussion about using patterns and technical indicators to analyze charts before trading trades or trading ranges can be found in the next chapter.

Chapter 11: Should You Trade Trends or Trading Ranges?

Traders generally gain profits by trading trends, trading ranges, or both. Prices that persistently move up or down becomes a trend. It may last from a few days up to years. On the other hand, trading ranges are characterized by securities that move only within defined price levels.

A large portion of swing traders goes for strong trends only. After all, the profits earned from trends tend to be higher compared to trading ranges.

Trends are also easier to manage for most traders. During an uptrend, for instance, you are assured that the price of the security will rise consistently. Even if it falls, the drop is pretty much negligible.

If you enter a trend within just a few days after it has started, then you don't have to worry a lot about risks. However, if the trend you have entered has been going on for weeks or months, then you are likely entering when every else is preparing to get off.

The problem with trading trends is that it can be tough to recognize when a new trend has started, and when to exit when the trend is nearing its end. As a swing trader, the latter issue matters more because you have to make a somewhat quick decision about whether or not to treat the signals as genuine—not as urgent as day traders, but you must certainly be agile and sensitive enough to successfully pull off your exits.

In comparison, swing traders who engage with trading ranges normally have a higher win ratio than those who exclusively trade trends. Why? Because when trading ranges, your objectives for profit and risk are easier to identify.

In terms of profit objective, all you need to look at is the other end of the range. For example, if you plan to short a stock that is priced at $30 per share, your objective in order to earn a profit is to cover that short near $20 per share.

Risks in trading ranges can be established easily too. If you have bought near $30 per share, you should exit once the stock goes below $29.

The biggest risk you will face when trading ranges is when the security starts developing a new trend. What you want instead is for a range to continue as it is. Once a new trend begins, your chances of being on the right of it are quite small.

Given all these, which of the two should you trade? If you can't choose between trends and trading ranges, it advisable for you to try trading both?

The thing is, there is no universal answer to the first question. Ultimately, it depends on what you want to get out of trading, and how much you are willing to risk when making your trades.

As for trading both, experts suggest leaving that for more experienced traders. You may eventually go for it, but make it a priority to understand trends and trading ranges first.

Those who can trade both do enjoy more opportunities to take advantage of the market. So, to upgrade yourself as a swing trader, aim to master trading trends and trading rangers as well.

To get you started on this, let's go over the proper ways to trade trends.

The first thing to do is look for strong trends. As discussed in earlier chapters, traders may follow either the top down or bottom up approach. Meanwhile, the strength of a trend may be assessed through the eyeball technique or technical indicators, such as ADX or DMI.

Once you have found strong trends that are worth your time and effort, your next step is to identify when to enter that trend. Getting this wrong will expose you to one of the biggest risks faced by swing traders: buying or shorting when a trend is nearing its end.

According to professional trader Ian Woodward, those who do not care about this risk are like dogs who are chasing after cars. At a glance, it may seem like a fun thing to do, but in reality, it is a reckless and dangerous thing to do.

What can you do to minimize the chances of making this mistake? Some check out the daily list of stocks reported by reputable finance newspapers, while others rely on security programs that are designed to recognize new highs and new lows. Here are some more helpful strategies that you should consider:

- Enter upon receiving a genuine signal

This may be based on a chart pattern or technical indicators. Usually, chart patterns are faster in giving out signals, but technical indicators are easier to interpret.

- Enter on a day of strength

Wait for the stock to develop three consecutive bars that indicate falling highs. Your entry should be made on the next bar that has a higher high than the previous one.

- Enter on a day of weakness

This works similarly to the one explained above, but instead of declining highs, wait for rising lows. Again, you should enter the succeeding bar that has a lower low than the previous bar. Having entered a trade, your next step is to manage your risk by establishing your exit level. This exact price depends on when you have made your entry. Here are the common types of exit mechanisms that swing traders use:

- Exit signal from a technical indicator

This means you are going to exit a trade on the break that falls below a moving average, or upon a crossover of MACD

- Exit level based on price

If you have entered a trade on a new peak, then you have to set an exit level that is in the trading range that the stock is coming from.

- Exit level based on time

This means exiting a trade after a certain number of days have elapsed. Setting this exit level shows that the exit price is not that important for the trader.

Now that you understand better to trade trends, let's proceed with trading ranges.

In general, looking for a security in a trading range is a tougher feat to accomplish than finding one that has new highs or new lows. As such, many swing traders rely on oscillators or the non-trending technical indicators to conduct their search, and to analyze when to enter and exit that security.

When identifying securities in a trading range, you must also consider their strength. This quality depends on the following factors:

- Time

Trading ranges that have existed for a long time upon discovery tend to continue going on for a longer period of time.

- Tests of Support and Resistance

The support levels and resistance levels grow stronger the more times a security touches them.

- Flat Ranges

This refers to how much a trading range looks like a rectangle. You should look for one that is as flat as possible because that indicates that the trading range is true. Avoid that do not have clearly defined support or resistance areas.

Entering a trading range should be done on a day of strength, or upon a technical signal, such as stochastics.

In terms of profit objective, the target is just the opposite side. For the risk level, it should be established just below the support level.

Now that you have learned about trends and ranges, which of the two do you think you would go for as a swing trader? Do you want to earn higher profits by riding trades? Or are you okay with earning smaller profits gained through the more stable trading ranges?

Each type of trading has its advantages and drawbacks, but whatever you choose, remember that there will always be some form of risk that you have to manage. As such, the following chapter focuses on guiding beginners like yourself on how to measure and manage the risks of swing trading.

Chapter 12: Managing Risks

One of the most critical factors that would determine whether or not you would succeed as a swing trader is your risk management system. For many, this entails limiting your investment for a particular security, and diversifying your portfolio.

The thing is, while those are important, managing risk also means the executing of orders given by the risk management system. More often than not, this factor is the one that many traders find to be tough to carry out. After all, in this case, you are your own worst enemy.

It certainly doesn't help that the nature of trading itself is quite deceptive. What you may believe at first to be true may turn out to be false upon more careful observation. If you fail to exercise caution, then you would end up losing a lot—if not everything that you have.

The goal of risk management is to minimize the losses that you might experience as a trader. This is a two-fold approach: first in the level of individual security, while the second is concerned with the portfolio-level risks.

In this chapter, we will cover the various risk management rules that swing traders should observe. By the end of it, you will also learn how to combine these rules into a risk management system that would work for you.

Having this doesn't mean that you will never suffer a loss in your trades though. Instead, it is a means of protecting you as much as possible from any mistakes you make or unexpected occurrences in the market.

We shall start by learning how to measure the riskiness of an individual stock.

First things first, here are the various factors that you need to consider in order to do your assessment:

- Beta of the Stock

Beta refers to the risk of a given stock relative to the market. Institutional traders tend to pay more attention to this than individual traders. However, this is an important point to include in your examination because it provides insight into how volatile a stock is compared to the market.

Take note that a stock's beta is not a fixed number. It may increase or decrease even in a span of a day.

There is also no optimal beta that you should look for in a security. For example, a security that has a high beta could be attractive, but make to check out if trading would put you at a risk of losing your entire investment as well.

You don't have to automatically ignore stocks with high beta. However, you must be extra careful and allocate less of your money to that security in case you end up deciding to trade it in order to minimize the risks of its volatile nature.

- Liquidity of the Stock

How easy it is to enter and exit a security indicates how frequently the shares of a security have been traded.

Though the liquidity of a stock does not matter much when it comes to entry since traders can wait for the right timing, its significance is highlighted more when it is time for an exit. Just imagine the trouble you would be facing if you have to exit as soon as possible, but you can't find a buyer—or if you are shorting, a seller.

So, how liquid must a security's shares be before you buy a stock? The answer depends on the size of your account. If your investment is $25,000, then the optimal stocks to invest in must be trading at least 100,000 shares each day. Furthermore, the size of your position should not exceed 5% of the average volume of shares per day.

- Size of the Company

Again, institutional traders pay more attention to this factor compared to individual traders. Still, you need to take this into account because the stocks of small companies tend to perform better than larger companies in the long run. However, their stocks are also more volatile so engaging with them would affect how you establish your stop loss levels.

- Share Price of the Company

Large company stocks—or also referred to as large caps—have lower volatility than those from smaller companies. You might be wondering though how you could distinguish which one is a large cap and which one is the small cap.

Traders compute for the market capitalization to determine the value of a company. This is computed by multiplying the price per share of the company by its total shares outstanding.

Companies may be classified into one of the following categories based on their market capitalization:
- Large Cap

Market Capitalization: $15,000,000,000 or higher

- Mid Cap

Market Capitalization: Between $1,000,000,000 and $15,000,000,000

- Small Cap

Market Capitalization: Between $300,000,000 and $1,000,000,000

- Micro Cap

Market Capitalization: Below $300,000,00

As explained earlier, the smaller the company is, the less liquid it is. As such, many professional traders make it as a rule for them not to trade stocks that are worth $10 per share.

Stocks from micro cap companies are more prone to becoming manipulated, for example, through rumors in trading forums or networks. Such rumors would likely not make any significant effect on a large cap company. But for those under the micro cap category, an unverified rumor could send their stocks through the roof. Therefore, swing traders are advised against trading stocks from small, unknown companies.

Once you have determined the amount of risk that a stock entails, you may refer to that information when planning out your risk management system for the individual stock level. Your objective at this point is to ensure that none of your positions would ruin your portfolio. In comparison, portfolio-level risk management is all about preventing the accumulation of multiple small losses from annihilating your entire portfolio of investments.

Managing risk at an individual stock level is done through position sizing. To establish this, you must first get to know how you are willing to lose in case of a failed trade.

A lot of experienced swing traders set their tolerance level for each position at 0.25% to 2% of their overall capital.

Let's say that yours is at 0.75%. To compute for the amount of tolerable loss for you, just multiply your capital by 0.75%.

So, if your capital is $100,000, you are willing to lose $750 on a single position.

From here, you can proceed to set your position size. There are two ways to go about this:

- By a Certain Percent of Capital

To do this, multiply the total worth of your account by a predetermined percentage level. Though the computation part is simple, the tricky part is establishing that percentage level. Here are some tips on how to determine if you need to set a small or large percentage for a particular position.

- Small Percentage (2% to 4%)

Choose this is the security has the following qualities:
  - The share price is $10 or below
  - Beta is above 2.0
  - Illiquid relative to your account size
  - Small cap
- Large Percentage (4% to 8%)
  - The share price is above $10
  - Low beta
  - Liquid relative to your account size
  - Mid or large cap

Once you have chosen a percentage for yourself, establish your stop loss level next. Base this amount on your loss tolerance threshold.

Going by the same example earlier, your stop loss level should be at a price that would make a position loss to be of an equivalent amount to 0.75% of your overall capital.

- By Risk Level

This is considered by trading experts as the more strategic way of setting your position size.

Let's use again the earlier example. If you were to use this method, you will determine your position size based on your preferred exit level. To compute for your exit level, establish a key price level where you want to make your exit, and then use that as a reference to finalize your position size.

The price level of your exit should reflect the amount that would signal you that trade is taking a bad turn. It is not enough to wait until the price falls to an obviously bad point. What you need is an earlier warning sign. Experts recommend using a previous swing low to serve as your stop loss level.

So, putting these elements together, you may compute for your position size by dividing the amount of capital that is at risk by the difference of the entry price and your stop loss level. If your capital at risk is $750 (or the 0.75% of $100,000 capital), while the entry price is at $845, thus making your stop loss level at $805, your position size is 18.75 shares—which you may round down to 18 shares to further reduce the risk and keep you within your loss threshold.

After determining your risk management mechanisms for the individual stock level, you may proceed to build your portfolio while also keeping the risks to a minimum.

Other than making bad trades yourself, there are various external factors that could destroy your portfolio. Such events are typically out of your control so the only thing you could do is to monitor the risk level of your portfolio and then put in place the mechanisms that would minimize the impact of those risks.

Experts suggest the following ways to develop your portfolio with minimal risks:

    a. Follow the 7% rule.

This basically means limiting the cumulative capital at risk from all your positions to only 7% of your total capital. Through this, you will be assured that the total amount of capital that you could possibly lose in a single day is just 7% instead of all of your capital.

Traders usually choose to set the tolerable loss percentage between 0.25% and 2%. The ideal maximum percentage, however, is around 0.5% per position. With this, you would still be able to diversify your positions since it would allow you to hold at least 14 different positions. Remember, the fewer positions you hold, the higher the risk level becomes.

    b. Diversify.

As the popular saying goes, "Don't put all of your eggs in one basket." That sums up the main rationale behind this risk management rule.

In trading, portfolio diversification means investing your capital in different securities, industry groups, or asset classes. By doing so, the losses of a position will likely be offset by the gains of the others.

Let's go over the three different ways you could do to properly diversify your portfolio:

    a. By increasing the number of securities

The most basic way to diversify your investments is by buying several securities. Experts suggest holding 10 to 20 securities at a time in order to benefit from your diversified portfolio.

Having multiple securities is not as simple as it sounds though. In order to achieve true diversification, the securities must be from different companies that belong to different industry groups. It would be even better if you could also invest in securities from other countries as well.

Take note that the more positions you have, the less time you could spend on keeping track of them, and thus affecting the returns you may expect your investments. Given these, try your best to observe the suggested 20-security maximum limit.

b. By being exposed to more industry groups
According to the founder of Investor's Business Daily, William O'Neil, about 30% to 40% of a security's return is influenced by the industry group it belongs to. Because of this, expert traders know that limiting their investments to only a couple of industry groups would significantly increase the risks that they might face.

You might be wondering though what these industry groups are. In general, the following are the primary sectors and industry groups that traders may invest on:
- Consumer Discretionary
  - Automobiles
  - Retailers
- Consumer Staples
  - Drug Retailing
  - Food Retailing
  - Household Products
- Energy
- Financials
- Healthcare
- Information Technology
- Materials
  - Capital Goods
  - Commercial Services
  - Industrials
  - Transportation
- Telecommunications
- Utilities

To clarify, industry groups may be classified under sectors. For example, energy services, energy products, and energy drilling are types of industry groups that all belong to the energy sector.

Make sure to include the number of sectors and industry groups that you are planning to invest in into your trading plan. Again, there is no magic number that works for all, but many traders aim for at least four different sectors or six different industry groups.

c. By exploring other asset classes

Aside from securities, you should also consider other investment vehicles to further diversify your portfolio. Here are the two main vehicles that will allow you to expand to other asset classes:

o Exchange Traded Funds (ETF)

Through these funds, you will be able to trade commodities, currencies, and stocks from other countries.

o American Depository Receipts (ADR)

If you are based in the US, this will give you access to trade with companies outside the country without having to go there. Having international securities in your portfolio will enhance the benefits that you may expect from diversification.

c. Combine long positions and short positions.

This strategy will reduce the standard deviation of returns from your portfolio compared to when all you have are completely long or short positions. In case of a major market rally or decline, you will remain protected since the gains from either the long or short positions will offset the losses from the others.

How should you decide on the ratio of long positions and short positions for your portfolio? The answer depends on the strength or weakness of the market.

For instance, if the overall market is in a strong bull condition, then the number of your short positions should not be more than 20% of your total portfolio. On the other hand, if it is a strong bear market, then the long positions should not exceed 20% of your total portfolio.

Another way to lessen the risk of having too many long or short positions in your portfolio is by trading other asset classes that are in a trend that is contrary to the stock market. For example, in a strong bull market, consider entering short positions that come from either the currency market or commodities.

Regardless of whatever you have decided about the number of securities you will hold at a single time, the type of asset classes that you will invest in, and the ratio of long positions and short positions in your portfolio, remember to record every decision point you have established in your trading journal. You might have thought of the best risk management strategies for yourself, but if it is not in written form that is easily accessible to you, then chances are, you will forget or ignore them in the future.

Chapter 13: Improving Your Trades Through Performance Evaluations

To enhance your skills as a swing trader, you must take the time to evaluate how well your trades have done on a regular basis. There are various ways to go about this, but all of the evaluation methods basically aim to determine the returns of your portfolio.

A performance evaluation of your trades is not as straightforward as it may seem at first. Several factors may complicate your calculations, for example, commissions, SEC fees, taxes, and other types of expenses. Cash deposits may also add another layer of complexity to the computation of your returns.

Since such factors are natural parts of the process, the only way to handle them is to take them into account when doing your calculations. In this chapter, we will discuss how exactly you are supposed to do this.

Let's start with the easiest scenario, wherein the account you started with has had no deposits or withdrawals, and its growth in value over time is only due to trading.

To compute for your total return, in this case, you have to divide the difference between the ending and beginning value by the beginning value.

Here's an example to better understand this formula.

By the end of the year 2019, the account value of Trader Sean is $95,850. During the first three months of the following year, he buys and sells stocks every few days. As such, by the last day of March 2020, his account value has grown to $105,910. Within those three months, Sean did not make any deposits or withdrawals from his account. Furthermore, the ending value of his account reflects the commissions he had paid during that period. As for taxes, those are not reflected because he is using a tax-deferred account for his investments.

From these data points, we may be able to determine Sean's total return by, first, subtracting $95,850 from $105,910. The resulting amount—which is $10,060—must then be divided by the beginning value: $95,850. After this, you will learn that the total return that Sean gained from January to March 2020 is 10.49%.

While this formula is quick and easy to use, you would likely have to adjust it since most swing traders perform deposits and withdrawals from their accounts. As explained earlier, this simple total return formula just straight-up assumes that there is neither a deposit nor a withdrawal made.

To consider these account movements into your computations, you may try using either of the following: the time-weighted return method, or the money-weighted return method.

1. Time-Weighted Return Method

This is used to calculate the returns of an account regardless of the timing of the cash flow movements. Because of this, many consider this as the superior method between the two.

2. Money-Weighted Return Method

This uses a formula that determines the return based on the account's return and the added value caused by the timing of the cash flow movements.

Since time-weighted returns would provide you a clearer answer that is not distorted by any large cash flow movements into or out of the account, let's focus on learning how to apply this method.

A time-weighted return method is actually a three-step approach. I'll give you a rundown of what each step entails so that you could better understand how to apply this method to your account.

Step 1: Break down the time period.

First, you need to break down the time period according to the number of deposits and withdrawals that have been made within the said period. This is important because you need to calculate the returns for each discrete time period.

To use this value in calculating the returns, you need to add 1 into the number of actual cash flow movements.

For example, take a look at this summary of cash flow movements in Sean's account that has a starting balance of $50,000:

- Account Value Before Deposit
  - $58,500
- Deposit
  - Date: 3 February 2020
  - Amount: $5,000

- Account Value Before Withdrawal
  - $61,300
- Withdrawal
  - Date: 14 April 2020
  - Amount: $3,000

- Account Value Before Deposit
  - $63,780
- Deposit
  - Date: 16 June 2020
  - Amount: $9,000

- Account Value Before Withdrawal
  - $72,290
- Withdrawal
  - Date: 20 December 2020
  - Amount: $7,000

- Ending Balance
  - Date: 31 December 2020
  - Amount: $68,350

Since Sean has made 2 deposits and 2 withdrawals within the year 2020, the calculation of return has to be for five—not four—time periods, as listed below:
- 1st Time Period
1 January to 2 February

- 2nd Time Period
3 February to 13 April

- 3rd Time Period

14 April to 15 June

- 4th Time Period

16 June to 19 December

- 5th Time Period

20 December to 31 December

Step 2: Calculate the return for each time period.
To do this, simply apply the formula for the total return of accounts without any cash flow movement for each time period.

- 1st Time Period

Return: 17%

- 2nd Time Period

Return: -3.46%

- 3rd Time Period

Return: 9.40%

- 4th Time Period

Return: 0.67%

- 5th Time Period

Return: 4.69%

These returns must be connected to one another through the method called chain-linking to finally determine the total return of the account for the given year.
Step 3: Chain-link the returns of each time period.
     The formula for chain-linking the returns of each time period is:
(1 + Return of 1st Time Period) x (1 + Return of 2nd Time Period) x . . . (1 + Return of Nth Time Period) − 1 = Total Return
Take note that the return must be converted into decimal form before you could proceed with adding, subtracting, and multiplying the values. The resulting total return may be

turned back to percentage form so that it would be easier to understand later on.

Applying this formula to Sean's account, the chain-linking equation would look like this:

$(1 + 0.17)$ x $(1 - 0.0346)$ x $(1 + 0.0940)$ + $(1 - 0.0067)$ x $(1 + 0.0469)$ − $1 = 0.285$ or 28.5%

Now that you know how to calculate the total return of an account, what you should do next is to compare it to a particular benchmark that could tell you if you are outperforming the market.

Traders may refer to the following major benchmarks to evaluate their performance:

- For Cap Growth
  - Large Cap: Russell 1000 Growth Index
  - Mid Cap: Russell Mid Cap Growth Index
  - Small Cap: Russell Small Cap Growth Index

- For Cap Core
  - Large Cap: Russell 1000 Core Index
  - Mid Cap: Russell Mid Cap Core Index
  - Small Cap: Russell Small Cap Core Index

- For Cap Value
  - Large Cap: Russell 1000 Value Index
  - Mid Cap: Russell Mid Cap Value Index
  - Small Cap: Russell Small Cap Value Index

These indexes may be accessed for free through this link: www.ftserussell.com. You can also use international indexes as your benchmark. For example, the website of the Bank of New York provides several compilations of indexes that may be used to compare international stocks that are traded in the US.

If you also short securities, then the nine benchmarks have given above is not that applicable to you. Instead, establish an absolute return level to serve as your benchmark. Most swing traders set this at 15% per year.

Having identified the benchmark that you would like to use, you are now ready to compare your return for the given year versus the annual return of the benchmark you have selected.

In case that you do not have information yet about your annual return, then you may use your monthly return instead. How should you interpret the results of this comparison? If your actual return is greater than the return of the benchmark, then you are outperforming the average return as indicated in the index you have chosen.

There are various probable reasons for this, such as:

- Using margin or leverage
- Using cash well even though the market is declining
- Trading securities with higher beta compared to the benchmark
- Adding real value, which is possible as you increase your skills as a swing trader

Knowing how well you did in comparison to the market, in general, should serve as a basis on how you evaluate your current trading plan. You don't have to make any changes to the plan if it is not really needed, especially when your total returns have outperformed the benchmark. However, it would not hurt you at all to revisit the trades that you have made, and try to spot areas that could be further improved.

The market is ever-changing so it is best to keep upgrading yourself wherever you can. It is important to remember though that revising your trading plan should not be done too often. Only do so when there is a significant reason, like a concrete benefit or a probable solution for the problems you have noticed in your trades.

Making frequent changes to your plan would keep you from knowing if a certain plan is actually effective or not. After all, you cannot truly judge a trading plan with data from only a short period of time.

Trading experts suggest reviewing your plan at least once per month. Go through your trading journal, and revisit the trades that you have closed. Those are good indicators of whether or not you should make some adjustments to your strategy.

For example, if your trading plan resulted in returns that are less than the average returns stated in the benchmark, then try your best to search for a common denominator among all your losing positions. Once identified, you may then add or revise the rules stated in your trading plan in order to prevent similar losses in the future.

On the flip side, you should also review your wins to determine if there are any common points among them. Should there be any, consider if you need to add or revise your trading plan rules to incorporate what you have done right in those trades.

As a final note, keep in mind that no trading plan works 100% of the time. There has also never been an absolutely perfect swing trader.

Losses are inevitable parts of swing trading. As such, you should always be prepared to handle them.

Many good trading plans end up as a failure when the trader fails to take into account the volatile nature of the overall market. As a result, they end up setting unrealistic expectations for themselves. Keep yourself from becoming this kind of swing trader by staying grounded and sticking with your trading plan.

CPSIA information can be obtained
at www.ICGtesting.com
Printed in the USA
BVHW040850050521
606341BV00011B/734